THE SHADE OF SWORDS

'An unbelievably sophisticated work that is terribly daring… commenting upon issues that have created war after war, along with enmity and countless barbaric acts. Akbar has produced an innovative and lucid religious history of ideology, idolatry, betrayal and violence.' Seymour Hersh, Pulitzer Prize winner and staff writer for *The New Yorker*

'In the crowded category of works on the historical forces behind September 11, Osama bin Laden and al Qaeda, this book stands out. It's one of the few not written by an instant expert of the conflict, nor, more significantly, by a Westerner. In *The Shade of Swords*, Akbar blends that trademark scholarship with a novelist's story-telling power as he analyses the spread of fundamentalist fervour in the Islamic world.' Robin Elsham, *Reuters*

'Akbar makes some telling points … [a]nd it's hard to argue with his conclusion: "Defeat is only a setback in the holy war. The jihad goes on."' Thomas W. Lippman, *Washington Post*

'Muslims are often asked to take an honest look at what has happened to their religion in recent decades. Here is one such endeavour – a textured and honest account of the rise of belligerent fundamentalism in some parts of the Muslim world. To understand the complex forces – religious, political, and historical – that have fuelled the fervor for *Jihad*, read this book.' Fareed Zakaria, Editor, *Newsweek International*

'An excellent new book by the distinguished Indian journalist M. J. Akbar traces the centuries-long history of the conflict between Islam and Christianity, inflamed today by the world dominance of the US.' Alexander Chancellor, *Guardian*

'[The] recital of the incarnations of the jihad by a Muslim offers readers a fair account of Islamic conflict over the ages and, implicitly, a number of warnings for the West.' Steve Young, *Library Journal*

'…a graceful and sensitive writer.' Marguerite Johnson, *Time*

'…one of India's ablest journalists.' *The New York Times*

'Best at evoking sympathetically the religious emotion that drives holy wars … His book is a succession of vivid accounts of Muslims who fought Christians, Hindus and Jews. A wide, entrancing stretch of history [that] has a taste for

M.J. Akbar, founder and editor-in-chief of *The Asian Age*, a multi-edition daily newspaper, is a leading Indian journalist and author. *The Shade of Swords* is his fifth book, after four published to great international acclaim: *Nehru: The Making of India, India: The Siege Within, Riot After Riot* and *Kashmir: Behind the Vale*. During the 1970s and 1980s he successfully launched and established a weekly news magazine and a daily newspaper. In November 1989 he entered the Indian Parliament as an elected representative. He returned to writing and editing in 1993.

THE SHADE OF SWORDS

Jihad and the conflict between Islam and Christianity

M.J. AKBAR

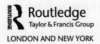

Routledge
Taylor & Francis Group

LONDON AND NEW YORK

First published in the UK in 2002
by Routledge
11 New Fetter Lane, London EC4P 4EE

Simultaneously published in the USA and Canada
by Routledge
29 West 35th Street, New York, NY 10001

In India, Pakistan, Sri Lanka and Bangladesh
by Roli Books
M-75, Greater Kailash-II (Market), New Delhi–48, India

This paperback edition first published in the UK in 2003 by Routledge

Routledge is an imprint of the Taylor & Francis Group

© 2002, 2003 M.J. Akbar

Typeset in Perpetua by Roli Books, India
Printed and bound in Great Britain by MPG Books Ltd, Bodmin

British Library Cataloguing in Publication Data
A catalogue record for this book is available from the British Library

Library of Congress Cataloging in Publication Data
A catalogue record for this book has been requested

ISBN 0-415-32814-4

To the memory of Ammiji and Abbaji, who are still with me

CONTENTS

ACKNOWLEDGEMENTS

Authors are loath to admit it but they labour under both conception and misconception. Time is one judge of the difference. This book has had an exceptionally tortured pregnancy, so the list of those in whose debt I am is long, much longer than the few names that will appear.

One of the first essays that I wrote on the shifting mood of the Islamic world emerged out of travel in the 1980s through the debris of a collapsing Soviet Union, and the sudden surge of Islam through some of the oldest Muslim countries in the world, in Central Asia. Faith quickly filled the space left behind by retreating communism.

My first visit to the region was in the same year that Margaret Thatcher tested Mikhail Gorbachev's dawn by lighting a candle in a church in Moscow. The cue was irresistible. I insisted to my guide on a conducted tour of Dushanbe that on the coming Friday I wanted to pray at a mosque since I had been informed that Comrade Mikhail had released religion from Marxist chains. Allah knows how many telex messages were exchanged between my guide and his masters in Moscow. (Remember the telex? This book began in the pre-e-mail age and this is as good a time as any to acknowledge that this book could never have been completed in time without the blessed e-mail. So thank you, Bill Gates, or whoever.) When Friday arrived they drove me through some exquisite country for a couple of hours till we reached a mosque adjoining the shrine of a Sufi *pir*, or master. They had not been able to locate a mosque nearer than that.

The startled *mullahs* offered me a mute and suspicious welcome, very apprehensive at the thought of Marxist Moscow bringing a believer to their doorstep. They spread the finest melons, pomegranates and dry fruit before me, hoping I would eat and go away. Conversation was difficult. Their English was on par with my Uzbeg, that is, non-existent. Finally, desperate to say something, anything, I asked them something quite inane. What was this mosque called? The answer came. Lenin Mosque. I shrugged, quite certain that my question had been lost in the maze of languages. I asked it again. Lenin Mosque. I did some quick thinking. Allah, I reasoned, would understand, hopefully, on the Day of Judgment, the variable life-long behaviour of an itinerant sinner like me. Allah is Merciful, and Muslims like me provide ample opportunity for Him to show His mercy. I am not a regular *nimaazi*, or prayer-goer, among other things. But I reckoned that however magnanimous Allah might be on other matters, He would never forgive me if I did not bow my head before Him in a mosque named after Lenin. I joined the half a dozen others who stood behind the *imam* that afternoon.

During my last visit to Central Asia, in 1992, mosques and *medressahs* were teeming through the old Muslim cities of Tashkent, Samarkand and Bukhara. Islam had simply shrugged off a century and half of defeat, subjugation and insult and reasserted itself through the minarets, across the skies of Central Asia.

The Muslim world, including the lost Muslim world of Spain and Portugal, traverses a marvellous geography of mountains and the unfathomable Sahara, to the fertility of the Nile and south to the heart of Africa. Then across the Red Sea to the conflicts of the Semitic nations; to the Holy Cities of Arabia and up to Jerusalem, claimed by three great faiths, each with enough reason to go to war for Jerusalem. The four ancient civilisations of Iraq, Turkey, Iran and South Asia form one arc, while a line from Albania through Caucasus across Central Asia establishes the northern frontier of Islam. The sultry charm of India opens up routes to the steamy ambience of south east Asia: a hundred races stretch across continents and countries through a welter of cultural differences but with a single and uniquely uniting faith that has bypassed the skepticism synonymous with religion in modern times.

Islam is a faith with a worldview, which sometimes surprises the world. The unity of response on basic issues, from a mosque in Baku to a mosque in Bali, startles a world that would prefer to divide this response into the preferred blocs of nationalism. This book also became one long travelogue through these lands. More correctly, the travel came before the book, and then the book demanded more travel. A chain of friends links these years of search. Do forgive me for mentioning only a few. Where does one start? Perhaps in the middle, where experience and reading were nudged towards an idea and the idea began its own journey. At that moment of departure I was privileged to receive the help of many distinguished friends and professional colleagues, but most of all from Patrick Wright who helped cajole thought into a sustainable viewpoint. One of these days I might even find a way of repaying my debt to Patrick, but I can't think of any now.

A host – I use the word advisedly – of Indian ambassadors were generous in countries where one had no friends, no language and a great deal to look for. Hamid Ansari comes instantly to mind. Dapper, impeccable and generous to more than one fault, he looked after me through a fortnight in Iran, where I had some memorable discussions in the seminary at Qum as well as with officials and academics who were familiar with both the theory and the practice of the emerging Muslim mind. There were at least a dozen trips to that great swathe between the Middle East and Spain: history, out here, is far from dead. Or, perhaps, the dead are not far from history. During my last visit I also performed the *umra*, or the lesser pilgrimage in Mecca. My good friend Talmiz Ahmad was our ambassador in Saudi Arabia: he provided undiluted help and diluted sustenance. Dilip and Shovana Lahiri were their ever-generous selves in Spain. Hardeep Puri is too mobile for a diplomat, or is that an oxymoron? He seems to have helped everywhere, often working in mysterious ways his wonders to perform. My visits to Pakistan began in the late seventies: Manju and S.K.Singh made Islamabad even friendlier than it is to a visiting Indian. Let me add this: if the governments of India and Pakistan behaved with each other the way Indians and Pakistanis do when they meet individually, this would be a region of laughter rather than tears. I cannot say how much the friendship of Hameed Haroon in Pakistan meant and continues to mean to me. Together we have explored his country, Pakistan, across village and town, through books and argument. The list of Indian friends who have sustained me with their affection and, even more, with their tolerance is always going to be incomplete when placed in print. Fatma and Rafiq Zakaria are better called mentors. Fatma was instrumental in giving me my first job, in the inestimable Khushwant Singh's *Illustrated Weekly of India* in 1971; now I feel adopted by them. It is a happy feeling.

This last decade has been a difficult period for me, for more than one reason, but if there is one friend who has remained at my side through this roller-coaster decade then it is T. Venkat Ram Reddy. I met Ram in the familiar tumult of the media, not the best place for bonds that survive mutual need. I am privileged to have received Ram's affection and support. Better still, we are colleagues in the daily newspaper we launched in 1994, *The Asian Age*. Ram is chairman of the company. Which brings me to the most tolerant company in Asia: the group of us who have remained with *The Asian Age*, and in particular Seema Mustafa, Kaushik Mitter, Suneel Sinha, Rupa Sarkar, Tikli Basu, Sarju Kaul, Aditi Khanna, Venkatesh Kesri, Nazreen Bhura and Rachna Grover. Thank you all in *The Asian Age* for your amused forbearance as this book made me a difficult recluse. I especially want to thank Rithika Siddhartha for the help she gave me in the last, nerve and muscle-wrenching phase. As the manuscript wandered towards the status of a book I was particularly fortunate to find my friends Pramod Kapoor and his wife Kiran, who run Roli Books with such elan. Through them I reached Christoph Chesher at Routledge. Christoph was invaluable with help in every way, including excellent advice. One of the rewards of writing this book is that we have become friends. If you ever want to be bullied, incidentally, then I recommend that you opt for Harinder Baweja at Roli, who weds steely professionalism with an engaging smile. The combination is devastating. Humble authors surrender and deliver. Thank you, all of you.

There is no sustenance greater than the affection of friends and family: the two become indistinguishable when you have friends like Sunil and Gita Gujral, Prabeen, Aruna and Anil Lal, and family like my sister Ghazala and brother-in-law Lokesh Sharma; and Shama and Madhu John. My children Mukulika and Prayaag have improved distinctly ever since they left home. There may be a cause and effect factor involved. They are now ready to start their own lives; but their love and concern and their ideas are an enormous source of joy. What good fortune it is to celebrate one's family! Life would be meaningless without the person who is the heart of this family, my wife Mallika, the calm centre around which all of us swirl, and who is the most precious part of our lives. Her love is the first and last acknowledgement.

PREFACE

In its traditional end-December view-and-review issue, *The Economist* closed the startling year 2001 with a cartoon in which a beleaguered Father Time passed on the world to a less-than-chirpy Child Time. Two parts of this globe were in flames: the Middle East and South Asia, the epicentre of the second conflagration being the contiguous region of Afghanistan, Pakistan, and Kashmir in India.

While the war between Israel and her Arab neighbours has been a staple of books, journalism, and even fiction, the tensions of South Asia are neither familiar nor fully understood. Yet it is in Pakistan and Afghanistan that American and European troops have landed to fight a jihad launched against the Christian West, with the United States as its primary target. This is no accident, but the culmination of a long process. American troops will stay here longer than they expect. Kabul has always fallen without a fight, as it did in 1838, 1879, 1978, and 2001. Equally, it has always been easier to enter Kabul than to leave it.

How did Pakistan become the breeding ground for, in the words of an architect of the idea, Lt. Gen. Hameed Gul, the 'first Islamic international brigade in the modern era'? How was Pakistan swamped by the Kalashnikov and jihad culture, terms used in a national broadcast by a man seeking to change it, President Pervez Musharraf? How did Osama bin Laden find refuge and opportunity in this culture? The answers lie in the sources of anger, for this is a war being fought in the mind as much as anywhere else.

We tend to define war in terms of nations, interests, and uniformed armies. This jihad is also a proxy war, fought by elliptical strategies, through irregular armies. To define this singular aspect of one Islamic response to the perceived world-domination by the United States is complex enough. There are, as implied, other responses as well, but jihad stands out through its ability to shift the tides of history on a day like 11 September 2001.

This present work seeks to explain the origins and nature of both the battle and the battlefield. This unique war, that has brought American and European troops to South Asia, is shaped by the history of Islam and the history of the region. The first eight chapters explain the doctrinaire and historical roots of the conflict between Islam and Christianity (no two faiths, avowedly separate, could be more linked): the wars that began from virtually the lifetime of the Prophet for political control of the known world, and the spill of hatred into literature and rhetoric, leaving wounds more permanent than the fortunes of battle.

Two years after the fall of Constantinople, that great symbol of Christian power, to Muslims in 1453, a Papal Bull gave authority to Catholic Portugal to go on a Holy Crusade eastwards; to hunt in India for wealth and allies against the Ottoman 'Saracens' who had revived Islamic power. Portugal however discovered that Muslims, who had begun to rule substantial parts of South Asia by the twelfth century, were not as yet a spent force: indeed, another Turkic-Mongol dynasty established India's greatest empire a little after the Portuguese created a foothold in Goa. It was left to anti-Catholic Britain to gradually displace and then replace the Mughal empire. Britain generally preferred the language of commerce rather than that of the Crusades, but the Muslim response, whether in dialectics or war, drew constant inspiration from the ever-present concept of jihad. The later chapters guide the reader through confrontations in the east in all their splendid variety, from the Caucasus through Afghanistan to the political battles in India from which emerged what no one had envisaged: a modern homeland for Muslims, Pakistan. A moderate liberal leader created Pakistan, but Pakistan soon slipped out of the conceptual confines of its founder to become a homeland of fundamentalists who constitute as great a threat to their haven as they are to the people and nations they seek to subdue.

The axis is large, lateral, and swings through time, memory, faith, victory, defeat, history and geography. *The Shade of Swords* traces a line that begins in the deserts of Arabia and flows through the lifeblood of a decisive battlefield in the war against terror, Pakistan and Afghanistan.

INTRODUCTION

The shade of swords is not an invitation to kill; it is an invitation to die. When Muslims take the name of their Prophet, Muhammad, they always add a prayer: Peace be upon Him. Peace is the avowed aim of Islam, a word that means surrender; as-Salam, or the Peaceful, is one of the names of Allah. But the Islamic faith also demands, from time to time, in a holy war defined by specific circumstances, the blood of the faithful in the defence of their faith. This is jihad.

The profession of faith is the *shahada*: *Lailaha il-Allah, Muhammad ur Rasul Allah*. There is but one Allah and Muhammad is His Prophet. Those who become martyrs for Allah are the *shaheed*. The martyr smiles his way to death and death opens the door to paradise. Believers do not surrender to anyone except Allah. They may occasionally have to submit, but defeat is only a pause in the process of renewal. They are not defeated by defeat. They wait, they keep the faith, and renew their jihad until they achieve the victory that Allah promised in His bargain with the believer, specified so clearly in the Quran. Islam has always recognized the reality of war in human affairs, and set its moral and political compass.

Such definition is as open to abuse as it is to use. This book is an effort to sift the difference by a search through text and history. The temptation to reinterpret both text and history to suit contemporary 'politically correct' requirements is the first trap to be avoided. There are Muslims today, for instance, who will convert jihad into a holy bath rather than a holy war, as if it is nothing more than an injunction to cleanse yourself from within.

It is true that the Prophet insisted that a greater jihad was the struggle to cleanse impurity within, but that does not take away from the fact that the lesser jihad inspired the spirit that once made Muslim armies all-conquering, enabled Muslims to protect their holy places, and ensured that most of the community lived within the protection of Muslim power despite formidable challenge from Christian alliances in a world war that was virtually coterminous with the birth of Islam. So often did Muslim armies, whether in the west or the east, triumph against odds that it conjured up a sense of a self-replicating miracle. Faith in Allah's bargain was reinforced by each victory, particularly against Christian armies who mobilized repeatedly not only to destroy Muslim empires but also Islam, which they called a heresy against Christ.

Jihad is the signature tune of Islamic history. If today's Muslim rulers are reluctant to sound that note, it is often because they are concerned about the consequences of failure. As in every bargain, there are two sides. Allah promised victory to the Muslim, but only if the believer kept faith with him. Defeat becomes an indictment of the ruler, and is therefore risky, particularly as Muslims have a long tradition of holding their rulers accountable. They are enjoined to do so.

Most governments of Muslim nations are seen today as unrepresentative, undemocratic, and evasive about the needs and demands of the community, the *umma*. The traditional Islamic polity has disappeared, and in its place undemocratic élites have emerged who have arguably neither the sanction of popular will nor the ballast of success to keep them afloat. The space for struggle is therefore occupied by movements outside the parameters of official authority.

Radical movements in Islam turn to the past for inspiration, with faith as their sustenance. Kings and dictators across the Muslim world are not necessarily displeased by this. Radical groups can divert public attention from their failings towards larger, 'heroic' international causes. Such duplicity is common, until it is exposed, or until it rebounds. It is also useful to leave jihad in the hands of an organization that can be sacrificed if it fails and exploited if it succeeds.

After the collapse of the Caliphate in 1922, and its abolition by Mustafa Kemal Ataturk in 1924, Muslim nations have not really been able to find a modern idiom for governance. The Caliphate, a remarkable institution that took nearly thirteen centuries to outlive its utility, is synonymous with the history of Islam. The first Caliph, Abu Bakr, took charge of the *umma* after the death of the Prophet. As the community grew at an unforeseen pace, it was impossible for one Caliph to remain the executive head of every Muslim. A mixture of temporal and spiritual responsibility devolved on what might be called the pre-eminent power within the Muslim world. This was based in Medina to begin with. It shifted to Damascus and Baghdad, and then to Constantinople where the Ottomans provided the last line of Caliphs. For all his actual and vaunted power, the Caliph was never omnipotent. After the Caliphate withered, defeated in its last jihad (the First World War), Muslim nations have been unable to create a sustainable representative system of government.

The last two great Muslim empires were the Ottoman and the Mughal in India. These two jigsaw puzzles re-sorted themselves out in the name of nationalism, but no Muslim country from the old empires has had an honest and sustained democracy. Where it is currently honest, as in Bangladesh, it is not sustained. The uniform of the army looms over even liberal Turkey; ironically it is the army that has taken upon itself to protect a secular state, as if adult franchise alone could not be trusted to do so.

The Arab nations slipped into authoritarian rule, some via royal families sponsored originally by the British over toast and tea or gin and lime, and now reinforced by the blinkered view of the West, keen to defend its oil supplies at all costs. In the richer kingdoms a thin veneer of support for royalty has been purchased by prosperity, while other citizens are assured certain comforts in return for obedience. Critics argue that there is neither political freedom nor free speech.

Kings, emirs, and dictators, more petty than powerful, prevail, forcing a question that Muslim élites are reluctant to answer: if you do not represent the people, then who do you represent?

Some governments try and fool Muslims into believing that they are there to defend the faith. They are quickly exposed by Islamic fundamentalists as puppets of foreign powers, or as profligate wastrels further removed from the principles of Islam than many an infidel. The most notable of the fundamentalist's scorn is, ironically, the land where the Prophet was born, Arabia. It is today ruled by the Sauds, who, they argue, have converted the Prophet's Arabia into a family estate with the help of the Anglo-American powers. They even changed the name of the country to Saudi Arabia just in case you forgot that it had become family property.

Jihad is permitted against the infidel; it is compulsory against the apostate or the *murtadd*. One group that troubled the Prophet deeply were the Hypocrites, or the *munafiqeen* (a word, incidentally that was earlier used by the Christian church in Abysinnia). The Hypocrites were a group

of Medinaites who became Muslims and then turned into agents provoca-
teur. There are at least twenty references in the Quran to them, one more
uncomplimentary than the next: deceivers, mischief-makers, fools, mock-
ers, deaf, dumb, blind, arrogant, cowardly, over-reaching, liars, renegades.
The Quran promises them terror, darkness, and the lowest depths of hell.
On par is the apostate, he who turns back after guidance has been shown
to him. Apostates are 'men whom Allah has cursed for He has made them
deaf and blinded their sight' (Surah 47, Verse 23). Their fate is sealed:
'They shall have a curse on them: wherever they are found, they shall be
seized and slain [without mercy]. [Such was] the practice [approved] of
Allah among those who lived aforetime: no change wilt thou find in the
practice [approved] of Allah.' Jihad is obligatory against an apostate Muslim state. This logic is extended by some groups to a Muslim government
that they describe as an agent of the enemy. In its issue of 13 October
2001, *The Economist* reported that the Saudi authorities had summoned
a blind, 80-year-old authority on Islamic law, Sheikh Hamoud bin Ogla
an-Shuaibi, who had earlier advised the chief justice of the country, to
check whether he had issued a *fatwa* against the ruling al-Saud family.
Sheikh Hamoud, who is spending his last days in Burayda in Nejd, a bastion of the Wahhabis, answered simply: 'Whoever backs the infidel against
Muslims is considered an infidel.' The infidel that Sheikh Hamoud is referring to is Christian America.

The irony is heavy, for the 'apostate state' has all too often provided
tacit support to fundamentalist groups in a bid to buy its way out of
trouble, and discovered that the hand that feeds is also being bitten. Osama
bin Laden positioned himself as a new *imam*, at once at war with the
infidel Christian and their apostate agents in the Arab world. Sections of
the clergy will also accuse those Pakistani leaders who supported the
United States against the Taliban and Al-Qaida of apostasy.

The experience of Pakistan is particularly important in the context of
modern Islam and the continued tug of war with the Christian world. If
the political centre of Islam for over half a millennium was Constantinople,
then its demographic centre shifted to South Asia, or India as the entire
region was referred to prior to 1947. Through the vagaries of history, many
of which are examined in this book, the British empire became the largest
home of Muslims in the world, and the Muslim-Christian relationship
acquired two dimensions. One was the Ottoman effort to preserve the
empire in the quicksands of nineteenth century European politics, even as

a resurgent West dreamt of the reconquest of Christian Constantinople from those who had renamed it Istanbul. The second was the experience of Muslims as a subject race of the British empire. A third element was added to this combustible equation by rising Hindu anger against Muslim rule in India among the emerging professional and educated middle classes of the nineteenth century, particularly in the capital of the British Raj, Calcutta.

The nineteenth century was one during which Indian Muslims declared more than one jihad against the British, who were forced into a serious enquiry into the nature of the Muslim mind and asked if rebellion was compulsory in Islam. The British protected their empire – and who can deny them that right – by playing Muslim anguish off against Hindu anger. They were subtle and successful, but India paid the price. A division in the mind became, through the agitational politics of an extremely determined leader, Mohammad Ali Jinnah, a division of the land. Pakistan was born along with India in 1947. As a new country, without the baggage of royalty from the past or the dilemma of defeat and dejection, Pakistan should have become a model modern Muslim nation.

Instead, unable to agree on a constitution, it slipped into civilian chaos at the top, which gave way to martial law, which in turn dissipated into military chaos and a second partition. After 1971 came a patch of democracy that was so authoritarian that people welcomed the return of the army. The see-saw swung on parallel lines in the nineties. The armed forces are back in power.

What then do the generals represent if they do not represent the people? Patriotism comes easily to the army uniform. Patriotism for a cause is positive, and helps nations to prosper. History has however repeatedly shown that when governance is unhinged by the absence of a stable and accountable system it is virtually impossible for anything positive to flower. Uncertain rulers need props, and the promotion of religious fundamentalism, especially to an external threat, is often the safest one and a welcome convenience.

Pakistan, born to protect Islam, quickly politicised jihad and turned it into a mechanism for the protection of élites who had usurped power. 'Infidel' India was next door. Popular emotions could always be aroused, particularly in view of the bitterness that accompanied Partition, when millions died in the most senseless and vicious massacres of South Asian history; when people killed people as armies watched helplessly, or, sometimes, helpfully. The politics of poison had asked for its dues. It was almost inevitable that fundamentalist elements would find refuge and even prosper in such an environment. Simultaneously, the collapse, through weakness and compromise, of secular elements in India, encouraged the rise of Hindu fundamentalism. One extreme fed the other.

The intervention of the Soviet Union in Afghanistan legitimized jihad for a while in the West, as America's foreign policy also made political use of something that it did not fully understand. Its understanding has somewhat improved after 11 September 2001, but it has yet to come to grips with a true appreciation of the historical context in which Islamic fundamentalism has arisen. The saving grace in both Pakistan and India is that there remains a strong urge towards secularism, sense, and democracy born out of South Asian traditions and culture. If that finds its political balance in both countries then there is hope for the return of common sense. Is common sense too much to ask for in the region of the jihad against Israel? For many, the case for a Palestine state is so obvious that it barely needs reiteration. Indifference and procrastination have allowed the conflict to turn cancerous. However, Palestine is also being used by many non-democratic Arab states as the cause they can focus public opinion on, deflecting criticism from their own regimes.

Perhaps the West became too complacent, and too certain that Arab regimes that owed their survival to Western patronage had ended their last jihad against Israel in 1973. They underestimated the Muslim will to martyrdom. They did not recognize the child who would walk with complete calm under the shade of swords.

INTRODUCTION TO THIS EDITION

The statue of the father of the KGB, Feliks Dzerzhinsky, erected in 1958, was pulled down rudely in August 1991 by revelers celebrating their liberation from totalitarian Communism. In 2003, the conservative mayor of Moscow, Yuri Luzhkov, began to suggest that it might be a good idea to restore it to the traffic island in front of the KGB headquarters, for old Feliks was not quite the monster he was made out to be, was he? It seems sensible to check in about fifteen years whether a statue has returned to its pedestal. Or not.

Saddam Hussein was out of the ordinary. He did not wait to die before his statues could be erected to his memory. He established a looming presence over Iraq with rather horrendous, and certainly badly wrought, images of himself. Some of them played up to his ego by more than just dressing up his looks; they refashioned him in the mould of Islam's great warrior-heroes like Khalid ibn Walid and Saladin. The father of all Saddam statues stood in Firdous (or Paradise) Square in Baghdad. Every Paradise needs a god. This monument to idle worship was brought down in full view of the media on 9 April. The media had little choice. War correspondents stationed in Baghdad in March-April 2003 were crowded into the Palestine Hotel, with the statue as room view. Footage of the fall shown repeatedly on BBC and CNN was carefully framed to exclude American tanks that had cordoned off the square.

The Iraqis bringing down the statue were not local Baghdadis. They were believed to be 'fighters' loyal to Ahmad Chalabi, a wealthy banker and leader of the Iraqi National Congress. He was the prime mover of a project authorized by Bill Clinton in November 1993, funded and supervised by the CIA, and launched in March 1995. It was meant to provoke an 'insurrection' that would seed an instant uprising by terrorized citizens and Army units to overthrow Saddam Hussein. The uprising sank without a ripple. Chalabi returned to Baghdad in 2003 as a frontrunner for the leadership of a US-controlled Iraqi government.

No one in Washington seemed perturbed by the fact that in April 1992 Chalabi had been convicted in absentia on more than 30 counts of theft, embezzlement and fraud. This was not the vindictive work of some pro-Saddam judiciary. The verdict was delivered in the courts of Jordan, an American ally, after authorities investigated missing deposits of $300 million from the Petra Bank, owned by Chalabi, which subsequently crashed. Investigators described him as 'one of the most notorious crooks in the history of the Middle East'. Chalabi fled Amman before he could be arrested. That such a person could be considered for the leadership of post-Saddam Iraq is a source of embarrassment to anyone with common sense, and sufficient reason to anger any Iraqi. If George Bush had succeeded in making Chalabi head of a puppet government, the one country Chalabi could not have visited was neighbouring Jordan: he would have been arrested. A few days after the fall of the Saddam statue, graffiti appeared on the pedestal. Its message was: Saddam has gone, thank you very much; it is now time for the United States to go home.

The second Gulf war might have ended even before it started, literally. In Washington on the afternoon of March 19, 2003 George Tenet, the now controversial CIA director, learnt from a source that Saddam Hussein would spend the night in a bunker in southern Baghdad. At 3.30 Tenet, along with Defense Secretary Donald Rumsfeld and General Richard Meyers, Chairman, Joint Chiefs of Staff, briefed President George Bush in the Oval Office. A little more than four hours later, the President made up his mind. At 9.30 pm, Washington time, the bunker in Baghdad was bombed. At 10.15 Bush went on television to tell the world that war had begun (later, the BBC discreetly apologized for screening a shot of make-up being applied on the President).

Those missiles never found Saddam Hussein; indeed the whole American army would encounter the same difficulty. The initial phase of the war surprised the western allies, who had prepared for a pushover through welcoming crowds. On 27 March Lt. Gen. William Wallace, from the centre of the battle zone, noted that 'The engagement we are fighting is a bit different than the one we war-gamed against,' irritating his Commander-in-Chief, Bush. On 1 April the momentum shifted. On

3 April Baghdad airport was within reach; the next day, the US Army's 3rd Infantry Division took control of the airport. By 9 April it was all over, bar the consequences.

During the war Saddam Hussein used all the rhetoric and imagery that he could think of to arouse Iraqis, and Islam was a standard reference point. It was not the first time that Islam was being used as a veil by a tyrant.

It is extraordinary that after so many centuries of proximity the worlds of Christianity and Islam should remain so widely separated by misunderstandings over religion, culture and power. Plastic images abound. Sometimes it seems as if Bede the Venerable were still alive to shape the discourse. In the 8th century he argued that since the Arabs of Mecca were descended from the spurned wife of Abraham, Hagar, and their son Ishmael, the whole race was illegitimate. The lineage was then stretched back to Cain, making Muslims by extension responsible for the second original sin, fratricide. Revenge became thereby obligatory on the descendants of the other children of Adam (Christians were said to have descended from Seth, through Noah). Muslims are equally willing to demonize the 'Christian' West when reality is subtler than the dark claims made by fundamentalists.

The problem operates at the intellectual as well as the popular level. One serious point of departure is the unwillingness of western writers to take Islamic historiography seriously. One example will suffice. Muslim accounts of the life of the Prophet in the seventh and eighth centuries might be as prone to adulation as any biography in any century, but this does not render their research inauthentic. Certainly the care and scholarship of Muhammad ibn Ishaq, who wrote the *Sirat Rasul Allah* is evident in his voluminous work and has been handsomely acknowledged by his translator, A. Guillaume (*The Life of Muhammad*, Oxford University Press, 1955).

One of the incidents from the Prophet's life in Guillaume's translation is related to the letter sent by the Prophet Muhammad to the Byzantine Emperor Heraclius. A copy can be found in the Islamic section of the museum at Topkapi in Istanbul. This document is obviously an important element of the Muslim-Christian relationship in the Islamic perspective, and has been a consistent point of reference through the centuries.

Ayatollah Khomeini wrote a letter in a similar vein to Mikhail Gorbachev, fully conscious of the analogy. But too many writers in the West dismiss this letter as inauthentic, unwilling to even consider the place it might have in Muslim thinking. When such a piece appears in as sober and influential a publication as the *Washington Post* then one must pause to consider the bias in less worthy media.

Muslims, in turn, often fall victim to a one-dimensional view of the conflict. Misunderstanding can be as hazardous as ignorance; and an accidental incident can so easily be nurtured into 'evidence' of deep intent. Of course, the Iraq war is an exceptional case: you do need some serious intent to make the effort to conquer a country. But simple mistakes can so easily be blown up into battle scenes from the Crusades.

On 26 June 2003 American soldiers rushed into a Baghdad home from where they had heard gunshots. They did not discover a secret cell of assassins; they had merely interrupted a wedding. In the process they must have convinced a few dithering Iraqis about the virtues of jihad against the infidel. Ordinary citizens who are dead because they came in the way of American misunderstanding, or edginess, are being glorified as 'martyrs' by newspapers like the *Shia Al Dawa*: the name will mean more after a reading of the section on Iraq.

The first edition of *The Shade of Swords* ended on a somber, and perhaps bleak, note: 'The jihad goes on.' At that moment it was not apparent where precisely the larger confrontation would develop, even if it were obvious that skirmishes would break out all across the Islamic arc, from the Philippines and Indonesia to Morocco via a turbulent South Asia and an incandescent Middle East.

Less than two years after a regime change in Kabul, the Taliban is back on the battlefield in Afghanistan while Osama bin Laden remains hidden in the shadows of Pakistan. Less than three months after the fall of Baghdad, the Qatar television channel Al Jazeera can find Saddam Hussein but not the combined might of the United States of America and Britain. It seems improbable that Saddam can hide forever. Every bounty hunter must be sniffing for a scent and every satellite scouring for a trace.

Saddam Hussein was a villain who was mistaken for an enemy; but his defeat has put into play forces that are far more significant than him. Saddam will not come back, and neither will his derided statue. But eventually power in Baghdad will go to the majority. This means some form of Shia rule, whether under a revived Dawa (the political party begun in the late 1950s by Shia leaders like Hakim and Sadr) or another political party or alliance.

This changes the geopolitics of the region dramatically, since for the first time the two most powerful countries of the Muslim Middle East, Iran and Iraq, will have Shia-dominated governments. This will not lead to the creation of a single nation; nor will either Baghdad or Tehran accept any erosion of its national self-interest. (Incidentally, Bahrain is a third country with a Shia majority). But, as Ayatollah Khomeini often said, the division of Muslims into separate countries would not matter if they had unity of thought and clarity of purpose.

George Bush has cleared the way for a future his hawks did not fully comprehend. The presence of 'infidel' armies, and the use of violent anti-Islamic language by some leading lights of the Bush entourage has revived the anger of the Crusades on the Muslim street. Whether this anger will also lead to unity depends on how events unfold. But time is never on the side of the invader. A story from Saladin and Richard the Lionheart (not apocryphal) makes this point well. In the last winter of his campaign, Richard sent Saladin a warning: if he did not get peace on his terms, Richard warned, he would stay another winter. Saladin's response was to laugh gently. Richard was welcome to stay another winter or return home as he wished. All the winters of his own life, Saladin said, would be spent on this soil. He was already at home.

America, George Bush said before life darkened on 9/11, was not an imperial power; it had, despite its strength, preferred morality to subjugation. While this was not wholly accurate, it was substantially true. But that might be the problem. Power is vulnerable in the grasp of puppets. In Iraq, it has all been tried before. History is a continuum in which 1920 can nudge 2003 into unpredictable postures. Jihad has been interpreted, or misinterpreted, in wildly differing ways by sultans and emirs who chose to confuse it with their own selfish interests, and often attributed improbable sayings to the Prophet to justify their less than pious wars. But there is no confusion about the legitimacy of a jihad when a *Dar ul Islam*, or a House of Islam, has been subjugated by those hostile to Islam. That makes the land a *Dar ul Harb*, or a House of War.

The British in India went to great lengths in the 19th century to persuade Muslims that their rule was not an invitation to a holy war. Americans in Iraq in the 21st century might find their eloquence less persuasive.

M.J. Akbar
July 2003

1

CHAPTER AND VERSE

Narrated Abdullah bin Abi Aufa: Allah's Messenger (May Peace Be
Upon Him) said, 'Know that Paradise is under the shade of swords'.
[From the Book of Jihad in Sahih al Bukhari]

In the beginning was a miracle and the miracle was a word: *iqra*. Read. Read, said the angel of God, Gabriel, and the illiterate Muhammad began to read the word of God out to the world in an enchanting prose that was later compiled and called the Holy Quran.

Islam was twice-born. The Christian calendar begins with the birth of Jesus, but the Muslim calendar begins its journey not from the birth of the Prophet, or the day of the revelation, but from the moment of survival, the Hejira, or the migration of the Prophet from Mecca to Medina along with his devoted companion Abu Bakr, a friend who also became a father-in-law when the Prophet married Aisha.

The Quraysh, his tribe, persecuted the Prophet when he announced his revelation; and when he sought refuge in Yathrib, soon to become famous as Medina, they wanted the life of this kinsman who promised to destroy idol worship in the Kaaba and thereby hurt the lucrative benefits of the pilgrimage. The Quraysh sent an army, between nine hundred and a thousand strong, led by their best nobles, to, in the words of the most formidable Muslim-baiter, Abu Jahl (nicknamed by Muslims as the Father of Folly), 'destroy . . . him that more than any of us hath cut the ties of kinship and wrought that which is not approved'. The Muslims, some three hundred strong, took position at the well of Badr, blocking the water from the advancing Quraysh. Battle was joined on the seventeenth day of Ramadan, and some indication of the apostle's anxiety is evident in this story. As he prayed to Allah, the Prophet cried out: 'Oh Allah, if this band of Muslims perish today Thou will not be worshipped any more'. Muhammad then slumbered, and when he awoke he was reassured for he had seen Gabriel holding 'the rein of a horse and leading it. The dust is upon his front teeth' (the quotations here are from *The Life of Muhammad, A Translation of Ishaq's Sirat Rasul Allah,* ed. by A. Guillaume, Oxford, 1955). After victory, Muslim soldiers insisted that angels, in white turbans, had come to their aid in a battle in which they were heavily outnumbered; believers to this day are convinced they will receive Allah's help in the midst of battle. Stories of Badr are part of the Islamic inspiration.

The spirit of jihad entered Islam at Badr. It is a spirit that inspires among believers a heroism beyond the bounds of reason; equally, it inspires dread among those outside the fold of Allah. Its root lies in the Arabic *jahd,* meaning exertion or striving. Its resonance comes from the nature of this strife: jihad is the holy war, the war of righteousness, the struggle against tyranny. It is a passion indifferent to the fate of battle because the jihadi wins either way: in the long run, the war will be won; and in the short run, death will bring martyrdom and paradise. Simultaneously, the strife is also to cleanse one's soul, for no martyrdom is possible without that inner purity.

The greater of the two kinds of jihad, the Jihad al Akbar, is the war against the enemy within; against one's own weakness and wandering. It is the Jihad al Asghar, or the lesser jihad, that is fought on the battlefield.

Islam, as the word itself implies, does not seek violence. Equally, Islam does not permit meek surrender either. There are circumstances in which all Muslims are *commanded* to fight to defend their faith. In such times war becomes a duty, and those who shirk it are condemned by the Quran. It may only be a lesser jihad, but for some twelve hundred years only a comparative handful of infidel armies emerged from the lesser jihad either with their pride or their power intact.

The success of Muslim arms has been phenomenal. The beginning was astounding. Within just two years of the Prophet's death, during which insurrections of the apostates had also to be met, the armies of Islam had challenged and defeated the drilled, disciplined, and superbly armed forces of the two great powers of the age, the Persians to the east and the Byzantines to the north and west. Within two generations, armies chanting jihad had marched from Medina to Jerusalem, Damascus, Antioch, Alleppo, and further north into the body of the Byzantine empire; in the east to Qadisiyya and Madain, which stored the wealth of the Sassanids, and from there to Nehawand, Hamadan, and up to the Caspian. A detour took them to Basra and Isfahan, whence to Nishapur and the Amu Darya (Oxus) in Central Asia, a flank turning towards Afghanistan and another march taking them to Sind and the Indus valley on the Indian subcontinent. To the south they reached Fustat and Alexandria in Egypt, opening the door to the Maghreb through which they raced across to reach the shores of the Atlantic at Ceuta where, searching for fresh worlds to conquer, they eventually crossed to Jabel Tariq (Gibraltar) and then on to Cordoba, Toledo, and Sargossa to establish a glittering empire that would merge east and west for seven hundred memorable years.

The sheer excitement of this achievement, however, has tended to eclipse a basic impulse of the Muslim mindset. Jihad is not a sanction to empire-building, though empires did emerge in its wake. The most powerful manifestation of jihad is not when all is won, but when all seems lost: that is the spirit of Badr.

The political consciousness of Muslims is heavily influenced by the inheritance of a powerful history. A community spread across so much geography and through so many cultures is not going to display monotonous uniformity in its responses, but there is a point at which the community unites more readily than any other. This might be called the Medina Syndrome. It is the belief that Islam and Muslims are under threat from powerful enemies, and that the only answer is unity, faith, and war.

Once it was the Quraysh. Now it is the Christian West, a conclusion that has formed over a millennium, from the days of the 'Franj' in Palestine. The argument that 'Christian' as an adjective is misplaced generally falls on stone. A remark such as the one made by President George Bush in the aftermath of the attack on the World Trade Center and the Pentagon on 11 September 2001, promising a crusade against Osama bin Laden; or a speech by the Italian Prime Minister Silvio Berlusconi describing Christianity as a more civilized religion than Islam is sufficient to persuade and initiate the unconvinced. The frustration of loss and the memory of green standards that once commanded the heights of political power plays its part.

All empires rise and fall, but the Muslim believes in a three-phase cycle: rise, fall, and renewal. Since an empire is the achievement of man, corruption is inevitable. The Prophet foresaw this when he said that the best Muslims were those of his generation, and that each successive generation would see progressive decline. He understood the ability of power to corrupt, hence his notable dictum: the closer you are to government, the further you are from God.

The lean warrior who conquered a kingdom was bound to change into the obese ruler. The fifth Caliph, who seized power after Islam's first civil war, and must not be seen on the same page as the venerable first four (Hazrats Abu Bakr, Omar, Usman, and Ali), became so fat that by the time he died in 680 he was unable to climb to the pulpit during prayers.

The answer was not capitulation before an infidel, but a continuing moral renaissance from which would emerge the next stage of political success. The Prophet promised in the Sunna the appearance of a true *imam* (the al-Mahdi) – according to one tradition, he would appear every hundred years – who would restore the glory of power through the purity of faith and a return to those first principles that had made Islam into a world presence within a single lifetime. To understand Islam today, we need to understand that beginning.

Treat it if you like as only a poetic truth, but Muslim historians record that on the night that Muhammad was born, the palace of Khusrau, king of the Persians, shook, fourteen of its turrets collapsed, the fire of the Zoroastrians died out, and the lake Sawah sank. Reality would make this prophetic. Persia would become Muslim and the Zoroastrians survive in exile, largely in India. That however was still many travails into the future.

The tradition of divine blessing is strong. Inevitably, there were variations, but one will serve the immediate purpose. Abdullah, Muhammad's father, was walking by the house of the scholar Waraqah ibn Nawfal, along with his father, Abd al-Muttalib ibn Hisham, when Waraqah's sister, Quotila, called out to him to marry her. Waraqah was a *hanif*, a person who accepted monotheism but was neither a Christian nor a Jew. She offered him a hundred camels, but Abdullah would not disobey his father and went with him to the house of Wahb ibn Abdi Manaf, where he was married to Manaf's daughter Amina. He spent three days with his new bride, during which time Muhammad was conceived. On his way back Abdullah met Quotila again, and asked if her proposition still stood. Her reply was crisp: No. There had been a light on his face three days ago and someone had taken it away. She had wanted to be the mother of this child who would be the future Prophet.

Muhammad was not destined to enjoy the love of his parents for very long. His father died two months before he was born, on a journey to a city, Yathrib, that would also become his refuge, and his mother when he was about six. His grandfather Abd al Muttalib doted on him, but could not, obviously, substitute for a mother. Although the family belonged to the Quraysh nobility, they were not very well off. But Muhammad's natural talents soon began to draw attention.

His intelligence and integrity won early recognition. At a relatively young age, for instance, he was selected to arbitrate on a dispute that could have sparked off yet another round of bloodshed between the traditionally fractious tribes. The Kaaba is the great symbol of Islam. Believers everywhere turn to this cube-shaped structure at the centre of the mosque in Mecca to pray five or more times a day. Tradition has it that Adam (the Quran calls both Adam and David *khalifah*s or Caliphs of God) built it at the exact spot on earth directly below the perfect Kaaba in Heaven. Destroyed in the Noah flood, it was rebuilt by Abraham with the help of his son Ishmael from the stones of five mountains, Sinai, al Judi, Hira, Olivet, and Lebanon. Searching for a stone to mark one corner, Ishmael met the angel Gabriel who gave him the famous black stone inside the Kaaba. According to a tradition, the Prophet said that when the stone came from paradise it was whiter than milk, but it had now become black from the sins of those who had touched it.

The Kaaba had fallen into the hands of those who had rejected the Lord God of Abraham.

The man who introduced idolatry into the Kaaba is said to be Amr ibn Luhaiy, who brought the image of Hubal from Mesopotamia and placed it there. The Quraysh now controlled the Kaaba and its revenues; Muhammad's own grandfather was custodian of the Sacred House when it was decided to raise the structure. When the black stone was to be restored to its original place, each tribe was ready to shed blood for the honour of doing so. Muhammad called for a cloak, placed it beneath the stone, and gave a part of the hem to all the tribes. There was peace. They named him al Amin, the one who could be trusted. He was about 35.

His reputation had already brought him to the notice of a rich, twice-married widow of noble ancestry, Khadija bin Khuwaylid. She employed him to oversee her caravans to Syria. He was 25 and she 40 when she sent an emissary, Nafisa bin Munya, to sound out Muhammad on marriage. He agreed, but her father proved a more difficult proposition. Her will prevailed. Muhammad loved Khadija deeply, called her the best of women, and promised that she would live with him in paradise in a house of reeds amidst peace and tranquility. Muhammad of course married again, but only after Khadija passed away. He had three sons, Qasim, Abdullah, and Tahir, but they all died in infancy. His four daughters, Zaynab, Ruqayya, Fatima, and Umm Kulthum lived to normal age. Aisha, the love of the Prophet's later life, was often envious of Khadija, causing Muhammad to rebuke her. He cherished Khadija, he said, because of her loyalty and love: when others did not believe in him, she had faith in him; when others were afraid to whisper support, she stood like a rock. She was his best companion and the mother of his children. He could not forget the decade of trial when the message of Allah lay in his heart, and the faith of a few was mocked and persecuted by a jeering world.

That message came in a cave about three miles out of Mecca called Hira, to which the Prophet would often retire, sustaining himself with only *kaak*, which was flour cooked in oil. One night in the month of Ramadan in 611, the angel Gabriel appeared to him in a dream, held out a long silk strip with written letters and said: 'Read!' (the word in Arabic is *iqra* from which 'Quran' is derived).

The Prophet replied that he did not know how to read. Gabriel grasped the Prophet so tightly to his breast that he thought he would die. Thrice Gabriel commanded: Read! Finally Muhammad answered, 'What am I to read?' Then were revealed the first verses of the Holy Quran, Surah 96, 1–5: 'Proclaim! (or Read!) In the name of thy Lord and Cherisher who created man out of a [mere] clot of congealed blood. Proclaim! And thy Lord is Most Bountiful. He who taught [the use of] the pen taught man that which he knew not.' As Maxime Rodinson (*Mohammed,* Penguin, 1971) puts it: 'The Voice said three words in Arabic which were to shake the world: "You are the messenger of God".'

As he turned towards home, the Prophet began to shiver. He sank his face into his wife's lap and narrated his experience. She realized that the moment had arrived. She comforted her husband and then called on the scholar Waraqah, whose sister had once wooed the Prophet's father Abdullah because she had seen a special light on his brow. Blind with too much reading, old and infirm, Waraqah asked to be led to the Prophet's presence. He said, perhaps with a sense of foreboding: 'I should like to be in the land of the living when your fellow men send you into exile!'

That exile, and worse, including a plot to assassinate him, would come within a decade. A revelation of peace had launched Islam; the hard steel of war would be necessary to protect it.

Allah did not send His message and then leave the Prophet to his own devices; it was an active and interventionist Allah who gave continuing guidance on matters both strategic and personal, spiritual and temporal. That first decade was indeed the darkest in the history of Islam, and sustenance for the small community came from the verses of the Quran, as in Surah 93: 'Thy Guardian-Lord hath not forsaken thee nor is He displeased.' That period has a particular significance today, for crisis and the urge to despair is once again the lot of Muslims. (Quotations from the Quran are from the translation by Abdullah Yusuf Ali, published by Amana Corporation, 1989.)

A wife, a cousin, a companion, and a freed slave were the first four converts to Islam. Khadija was the first. The second was a ten-year-old boy, Ali, who would grow up to become the foremost warrior of the faith, the Lion of God. The third was Abu Bakr, who would deny the succession to Ali, who was praised by the Prophet for his purity and known as Siddiq, and who would be the Prophet's only companion during the emigration. The fourth was a freed man, Zayd. This however was obviously family, or close to it. The first arc of expansion brought in the idealistic young or those who were discriminated against and searching for social justice. Among the most famous was Bilal, an African slave, who was bought and freed by Abu Bakr and who became a cult figure. It was however only a trickle, and the Quraysh restricted their anger to ridicule. Abu Talib, the Prophet's uncle, loved him deeply, and gave him valuable protection, but did not become a Muslim. Another uncle, Abdul Uzza, nicknamed Abu Lahb or father of the flame, was the opposite: he hated the Prophet and the faith.

Matters reached a crisis point when Abu Lahb persuaded enough of the leaders of the Quraysh that they must physically eliminate Muhammad. A scheme was devised to clear the principal hurdle to assassination, the fear that his clan would extract reparation. One member of every clan in the conspiracy would plunge a dagger, making it difficult for Muhammad's people to confront everyone. The Prophet had prepared for the worst. He had made enquiries about a possible move to Taif, but there too encountered hostility. He decided finally on Yathrib, some two hundred miles from Mecca, called Medina, or the city. Three tribes of Jews lived in it, the Qurayza, the Nadir, and the Qayqune. The two dominant Arab tribes were the Aws and the Khazraj. When negotiations were successful the Prophet asked Muslims to precede him to Medina and await his arrival.

His own emigration was full of drama. Abu Jahl was at the door, waiting to ambush Muhammad as he came out, but he fell asleep. The Prophet left Ali on his own bed, the latter's face covered, to buy some time. Furious, the Quraysh offered a hundred she camels to anyone who could overtake Muhammad and Abu Bakr. They had not, in fact, gone very far: they had a rendezvous with a guide at a deserted cave in Jabal Saur. Abu Jahl was part of the group that followed the tracks up to this cave, but they found a shrub had risen, a pair of wild pigeons had built a nest, and a spider had spun a web across the mouth of the cave. They turned away. The Prophet took a route towards the Red Sea coast and then north, cutting across the main road to Medina.

It was a Jew who sighted him at noon near Medina on the twelfth day of Rabiul Awwal, at the foot of a solitary palm tree near an oasis called Quba. On Friday the Prophet entered the city and the first mosque was built in Medina where his camel halted of her own will.

It was at Medina that the believers began to organize themselves as a community. It was here that the practices that still symbolize the faith were laid down. The Muslims were commanded to turn to prayer towards the Kaaba rather than Jerusalem. The Prophet used to fast three days a month: Ramadan was declared a full month of fasting: 'And eat and drink until the white thread of dawn appear to you distinct from its black thread; and then complete your fast till the night appears.'

'To those against whom war is made,' says the Quran (Surah 22, Al Hajj, Verse 39), 'permission is given [to fight], because they are wronged – and verily, Allah is most powerful for their aid.' The meaning is clear enough. Permission to fight is given to those who have been wronged, not to those who take up arms, and this is stressed in the next verse. Over and over again the analogy of David and Goliath is used; David's war is jihad. If ever the Muslims needed a victory against Goliath it was in their first battle at the wells of Badr. The Quraysh had come there with their final solution for the Prophet and the Muslims.

The battle of Badr was fought on Friday the seventeenth of Ramadan, in the second year of the Emigration, at an oasis about fifty miles south west of Medina. Livid at the growing confidence of the Muslim community, a force of over nine hundred well-armed men, including their finest warriors, set out from Mecca with seven hundred camels and a hundred horses. The Muslims could muster an ill-equipped force of about three hundred, with barely four horses between them.

A deeply worried Muhammad turned in only one direction, towards Allah. He prayed fervently in the small hut on the edge of the battlefield where he was billeted with Abu Bakr. If the Muslims were defeated that day, said the anxious Prophet, Allah would never be worshipped again. Abu Bakr intervened to say that this was enough; the Prophet had prayed to Allah, and Allah would save His believers. Too much entreaty would only annoy Allah, he added. Anxious, tired, the Prophet seemed to faint. When he opened his eyes there was a smile on his face; he had good news. He had seen Gabriel in a dream coming to help the Muslims, and sand rising like a whirlwind under the hooves of his horse.

The Prophet announced to the faithful that he had seen the enemy in full flight and recited from an early Meccan Surah (54: Verses 45–6): 'Soon will their multitude be put to flight, and they will show their backs. Nay the Hour (of Judgement) is the time promised them [for their full recompense]: and that hour will be most grievous and most bitter.'

The Prophet made the promise: 'By God in whose hand is the soul of Muhammad, no man will be slain this day fighting against them with steadfast courage, advancing not retreating, but God will cause him to enter Paradise.' Umayr bin al-Humam was eating some dates when he heard this. He flung them aside and asked 'Is there nothing between me and my entering Paradise save to be killed by these men?' He seized his sword and plunged into the enemy, fighting until he was slain. When the Prophet was asked what made Allah laugh with joy at His servant, he replied: 'When he plunges into the midst of the enemy without mail.'

Martyrdom was the Muslim's duty; victory was Allah's responsibility. Those who died would be welcomed by Allah to paradise. At a critical moment in the battle at Badr a dust storm blew into the faces of the Meccans; Gabriel's horse was galloping in. By mid-day the battle was over. The Meccans fled. Among the dead lay Abu Jahl.

Angels are friends and protectors of the believers, particularly those who shape their earthly existence on the lines of Allah's truth and reality, ensuring them the reward of paradise: 'In the case of those who say, "Our Lord is Allah", and, further, stand straight and steadfast, the angels descend on them [from time to time]: 'Fear ye not!' [they suggest], 'Nor grieve! But receive the Glad Tidings of the Garden [of Bliss], that which ye were promised!' (Surah 41, Verse 30).

Such inspiration was enough for the role models of Islam, the names that echo in Muslim hearts. This is the spirit that enabled Ali to tell the

9

Caliph Umar, during discussions on how many troops were required for the battle of Nehawand against the Persians in 642: 'Oh chief of believers! This matter cannot become victory or defeat because of a greater or smaller number. It is Allah's religion which He made superior, and His troops which He has honoured and supported till they have reached where they have reached. We have been promised victory by Allah, and Allah fulfills His promise.' Faith proved stronger than numbers at Nehawand, in the battle that broke the mighty Zoroastrian empire and is described in Muslim chronicles as the 'Victory of Victories'. Obviously, great battles are not won without military strategy, of which Nehawand was a superb example, but at the heart of jihad lies trust in Allah; confidence in human intellect takes second place. When Khalid ibn Walid, who wheeled through a thousand miles of desert to defeat the Byzantines and helped to take Jerusalem, was asked by a Christian Arab how great was the number of the enemy and how many Arabs he had, Khalid replied: 'Woe to you! Do you make me afraid of the Romans!' Once the wounds of his horses and camels had cured he would attack them again, even if their numbers had doubled. Again, when Saad ibn Abi Waqqas crossed the swollen Tigris against the incredulous Persians, they could only exclaim: '*Diwaane! Diwaane! Diwaane!* (Mad! Mad! Mad!) We are not fighting against men but against *jinns*!'

John Bagot Glubb pays the warriors a rather English compliment in *The Great Arab Conquests* (Prentice Hall Inc. Englewood Cliffs, New Jersey, 1963): 'They relied on their military spirit and on individual personal courage rather than on the science of war. The tradition has survived to this day, and has often cost the Muslim dear in contests with more businesslike killers who fight to win. Every Muslim child is brought up on the accounts of the Prophet's life and the Arab conquests, and thus the tradition of personal bravery to the neglect of skill has been perpetuated until now . . .' As Glubb adds, 'Islam is essentially a soldier's religion.'

Stories from the Hadith complement the message of the Holy Quran. There has been more than one compilation of the Prophet's sayings and deeds recounted by those who knew him personally, called the Hadith, or also known as the traditions. Imam Hanbal (780–885) was believed to have memorized a million. The best known work is by one of his students, Abu Abdullah Muhammad ibn Ismail ibn Ibrahim ibn Mughirah al-Jufi al-Bukhari, born in the Central Asian city of Bukhara in 810, who selected some 7,000 traditions culled from 600,000 he had heard. He narrates that the Prophet was once asked by Umar whether it was true that Muslims who died for the cause would go to paradise and pagans to hell. Yes, replied the messenger of Allah, adding: 'Know that paradise is under the shade of swords (*al Jannat-a tahata silal es sayoof*)'. The Prophet said that a single spell of fighting in Allah's cause was better than all the world, and a place in paradise as small as a bow was better than all the world and whatever was in it. The only reason why a person could ever want to leave paradise for this earth would be to get martyred again. Death was only a welcome release; there was no possible deed in this life that could equal jihad in reward after death. The Prophet urged Muslims to seek Firdaus, the best and brightest part of paradise, just below Allah's throne. Allah had reserved one hundred grades of paradise only for the martyrs. The blood of the wounded would smell like musk on the day of resurrection; and nothing could interfere with Allah's reward.

Islam's principles are clear: *La iqra fi ad din* (there shall be no compulsion in religion) and *Lakum dinakum wa layeddin* (your religion for you, and mine for me). However, after Medina, Muslims refused to offer the other cheek to those who would persecute them. Death became a trifle on the way to martyrdom. That too is the romance and conviction of Islam; it is a belief whispered from mother to son. Allah entered into a bargain with the believer. It was a bargain called jihad and it was made in Medina.

2

THE JOYS OF DEATH:
A BARGAIN WITH ALLAH

Says the Holy Quran to believers:

> 'Ye are the best of peoples evolved for mankind, enjoining what is
> right, forbidding what is wrong, and believing in Allah.'
>
> [Verse 110, Surah Ali Imran.]

And Surah 9, Al Tawbah, says in Verse 111:

> 'Allah hath purchased of the Believers their persons and their goods;
> for theirs [in return] is the Garden of Paradise. They fight in His
> Cause and slay and are slain: a promise binding on Him in Truth,
> through the Law, the Gospel, and the Quran. And who is more
> faithful to His Covenant than Allah? Then rejoice in the bargain
> which ye have concluded: that is the achievement supreme.'

The sun sinks into the desert like an eclipse, with the diamond ring
glowing on the top like stone melted by fire. Light sits on the flat
horizon, seeping like a long tide on either side of the sparkling jewel,
reluctant to leave. To the left, a thin moon begins to glow in the twilight.
There are no stars yet. Below me, as we begin to descend over Medina,
the six minarets of the Prophet's mosque glitter like sentinels of a world
within this world. There is only one other mosque with six minarets, built
in 1609 by Sultan Ahmed in Constantinople.

The first brick of the Medina mosque was laid by the Prophet himself;
it was here that the revelation came, in the seventeenth month after the
emigration, asking the faithful to turn towards Mecca instead of Jerusalem
during prayer. It was here that the Prophet received the message of Allah

and the homage of men; where he laid the law, instructed the *umma,* gave strength and shape to a community after his emigration from his birth-place, Mecca; it was in this mosque that he died and is buried. Beside his grave are those of the first two Caliphs, Abu Bakr and Umar. From mod-est beginnings, the mosque has grown to a splendour enabled by fourteen hundred years of devotion. In some indefinable way, the magnificence has not changed the simplicity.

The first *azaan* trembles through the cool morning about an hour before the call for the *fajr* prayer; this is for those who begin their worship earlier than prescribed. My room in the Medina Oberoi has a prized view, overlooking the huge quadrangle through which walk and bustle Muslims from every continent during every day of the year; men and women at peace with themselves and at ease with God in this mosque. Dark moun-tains trace a pattern against a sky that is beginning to awake behind the minarets. The men wear loose cotton trousers up to their ankles or robes; the women cover themselves up to the head. There is no question of a woman hiding her face. Some of the tall, handsome faces of women, a striking contrast against the dark *chador,* dare you to treat them as less than equal.

We reach the Gate of Gabriel, the angel who is known as *Ruhu al Quddus* (the Holy Spirit), in time for the dawn prayer; seven hundred thousand of the faithful can now bow before Allah behind a single imam. A large area is reserved for women. After *namaaz* the momentum shifts to the grave of the Prophet. The inching queues in search of a reverential glance are five deep although it is the month of Shaban and therefore comparatively uncrowded. The numbers multiply in the month after this, the holy thirty days of Ramadan, which draws Muslims like a sacred magnet to Mecca and Medina. The peak of course is during *hajj.*

Normally, Muslims travel to Medina, the city of the Prophet, after they have visited the Kaaba at his birthplace, Mecca. I am not however on the *hajj*; the pilgrimage can be performed only during the eighth, ninth, and tenth days of Zul Hijjah, the twelfth month of the lunar Muslim calendar. I am on *umra,* or the lesser pilgrimage, which can be performed at any time of the year, but does not earn the same merit and is no substitute for the *hajj,* which is compulsory for every believer who can afford to undertake it.

There is no emotion for a Muslim to equal the first sight of the Kaaba; and no feeling close to the sense of complete submission that overtakes him when his forehead touches the ground as he prays to Allah. In that physical act of *namaaz* there is the power of faith, the strength of surrender, and recognition of both the significance and insignificance of life.

Before he leaves for the Kaaba, the pilgrim must bathe, offer two *rikaah* of *namaaz*, and then change into *ihram*: two unstitched, seamless pieces of white cloth that become a monk's liberation. Then is recited the verse of intention, asking Allah to accept this pilgrimage; from thence to the spirit of *labbaika*, the praise and adoration of the unity of God.

The world of Islam swirls around the Kaaba, ceaselessly. During Ramadan and of course the *hajj* the crowds are such that even a camera cannot distinguish individuals from the collective movement of a brotherhood. The guards alone wear perfunctory, job-weary looks, but even they are transformed the moment the *azaan* calls the faithful to prayer. Lines form quickly and effortlessly, beside and then behind; there is no master here save Allah, the rest are equal. They consider themselves fortunate who are able to touch the walls of the chamber that is home to the black stone of Abraham, the first place of prayer, Muslims believe, founded for mankind. Just outside the Kaaba, now encased, is preserved the footprint of that great Prophet of Islam, Christianity, and Judaism. A hundred-odd feet away are the mounts of Safa and Marwah, between which Abraham's wife Hagar ran frantically in search of water for her son Ishmael, and despaired until the angel Gabriel showed her the spring called Zamzam. Muslims simulate that desperate prayer to Allah by running and walking seven times between the two mounts, and still slake their thirst from the water of Zamzam, the spring that will never run dry.

Beyond the holy places, Mecca and Medina fuse first world goods, first class food, and third world ambience. Medina slips into a warren of shops waiting to profit from the secondary pilgrim thirst, for merchandise. The Prophet's mosque is ringed with shops laden with gold jewellery, whose keepers prefer cash to credit card and dollars to any other currency. In the busy months there are human traffic jams at every door. On the streets, veiled women sell light, luminous Arab scarves. Elsewhere, beady-eyed men gossip amidst bedraggled bales of cloth, or scattered Molineux kitchenware, waiting for the woman who must return home with both gifts and necessities from perhaps her only visit to a foreign land.

Restaurants and foodshops fit every budget. The jester of McDonald hamburgers is not too difficult to find in either city, and Coke is sold alongside religious cassettes at the entrance of the Masjid al Quba.

Quba is where the Prophet paused, on the outskirts of the city, on his way to Medina; today it is part of a metropolis that has probably changed more in the past thirty years than it has in the last three hundred. The first man to spot Muhammad was a Jew, who passed on the glad news to the Muslims who had arrived earlier and were anxiously awaiting his arrival. He reached Quba on Monday the twelfth of Rabiul-awwal at high noon. Inevitably there was a competitive clamour to be the host. Muhammad let free the rein of his camel, named Ibn al-Rida, and allowed her to walk or stop wherever she chose. She finally sat down before a place, owned by two orphans, that was used for drying dates. The Prophet paid for the place and ordered a mosque to be built on the site. He himself worked with the Muhajirs and the Ansar on its construction, and they sang a ditty:

> If we sat down while the Prophet worked
> It could be said that we had shirked.

Today a chandelier hangs over the precise spot where the camel stopped; in front is the *mimbar*, and an imposing mosque stretches behind. The Prophet loved this first mosque so much that he came as often as he could, on horseback or on foot, and said that two *rikaah* of prayer here were equivalent to one *umra*.

No one leaves Medina without a visit to the battlefield of Uhud. Our vehicle finds a place among dozens of haphazardly parked tourist buses next to the mound of archers. This was the nether point of the field where the Prophet placed fifty archers on raised ground to guard the rear while the fighting took place on the plain between the mound and a hill. With some shock the pious discover that most of this battlefield has been converted into a housing colony. The decision is deliberate; the colony is not a slum that has been taken over by trespassers. The purist Saudi government has been consciously following a policy of reducing veneration of places associated with the Prophet's life. The explanation? It is Allah who must be worshipped, not Muhammad, His messenger and a man. There was a time when guards used to whip any believer who lingered at the grave of the Prophet in the mosque at Medina; they are less harsh now, but ensure that the queue moves rapidly, and that there is none of the adoration and near-worship that is part of the ethos of so many other Muslim cultures. This is why Uhud has been built over. The graveyard of the 65 martyrs, however, lies untouched. It is surrounded by a wall that protects it, mainly from pilgrims. Notices in Bengali, Urdu, and English warn the believer that Islam permits you to visit the grave of ancestors and heroes because it reminds you of the afterlife, but you can pray only to Allah, not to martyrs and saints, not even to intercede on your behalf to Allah.

The graves of those martyrs tell one of the most powerful stories in the history of the faith.

The Quraysh could not reconcile themselves to the defeat at Badr, which they treated as a fluke. With men like Abu Jahl having lost their lives in the last battle, Abu Sufyan became the pre-eminent leader of the Quraysh. His wife, the spirited Hind, had always hated Muhammad, and the loss of her father and two sons at Badr had increased her bitterness. She refused to sleep with her husband until Badr had been avenged. Abu Sufyan planned his moves with care.

In the meanwhile, the Prophet quickly established his leadership in his adopted city, binding the three communities, Jews, Pagans, and Muslims, through a convenant or a constitution that assured equality and the commitment of mutual assistance in the event of any community being attacked. The Prophet would be arbitrator in the event of any dispute. However, the theory worked less well in practise, not the least of the reasons being jealousy and the worst being treachery. Abu Sufyan established contact with at least one Jewish tribe, the Bani Nadir, and was entertained by their chief Sallam ibn Mishkam. Abu Sufyan wanted to ensure that the Quraysh would not face a united Medina when they attacked the Muslims. He had sufficient evidence to be confident. One of the principal enemies of the Muslims, a poet who used evocative verse to stir the sprit of vengeance among the Quraysh, was Kab ibn al-Ashraf, a member of the same tribe.

It took them a year to prepare, and the wealth of one caravan was the budget. The Quraysh army that headed for Medina had a force of 3,000, with 3,000 camels and some two hundred horses. They were so confident of victory that they brought their women along, with Hind as the principal cheerleader. She had promised herself that she would eat the liver of that great Muslim warrior Hamza, uncle of the Prophet. The Muslims learnt of their arrival when the Quraysh were near Medina. Disputes arose about what they should do. The more ardent Muslims, with Badr as their example, demanded war despite their huge disadvantage in numbers and equipment. Others warned that this would be suicide. The Quraysh, on the other hand, had clarity. They wanted to see the Prophet dead and the faith annihilated.

Muhammad finally donned his armour on Friday, the sixth of Shawal, and decided that he would meet the Quraysh at Uhud, some three miles north, the following day. Doubts lingered through the evening but, as he said, a Prophet does not take off his armour once he has worn it. The Jews did not honour the Medina covenant; they said they would not fight on Sabbath. There was more bad news. Muhammad had about a thousand men under his command. Of these, three hundred deserted him on the morning of the battle at the urging of Abdullah ibn Ubbay, who dreamt of taking over the leadership of the community after, as he expected, the Prophet had been defeated. This group has become infamous as the *munafiqeen* or the hypocrites; the betrayal could not have come at a worse moment.

Abu Sufyan was at the centre of the Quraysh forces; on his right was Khalid ibn Walid and on his left Ikrimah, son of Abu Jahl. Before the fighting began, Abu Sufyan asked the Aws and Khasraj tribes, who were allies of the Muslims under the pact, to leave the field as the Meccans had no quarrel with them. They answered with an insult. Quraysh morale was however high, lifted higher by Hind, who sang to tambourine music: 'If you advance we will hug you and spread soft rugs for you; if you retreat we will leave you and deny you our love.' She had certainly denied hers to her husband for a year.

Muhammad posted fifty archers at the back, atop a mound, with strict orders to prevent an assault from the rear, irrespective of the fate of the main battle; the rest of his force faced the enemy in the manner of Badr. The aggressive Muslims dominated the first phase of battle; this proved their undoing. The archers, assuming that victory was theirs, disobeyed orders and raced forward, anxious not to be left behind in the scramble for booty. Khalid ibn Walid, seeing his opportunity, used his horses in a splendid cavalry charge that won the day despite severe hand-to-hand fighting towards the end.

As the Muslims fell back, a cry went up that the Prophet had been killed, but that was wrong; he was only wounded and lost one tooth. This incident led to the famous revelation: 'Muhammad is no more than a Messenger: many were the Messengers that passed away before him. If he died or were slain, will ye then turn back on your heels? [3:144].' The Prophet rallied the Muslims and prevented defeat from becoming a rout.

Abu Sufyan actually went within hearing distance of the group around Muhammad to check whether what he had heard from a person called Ibn Qamia was true; had the Quraysh killed the Prophet? Umar replied, 'By God, you have not, he is listening to what you are saying now'. Abu Sufyan then regretted the desecration of Muslim corpses after battle but, before he turned to Mecca, he threw a last taunt: they would meet again in Badr next year. The Quraysh had not achieved what they wanted, and their reputation was blackened.

Abu Sufyan had reason for a personal apology. It was his wife who was responsible for the mutilation of bodies for she was determined to keep her promise and taste the liver of Hamza. An Abysinnian slave, Wahshi, an expert with a lance, had martyred Hamza only because he had been promised his freedom by his master, Jubayr, if he killed Hamza. The moment he did so, he left the field, his own role over. The savagery with which the Quraysh women behaved, shamed even their own ranks. Hind actually tore out Hamza's liver and tasted it.

The battle of Badr is known as *furqan*, or the first trial between good and evil; but there was much to be learnt from Uhud, a day of trial and test, and a jihad that ended in adversity. The verses of the third Surah, Ali Imran, constitute a lesson that is particularly relevant today, when Muslims see themselves as victims rather than victors.

Both success and failure come from Allah, says the Quran, and there are reasons for both. It is meaningless to exult at the first or grumble at the second, because both are part of Allah's plan. The real test of a Muslim's faith comes in adversity; sin is purified through resistance, struggle and faith, and in any case nothing can be more glorious than martyrdom. Sometimes victory for the unbeliever is nothing but the rope by which he hangs himself; the Quraysh destroyed their reputation by their behaviour after battle when they mutilated corpses after Uhud, alienating their own and thereby hastening the eventual victory of Islam.

'So,' says the Quran (3:139), 'lose not heart, nor fall into despair: for ye must gain mastery if ye are true in Faith.'

Mastery, and renewal, is yours, if you are true in faith. 'Allah's object also is to purge those that are true in Faith and to deprive of blessing those that resist Faith. Did ye think that ye would enter Heaven without Allah testing those of you who fought hard [in His Cause] and remained steadfast? [Verses 141 and 142].' The Prophet emerged from the wounds of Uhud stronger, and Islam never looked back.

Why did the Muslims lose? Because they fell victim to this world's gold, because of their greed for booty. 'Allah did indeed fulfill His promise to you when ye with His permission were about to annihilate your enemy – until ye flinched and fell to disputing about the order, and disobeyed it after He brought you in sight [of the booty] which ye covet. Among you are some that hanker after this world and some that desire the Hereafter. Then did He divert you from your foes in order to test you. But He forgave: for Allah is full of grace to those who believe [3:152].'

And, again, in Verse 166: 'What ye suffered on the day the two armies met, was with the leave of Allah, in order that He might test the Believers.' As for martyrs, 'Think not of those who are slain in Allah's way as dead. Nay, they live, finding their sustenance in the Presence of their Lord.'

For those who survive, defeat is paradise postponed. But only if they keep the faith. It is easy to believe in victory; the true strength comes from faith after defeat. Only that can ensure the miracle of renewal, and the return of victory.

This happened after Uhud. The Prophet was wounded, as were they, but they rallied around, confident that neither their limited numbers nor their initial reverses would prevent eventual victory. The Meccans left. Abu Sufyan's taunt was worthless; the Muslims kept the appointment at Badr the following year, but the Meccans did not. Uhud had removed, in a colourful phrase, 'the stain of Satan' (8:11). Uhud is triumph through inner cleansing, and therefore the greater jihad.

The 286 verses of the second Surah of the Quran, the Al Baqarah, constitute the longest chapter in the Quran and set out its moral principles, just as the seven verses of the opening chapter, Al Fatiha, sum up its essence. (The 'Verse of the Throne', or the Ayat-ul-Kursi, that describes the attributes of Allah, is in this Surah, Verse 255.) The defining story of jihad is one that should be as familiar to Jews and Christians as it is to Muslims. It is the story of David and Goliath.

Different prophets were given different missions, says the Quran: Allah spoke directly to Moses who led his people through wilderness for forty years and struggled with the unbelief of his own people; Jesus, 'strengthened . . . with the holy spirit' (Verse 253) had to fight without weapons; David, though a poor shepherd, was chosen by Allah to fight and slay the greatest warrior of the age. Shepherd, musician, poet, warrior, king and prophet, David refused Saul's armour and sword, and retained his sling and faith. Verses 249 and 250 narrate:

19

When Talut [Saul] set forth with the armies, he said: 'Allah will test you at the stream; if any drinks of its water, he goes not with my army; only those who taste not of it go with me; a mere sip out of the hand is excused.' But they all drank of it, except a few. When they crossed the river – he and the faithful ones with him, they said: 'This day we cannot cope with Goliath and his forces.' But those who were convinced that they must meet Allah, said: 'How oft, by Allah's will, hath a small force vanquished a big one? Allah is with those who steadfastly persevere.' When they advanced to meet Goliath and his forces they prayed: 'Our Lord! Pour out constancy on us and make our steps firm: help us against those that reject faith.'

By Allah's will, they routed them: and David slew Goliath: and Allah gave him power and wisdom and taught him whatever [else] He willed. And did not Allah check one set of people by means of another, the earth would indeed be full of mischief: but Allah is full of bounty to all the worlds.

This was the true jihad. The lessons are part of living Islam and are best enumerated by Abdullah Yusuf Ali:

1. Numbers do not count, but faith, determination and the blessing of Allah; 2. size and strength are of no avail against truth, courage, and careful planning; 3. the hero tries his own weapons, and those that are available to him at the time and place, even though people may laugh at him; 4. if Allah is with us, the enemy's weapon may become an instrument of his own destruction; 5. personality conquers all dangers, and puts heart into our own wavering friends; 6. pure faith brings Allah's reward, which may take many forms: in David's case it was Power, Wisdom, and other gifts . . .

The parallels with the twenty-first century are not hard to find.

The first war revelation, in Medina, gave Muslims permission to fight because they had been wronged. The tone of the second revelation is sharper, and as it is widely quoted we need to examine Verses 190 to 193 of Al Baqarah.

The very first of these verses is quite emphatic in its rejection of terrorism. 'Fight in the cause of Allah those who fight you, but do not transgress limits; for Allah loveth not transgressors.' What are these trans-gressions? Abdullah Yusuf Ali explains: 'War is permissible in self-defence, and under well-defined limits. When undertaken, it must be pushed with vigour [but not relentlessly], but only to restore peace and freedom for the worship of Allah. In any case strict limits must not be transgressed: women, children, old and infirm men should not be molested, nor trees and crops cut down, nor peace withheld when the enemy comes to terms.'

There is however no suggestion that you should be squeamish in a war against those who persecute Muslims; instead of the other cheek, the sword point emerges. 'And slay them wherever ye catch them, and turn them out from where they have turned you out; for tumult and oppression are worse than slaughter. But fight them not at the Sacred Mosque unless they [first] fight you there; but if they fight you, slay them. Such is the reward of those who suppress faith [2:191].'

Verse 192 is the antidote and requires little explanation: 'But if they cease, Allah is Oft-Forgiving, Most Merciful.' Neither does 193: 'And fight them on until there is no more tumult or oppression, and there prevail justice and faith in Allah; but if they cease let there be no hostility except to those who practise oppression.'

The Quran scorns those Muslims who shy away from a just war. Verse 216 of Al Baqarah says: 'Fighting is prescribed upon you, and ye dislike it. But it is possible that ye dislike a thing which is good for you, and that ye love a thing which is bad for you. But Allah knoweth and ye know not.' There is a clarification: fighting does not mean selfish aggression, and the highest censure is reserved for the bully and the oppressor. Conversely, there is no higher form of sacrifice than death in a jihad. Verse 38 of Surah 9, which was revealed when some Muslims did not want to follow the Prophet on a mission to Tabuk against the Christian Byzantines, says: 'O ye who believe! What is the matter with you, that, when ye are asked to go forth in the Cause of Allah, ye cling heavily to the earth? Do ye prefer the life of this world to the Hereafter?' One excuse that the shirkers had made was that it would be too hot during the Tabuk campaign. 'The fire of Hell,' says Verse 81 of Surah 9, 'is fiercer in heat.'

The Muslim who turns his back during a war of jihad has only one destination, hell. Verses 15, 16 and 17 of Al Anfal say: 'O ye who believe! When ye meet the Unbelievers in hostile array, never turn your backs to them. If any do turn his back to them on such a day – unless it be in a stratagem of war, or to retreat to a troop [of his own], he draws on

himself the wrath of Allah, and his abode is Hell – an evil refuge indeed!'
Al Anfal means the spoils of war, and the spoils are certain for believers
– even when the confrontation is with a great power, as the Christian
kingdom of the Byzantines undoubtedly was at the time. Also, as we have
seen repeatedly, numbers are not important, victory will come without
them. Verses 65 and 66 of Al Anfal state: 'O Prophet! Rouse the Believers
to the fight. If there are twenty amongst you, patient and persevering,
they will vanquish two hundred; if a hundred they will vanquish a thousand of the Unbelievers: for these are a people without understanding.'

Death is only a temptation, not a fear. 'And if ye are slain, or die, in
the way of Allah, forgiveness and mercy from Allah are far better than all
they could amass,' says Verse 157 of Surah 3, Ali Imran.

The translation of *Sahih al Bukhari* (the collection of 7,000 sayings of
the Prophet culled from 600,000 after sixteen years of painstaking scholarship by Imam Bukhari, born in Bukhara in 810 and died in 870) by Dr
Muhammad Muhsin Khan of the Islamic University of Medina (published
by Kitab Bhavan, New Delhi, 1987) uses a sermon delivered by Sheikh
Abdullah bin Muhammad bin Hamid of the Sacred Mosque of Mecca. He
traces the history of jihad from optional to obligatory, if the war is just
and in the cause of Allah, and reaffirms the terms of the second of the so-
called jihad chapters, Al Tawbah (chronologically however, the two are
separated by around seven years; it is among the last of the Surahs revealed and is the only one not prefaced by a Bismillah). As the verses here
make jihad obligatory, they are often quoted to prove that every Muslim
has to respond to any call for jihad. But there are qualifications. The
question is: what should be done if an enemy is treacherous, or a treaty
is violated? Four months notice has to be given of treachery before a jihad
is undertaken, and the door must always be kept open for repentance, and
only if this fails should war begin – and then be pursued with all vigour.
Verse 39 puts it succinctly: 'Unless ye go forth, He [Allah] will punish you
with a grievous penalty, and put others in your place.' Muslims can sus-
pend a jihad for tactical reasons but not abandon it.

The sermon dwells in detail on the rewards of the bargain: the souls
of martyrs could live wherever they liked in paradise, all their sins forgiven;
the martyr could intercede with Allah for seventy of his relatives. What
was Sheikh Abdullah's message? Allah will send the angels of Badr and
victory is guaranteed, but before victory comes, believers must believe.
The modern Muslim was leading a life of one who would not recognize

the Prophet, or understand the divine message; Muslims had become the illiterate pagans they had replaced. Muslims must cleanse themselves if they wanted success in this life.

Allah offers a bargain: this is the specific term used in the Quran. See Verse 111 of Surah 9 (Al Tawbah): 'Allah hath purchased of the Believers their persons and their goods; for theirs [in return] is the Garden of Paradise. They fight in His Cause, and slay and are slain; a promise binding on Him in Truth, through the Law, the Gospel, and the Quran: and who is more faithful to his Covenant than Allah? Then rejoice in the bargain which ye have concluded: that is the achievement supreme.'

It was surely the greatest bargain in history, for no other has powered such martial energy and such disdain for life. In a stirring passage in the third Surah (Verses 169 and 170), the Quran says: 'Think not of those who are slain in Allah's way as dead. Nay, they live, finding their sustenance in the presence of their Lord; they rejoice in the Bounty provided by Allah: and with regard to those left behind, who have not yet joined them [in their bliss], the [martyrs] glory is in the fact that on them is no fear, nor have they cause to grieve.'

What then is paradise like for the righteous? Verse 15 of Surah 47 explains: 'In it are rivers of water incorruptible; rivers of milk of which the taste never changes; rivers of wine, a joy to those who drink; and rivers of honey pure and clear. In it there are for them all kinds of fruits; and Grace from their Lord.'

The joys of paradise are strewn across the Holy Book. Take Verses 70 and 71 of Surah 43 [Al Zukhruf]: 'Enter ye the Garden, ye and your wives, in [beauty and] rejoicing. To them will be passed round, dishes and goblets of gold: there will be there all that the souls could desire, all that the eyes could delight in: and ye shall abide therein (for aye.)'

Surah 76 (Al Insan), after promising 'Chains, Yokes and A Blazing Fire' for those who reject Islam, says that the righteous 'shall drink a cup [of wine] mixed with *kafur*' – that is, camphor – just after the judgment. They will then enter paradise in garments of silk and brocade, decked in ornaments and jewels, a reward for their former humility; after which comes another cup of pure wine, mixed with *zanjabil* (ginger) from a fountain called Salsabil. At a divine banquet in the Realm Magnificent 'their Lord will give to them to drink of a Wine Pure and Holy' (Surah 76, Verse 21). In Surah 83 (22–36) the joys of paradise are described to those who mocked at believers in this life: 'Truly the Righteous will be in

Bliss; on Thrones [of Dignity] will they command a sight [of all things]. Thou wilt recognize in their Faces the beaming brightness of Bliss. Their thirst will be slaked with Pure Wine sealed: the seal thereof will be musk; and for this let those aspire who have aspirations. With it will be [given] a mixture of *Tasnim*, a spring from [the waters] whereof drink those nearest to Allah.' *Tasnim* means height and opulence and refers to the purest wine, a nectar.

And 'They will recline [with ease] on Thrones [of dignity] arranged in ranks; and We shall join them to Companions, with beautiful big and lustrous eyes' (Surah 52, Verse 20). The non-carnal case for houris has been well made by Abdullah Yusuf Ali: 'The Companions, like the scene, the dress, the outlook, and the fruit, will be beautiful. There will be life but free from all earthly grossness. The women as well as the men of this life will attain to this indescribable bliss.'

Verses 45 to 49 of Surah 37 (Al Saffat) promise that 'Round will be passed to them a Cup from a clear-flowing fountain, crystal-white, of a taste delicious to those who drink [thereof], free from headiness; nor will they suffer intoxication therefrom. And beside them will be chaste women; restraining their glances, with big eyes [of wonder and beauty]. As if they were [delicate] eggs closely guarded.'

Hell too is very specific. 'Those who reject Our Signs, We shall soon cast into the fire; as often as their skins are roasted through, we shall change them for fresh skins, that they may taste the Penalty: for Allah is Exalted in Power, Wise [4:56].' For the obstinate transgressor, this is the punishment: 'In front of such a one is Hell, and he is given for drink, boiling fetid water. In gulps will he sip it, but never will he be near swallowing it down his throat: death will come to him from every quarter, yet will he not die: and in front of him will be a chastisement unrelenting [14:16–17].' In Verses 49 and 50 of the same Surah, is written: 'And thou wilt see the Sinners that day bound together in fetters, their garments of liquid pitch, and their faces covered with fire.'

Before Abu Sufyan left the battlefield of Uhud, he went to the top of the mountain and shouted to Hubal, his god: 'Victory in war goes by turns . . . Today has come in exchange for Badr: show your superiority, Hubal!'

The Prophet heard this and asked Umar to reply: 'God is most high and most glorious. We are not equal. Our dead are in Paradise; your dead are in hell.'

That is the difference for the believer.

If there is a symbolic sword of Islam, then it is the one given by the Prophet to his son-in-law Ali, known as Zulfiqar. Ali is the lion of God, the hero of Islam. That sword was given to Ali not at the miracle of Badr but at the renewal of Uhud.

As for the 'victors' of Uhud, Abu Sufyan's son, Muawiya, established the great Ummayad dynasty after the death of the Prophet's grandson, Hasan, which ruled from 661 to 749. The dashing Khalid ibn Walid, whose cavalry charge defeated the Muslims, accepted Islam soon after Uhud. He led the Prophet's advance on Mecca and, before he died, ensured the victory of Muslim armies in Christian Jerusalem, Syria, and Iraq as far as the Euphrates.

As Allah pointed out, He has a plan.

3

REBELLIONS IN THE DARK OF THE NIGHT

The last injunction that the apostle gave was in his words 'Let not two religions be left in the Arabian peninsula'. (The apostle died on the twelfth Rabi-ul-awwal on the very day that he came to Medina as an emigrant, having completed exactly twelve years in his migration.) When the apostle was dead the Muslims were sore stricken. I have heard that Aisha used to say, 'When the apostle died the Arabs apostatized and Christianity and Judaism raised their heads and disaffection appeared. The Muslims became as sheep exposed to rain on a winter's night through the loss of their Prophet until God united them under Abu Bakr.'

[From *The Life of Muhammad* by Ibn Ishaq, born in Medina c. AH 85 and died in Baghdad in AH 151.]

Hind, who had tasted his uncle's liver, was understandably apprehensive as she waited in line to pay homage to Muhammad. Her husband, Abu Sufyan, leader of the Quraysh, had already become a Muslim. He welcomed Muhammad, who wore a red turban of Yemeni cloth as he entered his birthplace in triumph on the twentieth of Ramadan, in 630 by the Western calendar, at the head of ten thousand fully-armed Muhajirs and Ansars. Hind resisted to the end; outraged, she went up to Abu Sufyan, seized his moustaches, and cried to the Quraysh, 'Kill this fat, greasy bladder of lard! What a rotten protector of the people!' Abu Sufyan told his people not to be deceived by 'this woman' and accept the Muslim victory.

Muhammad, astride his camel, went to the Kaaba and circled it seven times. He touched the black stone with the stick in his hand, then took the key from the keeper, Uthman bin Talha, and went inside. He found a wooden dove and broke it into three. There were three hundred and sixty idols. The Prophet recited from the Quran (17:81): 'Truth has arrived, and falsehood perished; for falsehood is [by its nature] bound to perish.' After the noon prayer every idol was broken and burnt. All the pictures were erased, except two: those of Jesus and Mary.

Then the Prophet moved to the mountain, al-Safa, to accept individual allegiance. First came the men, then the women. As Muhammad would not touch the hand of a woman who was not family, a vessel of water was placed so that she could dip her fingers after him as a sign of her allegiance. Hind, defeated but not quite deflated, joined the queue, wearing a veil to disguise her identity, but she could hardly disguise her temperament. The conditions were announced. After submission to Allah and obedience to His apostle, came: 'And you shall not steal.' Hind replied: 'By God, I used to take a little of Abu Sufyan's money and I do not know whether that is lawful or not.' Her husband, perhaps with an air of resignation, answered that it was lawful in the past. The Prophet intervened: 'Then you are Hind?' he asked. She replied: 'I am; forgive me what is past and God will forgive you.'

Muhammad placed the next stipulation: 'And do not commit adultery.' Hind answered: 'Does a free woman commit adultery, O apostle of God?'

Muhammad then said, 'And you shall not kill your children.' Hind shot back: 'I brought them up when they were little and you killed them on the day of Badr when they were grown up, so you are the one to know about them!'

Umar, who was sitting by the Prophet, burst out laughing at her reply.

Muhammad continued, 'You shall not invent slanderous tales.' She said, 'By God, slander is disgraceful, but it is sometimes better to ignore it.'

The Prophet's last condition was, 'You shall not disobey me in carrying out orders to do good.' Hind answered: 'We should not have sat all this time if we wanted to disobey you in such orders.'

This remarkable exchange distils the spirit of Islam. The Prophet was the unquestioned leader, with the homage of men and the message of God, but there was no sense of any craven fawning. It was a community of equals, united through a common submission to Allah. This did not imply that there were no differences between the faithful, or that there could be no differences. Differences arose immediately after the death of Muhammad, over, predictably, the succession, culminating in civil wars and the epic confrontation between the grandson of Hind, Yazid, and the grandson of the Prophet, Husayn, at Karbala. Never did the Muslims need a rightly-guided leader more than on the day that the Prophet died.

Abu Bakr, his friend and closest companion, was leading the morning prayer on the twelfth of Rabi-ul-awwal (632 by the Western calendar) when Muhammad entered the mosque at Medina. There was a stir, and Abu Bakr stood aside to let the Prophet lead the prayers. Muhammad however, told him, 'Lead the men in prayer,' and took a place to his right. When the prayers were over, Muhammad said to the congregation in a loud voice: 'O men! The fire is kindled, and rebellions come like the darkness of the night. By God, you can lay nothing to my charge. I allow only what the Quran allows and forbid only what the Quran forbids.'

He then went to the residence of his wife Aisha, Abu Bakr's daughter, and died in her arms that day. She placed his head on a pillow, and stood up, beating her breast and slapping her face in grief.

Umar threatened to cut off the hands and feet of anyone who said the Prophet had died: Muhammad, Umar said, had only gone to meet Allah just as Moses had done for forty days. Abu Bakr rebuked Umar in a speech that has become a testament of faith. 'Oh men,' he cried, 'if anyone worships Muhammad, Muhammad is dead; if anyone worships God, God is alive, immortal.' He recited the famous verse from the Quran revealed eight years earlier after a cry went out during the battle of Uhud that the wounded Prophet had died: 'Muhammad is no more than a Messenger: many were the Messengers that passed away before him. If he died, or were slain, will ye then turn back on your heels?' (3: 144).

Three factions emerged almost immediately. One consisted of the original Medinaites, called the Ansar. The second were the Muhajir, from the original seventy two who had emigrated with the Prophet from Mecca, the first Muslims. Then there was the group who believed that succession should go only to the Prophet's family, the Banu Hashim, whose claims were represented by the Prophet's daughter Fatimah and her husband Ali. A fourth group, the aristocracy led by Abu Sufyan, the most recent converts, held its peace for the moment.

The Ansars gathered in the hall of Banu Saidah to press their claims. Abu Bakr and Umar went to meet them and a consensus emerged around Abu Bakr. He took quiet charge in a volatile vacuum.

Abu Bakr adopted the title of the Caliph of the Prophet of Allah. There is no better definition of that responsibility than the one given by him. He told the assembled Muslims in the hall:

I have been given authority over you but I am not the best of you. If I do well, help me, and if I do ill, then put me right. Truth consists in loyalty and falsehood in treachery. The weak among you shall be strong in my eyes until I secure his right if God will; and the strong among you shall be weak in my eyes until I wrest the right from him. If a people refrain from fighting in the way of God, God will smite them in disgrace. Wickedness is never widespread in a people but God brings calamity upon them all.

Then the crucial part: 'Obey me as long as I obey God and His apostle, and if I disobey them you owe me no obedience.'

This splendid and idealistic definition marks the beginning of what Bernard Lewis has called 'by far the greatest and most important sovereign institution in Islamic history' (*The Political Language of Islam*, The University of Chicago Press, Chicago, 1988). But in the idealism also lay the serious danger of continual challenge in the name of an elusive ideal.

There was always so much space between Allah's way and the waywardness of His followers. As the Prophet was the only man who could walk Allah's route with perfection, it was inevitable that those men who held office after Muhammad would leave small or large reasons for comparison, complaint, and, at some end of the tether, rebellion. Abu Bakr himself indicated that Muslims should obey him only as long as he obeyed Allah and His apostle, otherwise they owed him no obedience. If Muslims could find fault with Abu Bakr, the least controversial of the 'rightly guided' Caliphs, then there was little hope of docile obedience towards the men of variable ability that followed. The higher jihad was cleansing oneself, and a purge within became a recurrent reason for the call to jihad against rulers who were perceived to have betrayed the principles of Islam or the interests of Muslims.

Within the brief two and a half years that he was Caliph, Abu Bakr fulfilled the last injunction of the Prophet: the apostates were crushed in the wars of Ridda, and the whole of the Arabian peninsula came under Muslim rule. He however faced opposition at Medina from none other than a hero of the faith, Ali. Ali was incensed that he had not been consulted over the succession. This anger turned to bitterness when Abu Bakr passed him over as *his* successor, naming Umar instead. Umar was once so infuriated by Ali's wife that he threatened to set fire to Fatimah's house if she continued to use it as a rendezvous for dissent. There were companions of the Prophet who argued that Umar was too authoritarian, but he was also sagacious in administration and audacious in war. During his ten years in office, the city state became an empire that included Palestine, Egypt, the greater part of Iran, and then north to Azerbaijan and Armenia. Significantly, when he lay dying from a knife wound inflicted by a Persian servant, Umar made the elders promise that they would *not* consider his son, Abdallah, as his successor but choose, within three days of his death, one of six claimants. Among the six was Ali, and Umar left the final decision to others.

The elders narrowed the choice to Uthman, an Ummayad, and Ali; Ali again lost out. Uthman was over seventy, but remained Caliph for twelve years. His term was riven with controversy. As wealth began to pour into Medina from conquered territories, Umar's strict management of the state's treasury gave way to flexibility and accusations of corruption. Beneficiaries called Uthman generous; detractors called it nepotism. His opponents accused him of irreverence when he ordered all copies of the Quran burnt except the official version that was compiled in his time. Uthman complained that Muslims who had tolerated Umar's whip were now rebelling against his largesse; but he was clearly missing the point. Abstinence was part of the ideal Islamic ethic, as Muslims had seen practised by the Prophet. Uthman, said his enemies, had wandered from Allah's prescribed way. The third Caliph was brutally assassinated in 656 by a group instigated, among others, by companions of the Prophet and his favourite wife Aisha. Aisha's brother, also called Muhammad, was one of the perpetrators of the murder.

His death sparked such internecine violence, with each faction claiming the right to protect the faith, that the elders begged a now reluctant Ali to become Caliph. Under Ali, however, the civil wars became more intense. On one side he was challenged by Uthman's kin, the Umayyads. The governor of Syria, Muawiya, Hind's son, charged Ali with instigating the murder of Uthman. Ali shifted his capital from Medina to Kufa in Iraq to meet this threat; and there found that he had to face a Muslim army led by Aisha. Muslim commentators weep at the death of thousands of the faithful in what is known as the Battle of the Camel. In 657, Ali encountered the forces of Muawiya, at Siffin, in Syria. Ali said that he could have dealt with Muawiya but felt betrayed by Aisha, who was family. Muawiya offered a compromise to end the civil war; arbitration on the basis of the Quran. When Ali agreed, one of his own followers, from the dissenters who are known as the Khwarij, killed him – for betraying the faith by accepting this compromise. Even Ali was not considered faithful enough by some of the faithful!

Ali's son Hasan took his father's mantle, making the succession hereditary for the first time in Islam. But Muawiya's challenge was not over. He opened negotiations with Hasan and argued that a Caliph must combine commitment to faith with an ability to rule. Noting that Muslims had once chosen Abu Bakr over Ali, Muawiya wrote to Hasan: 'Had I believed that you had a better grasp over the subject people than I did and that you were in a stronger position to safeguard the lives and properties of the Muslims and in outwitting the enemy than I, I would have done what you have asked me to do. But I have had a long period of administration, and I am far more experienced. I have better understanding of politics and also I am much older than you.' Hasan accepted the argument, and Muawiya became Caliph. The peaceful transfer of power did not end the tension: when Hasan died prematurely, his followers accused Muawiya of having had him poisoned.

Muawiya was as good an administrator as he claimed to be: he ensured twenty years of internal peace and external advance across fresh frontiers. He renewed the Muslim challenge to the mighty Byzantines, but there was no prejudice against Christians during his regime. He opted for merit in administration, including Christians and Jews in offices of state. His chief secretary was a Syrian Christian. He was less generous to dissent by Muslims. When trouble arose in Basra, he sent Ziyad as governor who told the warring factions: 'Many heads do I see tottering; let each man see that his own remains on his shoulders.' With Muawiya, the Caliph also became a *malik*, or a king: Umar would have wept at the thought. The role of Caliph had adjusted to the needs of an expanding empire. By the time Muawiya died, Muslims ruled from Sind in India to the Maghreb, and Bokhara in the north. His success made serious opposition to his methods untenable. His philosophy of government (quoted from Ibn al-Ibri by Philip Hitti in *History of the Arabs*, Publisher, London, 1973) has become a classic: 'I apply not my lash where my tongue suffices, nor my sword where my whip is enough. And if there be one hair binding me to my fellow men, I let it not break. If they pull, I loosen and if they loosen I pull.'

What united Muslims in that unparalleled burst of initial success was faith, what separated them in the years after Muawiya was politics.

Contemporary Muslims, despairing of an Abu Bakr or Umar or Ali or

31

even a Muawiya to lead them, might find the son of Muawiya, Yazid (680–83), more familiar to their experience. He was the antithesis of his father, brutal, greedy, and a Muslim by the accident of birth rather than the virtue of conviction. In three terrible years he destroyed the stability his father had achieved. Advised by his father to be gentle with Hasan's brother Husayn, Yazid opted for aggression that made the schism between Sunni and Shia unbridgeable. In 680, in the heat of the month of Muharram, his far superior forces surrounded and massacred Husayn, his family, and his small band of companions at Karbala, some sixty miles from Baghdad. Yazid's general, Ubaydallah, brought him a macabre gift from Karbala: the severed head of Husayn, and his sycophants laughed while they kicked the head around till one man begged them not to show such disrespect to the grandson of the Prophet.

Blood and confusion travel together in this phase of Muslim history, as they tend to do at times when the rudder is lost. Within fifty years of the Prophet's death, there were three men in close proximity to one another, each claiming to be Caliph. In Damascus, Yazid's son could not succeed him and an official, Marwan, took charge. When he died in 684, his son Abdal Malik became Caliph.

In the deserts of Arabia, a rebel, Abdallah bin al Zubayr, seized the holy cities, and by virtue of this called himself the Caliph. In Kufa, Ali's capital, a fascinating figure called Mukhtar raised an 'Army of Penitents' because they had not been able to defend the rights of the Prophet's family, and declared for Ali's son, Muhammad ibn al-Hanafiya. Mukhtar took at least partial revenge for Karbala when he defeated and then decapitated Ubaydallah at the same spot where Husayn had fallen. Mukhtar was more than a warrior. He rallied the poor behind him with his stress on the equality promised in the Quran, and offered a dream that lifts depression to this day. He proclaimed that there would come a 'hidden Imam', the Mahdi, who would restore righteousness to this world and lead Muslim armies to victory.

Abdal Malik was one of the great Caliphs. He first waited for his rivals to settle their dispute. They did. Abdallah defeated Mukhtar. Then Abdal Malik turned on the victor. His army captured the holy cities. Abdallah fell in battle and his head received traditional treatment: it was impaled on a spear and sent to Damascus.

The rebellions had come thick and fast in the darkness of the night. The dawn, when it came, was glorious. Caliph Abdal Malik and his heirs created over the next hundred years an empire larger than any in history, fused by good administration and leavened by intellectual pursuit.

Decline was however almost inevitable: the Ummayads abandoned Islamic ideals, culture degenerated and politics followed. Rafiq Zakaria, the eminent Islamic historian, notes that 'it was their betrayal of the concept of Islamic brotherhood, irrespective of race or language, that brought them down' (*The Struggle Within Islam,* Viking, 1988). As we shall see, they were replaced by one of their generals, Abu al-Abbas, a distant relative of the Prophet. With the Abbasids began another cycle of rise, decline, and renewal in Muslim history.

The Caliphate was the one institution that survived the changing dynasties. What lay behind the strength of this idea? While Sunni Muslims, spread across three continents, recognized more than one king at any given moment, they generally accepted only one of them as Caliph. There had to be a rationale for such a status. This was ably laid down in the sixteenth century by the Turkish *ulema* after the great Ottoman Sultan, Selim the First, managed to wrest that honour from Cairo. They offered five reasons in support of their claim: the right of the sword; the sanction of the *ahl-uqd* or council of elders; nomination by the previous Caliph; guardianship of the Haraman, or the two holy cities; and possession of the relics of the Prophet (hair from the Prophet's beard, and his cloak, 'gifted' by the nominal Caliph in Cairo who had also 'gifted' the title to Selim).

Of these five, the most relevant are the power of the sword and the custody of Haraman. Indeed, the two are related, for without strength in the sword the holy cities cannot be protected. In addition, the reach of the sword must ensure the protection of Arabia: the Ummayads in Cordoba or the Mughals in Delhi might claim the title, but as they could not protect the holy places their claims were considered notional. The popularly recognized Caliph has always ruled from Medina, Damascus, Baghdad or, after the Turks conquered Hijaz, Constantinople. *Hajj* is central to Islam, and Muslims all over the world expected the Caliph to protect their holiest mosques and the routes to these mosques. (The monarchs of Persia, from Mahmud Abdullah in 1306, never claimed the Caliphate because Shias believe that only a man from the Prophet's family can be the rightful Imam: twelve generations of Imams extended from Ali to Muhammad al-Askari.)

Caliph is a corruption of *khalifah,* which comes from the Arabic *khalf,* meaning to leave behind, and so a successor or viceregent. The Quran mentions two Caliphs of Allah. The first was Adam. Says the Quran (2:30):

'Behold, thy Lord said to the angels, "I will create a viceregent (khalifah) on earth".' The angels had a relevant reply: 'They said: "Wilt Thou place therein one who will make mischief therein and shed blood – whilst we do celebrate Thy praises and glorify Thy holy (name)?"' The angels thought they knew something Allah did not and were rebuked. Allah asked them to bow before Adam, and only Iblis refused because, he told Allah, he had been created from fire and man from clay. Allah cursed Iblis till the day of judgment.

The second is David. 'O David!' says Verse 26 of Surah 38, 'We did indeed make thee a vicegerent on earth: so judge thou between men in truth (and justice).' Umar rejected the notion he could be a vicegerent of Allah; only Adam and David could claim that status, he said. The Caliph could, at best, be a representative of the Prophet. Some Muslim emperors, however, starting with the Abbasids, have been unable to resist the temptation to call themselves shadows of Allah on earth: the claim says more about them than it does about Allah.

The office of the Sunni Caliph, as we have seen, is technically consensual. This provision became a fiction after Muawiya, but the theory was preserved. The Ottoman Sultan received the sword of the Caliph by a process separate from the succession, and this required the consent of the ulema council. Of course, the results of this holy election were known in advance, without any untoward help from opinion polls.

However, that sword of the Caliph had two edges. The right to choose also implies the right to remove, and if a Caliph transgresses the law of God then it becomes, theoretically, obligatory on the part of the believer to disobey. A tradition of the Prophet, that there must be no obedience in transgression against God, provides the necessary authority. The Sultan cannot be above the law of Allah. This is important in understanding the dialectic of modern Muslim politics. The right to remove was applied in practice in the Ottoman empire – during a crisis, when the bargain with Allah appeared to be in suspension.

One example will serve. The meteoric rise of Ottoman power had paused by the sixteenth century, and begun to fall during the eight years of 'mad' Ibrahim and the long reign of his son Mehmet the Fourth (1648–87). A popular ditty in Constantinople summed up the two: 'The father was mad for the cunt, The son is mad for the hunt.' Even before Ibrahim, a reformist movement had begun in the mosques: the preachers, known as kadizadelier, advocated a ban on dancing, music, silk, pilgrimages to tombs, dervish practices, and even minarets in their call for a fundamental Islam that would inspire fresh glory to people and empire, themes that would echo in the Wahhabi movement. In 1656 the grand vizier, Koprulu Mehmet, banished the *kadizadelier* to Cyprus.

He however understood the reasons for such anger. His last piece of advice to the Sultan, who came to visit him on his deathbed on 31 October 1661, was that the government must have the appearance of religion and justice: the two bedrock virtues of a Muslim empire. In 1683 an ambitious Ottoman advance ended in disaster when it was on the brink of triumph. Kara Mustafa Pasha was defeated at the gates of Vienna by a coalition of the Holy Roman Empire, the Pope, Venice, and Poland. Mustafa Pasha paid for defeat with his life, but that did not change an emerging pattern. Buda fell to the Austrians in 1686 and Belgrade in 1688. Constantinople itself was threatened, and house prices collapsed as citizens fled. The Sultan continued to concentrate on the hunt.

Koprulu Fazil Mustafa had become a vizier in 1680; he had the virtues his master was lacking in: faith, integrity, courage, and prudence. On 8 November 1687, he invoked the Islamic principle of transgression against the law of God. He convened an assembly of the *ulema*, and read out a petition demanding the dethronement of the *padishah* (who 'thinks only of enjoying himself hunting') for misrule. He led a silent but unprotesting *ulema* to the palace, where Mehmet's frightened brother Suleyman had been hiding in the harem for forty years. Suleyman's first thought was that the Sultan had sent these people to kill him. Instead, they pulled him out of the harem and made him Sultan. He did not prove to be much better, and was replaced by a third brother, Ahmed II in 1691.

By this time Mustafa had become grand vizier and ran the government on principles closer to the Quran. That belief in the relationship between faith and renewal was reinforced. As the English ambassador to Constantinople, Sir William Trumbull, wrote to the Earl of Nottingham on 6 November 1689, Fazil Mustafa Pasha 'has already declared his intention to settle this government according to their ancient methods'. Vindication came in fine style. No less a czar than Peter the Great was defeated in 1711 when he sought to realize his dream of winning Constantinople back for Christendom. Belgrade was restored to the Ottomans by 1738. While the reasons were many, the faithful were content to equate the return of Islamic virtues with the hinge of their destiny. It could be argued that the institution of the Caliphate had proved stronger than the weaknesses of

Caliphs; that the laws of Islam, the Shariah, had saved Muslims from them-selves. Those 'ancient methods' had, once again, paid dividends.

Shariah, or the Quranic law, is the foundation of faith. After the Quran, the basis of the law is the Sunna, or the practice of the Prophet and the Hadith, or the sayings of Muhammad. To this can be applied, as required, *ijma* (consensus), *ijtihad* (independent judgment), *qiyas* (analogy), *istihsan* (equity and judgment), *istislal* (public interest), *urf* (custom), and *istidal* (legal reasoning). A *fatwa* is the decree of a recognized theologian on the Shariah. The Caliph must protect the Shariah to preserve the Dar al Islam, or the House of Islam. A Muslim does not have to live in a Muslim state, but he must have the right to live by his divine law; if that is denied, then he is in Dar al Harb, or the House of War, and jihad becomes obligatory upon him.

There is enough space in Islamic jurisprudence to accommodate the flux of history, but none for the imposition of another law. The problem arises with degrees of influence from the rest of the world – other civi-lizations, if you must. These tensions of influence and space are familiar in the contemporary world, particularly when the mores of non-Islamic, Western societies are advertised as synonymous with a modern, scientific ethos and the Islamic past denigrated as primitive. The excesses of the purdah in certain Muslim countries do not help the Muslim argument; and the excesses of the hamburger do not help the Western model, but neither the burqa nor the hamburger take away from the importance of this debate and modern tension. Islamic history has witnessed such ten-sion from a foreign influence before.

Hardly had Saladin saved the Muslims in the Third Crusade of the West, than a powerful whirlwind rose from the east, devastating every-thing in its path from Bukhara and Samarqand to Baghdad. Hulagu, brother of Kublai and grandson of Chengiz, taunted the Muslims with verses from the Quran which promised destruction to those who had forsaken belief: he was the scourge of Allah, he said.

Yet another miracle was needed; it came this time from Egypt. Baybars, the Mamluk Sultan, who had recently seized power, stunned the Mongols at Ain Jalut, ended their threat, and became the pre-eminent power of the region. At the street level, a major reformist movement arose in this time of despair, the Ikhwan al-Safa, or the Brothers of Purity. Their leader, Zahid, with his headquarters in Basra, was no bigot; he advocated a rational understanding of the Quran as the only means of return to glory. The restoration of Muslim confidence had its share of surprises: Hulagu's son became a Muslim and the new reverberations influenced the conversion of a Turkish tribal chief, Uthman, to Islam. Uthman founded the Ottoman empire. Within fifty years of the destruction of Baghdad by the Mongols, three major Muslim empires spread wing: the Safavids in Persia and Turkish tribes in Turkey, and India.

The Mamluks were also from Central Asia, and whether Muslim or pagan, this was the region that was on the ascendant. Cultural affinities were introduced that were different from the Arab-Persian past. Even after conversion, the Mongols did not lose respect for what they once held in awe, the famous law of Chengiz Khan, Yasa, which they had venerated as the secret of their rise to the status of a world power. This code has been described by J.J. Saunders (*The History of the Mongol Conquests,* Routledge and Kegan Paul Ltd, London 1971):

> Yasa, of which no complete text has come down to us . . . was a curious mixture of enlightenment and superstition: it enacted religious toleration, exempted the clergy of all faiths from taxation, forbade washing or urinating in running water (flowing streams were held to be 'alive' and sacred and were not to be polluted), and prescribed the death penalty for spying and desertion, theft, and adultery, the killing of animals in the Muslim fashion, and in the case of a merchant, a third bankruptcy! . . . From a superstitious belief that it contained the secret of the Mongol's success, the Yasa attained a wide currency and was adopted in a modified form as far away as Mamluk Egypt.

Elements of Yasa were quietly absorbed into Mamluk legislation, to the horror of the orthodox. In society, Mongols brought with them different hairstyles and attire, just as the British influenced styles of living when they colonized these regions. Bernard Lewis (in *The Political Language of Islam,* The University of Chicago Press, 1988) writes that the Mongol impact created

> a ruling elite of men who bear Muslim names and profess Islam, but who impose and administer non-Muslim laws, and thereby, in the eyes of the faithful, undermine and destroy the fabric of Muslim society, the preservation of which is the principal duty of

the Muslims. In the fourteen centuries of Islamic history, few Muslim governments have adhered strictly to the Shariah. But where they failed it was by error or avoidance, not by direct challenge . . . in the modernized Muslim states of the nineteenth and twentieth centuries, Shariah law was not merely neglected or tacitly disregarded; it was, in certain important areas, repealed and replaced . . . [This] is the ultimate betrayal, the worst of all disasters, worse even than infidel conquest and rule, since, under the semblance of Islam, it seeks to subvert the loyalty of the Muslims and destroy the faith by which they live. Those who impose infidel law are infidels; if they are or claim to be Muslims, then they are apostates, and must be treated as such.

The Ottoman Caliphs, who finally provided a single authority and stability to most of the region, took care to use the Shariah as widely as possible, until the Caliphate was brought to its knees by advancing Europe, unhinged by its reformist Turks in the twentieth century, and then abolished by Mustafa Kemal. By this time the Caliph was in any case a figurehead: he had already lost control of the holy places to the first world war armies of Britain and France. The Arab Muslims, however, were not particularly perturbed. Some were comforted by their *fatwas* against Turkish 'apostasy', others by rising nationalism, and yet others by the magic of British pound sterling. In distant India, however, which had the largest Muslim population in the world, there rose such an Islamic storm against British rule over the holy cities, that, when Mahatma Gandhi added the thunder of Hindu and Sikh anger against colonial rule, the mightiest Christian empire in history wobbled sharply.

When the Prophet, in his last days, asked Muslims to ensure that no two religions were left on the Arabian peninsula, what did he mean? It is obvious that he did not say that no two religions should be left anywhere in the world. A whole canon of Islamic jurisprudence deals with the behaviour towards infidels; implicit therefore is the fact that there will always be those who will not accept Islam.

The problems that the young Muslim community, now 'sheep exposed to rain on a winter's night' in Aisha's evocative phrase, faced were from the apostates, Jews and Christians. The Jews were not strong enough to pose a significant threat. The apostates, certain tribes who had given their allegiance to the Prophet but were reluctant to transfer their fealty to Abu

Bakr, were eliminated by the first Caliph. The Wars of the Ridda, which occupied most of Abu Bakr's Caliphate, ended the problem and left a precedence for traitors. The rules of war against the renegade are far harsher than the jihad against the infidel: there is no safe conduct, little mercy, no possibility of a truce, and death is the only option unless the apostate chooses to return to Islam.

Which religion could have been on the Prophet's mind when he asked Muslims not to let two religions exist on the Arabian peninsula? There was a mighty empire to the north of Medina, ruled in the name of a religion that Muhammad had been sent by Allah to replace, for Muhammad was the Prophet after Jesus.

The third on Aisha's list of those who had troubled nascent Islam were the Christians.

4

A MAP OF ISLAM

One-third of the Muslims would be defeated (which God would never forgive); one-third would be killed (making them the best of martyrs); one-third would be victorious and conquer Constantinople.
[A tradition in Sahih al Bukhari, quoting Muhammad on the jihad against the Byzantine Roman Empire]

Reynauld of Chatillon, a French carpetbagger who came to the Holy Land with the Second Crusade in 1147, was not renowned for delicacy. He placed the heads of his victims, whether Muslim or Christian, in a wooden box before throwing them over the high walls of his castle at Kerak in the hope that they would be conscious when they smashed into the rocks below. When the Patriarch of Antioch refused to fund an attack on the Christian island of Cyprus, the high priest was stripped, smeared with honey, and left under the West Asian sun to feed the flies. The baked Patriarch paid up.

In Cyprus, Reynauld's marauders confirmed his reputation with wanton rape and pillage. There was relief across the religious divide when he was caught rustling cattle by Muslims in 1160, and imprisoned for fourteen years until ransomed for 120,000 gold dinars. His powerful reserves of hatred now concentrated on one target: Muslims. He promised that he would defile the holy cities, drag the body of 'this accursed camel driver' from the tomb in Medina, and smash the sacred stone of Kaaba.

In 1182 Reynauld constructed a fleet of ships in his land-bound castle, sent them to the Dead Sea for trials, then dismantled and dragged them across the desert to Eilat on the Red Sea. From this mobile base his pirate fleet looted Muslim villages and communities, and planned an invasion of the holy cities. Reynauld's marauders were stopped by Saladin's brother, Malek al-Adil, only a few miles from Medina. This is the nearest a non-Muslim invasion has come to the holy cities.

Such raw passions have eased in a thousand years, but each age offers its own variation on a confrontation that begins with the birth of Islam. This is not a 'clash of civilizations' because both Islam and Christianity embrace more than one civilization and culture. At the heart of this conflict, often manifest as a political struggle for territory and power, is a basic, even fundamental, theological and ideological difference.

For Muslims, Muhammad is a man and the last prophet in a sequence that begins with Adam and includes Jesus; for Christians, Jesus is divine, and the final redemption of mankind. It is consequently incumbent upon the Church to declare Muhammad an impostor. To do anything else would be to make Christianity a 611-year-old religion and Christ's mission could not be deemed eternal. The Quran repeatedly tells Christians to return to the monotheism of Abraham, renounce the concept of the Trinity, and accept Muhammad as the Last Messenger. The Quran venerates Jesus; for the Church to return the compliment would be suicide.

The bedrock of Islam is *tawhid*, or the unity and indivisibility of God. Hence, God cannot have a son. Verse 171 of Surah 4 is specific: 'O People of the Book! Commit no excesses in your religion: nor say of Allah aught but the truth. Christ Jesus the son of Mary was [no more than] a Messenger of Allah, and His Word, which He bestowed on Mary, and a Spirit proceeding from Him: so believe in Allah and His Messengers. Say not "Trinity": desist. It will be better for you: for Allah is One God. Glory be to Him. (Far exalted is He) above having a son.'

'Christ disdaineth not to serve and worship Allah' says the next verse; how can Christians not do so? The virginity of Mary is confirmed, but not the divinity of Jesus (Yahya, phonetically closer to Jehu). Surah 19, named after Mary, says Joseph (Zakariya) is old and grey when he prays to Allah for an heir who would 'represent the posterity of Jacob.' Allah tells him that his prayer is answered. Joseph asks how, when he is decrepit and his wife is barren? Allah replies: 'That is easy for Me: I did indeed create thee before when thou hadst been nothing!'

The paradox is resolved: how can the child of a virgin, sent by God, not be a son of God? If that be the logic, then Adam should be called the son of God for Adam was created from nothing. Christians do not call Adam the son of God.

The first great piece of Islamic architecture, in Jerusalem, is the Dome of the Rock conceived by that Umayyad visionary Caliph Abdal Malik in 688. The Dome is not a mosque. There is no *qiblah* wall pointing towards Mecca. The mosque, Masjid al Aqsa, is next to the Dome. What is the Dome on the Rock meant to signify in the holiest city of the Christians?

Two walkways, marked by forty pillars, circle the rock over which the Dome rises; it dazzles above the Ascension Church, and the rotunda of Anastasis, or the Church of the Holy Sepulchre. It rises above the wailing wall, the Temple Mount, built by Solomon around 1000 BC, first destroyed by the Babylonians under Nebuchadnezzar, rebuilt by Ezra, defiled by pagans who worshipped their idols in it from 167 BC, restored by Herod, and then razed to the ground by Titus in AD 70. Solomon built his temple where Abraham had offered to sacrifice his son to God. (Jews say that son was Isaac; Muslims, the sons of Ishmael, take the name of their ancestor, who was Abraham's eldest, from Hagar: the Quran describes both Isaac and Ishmael as inspired prophets.)

In a beautiful phrase, Karen Armstrong calls the octagonal Dome of the Rock a 'map of Islam' in *A History of Jerusalem: One City, Three Faiths* (Harper Collins, 1997). Muslims believe that it was from this rock that the Prophet went to Heaven when Allah took 'His servant for a journey by night from the Sacred Mosque [Kaaba] to the farthest mosque [Al Aqsa], whose precincts We did bless – in order that We might show him some of Our Signs' (17:1). It is however also something more than that.

> The Dome itself, which would become such a feature of Muslim architecture, is a powerful symbol of the soaring ascent to heaven. But it also reflects the perfect balance of *tawhid:* its exterior, which reaches toward the infinity of the sky, is a perfect replica of its internal dimension. It illustrates the way the divine and the human, the inner and the outer worlds fit and complement one another as two halves of a single whole. The very colours of the shrine also convey a message. In Islamic art, blue, the colour of the sky, suggests infinity, while gold is the colour of knowledge, which in the Quran is the faculty which brings Muslims an apprehension of God.

The major inscription over the inner arcade is not the Quranic verse about the ascension of the Prophet but the verses where Allah admonishes the Christians for distorting the message of Christ. The Dome of the Rock is a challenge to Christians to renounce the Trinity, and return to monotheism and Allah.

Ideologically, Muhammad and Jesus also offer two radically different constructs of the ideal, a fact that has been used to spawn a swarm of negative images about the former. The Quran explains that different Prophets were relevant for different times, with different degrees of honour. Allah spoke directly to Moses, who spent forty years in the wilderness fighting the disbelief of his own people. Moses was given the Book, but not mastery of the sword. David was born a shepherd, but became warrior, king, musician, poet, and Allah's Caliph. Jesus was given the holy spirit, but no weapons for war, his mission was peaceful. Muhammad, as the last Messenger, combined the characteristics of all the Prophets, as his mission was greater than that of any of his predecessors.

The very proximity of Christianity and Islam was a source of their antagonism. Jesus said he was the son of man; why did Christians call him the son of God? The Jews are people of the Book as well, and closer in their monotheism to Islam than Christianity; but they are one Prophet further removed from Islam, because they have not accepted Jesus' mission. Such volatile proximity merely needs the spark of human conviction, or ambition, or sometimes even folly, to ignite.

The sixth was a century of great empire builders: the Tang dynasty in China, Harshavardhana in India, Justinian in Byzantium, and the Persian whose name Anawshirwan also became synonymous with justice. As powerful neighbours make the most natural enemies, the Byzantines and the Sassanians were in continual conflict. In the first decade of the seventh century the Persians, under Khusraw II, seemed invincible on every side, Armenia, Asia Minor, Syria. By 610 their advance scouts were within sight of Constantinople, and it was during this crisis that the Byzantines found a saviour in Heraclius who, according to a contemporary chronicler, killed lions in the arena unarmed. Antioch fell to the Persians in 611, and on 5 May 614 Jerusalem was captured. The Church of the Holy Sepulchre was damaged and the True Cross carried away as booty to Persia.

In Mecca the pagans greeted the fall of Jerusalem with joy. Through their local prism they saw it as the defeat of monotheists like Muhammad, and taunted him that his Allah had not been able to save Jerusalem. A fascinating revelation came down to comfort the Prophet against the pagans after the fall of Jerusalem (Surah 30, The Romans, Verses 2 to 6):

'The Roman empire has been defeated in a land closeby: but they, [even] after [this] defeat of theirs, will soon be victorious – within a few years, with Allah is the Decision. In the Past and in the Future: on that day shall the Believers rejoice – with the help of Allah. He helps whom He will, and He is exalted in Might. Most Merciful. [It is] the promise of Allah. Never does Allah depart from His promise: but most men understand that not.'

The next phase of the war did not seem to match the Quranic prediction: Persian armies annexed Egypt in 616 and reached as far as Tripoli, while another thrust besieged Constantinople. However, the Quran could not be wrong: by 622 Heraclius had turned the tide, perhaps literally, for he used sea power to outflank the Persians. He sent an army through the Aegean Sea and surprised the Persians at Issus, where Alexander had won his important battle nearly a thousand years earlier. By 625 Heraclius' armies had restored the status quo and won back the True Cross. In 628 Heraclius, honouring a vow, went on foot to restore the True Cross to Jerusalem.

Heraclius, congratulated by India and feted by Europe on his achievements, was in the holy city when he received a letter from Medina. It invited the Emperor of the Holy Roman Empire to become a Muslim.

Muhammad sent similar letters to the rulers of Persia, Abysinnia, Bahrain, Oman, and Egypt. The king of kings in Persia treated the letter with contempt. He tore it up. Muhammad prophesed that the Persian empire would be torn up soon. The king of kings ordered his governor in Yemen Badhan, to arrest this man who had dared to treat himself as an equal and lay waste the country if he did not obey. Muhammad replied: 'Tell him that my religion and my sovereignty will reach limits which the kingdom of Khusraw never attained.' The governor of Yemen, instead of arresting Muhammad, became a Muslim and merged Yemen into the growing Muslim state.

The Prophet was told that the emperor of the Romans did not read any letter unless it bore a seal, so he took out a silver ring and identified himself: Muhammad, Apostle of Allah. Dinya bin Khalifa al-Kalbi al-Khazraji was selected to take the letter. The message was short and simple:

> In the name of Allah the most Beneficient, the most Merciful: this letter is from Muhammad, the slave of Allah, and His Apostle, to Heraclius, the ruler of Byzantines. Peace be upon the followers of

guidance. I invite you to surrender to Allah. Embrace Islam and you will be safe. Embrace Islam and Allah will bestow on you a double reward. But if you reject this invitation you will be misguiding your people.

Heraclius treated this letter with grudging respect. He made enquiries about this man who claimed to be another messiah and asked if any traveller was present who had come from the Hijaz. As it happened, Abu Sufyan was in Jerusalem with a caravan and described the Prophet to the Emperor in respectful terms. Unlike the Persian, Heraclius was not contemptuous.

The nearest that the Prophet came personally to war with Christians was when he led an expedition to Tabuk, on the Syrian border, against a perceived threat from the Byzantines. There was reluctance on the part of some Muslims to answer the call for jihad, partly because of the heat (the expedition left in September or October) and partly out of fear of the Byzantine army. The more imaginative of this group, known as the Hypocrites, even claimed that they would not be able to withstand the charm of Syrian women and it would be best therefore for them to stay at home. After the expedition left, they rejoiced that they had escaped the heat: Allah pointed out to them through the Quran that the fires of hell were hotter. The Hypocrites participated in an unsuccessful plot to kill Muhammad on his way back from Tabuk.

Bukhari provides sufficient evidence that Constantinople was on Muhammad's mind in his last years. He reports in the *Book of Jihad* (a part of the Hadith) that Muhammad told a woman called Umm Haram that paradise would be the reward of the first batch of jihadis to undertake a naval expedition. She asked if she would be among them and he replied in the affirmative. Then Muhammad added: the first Muslim army to invade Caesar's city would be forgiven their sins. Umm Haram wondered if she would be blessed with such a reward, and the Prophet said no.

Bukhari records a tradition quoting the Prophet as having said that in the conflict with the Romans, one-third of the Muslims would be defeated (which God would never forgive); one-third would be killed (making them the best of martyrs); one-third would be victorious and conquer Constantinople. Facts bore him out, but the tradition also works as a metaphor. Death, defeat, and victory are equal parts of the experience in the confrontation between Muslims and Christians.

Muslim armies opened up a front against the Christian empire shortly after Muhammad's death, even before the problem of the apostates had been fully dealt with. Abu Bakr sent his best generals, Amr ibn al-Aasi and Khalid ibn Walid (the same warrior who had defeated the Muslims at Uhud) towards Syria, then a largely Christian country. The first Caliph's instructions on how to behave in war are exemplary: a jihadi must not betray a trust; misappropriate booty; be treacherous or mutilate a body. He could not kill a child, a woman, or an old man, uproot trees or burn palms. No animal could be slaughtered except for food. No hermit could be touched. For some inexplicable reason, however, Abu Bakr asked jihadis to kill anyone with a tonsure.

Amr took a route west, and Khalid an eastern line towards Amman, the Dera pass and towards the great prize, Damascus. Heraclius sent his forces down the centre of the fork, with orders to overwhelm the weaker of the two lines, that of Amr. In one of military history's more amazing feats, the camel-cavalry of Khalid wheeled around, raced through pitiless desert and reached the embattled Amr in time to change the course of the war. The Byzantines were defeated at the battle of Ajnadain in July 634, marking the first great victory in the Muslim-Christian confrontation.

Abu Bakr was ill with fever when news of the victory reached him; he died on 23 August 634. Under Umar, who became commander in chief, the Muslims operated in columns led separately by Amr, Shurabil ibn Hasana, and Khalid under the loose overall charge of Abu Ubaida. Damascus fell to the forces of Abu Ubaida and Khalid: the city was spared punishment but a *jiziya* of one dinar and one measure of wheat was imposed. Heraclius was surprised, but not complacent.

He still had command of the sea, and the resources to rebuild an army for Syria. The Arabs fell back to take up position south of Yarmouk: they preferred fighting with the desert behind their back, for that landscape meant freedom for them and peril for the enemy. Heraclius padlocked his army on the reoccupied Dera pass, and there was a stalemate for four months. The Muslims made better strategic use of the standstill, bringing fresh troops up from Medina and gradually throwing a pincer from three sides around the imperial forces. Opportunity came on the evening of 19 August 636, when one of those blinding sandstorms blew straight into the eyes of the enemy; that help from the heavens that is part of Islamic lore.

By the morning of the 20 August the storm had become a gale. A Muslim detachment slipped around and seized the bridge over the Wadi al

Ruqqad, surrounding the Byzantines completely. Then came the classic charge into the blinded enemy: between the natural and human force, the imperial army withered away. One of the cheerleaders on that day, incidentally, was the indefatigable Hind, urging her sons to cut off the limbs of the uncircumcized Christians. Heraclius returned to Constantinople.

The following year, Jerusalem was taken. It was the only conquered city that Caliph Umar visited.

Broad sweeps of history are not always amenable to a handful of sentences; but the legacy of history is always a mixture of fact and perception. No success is ever so glorious as to be free from fault; failure never so absolute as to deny space for a dream. Moreover, there is no theory that is immune from exceptions, and yet the challenge is to discover a meaning in the accumulation of facts. To tell it like it is – as later European objectivity demanded – cannot exclude the cycles that Ibn Khaldun saw in the rise, fall, and renewal of Islamic world power.

Purist Muslims mark the first decline from no later than the death of Umar, assassinated by a Christian slave from Syria called Firoz while he was praying in a mosque. Such were the tensions of the early days that Abu Bakr was the only 'rightly-guided' Caliph to die a natural death. Both Usman and Ali were assassinated by fellow Muslims. Nonetheless, the crises at the top did not abort the successes of jihad as it expanded Islam's borders across Asia and Africa. Jihad had an unprecedented fervour and momentum of its own as it found opportunity both in the east and west. Gibbon explains:

> While the [Byzantine] state was exhausted by the Persian war, and the Church was distracted by the Nestorian and Monophysite sects, Mohamed [sic] with the sword in one hand, and the Koran [sic] in the other, erected his throne on the ruins of Christianity and of Rome. The genius of the Arabian Prophet, the manners of his nation, and the spirit of his religion, involve the causes of the decline and fall of the Eastern Empire; and our eyes are curiously intent on one of the most memorable revolutions which have impressed a new and lasting character on the nations of this globe.

For the Muslims it was a miracle. Having conquered the cradle of Christianity, Jerusalem, Muslim armies aimed immediately for the heart of Christian power, Constantinople.

The first attempt on the capital of the Byzantine empire was made by the third Caliph, Uthman. In 653 his kinsman Muawiya, then governor of Syria, marched to the Bosphorus, while a fleet led by Busr ibn Artah sailed from Tripoli. Emperor Constans II advanced to challenge this fleet and both sides claimed victory in the naval battle. But Muslim losses were too heavy for them to continue to the walls of Constantinople.

Muawiya resumed his attacks on the eastern Roman empire after he became Caliph. In 664 he sent an expedition under Khalid ibn Walid, who crossed Anatolia and reached Pergamos, accompanied by another fleet under Admiral Busr, but winter forced them back. The most ambitious offensive was launched in 668, commanded by Fodala ibn Obeid al Ansari, and glittering with an array of heroes and companions of the Prophet, including Ayyub al-Ansari. Once again Busr ibn Artah had charge of the ships. There is some dispute over the precise year, but it is generally agreed that the Muslim armies and fleet reached the walls of Constantinople by 670. For eight years after that the war followed a pattern. The siege would take place during the summer months, while in winter the Muslims would retire to an island some eighty miles south of their target. It was a policy designed to wear out the assailant and hearten the defender. The Muslims finally turned back in 678, marking the first serious failure of their early campaigns.

One of those who fell at the walls of Constantinople was Ayyub al Ansari. His grave was discovered when the Turks conquered the city eight centuries later, in 1453, and was treated as a great religious event. It was at the mosque of Ayyub Ansari that a Sultan of the Ottomans was given the sword of the Caliph of all Muslims. After the failure of 678 Muawiya concluded a truce with Constantinople. It lasted forty years.

When Suleyman ascended the Damascus throne in 715, he was told by some theologians that as he was the first Caliph to bear the name of a prophet (Solomon) he would succeed where his predecessors had failed. He must have had better reasons for the campaign begun against Constantinople in 716, when a far more ambitious offensive was launched by the Arabs. His brother, Maslama ibn Abdul Malik, had uncomplicated orders: either conquer or stay. Do not retreat without instructions from Damascus. Suleyman did not make the mistake Muawiya had made; his armies were provisioned for winter too. Fortune was however was on the side of Constantinople: six months before the Arabs reached its walls, a brilliant soldier, Leo, seized power from Emperor Theodosius III, who retired to a monastery. It was the best thing that he could have done for his people.

The Muslims began their second siege of Constantinople on 15 August 717 with a massive force of some 180,000 Arabs, on land and sea; and about 1,800 large and small ships vessels under Suleyman ibn Maaz. Against Muslim determination, the Christians had two weapons: the first was Leo himself, and a miracle they called the Greek fire. Sulphur was known to be, well, sulphurous; and the Spartans are on record as having tried to burn Platia down in 429 BC by throwing balls of wood coated with tar and sulphur, but the Byzantines believed that the secret of their weapon was given by an angel to the founder of their capital, Constantine.

Greek fire is said to have been a combination of sulphur, naptha, and tar. Even water could not extinguish it; only sand and vinegar would do so. Defenders waited for a favourable wind and then launched missiles of Greek fire against Arab ships, where it spread terror and havoc. The Arabs had tasted its power during the first siege, but not in such intensity. They had yet to discover the chemistry of this weapon, but when they later did, they used it with devastating effect against their foes.

The Muslims thought they had prepared for winter, but that was in theory. Reinforcement and replenishment came in spring, but by that time their belief in victory had evaporated. Maximizing his slender resources with intelligent use of deception, counter-attacking with Greek fire, Leo outlasted the siege. Suleyman died during this offensive; Muslims say of a broken heart, but that may be overestimating the sorrow. The army he had sent dragged itself back to Damascus by 717. The ships were scattered by storms or looted by pirates who feed on any retreat.

As the Prophet had said, the first Muslims would be defeated. The Arab assault against the Christian empire of the east was over. The battleground shifted south, to the Mediterranean; the Arabs of the desert proved adept in handling the sea. Muawiya's forces conquered Cyprus and Rhodes, and invaded Sicily. Abdal Malik established a base on the edge of Spain when the Arabs took Majorca and Minorca, while Muslims, either in the name of the Caliph, or some emir, or indulging in more lucrative piracy, terrorized the rich ports of the Italian and Byzantine waters. One such independent band took Crete; while the emir of Tunisia, Ziadatallah's men, created a Muslim state in Sicily by the first quarter of the ninth century. For a while the Pope paid a tribute to keep Muslims out. The dream of Constantinople was forgotten till the Turks resurrected it in another millennium.

Within fifteen years of the defeat in Constantinople in 717, the western gates of Christian Europe were also shut upon the forces of Islam, in a battle that Muslim chroniclers call the Pavement of Martyrs, and Christians the battle of Tours. The astonishing fact was that those doors were so far within Europe. The confrontation took place on the banks of the Loire in October 732, exactly a hundred years after the Prophet died. While the world was amazed that the Muslims had reached this far, believers were amazed that they had not gone further. If faith had brought them this far, what could have stopped them at Tours? Had faith weakened?

Caliph Abdal Malik's most brilliant generals, Tarik ibn Ziyad and Musa ibn Noosier, asked Allah for fresh lands to conquer in His name when they reached the shores of the Atlantic. They got them. The kingdom of the Goths was delivered to the Caliph by 711. Over the following decades, Muslim armies sprawled over the southern provinces of France, until they were stopped in Toulouse in 722. In 731 Andalusia (Muslim Spain) got a new emir, or *wali*, Abdul Rahman ibn Abdullah al-Ghafiki, a capable man who eased the tensions between the Berbers and the Arabs that threatened to split the new kingdom. The Berbers, new Muslim recruits from Africa, discovered that while they did most of the fighting, Arabs were appointed to most of the high offices. The stories of clash and intrigue between Abdur Rahman, the Berber leader Munuza, France's Duke of Edo, and Karl Martel need not detain us. Suffice to note that early in 732 Abdul Rahman crossed through Aragon and Navarre and defeated the Duke of Edo at Arles on the banks of the Rhone. Abdul Rahman took Acquitaine, Bordeaux, and the city of Leon: his advance guards were now only a hundred miles from Paris.

The Franks, who had become Christians under Clovis, constituted the strongest power in Europe and their defeat would have had consequences which Gibbon has described in one of his more famous passages:

> A victorious line of march had been prolonged about a thousand miles from the rock of Gibraltar to the banks of the Loire; the repetition of an equal space would have carried the Saracens to the confines of Poland and the Highlands of Scotland: the Rhine is not more impassable than the Nile or Euphrates, and the Arabian fleet might have sailed without a naval combat into the mouth of the Thames. Perhaps the interpretation of the Koran would now be taught in the schools of Oxford, and her pulpits might

demonstrate to a circumcised people the sanctity and truth of the revelation of Mahomed.

It's a thought.

Karl Martel, as the cliché goes, was the power behind the throne of Theoderic. Arab accounts say that Karl deliberately delayed giving battle to Abdul Rahman, waiting for the latter's troops to be so laden with loot, that old enemy of Muslim armies, that they would be weakened by dispute and the desire to return. The adversaries finally met at Tours. Abdul Rahman was surprised by the size of the enemy army; his advance guards had underestimated their strength. Skirmishes began on either 12 or 13 October. The first important encounter took place after nine days; by the tenth day, the Muslims seemed to have the edge but the Franks had made one decisive breakthrough. They had opened up a line to the camp where the Muslim booty was stored. Abdul Rahman could not control his army as sections of the cavalry and infantry broke order to defend the booty rather than defeat the enemy. On 21 October, as he attempted to restore discipline, he was struck either by an arrow or a lance and killed. That night, the Muslims gathered what they could of their spoils and retired.

Someone should have recalled the verses of the Quran about the battle of Uhud, where Muslims lost because of greed for booty. The logic of the Muslim defeat was written there.

Historians are divided over whose victory was greater, that of Leo or Karl Martel. The debate is academic. Both won.

5

CIRCLE OF HELL

O shame upon Muslim rulers! At such an event tears fall, hearts
break with sighs, grief rises up on high . . .
[Imam Sheikh Shams ad Din Yusuf, in a sermon on Jerusalem at
the Great Mosque in Damascus after the truce of 1229 between
Frederick and al Kamil in which Muslims peacefully handed over
Christian holy sites to the Fifth Crusaders]

First, the good news. Frederick II's official astrologer, Michael Scot, had
class. He predicted his own death. Charting his horoscope he found
that he would be killed when a stone of a particular weight fell on his
head, so he began wearing a helmet at all times. Once, during mass in a
church, he lifted the helmet and a small stone fell from the vault, injuring
him slightly. He weighed the stone, found it was the predicted weight,
went to bed and died. The year was 1235. He had joined the Holy Roman
Emperor's court in Italy in 1220 as resident alchemist and astrologer. His
most singular achievement, apart from predicting his death, was the
translation of Aristotle that reached Europeans through that great Arab
scholar, Ibn Rushd, known to the West as Averroes. Frederick was one of
those great princes who sought to build personal and intellectual bridges
between the worlds of Christendom and Islam during the first half of the
thirteenth century.

As was the norm, Frederick had many titles, including Prince of Princes
and Wonder of the World. The second may even be justified as he led the
only bloodless Crusade. According to the Arab historian Jamal ad Din ibn
Wasil, he was 'distinguished and gifted, a student of philosophy, logic and
medicine and a friend to Muslims, for his original home was Sicily, where

he was educated. He, his father and his grandfather were Kings of the island, but its inhabitants were mostly Muslim.' Frederick was sufficiently fluent in Arabic to correspond with scholars. He had nothing but admiration for Muslim scholarship and civilization and utter contempt for the 'Franj' of western Europe, including the Pope. Muslims numbered among his palace guard, and prayed toward Mecca at the muezzin's call. Two surviving letters indicate deep familiarity with Arabic poetry and imagery. When in 1229 he wrote to his friend Fakhr ad Din, an emir in Cairo, about how 'the Pope has treacherously and deceitfully taken one of our fortresses, called Montecassino, handed over to him by its accursed Abbot' he described his personal anguish through the lines of a tenth century poet Al Mutanabbi: 'Death is tired of us, he has taken others in our place; he has chosen to leave us and forgotten our love . . . When you part with those who could have prevented that parting, it is they who are really going away.'

Unlike Gregory the Fourth, who became Pope in 1227, Frederick had no desire for war with Muslims. While he commended Jerusalem as a fine place for pilgrimage, he did not consider it worth a Crusade. He was however also King of Jerusalem through marriage to Yolande, daughter of John of Brienne, and the Pope, undeterred by the defeat of the Fifth Crusade at Damietta in 1221, used the popularity of revenge to undermine good sense. Frederick reached Acre in 1228 at the head of yet another army, although it was a small one. Then, instead of spilling blood, he opened negotiations.

His contemporary, Sultan al Malik al Kamil, was clearly the Anwar Sadat of the thirteenth century. Son of Saladin's brother, al Adil, he had nearly lost Egypt and Jerusalem to the Fifth Crusade in 1218, before he regained all in August 1221. He understood the cost and risks of war. At one point, in October 1219, al Kamil offered not only Jerusalem and the True Cross but the whole of Palestine, west of Jordan. Only the fanaticism of Cardinal Pelagius, a Spanish priest put in charge of the Fifth Crusade by the Pope, prevented a deal. He was equally amenable to peace, although not on the rather too peaceful terms that Frederick proposed. The emperor asked the Sultan to hand over Jerusalem as its strategic significance had ended with its walls. Those walls had disappeared when the ruler of Syria, al Muazzam, al Kamil's brother, took an ingenious decision to make Jerusalem useless as a garrison town in the event of Fifth Crusaders capturing the city: he destroyed its famous ramparts. Frederick argued that a few Franks in Jerusalem would be less of a threat to Muslims than a Frankish army on the road.

Frederick and al Kamil had been in touch long before Frederick arrived; they now played diplomatic chess with finesse. Cairo's negotiator, Emir Fakhr ad Din, became a personal friend of Frederick. The emperor used the negotiations to send 'queries on difficult philosophic, geometric and mathematical points' to Cairo's scholars. They were all answered. Frederick confided to Fakhr ad Din: 'I have no real ambition to hold Jerusalem, nor anything else; I simply want to safeguard my reputation with the Christians.' On 18 February 1229 an accord was signed between Frederick and Fakhr ad Din for a truce of ten years, five months, and forty days by the Muslim calender. The Christians got their holy sites in Jerusalem, plus Bethlehem and Nazareth but were not permitted to fortify them; Muslims retained their sacred Haram. Sultan al Kamil argued, 'We have only conceded to them some churches and some ruined houses. The sacred precincts, the venerated Rock and all the other sanctuaries to which we make our pilgrimages remain ours as they were . . .' Disingenuously, he added that Muslims could always take back what had been given once the truce was over. They did; but for the moment the street was incandescent. Muslims burned with shame and anger at the news that an heir had betrayed the greatest achievement of the incomparable Saladin.'

In scenes that television would have made international today, outraged crowds came out on the streets of Aleppo, Baghdad, Mosul as stories reached them of the loss of Jerusalem. Al Kamil's nephew, al Malik an Nasir, now ruler of Syria, encouraged the anger as he sought to settle personal scores. He asked the orator-preacher Sheikh Shams ad Din Yusuf to give a sermon on Jerusalem at the Great Mosque in Damascus; the congregation raised great cries and groans as the imam declared Al Kamil a traitor: 'The road to Jerusalem is closed to the companies of pious visitors! O desolation for those pious men who live there; how many times have they prostrated themselves there in prayer, how many tears have they shed there! By Allah, if their eyes were living springs they could not pay the whole of their debt of grief . . . O shame upon Muslim rulers! At such an event tears fall, hearts break with sighs, grief rises up on high . . .'

Christians too were screaming betrayal. When Frederick, who had the right to be crowned in the holy city, reached Jerusalem he discovered that no priest would oblige: the Pope, who wanted a holy war rather than a reasonable peace, had excommunicated him for delaying his Crusade. He therefore picked up the crown and placed it on his own head at the altar of the Holy Sepulchre. His behaviour in Jerusalem was not destined to make him more popular with Christians. When he visited Al Aqsa, Frederick found an emboldened Christian priest flaunting a Bible inside the mosque. He walked up to the priest and cried, according to the Arab historians: 'Swine! The Sultan has done us the honour of allowing us to visit this place, and you sit here behaving like this! If any of you comes in here again in this way I shall kill him!' When visiting the Dome of the Rock, Frederick asked why there was a wooden lattice at the door. To keep the birds out. 'And to think', responded the Emperor, referring to the first Crusaders, 'that God allowed pigs in!'

Shams al Din, the *qadi* of Nablus, who received the emperor, told the muezzins, as a gesture of courtesy, not to recite the *azaan* during Frederick's visit. However, at dawn the muezzin of Al Aqsa, Abdul Karim, ascended the minaret and deliberately began to recite those verses in the Quran which said that God had no son and those that spoke too of Jesus and Mary. The *qadi* rebuked the muezzin, and there was no further call to prayer. Frederick enquired. When told why, he said: 'You did wrong, *qadi*; would you alter your rites and law and faith for my sake? If you were staying in my country, would I order the bells to be silenced for your sake? By God, do not do this; this is the first time we have found fault with you!" Frederick then gave ten dinars each to every man in the mosque.

Frederick stayed for only two nights in Jerusalem before he moved to Jaffa. He was worried about his safety. The Templars, knights of the Christian mood, wanted to kill him. The Templars were in Palestine, and the world had become a darker place.

The behaviour of a thirteenth century Crusader prince like Frederick is remembered precisely because it is so unusual. Karen Armstrong notes in *A History of Jerusalem, One City, Three Faiths*:

> But after the bloodshed and the wars, Jerusalem had become a symbol of Muslim integrity and no Islamic ruler could easily make concessions about the Holy City. The Christians were equally shocked. To make such a treaty with the infidels was almost blasphemous. The very notion of allowing the Muslims to remain on the Haram in a Christian city was intolerable. They were utterly scandalized by Frederick's behaviour...This was no way for

a Crusader to behave! The Templars plotted to have Frederick killed, and he hastily left the country; as he hurried to his ship in the early hours of the morning, the butchers of Acre pelted him with offal and entrails. Jerusalem had now become such a sensitive issue in the Christian world that anybody who fraternized with Muslims or appeared to trifle with the Holy City was likely to be assassinated. The whole story of Frederick's extraordinary Crusade shows that Islam and the West were finding it impossible to accommodate each other: on neither side was there any desire for coexistence and peace.

The first Islam-Christianity conflict, between the Arabs and the Byzantines, was fierce, but it was not vitiated by an excess of venom. St John of Damascus, born about forty years after the Prophet died, established the dialectic of the Christian theological response, first rebutting the Quran's verses on Christianity, then disputing the basic concepts: was the word of God created or uncreated? Was God ever wordless? Then came the ridicule that was to become a constant Christian theme, accusing the Prophet of sexual indulgence. A doctrine of Christian sin complemented this dialectic. The only explanation for the defeat of mighty Christian kingdoms was that God had punished them for their sins; Latin theologians would include Heraclius' 'heresy' in deviating from the Catholic church of Rome in the litany.

There were however also other inclusive traditions: some Arab Christians began to venerate Bahira, the monk in Islamic lore, who recognized and foretold Muhammad's destiny. They believed that this monk taught their mysteries to the Prophet. As the wars continued in Byzantium, the Mediterranean, and Spain, the rhetoric became sharper. It was was only after the Crusades of the Roman Popes, with Jerusalem as the epicentre of transcontinental bloodshed, that a sustained and vitriolic campaign was launched against the person of the Prophet.

Time shifted elements of the Christian response till one became so volatile that it inflamed minds even more than the massacres of war. In the ninth century, Nicetas of Byzantium went over the same intellectual territory ('Muhammad's God does not accept Christian law and therefore cannot be the true God', etc) but ended on a harsher note. Muhammad was called a devil. Defeat, and even more than defeat, submission in conquered lands encouraged Christian diatribes against the person of Muhammad. It is not accidental that the war of words was fiercest in

Spain. Bile infected the conflict with a disease that has not healed. The Muslim reply to character assassination was the death sentence.

The sentiment of the second millennium was more evident in the demagoguery of Popes and the denunciation of philosophers; in the conversion of Muhammad into 'Mahound' by the church militant before the Crusades and the poetry of Dante, who sent Muhammad to the eighth circle of hell for sowing religious discord. Muslims have always asked one question to which they have found no adequate answer: if they could show respect for Jesus, why could Christians not extend a similar courtesy to their Prophet?

Having turned Jesus into an image of unrelieved virtue, Christians always compared Muhammad against the God he never claimed to be. Virginity was not a moral virtue to him. He had an active sex life, whose reputation was unnecessarily enhanced by the self-defeating if probably well-intentioned claims of some of his companions. Stories from the Sahih al Bukhari became ammunition for the most powerful writers and orators of Christian west Europe, before, during and long after the Crusades: Voltaire was in the same procession as Dante. Thus emerged Muhammad the sex-fiend, or the Mahound-impostor.

His message was discredited. The false revelation, a reference to the verses which Muhammad denied, said to be in praise of Al lat, Al Uzza and Manat, the pagan goddesses, were trotted out as 'evidence' of fraud; these, of course, are the now-famous 'Satanic Verses'. Pedro de Alfonso, a Spanish Jew who got himself baptized in 1106 and became godson of Alfonso 1 of Aragon, mocked that Muhammad would not have withdrawn these verses had he not been forced to do so by his followers. Peter the Venerable, abbot of Cluny, saying that he preferred reason to force, and words to arms, injected enough malice into those words in his *The Abominable Heresy or Sect of the Saracens*. He accused Muhammad of pretending that God spoke to him, and called him an evil liar. He wrote to Louis VII, about to set off on a Crusade, that he should destroy this heretic faith just as Joshua had the Amorites and Canaanites. Instances can be multiplied. The revelations of the Quran were ridiculed. It was not Gabriel who had spoken to Muhammad, said Thomas of Pavia, only an evil counsellor who taught him tricks to fool the illiterate and ignorant Arabs. Other stories were circulated which often got the iconography mixed: Muhammad had trained a dove to eat a grain of corn from his ear, so that he could flaunt it as the Holy Ghost. These were variations on an old theme. When the Prophet was alive his enemies dismissed the verses of the Quran as the ravings of a *majnoon* or a mad poet. The Quran answered: 'We have not instructed [the Prophet] in poetry' (36:39) and 'It is not the word of a poet: Little it is ye believe! Nor is it the word of a soothsayer" (69:41 and 42).

The case of the licentious Prophet has been a consistent element in Christian minds. For Christians, who saw salvation in suffering, a Prophet of many marriages and battlefield booty would be an object of scorn even if there were no other reason for distortion. I have noted the reason before: Islam can survive with Jesus as a Prophet; Christianity cannot survive if Muhammad, and not Christ, is the last Messenger. Muhammad, therefore, had to be a 'sower of discord', father of a heresy, just as for Muslims Christianity was an incomplete faith. The levels of linguistic violence indicate a hatred that had become almost unbridgeable by Dante's time. A poet as incomparable in Christian literature as Dante Alighieri flaunts images that go beyond the liberty of art (the translation is by John Ciardi, Penguin, Harmondsworth 1954), when he meets Muhammad and Ali in hell:

A wine tun when a stave or cant-bar starts
Does not split as wide as one I saw
Split from his chin to the mouth with which man farts.

Between his legs all of his red guts hung
With the heart, the lungs, the liver, the gall bladder,
And the shrivelled sac that passes shit to the bung.

I stood and stared at him from the stone shelf;
He noticed me and opening his own breast
With both hands cried: 'See how I rip myself!

See how Mahomet's mangled and split open!
Ahead of me walks Ali in his tears,
His head cleft from the top knot to the chin.

And all the other souls that bleed and mourn
Along this ditch were sowers of scandal and schism:
As they tore others apart, so are they torn.

Behind us, warden of our mangled horde,

The devil who butchers us and sends us marching
Waits to renew our wounds with his long sword

When we have made the circuit of the pit;
For by the time we stand again before him
All the wounds he gave us last have knit.

But who are you that gawk down from that sill—
Probably to put off your own descent
To the pit you are sentenced to for your own evil?'

In Dar ul Islam such spleen was mopped up by the sword. Dar ul Harb remained a battlefield of many fronts. The Crusades were first launched in the mind. Stray references from Ibn Ishaq's biography of the Prophet and the traditions were picked up, distorted and disseminated; Muhammad was called both a pervert and an impostor. The sexual angle was rich fuel for such propaganda, from Aisha's age at the time of her marriage to the titillation of the seventy *houris* reserved for each martyr in paradise. Even after the Crusades lost steam, the battle over the true faith remained intense. Subtler logic was used by the more subtle, for instance in Ricoldo da Monte Croce's dissertation on the Islamic *shahadah,* and its first principle, 'There is no God but God and Muhammad is His Prophet'. Ricoldo's response? 'And that word is to be noted which Muhammad puts in the Quran more than a hundred times, I believe. There is no God except God. For this proposition is true of everything: there is no dog except a dog; there is no horse except a horse.'

Too clever by half. Ricoldo also reiterated the accusation that the Prophet was a *majnoon*, or possessed, which he said explained the confusion he found in the Quran. San Pedro, anxious to prevent apostasy by Spanish Christians, painted a typical portrait: 'Muhammad put on purple and used scented oils, that he might smell sweet, and coloured his lips and eyes, as the leaders of Muslims and many others, of both sexes, are accustomed to do nowadays . . .'

Even Muhammad's death did not escape calumny. Crusade intellectuals like Alan of Lille or Guibert of Nogent said Muhammad had been eaten by dogs, or had suffocated and been eaten by pigs; for good measure Ranulphi Higden added that this had happened when he was in a drunken stupor. Norman Daniel provides a welter of such references in an excellent account of this war by blasphemy in *Islam and the West* (Edinburgh University Press, Edinburgh, 1958).

The Crusades were, consequently, advertised as a moral duty, a purification and a purging through the sword. Daniel comments:

> The essence of Crusading was 'to slay for God's love'. Occasional comments of more serious writers reveal a similar attitude. Fidenzio's whole purpose in writing was to encourage the Crusade, but his mind is most revealed by a chance comment on the unmentionable *scelera carnalia* which Islam seemed to encourage: 'And if there were no other cause but this, it would be the duty of Christians to fight against them, and to cleanse the earth . . .' The Muslims, said Benedict of Alignan, were not worthy of disputing with, 'but rather to be extirpated by fire and the sword'. As St Barnard had written: 'a Christian glories in the death of a pagan [i.e. a Muslim] because Christ is glorified; the liberality of the King is revealed in the death of the Christian because he is led out to his reward'.

Heaven was available for the Christian martyr as well. Behind this aggression lay a deep Christian depression at the success of the Prophet who had come after Christ. The depression doubled after Saladin's victories and the failure of the consequent Crusades to reconquer Jerusalem.

In 1239, the very year the truce of Frederick and al Kamil ended, al Nasir Daud, the governor of Kerak (ironically, Reynauld's old bastion) forced the Franks out of Jerusalem. He returned it to them a short while later in exchange for assistance in his war with Cairo, but this was a brief respite. In 1244 an army of Turks retook the city. Five years later the final offensive of the Crusades, the seventh, under Louis IX of France, dropped anchor at Damietta. The Egyptians abandoned the field. Ibn Wasil, a contemporary Arab historian, calls this shameful, as the port had sufficient provisions and arms to defend itself for at least two years. 'There was great grief in Egypt, the more so because the Sultan [Najm ad Din Ayyub] was ill, too weak to move, and without the strength to control his army, which was trying to impose its will on him instead.' On 30 August 1249 the Sultan died, and the Crusaders, although they had suffered reverses elsewhere, moved towards Mansura, where the Egyptian army was camped. His successor, al Muazzam, was in Mesopotamia at that time. An eloquent call for jihad by the regent, Emir Fakhr ad Din, still alive, was read out in the Great Mosque at Cairo. On 10 February 1250 the Muslim army, camped at Mansura, suddenly found Frank cavalry in its midst. Fakhr ad Din was having a bath, and leapt on his horse, unarmed, to rally his forces but was captured by Templars and killed. Certain of victory the Crusaders began to disperse through the streets.

At this decisive moment, yet another of those inexplicable reversals of fortune occurred, and a dying kingdom found sufficient fresh blood to defeat the might of Christian Europe. The Mamluk Turks of the Bahariya regiment of the Egyptian army, under the command of their leader Rukn ad Din Baibars, suddenly launched a ferocious charge and massacred the Franks. Cairo was trembling with anxiety; so far the messenger pigeons had only brought bad news. Next morning, a Wednesday, news of Baibars' victory reached the capital. 'The city prepared for a feast and the glad tidings were announced by a roll of drums. The victory over the Franks caused great joy and exultation. This was the first battle in which the Turkish lions defeated the infidel dogs,' reports ibn Wasil. The revived Muslims followed this up with 'a stupendous triumph' on 7 April 1250; once again the Mamluks were both the most courageous and the most audacious. 'They were Islam's Templars,' writes ibn Wasil. The whole army of the Seventh Crusade was taken prisoner. A eunuch, Sabih, was detailed to guard the king of France, raising some eyebrows among the Mamluks, while Cairo's poets celebrated with lines suggesting that Jesus himself would not breathe freely at the impiety of his followers. On 2 May, the leader of the Mamluks, Rukn ad Din walked into the camp of the Sultan, al Muazzam, struck him with his sword and walked away. The wounded Sultan appealed for help and got none. He fled towards his ships but was captured and killed. Passing boatmen buried him three days later. Thus ended the dynasty started by that authentic hero Saladin Ayyubi.

The Mamluk Turks, recent converts to Islam, restored some of the pristine energy. In 1260 Baibars astonished the world by defeating the rampaging Mongols at the battle of Ain Jalut in Galilee. Palestine and Syria once again were in the realm of Egypt. The Christian West was amazed, and no argument seemed capable of explaining yet another astonishing renewal of 'heretic' Islam; it had even reversed a Mongol tide. In 1291 the Mamluk Sultan Khalil destroyed the kingdom of Acre and eliminated Christian power, though not the Christian presence, from Palestine.

'The problem of the Islamic triumph presented itself most acutely in the form of the sufferings of Christians and their subjection to Islamic rule, particularly when it was directly observed,' writes Daniel. He quotes an evocative passage from Ricoldo's *Epistocae commentatorie de perditione Acconis*:

> It happened that when I was in Baghdad 'in the midst of the captives by the river Chobar' – the Tigris – in one respect the pleasantness of the garden delighted me, because it was like Paradise, for the wealth of the trees and fertility and variety of fruits; it had sprung up, irrigated by the waters of Paradise, and golden houses were built about it. In another respect, the massacre and capture of the Christian people and their overthrow after the lamentable capture of Akka drove me to sadness, when I saw the Muslims most joyful and flourishing, the Christians really neglected and mentally dismayed . . . I began more carefully than usual to reflect upon the judgements of God about the government of the world, and especially about Muslims and Christians . . . . From India to the regions of the West, peacefully and without opposition [the Muslims] at any rate possess the most choice and fertile kingdoms and those that are full of earthly delights . . . Mountains of salt, fountains of oil, manna of heaven, rivers of Paradise, aromatic spices, precious stones, vines of balsam and the sweetest of fruits.

Ricoldo's passion is palpable: Muslims multiplied because their Prophet had encouraged them to fornicate, he wrote with the anger of a Dominican, and yet God had given them power to crush other religions. He was forced to see Christian women and children sold into slavery after being paraded through streets, watch nuns become concubines, hear the Christians being taunted that their Jesus could not help them against Muhammad: God seemed to have become the God of the Quran rather than the God of the Bible! The similarity to the Muslim lament during their moments of distress is striking: Muslims had exactly the same complaint against Allah when the age of Christian victories came. It is a syndrome that has been well-described as half self pity and half bravado. Future compensation is generally inadequate balm for such a mood.

Muslims, who themselves were not short of invective against Christians, still viewed the onslaught against the Prophet as a deliberate and hurtful conspiracy. Muhammad, in the words of that ideologue of the Crusades, Humbert of Romans, had created Islam 'especially for the destruction of Christianity' (see again Norman Daniel). Dante too saw Christians and Muslims as children claiming the same Father, and realized that only one of the two could be legitimate. The next step was easy. Christianity was in danger. The Church demanded its own martyrs. One jihad had asked for another.

This war of three hundred years and perhaps more was intellectual, religious and military. With Popes leading the charge, priests inevitably played a prominent role in the mobilization of people as well as the ideas that would be needed to sustain them. The Dominican friars and the Franciscans were created to undertake missionary work amongst Muslims. In 1219 St Francis of Assissi crossed the Nile during the Fifth Crusade to try and convert none other than Sultan al Kamil. The Sultan was impressed with the spirit of this mendicant-missionary and treated him with honour before sending him back with a safe escort. However amenable he might be to peace, al Kamil was not ready for peace with the pope. Peace, in any case, was the last thing on the mind of the Franciscans. When nothing had been gained, as well as when all seemed lost, there was always the joy of martyrdom under the Muslim sword. In the year that St Francis preached to the Sultan, a band of Franciscan brothers deliberately provoked their martyrdom in Morocco. Their example was an accidental hero from the Spain of the ninth century.

The episode of the monk Perfectus in Cordoba links many levels of a complex relationship. In 850, Perfectus was confronted by a group of Muslims in a souk with the old question: who was the greater Prophet, Jesus or Muhammad? It was a set-up by Muslims, of course: to deny Jesus would be to deny his own faith; but to reject Muhammad meant an invitation to a beheading. It was a capital offence to insult the Prophet. Perfectus began his reply cautiously, but suddenly something snapped and he burst out into a torrent of passionate abuse, calling Muhammad a charlatan, a sexual pervert and so on. A street problem which could have been sorted out suddenly acquired dangerous proportions. An angry crowd took the monk to the *qadi*, who refused to pass a death sentence, ruling correctly that Perfectus had been unfairly provoked. Perfectus however got another fit of moral indignation and became so abusive that the law was forced to take its course. He was executed on the day of the Id festival.

On that Id, a group of Muslims enjoying their holiday on a boat cruise drowned when the boat capsized. Christians called this a sign; God had punished the Moor for the death of Perfectus. The monk became a cult figure in Spain, inspiring bands of potential martyrs. In the summer of 851, about fifty Christians – monks, priests, scholars, laymen – walked up to the *qadi* to denounce Muhammad and collect their death sentence. The Church was not terribly enthusiastic at this outburst of unofficial piety; the bishop of Cordoba, whose principal purpose was peaceful coexistence with the new rulers, publicly condemned such enthusiasm. The martyrs however found leaders in firebrands like Eulogio and Paul Alvarro who added an apocalyptic twist: the rise of Islam was a prelude to the end of the world. Was it not said that Jesus would not return till the Great Apostasy had taken place; until a rebel had established his rule in Jerusalem and converted many Christians? The Book of Revelations, they argued, mentioned a great beast marked by the number 666 who would crawl out of any abyss, sit on the throne at Temple Mount and rule the world. The Muslims had built two mosques on Temple Mount, and ruled a fair share of the world; the parallel was neatly rounded off by saying that Muhammad had died in the year 666 of the era of Spain. (If either of them had read the Quran, they would have discovered, possibly with horror, that the Beast as a sign of the last day is also mentioned in the Quran, in 27:82.)

At the end of the fourteenth century the Franciscans in Jerusalem were still doing what they had done in Morocco nearly two centuries earlier. On 11 November 1391 a group of them went to al Aqsa and demanded that the *qadi* hear them out. When he did, they called Muhammad a libertine, a murderer, a glutton, and a despoiler who thought the purpose of life was eating, sex, and expensive clothes. An angry Muslim mob collected demanding the punishment of death for slander. The Franciscans wanted the same thing. The *qadi* offered conversion before he announced death. They chose death because, by inverse logic, it would ensure damnation on the Muslims. A similar incident is recorded from 1393. This was, in either slaying or suicide, the Crusader spirit.

A familiar phrase describes the first Crusade as the victory of monarchy over anarchy. Muslim power had fractured by the last century of the millennium when Christian kings were uniting, or at least being forced by the Popes and public opinion to set aside their formidable differences and take on Muslim empires. The Umayyads did not long survive the battle of Tours; they lost their credibility and then their empire. After Caliph Hisham, who lost that war, four successors came and went in less than a decade. In June 750 Abul Abbas, a descendant of the Prophet and one of their generals, invited eighty Umayyad nobles to his home for dinner and slaughtered them while the other guests treated the massacre as part of the evening's entertainment (the only important prince to survive was Abdur Rahman who went on to establish an Umayyad dynasty from Cordoba in Spain). There was popular support for this revolt in the name of first principles. The historian al Tabari may have been obedient in addition to being colourful, but was also reflecting the popular mood when he wrote 'now are the dark nights of the world put to flight, its covering lifted, now light breaks in the earth and the heavens, and the sun rises from the springs of day while the moon ascends from its appointed place . . . Right has come back to where it originated, among the people of the house of your Prophet, people of compassion and mercy for you and sympathy towards you . . .'

The Abbasids of Abul Abbas, who called himself al Saffah, or the shedder of blood, however, would not be remembered so much for the purity of faith as the glory of some of his heirs, the most famous being Haroon ur Rashid (786–804). Actually the Arabian nights are a bit of an undersell. The culture of the Abbasid court lost its Arabic exclusivity and stretched to include Persians and Turks. The capital moved to Baghdad: construction began in 762 and ended four years later at a cost of some five million dirhams. Degeneration was perhaps inevitable. At the palace, truth began to compete with fiction. Haroon's grandson Mutawakkil is said to have had 4,000 concubines; more impressively, he claimed to have slept with all of them. Slaves and eunuchs appeared in abundance. The wealth was legendary, the spending gross. Harun might buy a ruby for 40,000 dirham; the Caliph Mustain order a rug worth 130 million dirham for his mother. There were however also substantive achievements, notably in the field of scholarship. Abu Sina, Al Farabi, and Al Ghazzali are still household names. An impressive statistic states that there were over a hundred bookshops in Baghdad at the end of the ninth century, a time when there were none in London or Paris.

Abbassid excesses might be borne by a people sharing some of the prosperity, but they were consistently challenged by the pious clergy. The Abbasids have the dubious distinction of harassing and even hounding all the four great imams who laid the foundations of Islamic jurisprudence: Abu Hanifa (700–67), Malik ibn Anas (710–95), Muhammad as Shafi (772–826), and Ahmed ibn Hanbal (780–95). The first died in prison; the second was flogged; the third did a prison term, and the fourth was flogged as well as jailed. This was the fate of the four great intellectuals of whom it is said that the gates of independent enquiry closed after them. Little wonder then that when the Mongol Hulagu Khan came to the doors of Baghdad in 1258, he taunted Caliph al Mustasim with verses from the Quran where Allah warns Muslims of the price of pride: humiliation and calamity. Baghdad was destroyed, the Caliph killed. The dynasty was finished and the centre of Muslim power in that region moved south to Cairo to witness another great revival.

The French victory in the battle of Tours that shook Damascus had an equally major, and positive, influence in Europe. With the unification of the Franks, power began to shift from the east towards the west of Europe. Fourteen centuries later the pendulum remains stuck, never having swung back. The Byzantines lost control over the papacy in the reign of Martel's son, Pepin, with the election of Pope Stephen in 752. Pepin's son, the great Charlemagne, a contemporary of Haroon ur Rashid, built on an impressive legacy with his own genius, and Christians began to dream seriously of Jerusalem, the city of Golgotha, the tomb of Christ, and the Holy Sepulchre Church. It was a dream reinforced by every arduous pilgrimage made in that era of poverty, disease, and war, encouraged by an activist clergy that sought sustenance in faith.

In the last century of the millennium the growing confidence of Christian Europe was spurred by an old prophecy that before the end of the world (it was nigh once again) an emperor from the west would become king of Jerusalem and destroy the anti-Christ there. Religion and politics were a working combination, but their most productive century was the first of the second millennium.

The great pilgrimage of 1033 was a sign of things to come. In 1061 Count Roger invaded Muslim Sicily, bringing it back to Christendom by 1091. In 1085 Frankish knights fought beside Spaniards to recover Toledo. Pope Gregory VII formed a militia called the Knights of St Peter, and ordered their mobilization when the Turks scored major victories over the Byzantines in 1071 and 1074. The Knights were meant to reconquer Jerusalem after they had dealt with the Turks. They did not, of course, but another Pope twenty-five years later did see a 450-year-old dream come true, when the standards of Godfrey of Bouillon were raised on the battlements of Jerusalem.

Robert the Monk, who wrote an account of this victory within ten years, called it the greatest event in history since the Crucifixion, for the Anti-Christ would soon arrive and the last battle before the Day of Judgment begin. The Anti-Christ came, but his name was Saladin.

6

ALLAH! MUHAMMAD! SALADIN!

Almighty God! Let his soul be acceptable to thee and open to him
the gates of Paradise, that being the last conquest of his hopes.
[Inscription on the grave of Saladin. He died on 4 March 1193]

It all began with a castration. The story has an Arabian Nights quality to it, but that does not make it a fantasy.

Najm ad Din, head of a prosperous Kurd family of Tovin, in Armenia, had a great friend, a charming man called Bihruz. Charm was both his strength and his weakness. He charmed the robes off the wife of the local emir but had the distinct misfortune of being caught in her company with his pants down. The emir promptly castrated him, and then, probably to make doubly sure, banished him.

Najm ad Din decided to accompany his friend; the two made their way to Baghdad and the court of the Abbasid Caliph Mustafi. To turn misfortune into opportunity reflected the spirit of the times, or at least the spirit of the two friends. Unlike in our very civilized era, eunuchs then were not ridiculed, insulted, prostituted, and ostracized merely because they were devoid of one facility. This absence was even considered a virtue, not merely for jobs that required contact with the family and women, but also in office. Their minds possibly focused better. Bihruz's infamous charm now brought dividends. He became a chess-playing friend of the Sultan himself. One reward that he received for high office was a castle in the city of Takreet, on the Tigris, north of Baghdad. Bihruz appointed Najm ad Din governor of the castle, and the latter invited his brother Shirkuh to join him in his good fortune.

In 1137 a son was born to Najm ad Din at Takreet, whom he named

Yusuf ibn Ayyub. (In the last decade of the twentieth century, an Iraqi, Saddam Hussein, would make it a point to advertise that he too was born in Takreet.) Yusuf's birth was not immediately propitious. That very night his uncle Shirkuh had an altercation with the chief of the castle gate which turned violent, and ended in the latter's death. A horrified Bihruz expelled the brothers. They left for Mosul to the principality of a man whose life Najm ad Din had once saved, five years ago.

The Atabeg of Mosul and Aleppo at that time was Imad ad Din Zengi, dark, with a bristly beard, one of the many claimants of fragile power. But he was also different. He slept with his soldiers and enforced such exemplary discipline that it was said his troops marched between two ropes so that they would not destroy cultivated fields. This was the leader who was called, by Ibn al Athir, 'the gift of divine providence to Muslims'; who would launch the counter-offensive against the Christian kingdoms of Palestine that reached its apex in fifty two years, thanks to Yusuf, known to the world as Salah ad Din Ayyubi, or Saladin. Zengi gave notice of his abilities in the year Saladin was born, with the conquest of the strong Crusader fortress of Mont Ferrand (or Barin, in Arabic) in which King Fulk of Jerusalem and his barons were defeated and trapped till they paid a ransom of 50,000 dinar for their freedom. There was a great uproar; monks swept through the Byzantine empire warning the Christian world that the Muslims had only one real ambition, and that was Jerusalem. Emperor John II Comnenus was cool; he used the opportunity to claim Antioch from the shaken Crusaders

In 1144 Zengi changed the geopolitics of the region. He took Edessa, the first of the four kingdoms established in the first Crusade.

Zengi gave a call for jihad. Eager troops came from the Turkish tribes, specialist sappers arrived from Khurasan and Aleppo. His army first devastated the countryside around the fortified city until it was said that not a bird dared to fly near Edessa. The sappers, working through tunnels, reached under the towers of the city walls. Wooden supports were set on fire directly under the towers, weakening the walls until they crumbled, and Zengi took Edessa by storm at dawn two days before Christmas in 1144. The 'Franj', outsiders, were stripped, looted, chained. But Zengi treated the eastern, local, Christians, Syrians and Armenians, well, saying that they were of the land unlike the Franks from Europe. (Muslim accounts, lavish in their praise for Zengi, tend to ignore the fact that he liked a drink or two – or three.) The loss of Edessa stunned Europe. A very interesting story indicates the impact of this victory. The King of Sicily, Roger II, in the tradition of his land, had Muslims in his court, one of them an old sage. One day, looking out at the sea, he saw a ship that brought news of the expedition Roger had sent to Tripoli. It had been victorious. Roger turned to the Muslim sage who was dozing nearby and teased him: 'Do you hear what they said?'

'No,' replied the sage.

'They told me that we have defeated the Muslims in Tripoli. What use is Muhammad now to his land and his people?'

'He was not there,' answered the old man. 'He was at Edessa, which the Muslims have just taken.'

The other courtiers laughed but Roger reminded them that the sage always spoke the truth. A few days later the loss of Edessa was officially confirmed. The clergy picked up currents of that shock and spread it across Europe.

During Easter in 1146 Louis VII of France and his beautiful wife Eleanor of Aquitaine knelt before St Bernard of Clairvaux at Vezelay, who promised the couple permanence in paradise if they undertook what became known as the Second Crusade, a direct reaction to the fall of Edessa. For Eleanor, 25-years-old, that Crusade proved to be less than divine: she was accused by her husband of seducing her uncle, Raymond of Antioch, and placed under guard. Eleanor's marriage to Louis was later dissolved, officially because she was unable to produce a male heir. Eleanor went on to become more famous as the wife of England's Henry II whom she married in 1152, taking Aquitaine along with her. Arab historians do not credit Louis VII with much of a role in that Crusade: the fierce assault on Damascus was led by the German emperor Conrad III where, once again, the Crusaders lost a crucial encounter on the point of victory. Zengi had died at the age of 60 by the time of the Second Crusade. One September night in 1146 he fell asleep, drunk. A little later, he was woken by a noise and discovered his servant, a eunuch, drinking from his goblet. Terrified that he would be punished the next day, the eunuch killed the great Champion of Islam.

Zengi's successor, his second son, Nur ad Din Mahmud, was 29. He was both more pious and more zealous than his father. He lived by the classic code of the faith, frugal with himself and generous to others. Jihad was his obsession at a time when compromise and caution were the pre-ferred policies of other Muslim rulers. The principal ally of the Kingdom of Jerusalem was in fact Unur, the ruler of Damascus, and therefore it was something of a shock to Unur when in July 1148 the Second Crusade ended up at his doorstep rather than at the gates of Edessa. Muslims rallied from all over the region to protect Damascus; and when the Franj heard that Nur ad Din was also on his way, they simply dispersed before the amazed Damascenes. Nur ad Din built an exquisite pulpit that would wait for the liberation of the al Aqsa mosque; a young man in his court would one day install that pulpit.

Saladin was this young man, of course. He inherited another conviction from his mentor: that the key to this jihad lay in the unification of Syria and Egypt. As long as Arab power was split, the Kingdom of Jerusalem was unshakeable. Understandably, the official policy of the Franks, holding the space in between, was to keep the two divided.

In 1163, Nur ad Din asked Shirkuh (who had also served in Zengi's army) to lead an invasion of Egypt. A reluctant, 26-year-old Saladin was ordered to accompany his uncle. In Cairo, the faltering Shia Fatimid dynasty resisted Shirkuh and Saladin for five years with help from Jerusalem but on 8 January 1169 Cairo fell and Shirkuh proclaimed himself king of Egypt. Within two months he was dead, allegedly poisoned. Nur ad Din made Saladin king of Egypt assuming that a 32-year-old would be obedient. Saladin had his own views on war strategy and his interests. In 1174 Nur ad Din began to raise an army against Saladin, but died of a heart attack on 15 May, before he could march. In 1175 Saladin took the offensive, reached Damascus, removed the boy who had succeeded Nur ad Din, and was proclaimed Sultan of Syria and Egypt, and guardian of the holy places.

He knew what he wanted. He said, later, that when God gave him Egypt it was only because Allah wanted him to liberate Jerusalem. He was ready for a mission that had been searching for a missionary since the turn of the century.

The Crusades began, officially, on 25 November 1095 when Pope Urban I, addressing a tumultuous gathering of knights, priests, and laymen, granted remission of all sins to anyone who joined the holy war against Muslims. The Muslim Turks, said the Pope, had become 'an accursed race, a race utterly alienated from God'; it was a Christian duty to 'exterminate this vile race from our lands'. Once the Turkish filth had been cleansed from holy Byzantine territory, the army of Christ would march to Jerusalem and liberate the tomb of the saviour from infidels. '*Deus hoc vult!*' ('God wills this!') roared the audience.

By March 1096 nearly a hundred thousand men, from nobles to robber barons to priests to peasants were on the move as part of five armies. Every section of society had been inspired by the holy war. That autumn an equal number or more followed them as part of five more armies. The Byzantine emperor Alexius Comnenus I had asked for help in 1095 to clear the Turks from Anatolia which they had occupied after the battle of Manzikurt in 1071, and was expecting a contingent of mercenaries. He was horrified by the hordes that reached Constantinople to save him and pushed them on towards the Turks as quickly as he could. However, against the odds, this army defeated the Seljuks, reached Palestine, and created two principalities, Edessa and Antioch, before, in 1099, standing at the walls of a vision: Jerusalem.

On 15 July 1099, during the holy month of Ramadan, a trooper in the army of Godfrey of Bouillon broke through from the north towers, and the rest of a thirsty and inflamed army followed. It was inflamed by faith and thirsty for blood. For three days Muslims and Jews, male or female were massacred. A group of ten thousand Muslims who thought they were in the sanctuary of the al Aqsa mosque were slaughtered; Jews met a similar fate in their synagogue. An eyewitness, Raymond of Aguiles, reported, with pride: 'Piles of heads, hands and feet were to be seen . . . If I tell the truth it will exceed your powers of belief. So let it suffice to say this much, at least, that in the Temple and the Porch of Solomon, men rode in blood up to their knees and bridle reins. Indeed, it was a just and splendid judgment of God that this place should be filled with the blood of unbelievers since it had suffered so long from their blasphemies.'

The rotting bodies had not been removed till Christmas; their stench has not gone nine hundred years later. The glorious Caliph of the world of Islam, al Mustazir, reacted to this cataclysmic catastrophe by appointing a committee.

A straggle of survivors, and fearful Muslims from the region, poured into Damascus and Baghdad, weeping and inconsolable. Qadi Abu Saad al Harawi comforted them with the memory of the Hijra, when Muslims had to escape from Mecca, and said they would return to Jerusalem in triumph as the first Muslims had returned to Mecca. He took a delegation to the Caliph, who paid lip service and returned to his mismanagement. The Qadi noted ruefully that men of faith had become weak. Only poets remained to stir passions in a manner that Sir Muhammad Iqbal was to do in the twentieth century, another time of despair for the community. Muzaffar al Abiwardi wrote:

71

To shed tears is a man's worst weapon when the swords stir up the embers of war,

Sons of Islam, behind you are battles in which heads rolled at your feet.

Dare you slumber in the blessed shade of safety, where life is as soft as an orchard flower?

How can the eyelids close lids at a time of disaster that would waken any sleeper?

While your Syrian brothers can only sleep on the backs of their chargers or in vultures' bellies

Must the foreigners feed on our ignominy, while you trail behind you the train of a pleasant life?

When blood has been spilt, when sweet girls must for shame hide their lovely faces in their hands

When the white swords' points are red with blood, and the iron of brown lances is stained with gore!

At the sound of sword hammering on lance young children's hair turns white

This is war, and the man who shuns the whirlpool shall grind his teeth in penitence.

This is war and the infidel's sword is naked in his hand, ready to be sheathed again in men's necks and skulls.

This is war and he who lies in the tomb at Medina seems to raise his voice and cry: 'O Sons of Hashim!

I see my people slow to raise the lance against the enemy, I see the Faith resting on feeble pillars.

For fear of death the Muslims are evading the fire of battle, refusing to believe that death will surely strike them.

Must Arab champions suffer in resignation, while gallant Persians shut their eyes to dishonour?'

Those Arab champions and gallant Persians finally found their leader in a Kurd, Saladin. In 1183 Saladin completed his task of uniting Arab power under a single banner when he took the Gray Castle of Aleppo in the month of Safar. A young *qadi* called Muhyi ad Din penned some verse around an old saying, that became very popular: he who takes the Gray Castle in Safar will take Jerusalem in Rajab.

As Saladin gathered Muslims into one kingdom under the banner of the true jihad, the disease that had cost the Muslims Jerusalem now grew rampant among Christians: disunity. The principal schism was around, inevitably, the policy towards Muslims between the peace party and the war party. The argument travelled from the bottom to the top. At a social level, the raw and powerful Crusader spirit had been replaced by settler comfort amongst second and third generation Christians. Many of them, some with eastern mothers, had begun to think of themselves as Orientals. They took something as decadent as a bath, used soap, spoke Arabic, listened to local music, wore the *keffiya*, and some women even took to the veil when shopping. It was convenience rather than conversion. Inevitably, Europeans married local women, and a mixed race called the *poulains* was born. The problem became far more serious as it reached the decision-makers at the top. The hawks wanted permanent holy war, while the doves argued that the realities of the neighbourhood demanded a spirit of accommodation. The Arabs, by and large, had an amused contempt for everything Crusader except their raw courage. There was no art, no learning, no sophistication that came with them, but there were excellent forts, heavily fortified churches and a culture of confrontation. Priests had formally donned armour and nobles the gown. The Order of the Hospital had been created to care for the sick; in 1113 the Pope, through a bull, placed it under Rome's direct authority, and in 1136 gave it the right to use arms: they formed an important part of the failed Second Crusade. In 1119 the Order of the Temple was created to protect pilgrims, drawing its message from St Bernard of Clairvaux who, as we have noticed, did not mince any words: killing a pagan for Christ, said the saint, was the way to glory. These knight-priests were true Christian jihadis, with vows of poverty and chastity; they were also, in battle, the first to attack and the last to retreat. They were the hard steel of Christian arms.

Among the hawks, our familiar Reynauld of Chatillon swooped the hardest. The leadership was in disarray: the young Baldwin IV, struck with leprosy, died in March 1185; his son, Baldwin V died the following year, and Guy of Lusignan took over after more fratricide than even a healthy kingdom might have been able to afford.

In March 1187 Saladin gave the call for jihad. A truce he had negotiated with Raymond of Tripoli, one of the doves, had been broken by Chatillon. In 1186 he attacked pilgrims on the way to *hajj*, massacred or imprisoned them and when reminded of truce, taunted: 'Let your

73

Muhammad come and save you!' The response to the call for jihad was overwhelming. Force was accompanied by some brilliant strategy. Saladin understood the knights of the Kingdom of Jerusalem better than they understood him. His most famous victory, at Hattin, was a triumph of strategy as much as of arms. As Saladin massed 25,000 odd troops to the east of Galilee, King Guy in Jerusalem summoned the True Cross from the Holy Sepulchre: it had been used as a standard in war only twenty times before, at moments of severe crisis. On 1 July Saladin's forces gathered at the plain of Lubiya where he hoped to give battle. He wanted to lure the knights into the open, at the height of summer. Therefore, taking a risk, he split his army and personally led an élite corps to Tiberias, took the city, and waited outside the citadel. Besieged, the Countess Eschiva, wife of Raymond, sent a desperate plea to Jerusalem for help. Raymond himself warned his colleagues that this might be a trap, but the hawks sneered that he was a Muslim-lover. They won the battle in council and lost it on the Horns of Hattin – ironically, the spot where Christ is said to have delivered the Sermon on the Mount, promising the meek that they would inherit the earth. On 3 July Christian forces set out to rescue Tiberias. Saladin surrounded the Christian army, cut off all access to the fresh water of Lake Tiberias, and watched and waited for thirst to drain the spirit while his cavalry harassed the enemy from both sides. At noon the following day he ordered dry grass placed before the enemy to be set on fire. The demoralisation was complete by then. When King Guy asked his soldiers to defend the True Cross they refused. Saladin's cavalry decimated the Templars; and the rest of the army was defenceless as the Muslims completed a massacre. Count Raymond escaped because Saladin opened a gap to allow him to do so.

Saladin's son al Afdal, only 17, was with him on 4 July. The Crusaders, now desperate, fought with remarkable courage from the high ground around the tent of their leader, King Guy. Twice the young man screamed with joy that the Muslims had won, but Saladin silenced him. Only when that tent had fallen would he assume victory. When the tent collapsed, Saladin dismounted, weeping with joy, and knelt in obeisance to Allah. The True Cross was seized. King Guy and Chatillon were both made prisoner. Saladin was seated on a divan when the two were brought before him; he asked Guy to sit beside him, and offered him *sherbet*. The Sultan went out to inspect his troops, returned, and summoned his prize captives again. He offered the hated Chatillon the option of conversion; when he refused Saladin brought his scimitar down on Chatillon's shoulder, and left the head to be beheaded by his servants. King Guy trembled and fell to his knees. Saladin told him to rise: real kings, he said, do not kill each other. Chatillon had only paid for his perversity.

The road to Jerusalem was now open. Acre, Beirut, and Sidon fell; only Tyre resisted, and Saladin ignored the coastal city, a decision which Muslims would bitterly regret later. His aim was to encircle Jerusalem and clear the region of Christian enclaves. On 19 September Saladin broke camp at Ascalon and started the last stage of his march. The army had one dream: to hear the muezzin call the faithful to prayer from al Aqsa.

On 26 September the assault on Jerusalem began. Imad ad Din, a retainer who wrote the history of the conquest and Saladin's life, describes, with typical flourishes, the mission:

> Islam wooed Jerusalem, ready to lay down lives for her as a bride-price, bringing her a blessing that would remove the tragedy of her state, giving her a joyful face to replace an expression of torment, making heard, above the cry of grief from the Rock, calling for help against its enemies, the reply to this appeal, the prompt echo of the summons, an echo that would make the gleaming lamps rise in her sky, bring the exiled Faith back to her own country and dwelling place and drive away from al Aqsa those whom God drove away with his curse.

In 1099 the siege had lasted five weeks. This time it would take seven days. Saladin began battering the northern wall around St Stephen's Gate, exactly where Godfrey of Bouillon had been eighty eight years before. On 29 September, it was breached. The Patriarch of Jerusalem, Heraclius, who lived openly with a draper's wife from Nablus, offered a fortune for guards to defend the breach; there were no takers. Women began to cut the hair of their children in expectation of martyrdom. The defenders had however one trump card: the holy places. The threat to destroy the Dome of the Rock and al Aqsa softened Saladin. (In 1098 Muslims debated a similar option, but chose not to touch the churches before the Crusaders came and slaughtered them.) A deal was made: the Christians could pay ransom of ten gold *bezants* for each man, five for a woman, and one for a child, and leave.

On 2 October 1187, or 27 Rajab 583 by the Islamic calendar, Saladin entered Jerusalem. It was the day on which Muslims celebrated the ascension of the Prophet to heaven from Jerusalem.

Saladin kept his word. Not a single Christian was killed. Heraclius scandalized the Muslims by leaving with his chariots loaded with wealth while many poor Christians headed for slavery because they did not have ransom money. Saladin, moved famously to tears by the tragedy of families who were being separated for slavery, freed hundreds without ransom. When a generous man stumbles, God takes his hand, said the Prophet. Saladin was nothing if not generous. He released the widows of dead soldiers, and wives of prisoners, and sent them away with gifts. Saladin's brother, al Malek al Adil, asked for a thousand Christians as reward for his part in battle, and released them immediately. Christians everywhere, he said, would remember his behaviour and contrast it with their own. Meanwhile, the *ulema* reminded Muslims that only the lesser jihad was over; the greater jihad, that of cleansing themselves, of continuing the struggle to live in the just way of Allah had begun.

Saladin would not blame the eastern Christians for the Crusades and allowed Syrian and Armenian Christians to live on in Jerusalem. Hotheads wanted to destroy the Church of the Holy Sepulchre, but he did not permit a single sacred Christian site to be touched. The church was closed for only three days. He invited the Jews back to the city, and his name was celebrated throughout the Jewish world. When he destroyed Ascalon because he did not want to defend two cities, the Jews of Ascalon were given homes in Jerusalem and allowed to build a synagogue.

Saladin had, consciously, emulated the Caliph Umar, and taken Jerusalem without bloodshed or destruction. After the defeat of the Byzantine forces at the battle of Yarmuk on 20 August 636, the emperor Heraclius realized that he would not be able to hold the region. He went to Jerusalem, picked up the Holy Cross, and left Syria, never to return. In July 637 the Muslims were at the walls of Jerusalem. Their first siege lasted seven months. The patriarch Sophronius did his best, but was forced to surrender in February. It is uncertain whether Umar went to accept the surrender of Jerusalem or not, but the second Caliph did visit Islam's third holiest city. When the richly caparisoned Byzantine priests saw Umar, who, astride a white camel, wore only an old and patched tunic, they thought he was a hypocrite. Jerusalem's history is splashed with blood, before and after the Islamic intervention, but that transfer of power was the most peaceful in its history. No one was killed after surrender, no property destroyed, and no attempt made to convert any inhabitant. On the other hand, while Umar was touring the Church of the Holy Sepulchre with Sophronius as his guide, they heard the *azaan*, the call to prayer. The patriarch asked the Caliph to say his prayers right there, in the Anastasis. Umar refused. He told the priest that if he had prayed at that spot, Muslims would have converted the church into a mosque. Umar passed an order that no Muslim should ever pray at this church or at the martyrium of Constantine, or ever build a mosque there. Christians and Jews – and Christians were not a minority in Jerusalem then – were offered the protection of the Quranic law, as *dhimmi*: they were given freedom, but not complete equality, and they had to pay a poll tax (*jiziya*) of one dinar per family per year. Not all successors of Umar were equally sagacious, and the *jiziya* was later often abusive and insulting. Umar also lifted the Christian ban and brought the Jews back to a city which was holier to them than it was to Christians and Muslims. He invited seventy Jewish families from Tiberias and gave them permanent residence on the southwest region of the Haram, above the site of the temple.

The nobility of an Umar or a Saladin was not prevalent among all the victors when Saladin took Jerusalem. Saladin's own behaviour was exemplary, but his soldiers demanded booty, and as they had not been permitted to loot, they were hungry for slaves. Women, as usual, suffered the fate of concubinage, while Muslim propagandists gloried in their subjugation and rape. This made particular sense of the Christian lament that was to travel through Europe: 'Rachel weeps again, whose need for sons discredits her womb.' Such excesses do not however take away from Saladin's memorable conduct and the good sense of his policies. Of all human virtues, he gave primacy to generosity and courage. He often quoted the verse where Allah had praised the Prophet's generosity, and then would repeat a second saying of the Prophet: God loves courage, even in the killing of a serpent.

The highest honour that Saladin could confer at that hour was to choose the man who would deliver the first *khutba* on Friday from al Aqsa. Arab historians record that the venerable old men waiting for the honour began to sweat when Saladin named a 32-year-old *qadi* from Aleppo, Muhi ad Din, the young man who had written a poem after Alleppo. In a speech that is still remembered, and which did not hesitate to demand vengeance against infidels, the *qadi* had one central message for believers: victory had not come because of their sharp swords, fleet horses, or their courage in battle: it had come from Allah. He called Saladin the Sultan of Islam.

He remains one, as any television image from the Palestine battlefield will confirm. The irony is that the man who was hailed by Jews all over the world for bringing them back to Jerusalem has become an inspiration for a jihad against Israel, but perhaps no more ironic than the fact that the sling of the Caliph of Allah, David, is the preferred weapon of Palestinian children against armies flying the star of David on their banner.

Saladin's epic confrontation with the Third Crusade is also a living fact in a region that chooses its memories with care.

Before he died in 1181, Pope Alexander III was the first to warn European princes of the potential of this new power in the Holy Land, Saladin. No one took notice. The two great powers of the West were England and France, and the behaviour of their ruling families was exotic, to put it mildly. The Byzantines, who in 800 had refused to recognize the coronation of Charlesmagne by Pope Leo III on Christmas Day, 800 as Holy Roman Emperor because the hero of the Franks was illiterate, were now supplicants before other dynasties, begging for help to preserve the boundaries of an empire being steadily eaten up by Turks to their east.

What were England and France doing in the decade in which Saladin united Egypt and Syria and liberated Palestine? Louis VII of France, veteran cuckold of the Second Crusade, finally got an heir when he was 45 from his third wife Adele of Champagne, in 1165. The people called the child, Philip Augustus, 'God-given', at least partly because his father seemed unlikely to have given Adele anything potent. If this was Paris gossip, the second reason was more serious: an heir to the Capetian dynasty effectively blocked the Plantagenets from claiming the throne of France in addition to that of England. The French celebrated the birth of Philip on the streets by taunting the English and praying that the child would, when he became king, remove Henry II and his heirs from their continental base in Aquitaine. In England there was gloom at Philip's birth; royal astrologers saw two comets in the skies, and said that this meant either the ruin or death of a king. Philip was eight years younger than the most famous child of the competition, Richard. Eleanor, unable to give an heir to the pious Louis, proved fertile enough in her thirties with lusty Henry, giving birth to five sons of which the first died as an infant. Richard, her second surviving son, was her favourite.

The two families did not allow politics to interfere with their love life. Richard and Philip, son and stepson of Eleanor, became lovers. Gerald of

Wales (actually, the archdeacon of Wales, and a notable historian of the era) has left an account that is not finicky: the two ate from one dish and slept in one bed. In 1161, Philip's beautiful half-sister Alais was promised to Richard. He was only four then, but princely marriages were called alliances for good reason. Alais was consequently sent to the English court to learn English manners, such as they were, and be ready for Richard. Along the way, while Richard was in Philip's bed, Alais joined Richard's father Henry in his. Henry made more room for Alais by sending Eleanor to prison; her first husband had imprisoned her for cuckoldry, her second for his adultery. It was already a complicated who's whose when Philip fell in love with Richard's brother Geoffrey, despite the latter's reputation as a deceiver, dissembler, and hypocrite.

At the political level, Philip insisted that Richard should honour the pledge to marry a woman who was now his father's mistress as he wanted the castle in Gisors that had been promised as part of the marriage settlement. This was the castle in France where the two ruling families often met to confer, by an elm tree that became renowned. Richard was indifferent to his future wife's taste in boyfriends, but he was upset that he was not being made heir to the throne. Henry encouraged a civil war between his sons that lasted three years and ended only with the eldest son's death in 1183. Richard's obstacle was dead, but his father was bitter and stubborn. In 1186, the third son Geoffrey was trampled to death in an accident. Philip was so upset that he threatened to inter himself with Geoffrey. He went back to Richard to ease his grief.

It was after this that the family saw the light. Or, more accurately, was shown the light.

In November 1187 the Archbishop of Tyre, Josias, boarded a ship with black sails to indicate he was in mourning and headed for Europe with the bad news. Gregory VIII was Pope, and he urged Europe to turn its attention away from its own bitter quarrels and confront the Muslims in another Crusade. He died within two months, but Clement III took up the cause. He sent Josias to ask England to lead another Crusade against the 'unspeakable progeny of Ishmael'. Josias met Richard in France in December. The prince fell on his knees and accepted the cross, the first prince of Europe to declare for the Third Crusade. Henry and Philip went down on their knees as well after the persuasive Josias met them.

Henry rose from his knees quite quickly. He was doing enough, he thought for the cause by sending blood-money, or atonement-money, to the Templars and Hospitalers for the murder of Thomas Becket. He was soon demanding to know why he should worship Christ when Christ was not being very helpful to him in his fight against his son. By the time Henry and Philip met again, at the elm tree in Gisors, piety had once again been replaced by rancour. In his anger Philip had the elm cut down and Henry declared war – not on Saladin, but on Philip. He ranted against Richard's affair with Philip and cursed his son. In 1188 the two royal lovers decided to join forces against Henry. A defeated Henry died in lonely misery. Blood is said to have burst from his nostrils when Richard approached his father's body, but the former was now king, and ready for the holy war.

Only men were invited to his coronation banquet. A pogrom against English Jews set the mood for the Crusade (Richard enjoyed hearing stories about Jewish teeth being pulled out, slowly). He imposed on England what became known as the Saladin tax: one-tenth of a subject's income for three years unless he joined the Crusade. Perhaps appropriately, a Christian *jiziya* had been named after a Muslim.

In July 1190 Richard I and Philip II met on the fields of Burgundy with their armies. Philip, still a bachelor, had been king for ten years although he was younger than Richard by six, but Richard was the star of Europe. The two took different routes, but agreed to meet at Sicily before they mounted their joint offensive against 'the race of slanderers'.

Baha ad Din describes the Muslim reaction as Philip landed in six ships on 20 April 1191 and Richard followed on 8 June. 'His [Richard's] arrival made an enormous impression: he appeared with twenty-five ships laden with men, arms, and equipment, and the Franks made a great display of joy and lit fires that night among their tents . . . His arrival put fear into the hearts of the Muslims, but the Sultan met the panic with firmness and faith in God.' Saladin sent a summon for jihad against the united might of Europe:

> Where is the sense of honour of the Muslims, the pride of the believers, the zeal of the faithful? . . . They have become negligent and lazy . . . If, God forbid, Islam should draw rein, obscure her splendour, blunt her sword, there would be no one, East or West, far or near, who would blaze with zeal for God's religion or choose to come to the aid of truth against error. This is the moment to cast off lethargy, to summon from far and near all those men who

have blood in their veins . . . God willing, the Unbelievers shall perish and the faithful have a sure deliverance.

The 16-month war confrontation between Richard and Saladin was full of romance, with nothing more romantic than the last battle of the Crusade, when Saladin's forces swooped down on Richard's camp outside Jaffa. Heavily outnumbered, Richard still retained his lion's heart, and amazed the watching Saladin with his courage and skill. At the height of battle Richard was unhorsed, and vulnerable. Saladin turned to his brother al Malek al Adil and told him to take two Arabian horses as a gift to Richard, for a king as great as him should not fight on foot. Richard saved the day on Saladin's horse, but could not save the Crusade, which was effectively over after its retreat, on 6 July 1192, from Beit Nuba, when Jerusalem was in sight of the great armies and their spirit had risen as high as their hopes. Richard lost his nerve. Moreover, he was convinced that Saladin knew his every move, as indeed it appeared from the quality of Saladin's intelligence that there was a mole at the highest levels of Richard's council. This person, whoever he was, must rank as the most decisive mole in the history of secret services.

Richard was ready to follow if the others insisted on an assault of Jerusalem, but he resigned his command. Philip had already left for France. It all ended in bathos. The Duke of Burgundy, Hugh, composed a song questioning Richard's virility; Richard used his own artistic abilities to reply with a bitchy song about Hugh. Richard fell seriously ill after Jaffa, and was feverish when the treaty with Saladin was read out to him. The last exchange between two great men was a true measure of their temperament. Richard sent word to Saladin that he was only going home for the period of the three year truce and would return with an army that was even greater. Saladin replied that if he had to lose his dominions then he would rather lose them to a king of courage and honour such as Richard.

Richard took the last ship out, in October, and underwent strange adventures before a second coronation. Saladin barely survived his winter of content. In February he fell ill, and died on 4 March 1193, his dream fulfilled. He had not only won Jerusalem; he had also saved it for Islam. 'The day of his death was a day of grief for Islam and the Muslims, the equal of which they had not known since the days of the right-guided Caliphs,' writes Baha ad Din (quoted from *Arab Historians of the Crusades,* Dorset, 1989). Money was borrowed to pay for his funeral for he had no wealth of his own. Muslims wept and recalled that when the Prophet died his only possessions were his weapons, a white mule and a small piece of land in Khaibar that was given to charity. The *imam* who led the funeral prayers was Muhyi ad Din ibn az Zaki, the young *qadi* from Alleppo who had led the first Friday prayers at al Aqsa after Saladin took Jerusalem.

Allah! Muhammad! Saladin! reads a message inscribed in the small room in the modest mosque called al Khanagah where Saladin lived in the old city of Jerusalem after his great conquest in 1187. Saladin had led the most successful jihad since the Prophet.

7

THE DOORS OF EUROPE

'Do not weep as a woman over what you could not hold as a man.'
[Ayesha, mother of Boabdil, to her son when
he sighed at the loss of Granada]

Do not do what you want, nor what you can, but what serves your
interests . . . . If you visit a government office, you should enter
blind and leave deaf.
[Two maxims prescribed by Alexander Mavrocordato, a Greek
Prince who served the Ottoman empire, in the *Book of Duties,*
quoted in Philip Mansel's *Constantinople: City of the World's
Desire,* 1453–1924, John Murray, 1995.]

There is no pain in life, they say in Granada, so cruel as to be blind in
Alhambra. When the Arabs of the desert conquered Spain, they said
that they had reached heaven. From the ramparts of the Alhambra, sitting
on a spur of the Sierra Nevada, look out and you see a paradise created
by nature; look in and you see a paradise created by man. Those who
reduce romance from the story of Alhambra make themselves poorer;
memory is more fertile than arid fact.

The subjects of the Last Moor, Boabdil, called him El Zogoybi, or The
Unlucky. Others called him El Rey Chico, or the Boy King. Boys change,
but sometimes luck does not. His father, ibn Hassan, fell in love late in life
with a Christian captive Zoraya. Amble through the Court of Cypresses in
the gardens of Alhambra and guides will point knowingly to the nook in
the cool, shaded, and splendid bowers where the king courted his love.
Ibn Hassan's wife Ayesha would have hardly created a fuss over another

royal marriage, but she was concerned about Zoraya's two sons. She wanted the kingdom for her own son Boabdil. A younger wife is always closer to the king's ear. By 1482 Ibn Hassan and Boabdil were at war. The faltering Nasirid dynasty never recovered from that conflict. In 1483 Boabdil was captured by the Castilians, who welcomed a pawn in the game against his father. In 1485 they seized Ronda; Loja, Malaga, Baja, and Almeira fell in successive years. In 1491 the Castilians laid siege to the last Muslim fortress in Spain, and the most glorious of them all, Alhambra. In December the terms of surrender were negotiated. On the first day of 1492 Christian troops entered the castle.

On the morning of 2 January 1492 Boabdil handed over the keys of Alhambra. From the summit of a hill, now known as El Suspiro del Moro, or the Last Sigh of the Moor, as he turned, in tears, to take a last look at Alhambra, Ayesha told her defeated son: 'Do not weep as a woman for what you could not hold as a man.'

It was however asking too much of a boy-king to hold out against the swings and roundabouts of history. Christian historians of the time marked the start of the 'Reconquista' to the battle of Covadonga in 722, which was won by the Christians eleven years after their decisive defeat at Guadalete in 711 by a small Muslim army of about 11,000 troops. That is a comforting rather than a material date. The Muslim withdrawal from Spain is better marked by 1085 when Toledo was lost to Alfonso VI.

It was a season of triumph for the Church, from Spain to Palestine. By 1150, Muslims had lost all territory north of Lisbon and the Guadiana river. Nonetheless, at the same time as Zengi and Nuruddin refreshed the spirit of jihad in Palestine, the Almohads of Morocco intervened in Spain to check the Christian advance. The crucial difference was that there was no Saladin to consolidate after that initial burst in Spain. The Almohads peaked by the last decade of the century. In 1191 they threatened Lisbon after the capture of Alcacer do Sal but did not take it; and after defeating Castile's Alfonso VIII in 1195 they moved towards Madrid in 1197, but once more without success. The Church was understandably anxious. Spain was given the special status of a Crusade zone. Pope Innocent III ordered every bishop in France to send help to Castile; in complementary moves, the Lateran councils of 1179 and 1215 forbade Christians, under pain of excommunication and confiscation of property, to work in the homes of Muslims and Jews or trade with them. (In 1227 Pope Gregory IX banned the *azaan* in Christian dominions.)

In 1212 Alfonso VIII, with contingents from Aragon and Navarre, marched to Las Navas de Tolosa and destroyed the Almohads on 16 July. In 1236 Fernando III conquered Cordoba, capital of Andalusia and the prize of Spain, after a revolt by Christian mercenaries in January became the pretext for a siege that lasted till capitulation on 29 June. The great mosque was consecrated as a cathedral the following day, and mass was said. On 22 December 1248 the king of Castile, Fernando, entered Seville as victor: every Muslim had already been ordered to leave, and most of Spain was now ruled by Aragon, Castile, or Portugal. Such was the worldwide impact of these successes that Louis IX of France, head of the last crusade, threatened Ayyub, the Sultan of Egypt, in a letter dated 5 June 1249: 'We chased your people before us like herds of oxen (in Spain). We killed the men, made widows of the women, and captured girls and boys. Was that not a lesson to you?' One last flicker of the Islamic flame held out in Andalusia.

In 1237, without a known ancestry, Muhammad ibn Yusuf ibn Nasr established himself at Granada. For over two and a half centuries this family, called the Nasirids, ruled an arc of land from Granada south till Gibraltar, and in the process left behind some of the most brilliant art and architecture of Muslim Spain. Beneath the grandeur lay a sharp sense of reality that protected this dynasty. From 1246 the Nasirids began to pay an annual tribute to Castile. Realpolitik was reinforced by a chain of tough fortresses built by Muhammad II that helped preserve the independence of Granada and make it a subject of fables. Stories of hidden treasure guarded by a genie persuaded Napoleon's soldiers to blast the Tower of Seven Floors before they abandoned the fort during their campaign in Spain. They found nothing, but the rubble fell on the gate through which Boabdil had left, sealing it.

Muhammad V gave final shape to the most fabulous achievement of this dynasty, the complex of palaces, offices, and gardens in the fortress on a hill, Alhambra. On the arch of its imposing entrance a giant hand is engraved on stone, with a key below it. The hand is doctrine; the key opens the door of faith. A single phrase, the motto of the founder, Muhammad I, is inscribed in hundreds of places, on inner walls, and arches and on the walls facing the gardens, lest any ruler have the temerity to forget: *Wa la ghalib iz-la Allah! There is no Conqueror but Allah.*

Church bells pealed across Europe in celebration when Granada fell. That door through which Islam had entered Europe through the West was finally shut after a span of over seven hundred years.

Another one, however, had just opened in the east. Constantinople.

In 1204, seventeen years after Saladin took Jerusalem, Constantinople was sacked, not by Muslims but, bizarrely, by a Fourth Crusade, inspired this time by Venice and Genoa. Franks knights, landing in Venice to go to the Holy Land were diverted by the clever Doge to Constantinople which they ravaged, raped and looted. Ibn al Athir reports that a prostitute was placed on the patriarch's throne and drunken Franks raped Christian nuns in monasteries, while Baldwin of Flanders was crowned emperor of a desolate empire. The Byzantines returned in 1261, but never quite recovered their confidence. The pressure on the empire from Turkish Muslims intensified after Usman (whose heirs are known by a verbal variation, Ottoman) established himself in north-west Anatolia in 1299, with Bursa as his first capital. In 1366 Murad I shifted the capital to Edirne in Europe. Over the following thirty years the Ottomans defeated Bulgaria and Serbia, both potential claimants of Constantinople. Bayezid, who ruled between 1389 and 1402, besieged Constantinople but was checked by those famous walls running from the harbour at the Golden Horn to the sea of Marmara and then around the city.

In 1402, the rising Ottoman dynasty was brought back to earth by another Turk, a military genius from Central Asia, Taimur the Lame, who defeated and imprisoned Bayezid. However, after the death of Taimur, Ottoman expansion revived. Murad II, who became Sultan in 1421, led a second Ottoman expedition against Constantinople. His son would do better.

Mehmet II's mother was either a Jew or a Christian slave (Turk nobles would often marry impregnated slaves). His father's dream became his obsession. Mehmet was ridiculed, not least by his own grand vizier, who called this obsession a folly of youth. Mehmet ignored such sagacity. He prepared for the invasion by constructing the fortress of Rumeli Hisari on the Bosphorus to ensure the stability and security of his supply lines. In May 1453 Mehmet gave a call for jihad. Addressing his troops as *ghazis*, or warriors of Allah, he inspired them with the Prophet's prediction that Constantinople would one day be ruled by the faithful.

On 29 May 1453 his army made the blood flow like rain after a storm, and corpses float to the sea like melons on a canal, according to one observer, Nicolo Barbaro. The last Byzantine emperor Constantine II fought to the end of his life and his empire. Some 30,000 Christians were either enslaved or sold. Sultan Mehmet rode on a white horse towards the Cathedral of Hagha Sophia, mother of all churches, built in the sixth century by Justinian. He dismounted in front of the cathedral, picked up a handful of dust, poured it over his turban and proclaimed the *shahadah:* 'There is no God but Allah and Muhammad is His Prophet.' The cathedral in that instant became a mosque. Mehmet prayed for the success of the house of Osman.

He was only 20-years-old. One of his first decisions was to order the death of the grand *vizier* who had taunted him for dreaming of Constantinople.

Istanbul, its Turkish name, does not mean city of Islam. It is a variation of a Greek phrase, *eis teen polin,* and stands for 'into the city'; for the Turk peasant a visit to the capital was clearly an event. What Mehmet did was to corrupt a corruption, and devise a variation called 'Islambol', or city of Islam. Constantinople was to become the new centre of the power of Islam, the base from where *ghazis* or warriors could renew their thrust towards Christian Europe. Within two years of his *fatah,* or conquest, the *fatih* or conqueror was dreaming of Rome. Like his grandson Selim, Mehmet saw himself as another Alexander, and had Arrian's life of the Macedonian read out to him every day. Alexander is one of the ancient heroes referred to in the Quran, and a legitimate model for an Islamic warrior.

The ulema reminded Mehmet that victory had come from Allah, and he did not argue; he interpreted it as a sign of Allah's blessing for the House of Osman. Preachers put out stories that saints in white robes, led by the prophet Elijah had fought in Mehmet's army on the day Constantinople fell. As if to confirm this divine help, and to link this achievement with the Prophet's *hadith* on Constantinople, the grave of Abu Ayyub Ansari was discovered at the Golden Horn, against the walls that had not succumbed in 669. Ansari was one of the companions of the Prophet and one of the commanders of the Ummayad army during the second siege of the Byzantine capital. In 1459, Mehmet built a mosque at the site of the grave, which became a point of pilgrimage. The area, called Eyyup, is still a celebrated enclave. A second mosque, completed in 1470, on the site of the Church of Holy Apostles, has the Prophet's prediction for Constantinople inscribed in golden letters.

Titillating stories from the harems of Topkapi, with its warren of rooms lost in a secret world of slaves, concubines, power-hungry eunuchs, and Sultans immobilized by protocol and relatives immobilized by fear, should not obscure us to the fact that the system worked and that the state was proudly Islamic. No war was declared by a Sultan without a *fatwa* from the *mufti*. Every Friday when he was in the capital the Sultan went in a procession to the mosque for Friday prayers. The Prophet's birthday was celebrated each year with great illumination and colour, leading one awed visitor in 1841 to comment that the night looked like something out of his stories. This visitor's name was Hans Christian Andersen.

A high point of state celebrations was the circumcision ceremony of the Sultan's sons, a tradition started by the 32-year-old Suleyman on 27 June 1530 when his three sons Mustafa, Mehmet, and Selim were circumcised in the presence of dignitaries of the empire and obedient foreign princes. There was pomp for the nobles, circus for the people, poetry for intellectuals, and contests in recitation of the Quran for the religious schools (*medressas*). The occasion kept getting more ornate: Mehmet III's foreskin was presented to his mother on a golden plate while his grandmother received the knife and the blade-wielder went home with 3,000 gold coins, a golden bowl, cloth and, last but hardly the least, one of the Sultan's daughters in marriage. He was assuredly not the local barber.

After Selim I's conquests, the Sultan was also the Caliph and servant of the two holy places. The Sheikhyul Islam, the grand *mufti*, was one of the most powerful men in the empire, head of the *ulema* and a player in high politics since his interpretation of the law of Allah could be used, if opportunity arose and the moment was fortuitous, to depose the Sultan himself. The most curious such *fatwa* was surely that given against Osman II in 1622, preventing him from going on *hajj*, one of the five pillars of the faith, on the pretext that his absence would create disorder. Osman's motives were however hardly religious; he wanted to raise an Arab army during his pilgrimage to challenge the élite guard, the Janissaries, who, in alliance with the grand *mufti* and the grand *vizier*, had turned against him. On 9 May the Janissaries seized Osman 'in the name of the law' and took him to the Seven Towers where he was strangled around the neck and his testicles literally squeezed to death.

The most successful of the grand *viziers*, and *viziers*, used the authority of the Quran (those 'ancient methods' that had won and preserved the empire) for guidance in matters administrative and, occasionally, even in economic policy. The law was the *sharia*; indeed, some of the legislation went beyond the *sharia's* precepts, as for instance in the dress code applied to different communities. Only Muslims were entitled to wear green or white turbans; Christians and Jews were allotted light and dark blue, and yellow headwear. The legislation could get worse; in 1580, for instance, Murad III ordered that the attitude of the non-Muslims should be one of humility and abjection, and therefore they should not dress like Muslims, live near mosques or in tall buildings, or buy slaves. The next Murad (not his son, but a half century or so down the line) was young when he became Sultan, and refused to show any signs of growing up. His mother, Valide Kosem, said to be the most powerful woman in the history of the dynasty, ruled in his name. One of her principal concerns was that a lax empire might lose Yemen, the gate to Mecca. No Sultan would have survived loss of the holy cities.

This did not mean that a doctrinaire Islam was imposed on the people, or that non-Muslims were excluded from governance or the army. Far from it. The success of the Ottoman state lay in the opposite approach. Jews driven out by the Spanish Inquisition were invited to settle and lived in peace till the end of the Caliphate; a roughly constant Jewish population of about ten per cent began to fall only during that difficult century for Muslim empires, the nineteenth. In 1914, 22 per cent of Constantinople was Orthodox Christian, 25 per cent Armenian and 4 per cent Jewish. The conqueror Mehmet II made no effort to expel Christians in the manner that Spain had expelled Muslims. Instead, he created space for the Church.

Inevitably, time and stability encouraged the return of the Byzantine tavern, if indeed it had ever gone away. Mehmet II was no puritan; the artist Gentile Bellini was commissioned to draw erotica for his private apartments (he has left a splendid portrait of the Conqueror as well). However, his son Bayezid II was pious, and not only removed father's erotica but also closed the taverns for a while. They returned. Most Sultans enjoyed their wine and women, and some extended their joys to little boys. Suleyman the Magnificent once ordered prohibition, but did not allow such abstinence to interfere with his own preferences. His grandson Selim II overdid it, though; he was called, hopefully affectionately, a drunk, and is believed to have died from a fall during a bath, while inebriated.

The humble had a humbler drink, a sort of beer called *boza*. Ogier de Busbecq, the Hungarian ambassador who reached Constantinople on 20 January 1555, describes life among the commoners during the era of Suleyman (*Turkish Letters*, Sickle Moon Books, 2001).

> The Turks are so frugal and think so little of the pleasures of eating
> that if they have bread and salt and some garlic or an onion, and
> a kind of sour milk . . . which they call *yoghoort*, they ask for
> nothing more . . . Even their formal banquets generally consist
> only of cakes and buns and sweets of other kinds, with numerous
> courses of rice, to which are added mutton and chicken . . . There
> is one drink, however, which for completeness sake I must not
> omit.

This was 'Arab Sorbet', made from grounded raisins, fermented for two
days, and then drunk lots plenty of snow. It affected the head and feet,
reported the ambassador, no less than wine. Better still, it was within the
law.

West Europeans would paint a picture of lechery and the lusty Turk,
being particularly aghast at the open homosexuality and possibly envious
of stories from the harem. Venice forbade lads under fourteen from visiting
Constantinople for fear that they would be afflicted with the 'Turk disease'.
Mehmet II was said to have made Radu, brother of Vlad the Impaler (the
model for Dracula) the prince of Wallachia, after first having made him
his lover. As Philip Mansel (*Constantinople, City of the World's Desire
1453–1924,* John Murray, 1995) points out pertinently, while Venetians
settled in Constantinople in considerable numbers, no Ottoman Muslim
ever settled down in Venice. He also notes, for good measure, that towards
the end of the eighteenth century the best brothel in town was next to
the British embassy.

By this time, the Turk had become a strange composite caricature in
Europe, a dreaded, debauched Saracen-Turk Muslim whose harem-eunuch
belly dance orientalism was complemented by a military prowess that
obsessed the western European mind. Edward Said describes the syndrome in *Orientalism,* Pantheon, New York, 1978:

> Not for nothing did Islam come to symbolize terror, devastation,
> the demonic hordes of hated barbarians. For Europe, Islam was a
> lasting trauma. Until the end of the seventeenth century the 'Ot-
> toman peril' linked alongside Europe to represent for the whole of
> Christian civilization a constant danger, and in time European civi-
> lization incorporated that peril and its love, its great events, fig-
> ures, virtues and vices, as something woven into the fabric of life.

In Renaissance England alone, as Samuel Chew recounts in his classic study *The Crescent and the Rose,* 'a man of average education and intelligence' had at his fingertips, and could watch on the London stage, a relatively large number of detailed events in the history of Ottoman Islam and its encroachments upon Christian Europe. The point is that what remained current about Islam was some necessarily diminished version of those great dangerous forces that it symbolized for Europe.

Selim I (1512–20) believed that he had been ordered by Allah to conquer both the east and the west. Persia was however an inconvenient barrier to any ambitions further east. Selim brought the Caliphate to Constantinople after he defeated the Mamluks and hanged the last one from the gates of Cairo 1517. The emir and sharif of Mecca handed over the keys of Kaaba and descendants of the Prophet came to pay homage, albeit reluctantly, to the new Caliph. Constantinople was at last the capital of Islam. The proudest title that Selim possessed, and his successors inherited until the British made it irrelevant in the twentieth century, was servant of the two holy places. He had no contemporary rival in Islam or Christendom; Mughal power in India would only begin to flower a decade later; Morocco had been driven out of Spain; the Persians were content with Persia. All the great cities were part of the empire: Damascus, Baghdad, Cairo, and the three holy cities, Jerusalem, Mecca and Medina. The Sultan was 'God's shadow on earth', a claim which the orthodox might object to but could do nothing about.

The three ambitions of his son Suleyman the Magnificent (1520–66) reported Busbecq in his letters, were to complete his mosque, restore the Roman aqueducts to give Constantinople a good water supply, and conquer Vienna. Busbecq conveys some of the strain that Europe felt at another sign of 'the anger of heaven' against Christians, such as Attila of old and Taimur of recent vintage:

> Soleiman [sic] stands before us with all the terror inspired by his own successes and those of his ancestors; he overruns the plain of Hungary with 200,000 horsemen; he threatens Austria; he menaces the rest of Germany; he brings in his train all the nations that dwell between here and the Persian frontier . . . . Like a thunderbolt he smites, shatters and destroys whatever stands in his way; he

is at the head of veteran troops and a highly trained army, which is accustomed to his leadership; he spreads far and wide the terror of his name. He roars like a lion along our frontier, seeking to break through, now here, now there.

The ambassador is, however, confident that the Emperor Ferdinand will stand his ground to save 'his own faithful subjects' and 'Christianity in general'. Suleyman's empire extended from Hungary to Yemen and Iraq to Algeria. Belgrade was taken in 1521 and Rhodes in 1522. Vienna was within his sights. Suleyman the Magnificent started building his great mosque after Emperor Charles V agreed to pay him tribute. He deserved his accolade.

However, writing the obituary of the Ottoman empire started long before it fell ill. Some European ambassadors, who made up in judgment what they lacked in comprehension, were eager to be aggressive. The English ambassador in 1622, Sir Thomas Roe, a globe-trotting envoy who also served his nation's interests in India, thought that the Ottoman regime had become a sink of sluttishness, and the empire was close to collapse. In 1639 the Venetian ambassador threatened the grand *vizier* only to receive a contemptuous response that the alleged power of Christendom was a chimera. The Turks could afford to laugh for another century or two.

One of the first hints of trouble ahead was sounded by a Christian convert in 1731. In 1726 Ibrahim Muteferrika, a high official, persuaded the Sheykhyul Islam to permit a not-so-new technology called printing against the wishes of calligraphers. In 1731 he presented a treatise to Mahmud I entitled *Rational Bases for the Politics of Nations* whose central question was: why had Christian nations, so weak in the past, become so strong as to even defeat the once all-conquering Ottoman armies? His recipe would be repeated later and often, first in the form of suggestion and then, as the Sultans weakened, as virtual instructions. Reform, and imitation of the 'modern' European polity and law. Muteferrika's advice came at a time of familiar turmoil; Mahmud had become Sultan thanks to a street revolt encouraged by the clergy who denounced his predecessor Ahmed III's unIslamic profligacy and issued a *fatwa* against his treaty with Christian Russia and war against Muslim Persia.

The Conqueror of Constantinople, the Fatih, Mehmet II was the first to appreciate the dangers of a Christian fifth column joining hands with the major powers of Christian Europe. The Greeks took the lead, lobbying for an immediate Crusade. Hungary, Austria, and Venice were powerful neighbours who could readily use the united banner of a Crusade to open hostilities. 'What nineteenth century statesmen referred to as the "Eastern Question" – the design of the European powers to conquer Ottomon territory – began in 1453,' writes Philip Mansel. The "Eastern Question" became insistent in the nineteenth century when the Ottomans started to falter; for three hundred years before that their response was generally adequate if not always consistent. Mehmet's own answer was first to strengthen his defences. By 1455 the Yedi Kule (Seven Towers) had been built on edge of the Sea of Marmara, and the walls were still being reinforced twenty years later. Defence was always the best offence for Constantinople.

No sword could however be by itself sufficient. It required the scabbard of a policy acceptable to the people, to Muslims, to Christians, and to the Jews who were proudly settled and protected so long as the Caliphs were in power. Christians were a priority; geopolitics made them so.

There was no patriarch of the eastern church when Constantinople fell because of various efforts at reconciliation with Rome. Mehmet sought out a learned monk, George-Gennadios Scholarius, made him patriarch, and restored all the rights and privileges of the church that existed under the Byzantines. Scholarius' chief merit was that he had opposed any reunion with Rome. On 5 January 1454, he was consecrated and enthroned in the Church of Holy Apostles. It was intelligent policy. It prevented Rome from asserting authority in a vacuum over the Christians of the fast-expanding empire; and it resurrected a church that could assure, as far as possible, loyalty to the Sultan, revenues to the empire, and a counterbalance to Rome. Mehmet checked Rome's power with an orthodox dam.

He also devised a cosmopolitan structure to protect an Islamic empire. One of the more remarkable consequences was the creation of an institution that became a bulwark – until nearly four hundred years later when it self-destructed. It was also the most unusual instance of the Muslim-Christian interaction.

Slavery, in the words of Sultan Abdulmecid was shameful and barbaric, although he was probably right when he pointed out that slaves were comparitively better treated in Turkey. He shut the city's slave market in 1847 but did not go so far as to ban this evil. There was nothing pretty about that market. Dealers led small children through the *bazaar*, shouting out their price. All those stories about teeth and genitals being checked greedily, and virgins fetching a higher price are true. It was forced labour and sex-bondage, and the more finicky buyers could take a woman home to check whether she snored. Slaves came from as near as Poland and as far away as Sudan (Pushkin's ancestor was a black bought in Constantinople).

In theory slaves could buy back their freedom, but the theory was largely fiction. The universality of the practice was an explanation, not a justification; conquered Muslim populations faced the same fate, if not worse, assuming death is worse than slavery. Such consequences of defeat must have lent an extra edge to the search for victory. Slaves have been wartime booty ever since wars began; fortunately, slavery has ended before wars have.

There was one option, which sometimes produced remarkable results in Islamic history, as in the case of the so-called 'slave dynasties' of Delhi or the Mamluks of Egypt. Conversion not only offered possible escape from bondage, but also equal opportunity if not always complete equality. (Muteferrika, mentioned above, had saved himself from slavery by conversion.) New converts with strong community bonds, or groups with a military ethos could even go so far as to exploit an opportunity to seize the decayed realms of rotting kingdoms. The House of Osman, in the tradition of most Muslim dynasties, had no trouble with class distinctions, and slaves were freely promoted to the most sensitive positions in the palace and entrusted, literally, with life and death. Four pages slept at each corner of the bed of the first Sultans.

Mehmet gave a creative twist to slavery. He turned them into the guardians of the empire. He created the 'janissaries', a word that comes from the Turkish *yeni ceri* or, simply, new troops. The process of recruitment was called *devshirme,* or gathering; and this was literally true. A *firman* would be issued, and officials go to Christian territories like Bosnia to gather Christian Slav boys between the ages of eight and sixteen (no Turks could be so gathered). They were taken to Constantinople, circumcised, and converted. Pedigree then came into play. The best would go to a palace school or a pasha household, and then down the line till some reached farms.

A chosen few were trained to become the Janissaries. This élite palace guard also became a spearhead of the empire: it protected the Seven Towers, patrolled the walls, and enforced law and order in the city. Deprived of family, these young men diverted their loyalty to the state even more than to the Sultan. In return, the state gave them power and comfort (the head of each unit of the guard wore a soup ladle in his belt). Their barracks were between the Suleyman mosque and the Golden Horn, while their Aga lived in a splendid palace. On Tuesday, once every three months, came pay day; the Sultan, as a Janissari of the sixty first unit himself, also received his small leather bag. He had the good sense to return it, with a hefty tip, to the commander. Whenever the Sultan visited the barracks he would drink *sherbet* and fill the emptied glass with gold coins before returning it. During Ramadan, baklava would come from the harem.

The Janissaries were constantly praised and pampered in proclamations. Unsurprisingly, it occasionally went to their head. The sign of the barrack's anger was an upturned *pilav* cauldron. A hungry Janissari was bad news. Even Selim II faced trouble when he did not give them their customary bonus, but trade unionism was the least of the worries. Their power was such that they forced Suleyman to abandon the siege of Vienna (his magnificent dream) and abort an attack on Persia. In 1622 they did to Osman II what we have seen. They had a running battle with Murad IV and revolted against the reforms of Mahmud II who began to Europeanize the army, forsaking those 'ancient traditions'. Mahmud obtained a *fatwa* indicating that the new drill and uniform were not Christian but 'modern Muslim'. The grand *vizier* tried to help by explaining that the new drill was in accordance with the Quran and had the approval of the *ulema*. However, when on 11 June 1826, four drillmasters began exercises on the European model, trouble began. On 13 June 20,000 Janissaries swept through the streets and stormed the Topkapi, shouting that they did not want the practices of infidels and demanding preservation of the past in the name of Muhammad and Haji Bektash, their patron dervish. Mahmud was accused of wanting to become a Christian, a suggestion that the Greeks spread with great glee, claiming that they had seen the cross of Constantine over the Aya Sofya. Mahmud brought out the artillery. On 17 June the Janissaries were abolished; 6,000 were executed and 5,000 exiled. Whether it was a coincidence or not, the decline of Ottoman fortunes became terminal after that. The West began to eat back what it had lost to Muslim appetite for hundreds of years.

The nineteenth was the century of loss for Muslims. As early as in 1808 the Serbs were encouraged to revolt, and by 1830 a Serbian state had been established. In 1821 it was the turn of Greece, encouraged by the music of Byron's poetry, to demand freedom from the Ottomans. Greece became independent in 1833. In the Caucasus, Russia moved into the Turkish penumbra. In 1839 Britain occupied Aden to consolidate her control over the sea routes to the jewel in her crown, India. Aden became the base from which Britain operated through the Arabian peninsula, eventually creating alliances with the Trucial States, Abu Dhabi, Dubai, and Sharjah. When you weaken you become vulnerable everywhere. France occupied Algiers. In contrast to the British experience in India, the capital was occupied before the country. The French had their taste of jihad when Abdul Qadir (1808–83), with the support of the *ulema* and villagers, went to war with the infidel. He was defeated and exiled in 1847 to Damascus, where apparently he got along quite well with resident Frenchmen until he died. 1860 witnessed a civil war in Lebanon, and an attack on Christians in Damascus provoked European intervention. A special regime was created for Lebanon after an agreement between Muslims, Druzes, and Christians. (During that decade Tunisia experienced what might today be termed World Bank treatment. Following an escalation of its foreign debt, an international finance commission was set up in 1869 to reform finances, reassert law and order, and invest in education. In 1881 the French took over Tunisia for equally well-known reasons: financial stability, frontier stability, and to prevent the Italians from becoming equally conscientious about the welfare of Tunisians.)

Moscow was encroaching elsewhere. The competition between the European powers helped Turkey to save something from what could have been a complete wreck. Peter the Great had dreamt of winning Constantinople back for Christianity and Tsar Alexander I called the city 'the key to the door of my house'. In 1853 Nicholas I made the remark to the British ambassador in St Petersburg that echoed through the next century. 'We have a sick man on our hands, a man gravely sick,' he said, referring to Turkey, and wanted the European powers to divide the Ottoman empire by mutual agreement and turn Constantinople into a free city. Russian insults provoked the students of Turkey's *medressas* (the Taliban of their time) to come on to the streets, and Abdulmecid obtained a *fatwa* to declare war on Russia on 4 October 1853. This was however one war that the House of Osman could not fight alone. Britain and France, determined to keep Russia out of what would become their prize, joined Turkey in what is famous as the Crimean War. By 1856 the alliance had defeated Russia and Abdulmecid presented himself with a new palace, deserting Topkapi.

There was however a price to a seat on the same table as England and France. In 1856, for the first time since 1453, church bells were permitted to ring, by the authority of an imperial decree, in Constantinople. Many Muslims declared it a day of mourning. By 1877 Bulgaria had been given autonomy; Crete won similar terms in 1898 (and joined Greece in 1913). The weakness of Constantinople had gone to the heart. It was in huge external debt, and its revenues were being scanned by lenders. Muslims all over the world shuddered when a Bulgarian army reached the walls of Constantinople during the Balkan wars.

The largest Muslim population in the world at that time was not in the Ottoman empire but in the British empire, in India. Agitated by the fate of their Caliph, Indian Muslims sent a medical mission to Turkey during the Balkan wars under the leadership of Dr M.A. Ansari. That mission of 1912 initiated a wave that became tidal in ten years.

Ten years later, in 1922, the Caliphate that had stirred Indian Muslim passions, was dying. On 10 November 1922 the heirs of Mehmet II and Suleyman the Magnificent suffered what was perhaps the ultimate insult: the royal band deserted. On 16 November Mehmet Vahideddin, Caliph of the Muslims and Sultan of Turkey wrote to General Sir Charles ('Tim') Harington, commander of the British forces:

> Sir,
> Considering my life in danger in Istanbul, I take refuge with the British Government and request my transfer as soon as possible from Istanbul to another place.

At 8 in the morning on 17 November the last Caliph, Mehmet VI, left his palace by the Orhaniye gate in a winter storm, protected by British Grenadier Guards, and accompanied by his son, Ertugrul, his chamberlain and the bandmaster, who had not deserted along with the band. The British took him to a launch from which he boarded the *Malaya* to Malta; he died in San Remo in 1926. Creditors refused to let his body be buried for two weeks. There was one more Caliph, but not Sultan; Kemal Ataturk did not as yet feel strong enough to dispense with the Caliphate. Abdulmecid II lasted with ceremony and nothing else till 1924. On 3 March that year the Caliphate was abolished. The Caliph was instructed to pack for departure at dawn. He left at 5.30 and reached the Catalca railway station at 11. The stationmaster was the only official to show any kindness. He was a Jew and he thanked the Ottoman dynasty for being the saviour of Turkish Jews whose ancestors had been driven out from Spain. At midnight the Orient Express drew in. The Caliph was given a visa for Switzerland and two thousand pounds sterling to find his way in the world. For the better part of 469 years the Ottoman dynasty had held the balance of power in that world, and shaped the fortunes of Islam. Its only enthusiasts now remained in India.

The nineteenth century had also been fatal to the other great Muslim empire in the world, the Mughal, in India. The Mughal empire of India had, during the glory years of Akbar, Jehangir and Shah Jehan, considered itself superior to the Ottoman, a claim that the fellow-Turks of Constantinople shrugged off as insolence. After a century of dismal degeneration, the British buried the Mughals in 1857 after a war that changed the British as much as it changed India. The Mughal empire died unwept, but not unloved.

8

JIHAD IN THE EAST:
A CRESCENT OVER DELHI

'You walk on the water!' they said to the Sufi Abu Yazid al Bestami.
'So does a piece of wood,' Abu Yazid replied.
'You fly in the air!'
'So does a bird.'
'You travel to the Kaaba in a single night!'
'Any conjurer travels from India to Demavand in a single night.'
'Then what is the proper task of true men?' they asked.
'The true man attaches his heart to none but God,' he replied.
[From *Muslim Saints and Mystics* by Farid al Din Attar]

The last sigh of the Moor was not the last sigh of the Muslim. Spain settled her scores with the Arabs, and was content to protect what she had recovered, with brutality if necessary. The Inquisition removed all Muslims and Jews from the Catholic empire; those who stayed, converted. No option was offered. Spain's Jews found shelter in the Ottoman empire, and lived in comparative peace under the Caliph. Muslims resettled across the Atlantic in north Africa, but nostalgia was their only consolation, for Muslim Africa did not have the energy for another conflict with Europe.

There was however another continent on which the next phase of wars between the nations of Islam and those of Christian Europe would take place, Asia, and in particular the Indian subcontinent and the Indian ocean. Muslim power swept into the heart of India at the beginning of the second millennium. Christian nations began to challenge it halfway through that millennium. The language remained that of a holy war.

On sea, the Portuguese, in caravels and *naus,* with the authority of the Pope, launched a crusade against Moors, even as they picked up (or looted) spice along the western and eastern rims of the Indian Ocean for huge profits in Europe. It was havoc while it lasted, but the more substantive confrontations still took place on land. The British, less inflamed than the Portuguese, and with better timing, displaced, and then replaced, Muslim rule in wealthy India. Beyond the Himalaya and the Pamirs, formidable Russia gobbled up vast territories to her vacant east, and subdued the weakened if obstinate Muslim nations of Central Asia.

After they had destroyed Muslim empires and kingdoms, Calcutta and St Petersburg sparred for the one independent Muslim nation in between them, Afghanistan, in what became known as the Great Game. That game of snakes and ladders between the two great Christian powers of the age was played on an Islamic board. Afghanistan has been both the wedge and the door in the geopolitics of the region. The traditional route to the conquest of Delhi was through the Khyber Pass; Delhi was vulnerable without control of Kabul. The British understood this, although they were the only foreign power to reach Delhi from the east.

The first Christian to come to India, according to local belief, was Jesus' disciple, St Thomas, famous for his doubts. Muslims came as traders to the western ports, from Gujarat to Kerala, hundreds of years before any Muslim army entered the heartland. The first Muslim armies in search of the wealth of central India came in the eleventh century, and in search of kingdom in the twelfth. The first European ships, armed with the cannon of holy war, were from Portugal. Portugal could not take a second step after obtaining her foothold in Goa; it was stopped by another Muslim dynasty that blazed its way into Indian history, the Mughals. The first Christian power to establish an empire was Britain, which ended Mughal rule and shaped modern India.

The story of the Muslim conquest of central India may have begun with a misunderstanding: one man's pronunciation can become another man's poison. The three most revered pagan goddesses of pre-Islamic Mecca were Al Lat, Al Uzza, and Manat, denounced in the Quran as false deities and the source of the infamous controversy about the alleged 'Satanic Verses'. According to an old belief, when the Prophet smashed the idols at the Kaaba, the image of Manat was missing: it had been secreted away, and sent in a trading ship to a port-town in India called Prabhas, which imported Arab horses. According to this belief, idol-worshippers built a temple to Manat, and renamed the place So-Manat, or Somnath. The warrior king Mahmud, who built an empire from the Afghan city of Ghazni, waged the first jihad in the heart of India. His most famous raid was the one in which he destroyed the idol at Somnath and carried away enough booty to appease avarice.

One of the intellectual giants of the time travelled in Mahmud's entourage during this campaign, a historian, sociologist, astrologer, astonomer, linguist and scientist who translated Euclid into Sanskrit and wrote a treatise on the astrolabe for Indians. Abu Raihan al Biruni (*Al Biruni's India: An Account*, trans. E. Sachau, Delhi, Chand, 1964) has left a record of the destruction of Somnath in 1026, but does not mention this fascinating, and alleged, connection between the life of the Prophet and a temple in India. Al Biruni narrates that a bejewelled stone idol was worshipped at Somnath. This, for the Manat school, served as further evidence. Lat had a human shape, Uzza appeared in a sacred tree, and Manat was a stone image. One of India's most respected historians, Romila Thapar, comments: 'The identification of the Somnath idol with that of Manat has little historical credibility. There is no evidence to suggest that the temple housed an image of Manat. Nevertheless, the story is significant to the reconstruction of the aftermath of the event since it is closely tied to the kind of legitimation which was being projected for Mahmud.'

The belief prevailed. The thirteenth century Muslim theologian Maulana Minhaj us Siraj wrote in *Abqat-i-Nasiri:* 'He [Sultan Mahmud] led an army to Naharwala of Gujarat, brought away Manat, the idol from Somnath, and had it broken into four parts, one of which was cast before the centre of the great Masjid at Ghazni, the second before the gateway to the Sultan's palace, and the third and fourth sent to Mecca and Medina respectively.' Somnath was hardly the only temple Mahmud destroyed, but he considered its destruction an achievement worthy of recognition by the Caliph himself. 'The link with Manat,' says Thapar (*Somnath and Mahmud, Frontline*, 10 April 1999)

> added to the acclaim for Mahmud. Not only was he the prize iconoclast in breaking Hindu idols, but in destroying Manat he had carried out what were said to be the very orders of the Prophet. He was therefore doubly a champion of Islam. Other temples were raided by him and their idols broken, but Somnath receives special attention in all the accounts of his activities. Writing of his victories to the Caliphate, Mahmud presents them as major accomplishments in the cause of Islam.

The cause of Islam arrived in India some three hundred years before Mahmud did. A Muslim army, of roughly the same size as the one in Spain, entered Sind in exactly the same year, 711. It was commanded by a young man, Muhammad bin Qasim, son in law of the governor of Iraq, Al Hajjaj, during the reign of Caliph Walid. Sindhi pirates had plundered Arab trade ships returning from Sri Lanka and enslaved Muslim women and children. The Brahmin king of largely Buddhist Sind, Dahir, shrugged off any responsibility and refused to pay reparations. In 1712 Muhammad bin Qasim drove him out of his capital, Debal, but Dahir died in a more decisive battle in June, when an arrow of Greek fire felled him from his elephant. By 714 the Arab conquest of what is now the south of Pakistan was complete, but Islam, uncharacteristically, remained confined to this region for three centuries, checked by powerful Hindu monarchs to the north and the east. Until there came Mahmud Ghazni, a military genius who never suffered defeat in three decades of constant war.

Muslim kings established themselves in Afghanistan in 870 when Yaqub ibn Lais won Kabul from the Shahis, a Hindu dynasty that ruled from Kabul to the Beas river in the east from their capital near Peshawar. Yaqub founded the city of Ghazni. In 977, Subuktigin, yet another Turkish slave, ascended his father-in-law Alptigin's throne in Ghazni and inflicted serious defeats on the neighbouring Shahi Raja Jaipal.

In 1008 his son Mahmud was the first of the family to cross the Indus. The rulers east of Indus were prepared. Anandpal, the Shahi king of Peshawar, was at the head of an alliance that included Ujjain, Gwalior, Kanauj, Delhi and Ajmer, with the single purpose of holding the invader at the gates of India. Contemporary reports indicate that the fervour percolated to the citizens, with women selling their ornaments and donating their savings to finance this army. Mahmud won the day after Anandpal's elephant took fright and bolted. That victory opened the way to India, and to the wealth of its fabled temples that Mahmud used to create a court in Ghazni that rivalled Baghdad in the quality of its intellectuals, artists, and poets, among them al Biruni. Al Biruni was genuine in his extravagant praise for the degree of sophistication in Indian mathematics, astrology, philosophy, and architecture, noting that Muslims could only marvel at the reservoirs and tanks in India. However, he criticized the Brahmins for a 'folly . . . for which there is no medicine.' Hindus, he said, 'believe that there is no country but theirs, no nation like theirs, no king like theirs, no science like theirs'. This made them 'haughty, foolishly vain, self-conceited' and reluctant to share knowledge even with other castes in the country, let alone foreigners.

In October 1024 Mahmud of Ghazni set off towards Somnath, through Multan and Ajmer where the king fled rather than face him. His army reached Somnath without much trouble. The roof of the temple, said to have fourteen golden domes, rested on fifty six wooden pillars inlaid with precious stones. Inside a dark chamber stood the *lingam* of the Lord Shiva set with jewels, and worshipped by thousands of pilgrims who came each year bringing their riches along with their devotion. It is pointless repeating estimates of how much wealth Mahmud carried from Somnath; all too often the amounts mentioned are only evidence of a historian's adulation or irritation. The principal objective of this fighting army on its return journey was to protect the loot. Al Biruni, hopefully without a touch of pride, describes the havoc that Mahmud caused in India: he

> utterly ruined the prosperity of the country, and performed won-
> derful exploits by which the Hindus became like atoms of dust
> scattered in all directions, and like a tale of old in the mouth of the
> people. Their scattered remains cherish, of course, the most invet-
> erate aversion towards all Muslims. This is the reason, too, why
> Hindu sciences have retired far away from those parts of the coun-
> try conquered by us, and have fled to places which our hand can-
> not yet reach, to Kashmir, Benares and other places.

Mahmud had no interest in ruling what he had conquered; but he kept the key to the door of India in the hands of a governor in Lahore. His successors continued the policy of turning India into a treasure hunt. It was however the destruction of Somnath that made Mahmud into an archetypal Muslim *yavana* (foreigner) invader-plunderer-rapist of popular mythology.

A second emotive narrative marked the start of the greatest Muslim empire that the subcontinent has known, the Mughal. It was the reputation of the Mughal empire that drew the British towards India. James I sent an envoy, Sir Thomas Roe, who we have encountered before, in Constantinople. Sir Thomas was awed by the ceremonial attire of Emperor Jahangir: the unset walnut-sized ruby on one side of the turban, an equally large diamond on the other, and at the centre an emerald larger than a heart; pearls, rubies and diamonds in the sash; diamonds at his elbows and armlets; and a chain of huge pearls around his neck. Francois Bernier, the French traveller, estimated that Mughal revenues were probably greater than the joint revenues of the Ottoman empire and Persia. Such pomp began in simpler circumstances. The first of the great Mughals, Babur, preferred the pen to diamonds.

Zahiruddin Muhammad had three titles. The first, *Babur*, was descriptive; it meant tiger. The second, *Padishah*, or king, was his achievement. He gave himself the third, *Ghazi*, or warrior of God, after the great victory by which he established the empire.

On 6 December 1992 zealous Hindus, encouraged by senior national leaders, destroyed a mosque in the city of Ayodhya called the mosque of Babur, because they believed that Babur had built this mosque on the spot where a temple commemorating the birthplace of Lord Ram had stood.

Babur may have been more prude than prudent. The only idols that he claims, without any bombast or guilt, to have destroyed in his remarkably honest and brilliantly evocative diary, *Baburnama,* were at Urwah in Gwalior. He visited Urwah valley on 28 September 1529. His principal problem seems to have been that 'These idols are shewn quite naked without covering for the privities . . . I, for my part, ordered them destroyed' (translated from the original Turki by Annette Susannah Beveridge, 1922).

There is no mention in the *Baburnama* about any temple to Lord Rama being demolished either on his direct orders or by troops moving east to subdue the Afghans who had lost an empire in Delhi but not lost hope. Going by the temper of the memoir, Babur would not have hesitated to report as important an incident as the destruction of the birthplace of the Lord Ram in a journal of record. That however is not conclusive, as some pages have been lost despite the diligence of his heirs who ensured that this masterpiece was translated into Persian as early as in 1589. However, neither does the well-known and oft-quoted chronicler of the time of Babur's grandson Akbar, Abul Fazal, mention any demolition of a temple in Ayodhya, the home of 'Ramachandra, who in the Treta age combined in his person both the spiritual supremacy and the kingly office'. That great Indian poet Goswami Tulsidas, author of an epic on Lord Ram, *Ramcharitamanas,* is also oblivious to any such incident.

Babur was not the most rigorous of believers (entry for 24 April 1519: 'At the midday prayer there was a wine party at the place.' 25 April: '. . . At noon we mounted and started for Kabul, reached Khwaja Hasan quite drunk and slept awhile . . .'). What is undisputed about the three-domed mosque built at the time of Babur in Ayodhya is that it was constructed by Mir Baqi, a noble, in 1528. The inscriptions confirm that 'this alighting place of angels' was built 'by the command of Emperor Babur' and 'in thanksgiving to the Prophet of all prophets in the two worlds, in celebration of the glory of Babur *qalandar* (recluse) who has achieved great success in the world'. There is however no evidence to confirm that a temple to honour the birthplace of Lord Ram was destroyed to build this mosque. For all his battle-rhetoric, Babur was no bigot. Bigotry, in fact, would have been poor policy for a small band of Turkish-Mongol invaders surrounded by hostility from both displaced Afghans and unfamiliar Hindus. There were those we might describe as fundamentalists today, urging the immediate imposition of *sharia* in Hindu-majority India. As the historian Bimal Prasad comments: 'It is a tribute to the sense of realism, wisdom and generosity of the Turkish rulers of India that they did not pay heed to such outpourings, openly asserted their right to do what they considered best for their rule, regardless of the injunctions of the *sharia* or the preachings of the *ulema*' (*The Foundations of Muslim Nationalism,* Manohar, Delhi, 1999). The claim that Mir Baqi's mosque was built on the site of the birthplace of Lord Rama rests on belief, amplified into a conviction by some careful fanning of Hindu-Muslim flames at the time of the last Muslim *nawab* of Awadh, Wajid Ali Shah. That fan was in the hands of the British who were just a step away from becoming masters of India.

Babur's real encounter with Indian interests was not over a temple in Ayodhya but on a battlefield near Agra. Babur entered Delhi by defeating the Afghan Ibrahim Lodi at the battle of Panipat in April 1526. He became a true emperor of India after victory in a jihad at Khanwa less than a year after the battle.

An astrologer, Muhammad Sharif, forecast that Babur would lose. He may have been watching the mood in Mughal camp more than the stars. A powerful alliance confronted the Mughals, led by Rana Sangha. According to the historian of the Rajputs, Colonel James Tod (*Annals and Antiquities of Rajasthan,* London, OUP, 1920), Rana Sangha's army had 'Eighty thousand horses, seven Rajas of the highest rank, nine Raos, and hundred and four chieftans bearing the titles of Rawul and Rawut, with five hundred war elephants'. Against them, Babur had about the same number that he commanded at Panipat, some 12,000 men. All the initial skirmishes were won by the Rajput alliance, which included Hasan Khan of Mewat, and

Mahmud Khan of the defeated Lodis who hoped to recapture Delhi. There was a sense of doom in the Mughal camp.

On 26 February 1527 Babur gave orders for two jihads: one against the 'pagan' and the other for spiritual cleansing. He renounced alcohol and prayed to Allah. His servants destroyed gold and silver drinking vessels: 'dashed upon the earth of contempt and destruction the flagons and the cups, and the other utensils in gold and silver, which in their number and their brilliance were like the stars of the firmament. They dashed them in pieces, as, God willing! soon will be dashed the gods of idolators'. He then summoned all the *begs* and braves and told them: 'Better than life with a bad name is death with a good one! God the Most High has allotted to us such happiness and has created for us such good fortune that we die as martyrs, we kill as avengers of His cause. Therefore each of you must take oath upon His Holy Word that he will not think of turning his face from this foe, or withdraw from this deadly encounter so long as life is not rent from his body.' They took this oath upon the Quran.

On 13 March, new year's day by the Persian calendar, Babur set his formations. On the seventeenth battle began between nine and ten in the morning. Babur was at the centre, surrounded by those *that strive in the way of the Lord* (the description of jihad in the Quran; the account in *Baburnama* is full of references to verses from the Quran depicting the faith of martyrs and the promise of victory to believers). The Mughals reeled under a heavy charge on the left wing, but the line held. Babur ordered a special corps of infantry to move forward while his matchlockmen, under the 'marvel of the age' Ustad Ali Quli made effective use of cannon and musket from behind a chain of carts. (The same tactics had been employed at Panipat.) Then, from the centre, Babur himself advanced 'towards the pagan soldiers, Victory and Fortune on his right, Prestige and Conquest on his left . . . Between the first and second Prayers, there was such a blaze of combat that the flames thereof raised standards above the heavens, and the right and left of the army of Islam rolled back the left and right of the doomed infidels in one mass upon their centre'.

There was a last, determined charge by the enemy on the Mughal left, but 'the holy warriors, their minds set on reward' forced them back with arrows. Finally, 'victory the beautiful woman whose world-adornment of waving tresses was embellished by *God will aid you with a mighty aid* [48:3], bestowed on us the good fortune that had been hidden behind a veil, and made it a reality. The absurd Hindus, knowing their position perilous, *dispersed like carded wool before the wind* and *like moths scattered abroad* [48:3]' (the italics indicate direct quotation from the Quran).

Babur claimed the title of *Ghazi*, or warrior of God, after this victory and wrote the following quatrain:

> For Islam's sake, I wandered in the wilds,
> Prepared for war with pagans and Hindus,
> Resolved myself to meet the martyr's death.
> Thanks be to God! a *ghazi* I became.

The battle of Khanwa is significant, for had Babur lost, the throne of Delhi would have gone to Rana Sangha of Mewar. The sequence of Muslim Sultans and shahenshahs who ruled Delhi from 1162, when Muhammad Ghori defeated Prithviraj, would have ended. As it happened, a Muslim continued to sit on the throne, in either Agra or Delhi till 1858, when the British exiled a hapless and desolate Bahadur Shah Zafar to Burma.

Two significant attempts were made to change this pattern, at Panipat, in 1556 and 1761. Both failed.

Babur's son Humayun is remembered for four things. He lost his kingdom to the governor of his eastern provinces, an Afghan from Bihar, Sher Shah Suri, at the battle of Kanauj in May 1540. He regained it in 1555 with the generous help of his father's friend and Persian contemporary Shah Tahmasp with less effort than he had lost it. On his return to Delhi after fifteen years, on 23 July 1555, he kept his word to a water carrier called Nizam who had saved his life, making him lord for either two hours or two days. Last, that he was father of one of the greatest emperors of India, Akbar.

Akbar's court historian Abul Fazl overdid the sycophancy in *Akbarnama* (translated by Annette's husband, H. Beveridge and published in three volumes in Calcutta in 1907–1929) by suggesting that the king of kings was born with 'a sweet smile' that 'rejoiced the hearts of the wise'. There was little to rejoice about. Humayun and his wife Hamida were in exile when Akbar was born, and the child would have to wait before there was enough to smile about. Akbar was 14 when Humayun died; four tutors had been unable to make him literate, although one, Abdul Latif, left him with a lasting love of Sufi poetry.

The boy-king was challenged for the throne by one of the strangest characters in Indian history, an ugly, puny man who could neither wield a sword nor sit on a horse, who belonged to one of the lower castes in the Hindu hierarchy but was an authentic hero. His name was Hemachandra, and he was known as Hemu. He started life selling saltpetre in the small town of Alwar and rose so fast during the brief interruption to Mughal rule, that the entire administration came under his control. What he lacked in martial skills he compensated with leadership and a splendid mind.

He marched against the brittle forces of Akbar in 1556. There were omens on both sides. Hemu dreamt, on the way to Panipat, that his elephant was swept out in a flood and he was saved from death by a Mughal chain. For the Mughals, Ahmad Beg, who read the future in the blade-bone of a sheep, predicted victory for Akbar. The battle went Hemu's way, while Akbar watched from a mound guarded by a personal force. The Mughals were on the verge of defeat when an arrow struck Hemu. Abul Fazl attributes this to Allah's 'divine wrath' against the infidel; a victory of jihad. Hemu was brought before Akbar, but he refused to decapitate a chained prisoner. His general, Bairam Khan, a 'warrior of the faith' was not hesitant.

Mughal power had come to stay, but preserving the dynasty also needed a crucial victory in bed. At 14 Akbar married his uncle Hindal's daughter Ruqaiya. Thirteen years and more wives later Akbar did not possess the one non-negotiable requirement of a dynast, a male heir. Neither his sexual inclinations nor the norms of the time were a problem. His visits to courtiers' households, in fact, became a bit of a problem thanks to a roving eye. One of his courtiers, Badayuni, offered sensible advice to anyone who complained about the emperor's predilections: either do not befriend a mahout, or make the house large enough for an elephant. Three children, a daughter, Fatima, and the twins, Hasan and Husain (all names from the Prophet's family), died as infants.

In despair Akbar turned for help to a disciple of India's most venerated Muslim Sufi saint, Khwaja Muinuddin Chishti, who had come to India from Iraq at the end of the twelfth century and settled in Ajmer. The emperor visited Selim Chishti, who belonged to this order, at his hermitage in Sikri, a village near Agra and vowed that if a son was born, he would go on foot to the shrine of Muinuddin Chishti. A Rajput wife of his, the daughter of Raja Bharamal, became pregnant. A son was born in August 1569, and named Selim. The emperor of India walked, barefoot, for more than three hundred kilometres, from Agra to Ajmer, to offer his thanks at the shrine of Khwaja Muinuddin Chishti.

If Islam spread in India, it was not because of the sword of Akbar, but because of the power of his Sufi mentors, mystic-saints like Khwaja Muinuddin Chishti. An emperor bowed to the saint. Mere monarchs could not demand obedience from a Sufi; his, or her, allegiance was only to God.

Sufi derives from *saf,* an Arabic word meaning wool; for the only possession of these inspired men and women was a piece of coarse woollen cloth. Their lives were dedicated to a mystical union with Allah, inspired by such verses of the Quran as the one in which Allah says that he is closer to man than his jugular vein and knows more about his innermost thoughts than even the ego. The wisdom of these masters is divine, but they neither offer explanation for nor glorify their powers. They treat life with the disdain of one who can see nothing but the Beloved.

Sufis have been part of the Islamic tradition from the earliest days: Hasan of Basra was born in Medina some ten years after the Prophet's death. One anecdote from Farid al Din Attar's *Muslim Saints and Mystics,* translated by A.J. Arberry (Routledge and Kegan Paul, 1966) illustrates the Sufi sensibility. 'Almighty God,' said Abu Yazid al Bestami, the ninth century Persian mystic, 'admitted me to His presence in two thousand stations, and in every station He offered me a kingdom, but I declined it. God said to me, "Abu Yazid, what do you desire?" I replied, "I desire not to desire".'

The first Sufi to reach India was Mansur al Hallaj, a saint so controversial that he lost his head, literally. He crossed the limits of the *ulema's* endurance and stepped into unacceptable blasphemy when he equated himself with truth. He was executed, cruelly, on 28 March 913, and entered legend as the ideal devotee of Allah. In India he travelled through the lands conquered by the Arabs, Sind and Punjab, and became the ultimate symbol of love in the popular poetry of the region. However, the true impact of sufism began with Khwaja Muinuddin Chishti.

Oral traditions recorded in Persian two or three centuries after his death are heavy with myth and miracle, but one constant theme is the willing conversion of those who accepted the superiority of his divine power. The *Siyar al Aqtab* (quoted by Dr P.M. Currie in *The Shrine and Cult of Muin al din Chishti of Ajmer,* Oxford University Press, Delhi, 1989) narrates the story of his encounter with the Maharaja of Ajmer, of the priest Shadi Dev, and the conversion of the most powerful magician in India, Ajaipal. These tales are, in a correct sense, fabulous; they are also believed.

Muinuddin was drawn to Ajmer in India by a vision he saw when in a trance at the tomb of the Prophet in Medina. He believed that he had been ordered to make Islam manifest to the people, and after years of travel he reached Ajmer with forty followers. The local *raja* (king) had been warned by his astrologers that if such a dervish came to his land, he should be killed but no one stopped them. They camped under a tree outside a city where the camels of the *raja* would rest. The royal camel-driver asked them to leave. Annoyed, the *khwaja* arose but cursed the camels so that they would never be able to get up. He moved to the banks of the lake, Ana Sagar.

A confrontation between the *khwaja* and some local Hindus over eating meat turned ugly and he was assaulted while in prayer. He picked up some earth, recited the *Ayat ul Kursi,* or the verse of the throne, which empowers the believer, and threw it at his assailants. They became numb and weak.

They went to a man they called Dev, and he suggested that only a powerful magician would be able to respond to this Muslim yogi. Dev met Khwaja Muinuddin, and he was so overwhelmed that he began to tremble from head to foot; however much he tried to protect himself by saying 'Ram, Ram' all that came out of his mouth was one of the names of Allah, 'Rahim, Rahim'. The *khwaja* gave him a cup of water. He drank it, fell at the *khwaja's* feet, converted, and became his disciple. Muinuddin asked him what his name was. Dev, he replied. The *khwaja* christened him Shadi Dev or Happy Dev. The maharaja in the meanwhile sent someone to plead for the camels, and only when the *khwaja* released them from his spell did they stand up. The greatest magician of India, a yogi called Ajaipal now came to test his powers against the *khwaja*. All his incantations and spells, his snakes and firebolts, were repelled; he surrendered and became a Muslim called Abdullah. Ajaipal asked for one boon. He wanted to live forever. Muinuddin prayed to Allah and the wish was granted with one condition, that he would remain hidden from the eyes of men. They say that Ajaipal/Abdullah still comes every Thursday night to the shrine of Khwaja Muinuddin Chishti.

This shrine has been a centre of pilgrimage from the time he died for slave and Sultan alike, but its fame multiplied after Mughal emperor Akbar came barefoot to give thanks for his heir. Akbar built the mosque named after him and visited the shrine fourteen times. Jahangir of course was convinced that he owed his life to this saint. A picture by that Mughal miniature master, Bichitr, in the Chester Beatty Library and Gallery in Dublin, shows Muinuddin Chishti offering the insignia of imperial office to Jehangir. His son Shah Jahan visited Ajmer five times, and built an exquisite mosque. Even Aurangzeb, who was puritan enough to resist 'shrine-worship' came here to give thanks for his victory over his brother Dara Shikoh.

It is entirely in character that a holy man should be more effective than a holy sword in India. Muinuddin died in 1236. His disciples, known as the Chishti order, were instrumental in spreading Islam among the people. Qutbuddin Bakhtiyar Kaki settled in Delhi. More important was the work of Fariduddin, popularly known as Baba Farid, in the Punjab, who died in 1266. Legends about him are still current in folklore. One says that he hung by a rope for forty days while meditating. A number of verses in the Sikh holy book, the *Guru Granth Sahib*, are attributed to Baba Farid. His successor, Hazrat Nizamuddin Auliya, who died in 1325, is the mystical lord of Delhi, with an enclave in the heart of the modern capital named after him. His successor, Nasiruddin Chirag Dehlavi, died in 1356; his disciple Gesu Daraz took the Chishti order south to Gulbarga. His reason was, however, not religious; he fled from the invasion of Taimur in 1398.

In the mid-thirteenth century a second Sufi order appeared, that of the Suhrawardis, who went east to Bengal. In the fourteenth century, in Bihar, the great mystic Sharafuddin Maneri established the Firdausi order. The Qadiris came at the end of the fifteenth century. The Naqshbandis, early in the seventeenth century, established what can only be described as a power base from the Punjabi city of Sirhind and were part of the politics of the Mughal empire, but none of the other orders shared their conservatism.

Harmony is the fundamental Sufi tenet, and they spread the faith without creating rancour. They endorsed the absorption of local social rituals. Sharafuddin Maneri, for instance, permitted Muslim women to wear *sindoor,* the red vermillion powder that is a mark of marriage. 'Reformist' organizations of the twentieth century like the Tablighi Jamaat were established to elimate such traditions from the practice of Islam in India.

When so much now divides the Indian subcontinent, one form of adoration still rises above the tragedy of separation and the constant threat of war: submission at the shrines of saints like Khwaja Muinuddin Chishti and Hazrat Nizamuddin Auliya. Even on a state visit, a Pakistani leader will place Ajmer on his schedule, and no Indian will ever obstruct such a pilgrimage. These saints were of the people, and they remain so. Their message protected the harmony of daily life even when the wars of élites turned bitter and the phrases of obsequious historians were laced with acid that would burn generations long after the sycophants were dead.

Islam came to the Indian subcontinent at the beginning of the eighth century, beginning a complex relationship that expressed itself in war, culture, civilization, dialogue, dress, ethics, literature, law, mysticism, philosophy, suspicion, myth, segregation, integration, fantasy, and nightmare. It was a relationship launched by war but not sustained by it. Muslims who came as invaders stayed to become Indians. This remained their country even after a strategy outlined in a papal bull of 1455, two years after the fall of Constantinople to the Muslims, succeeded, through a long and circuitous route, four hundred years later.

9

THE HOLY SEA: PEPPER AND POWER

Moreover, since, some time ago, it had come to the knowledge of
the said infante [Prince Henry of Portugal, also called the Naviga-
tor] that never, or at least not within the memory of men, had it
been customary to sail on this ocean sea toward the southern and
eastern shores, and that it was so unknown to us westerners that
we had no certain knowledge of the peoples of those parts, believing that he would best perform his duty to God in this matter, if
by his effort and industry that sea might become navigable as far as
to the Indians who are said to worship the name of Christ, and
that thus he might be able to enter into relation with them, and to
incite them to aid the Christians against the Saracens and other
such enemies of the faith, and might also be able forthwith to
subdue certain gentile or pagan peoples, living between, who are
entirely free from infection by the sect of the most impious
Mahomet [sic] . . .

[From a Bull issued by Pope Nicholas V on 8 January 1455,
who wanted an alliance between the Christian powers of the
West and Indians, who he mistook for heretic Christians as
they were not Muslims, in order to squeeze the 'Saracen'
empires in between].

A mighty armada appeared suddenly in the Indian Ocean in the fifteenth
century, establishing its command with overwhelming force from Java
to Calicut to Malindi, the richest port in east Africa, north of Mombasa
and south of Mogadishu. From a distance, their sails seemed like massed
and billowing clouds and their drums sent tremors through any port they

neared. The treasure ship that held their cargo had nine masts and was 400 feet long; by comparison Colombus's *Santa Maria* was only 85 feet. This armada was not proof of any European prowess. It had sailed from China.

Its commander was a Muslim, Zheng He. His father Ma He had performed the *hajj*, and was killed in the wars with the Mongols in 1381. Zheng, his second son, was sent to Beijing, where he was castrated to be made 'pure' for service in the royal household (he was called San Bao, or Eunuch of the Three Jewels; according to one interpretation, the title emerged from a Buddhist honour meaning Three Jewels of the Pious Ejaculation). He chose the right side in succession wars, and became a favourite of the emperor Zhu Di. The emperor did wonder whether, at 35, Zheng had not become too old for such hazards, but he was selected to command China's greatest naval enterprise because, as the Chinese proverb put it, 'the old horse knows the way'. He led seven such armadas from China to Africa between 1405 and 1433, reaching Malindi in 1418. That first fleet consisted of three hundred and seventeen junks carrying 27,000 men. The world had seen nothing like this. By 1433, Zheng had the oceans at his command, but not the mandarins at home. After Zhu Di died, they changed policy, stopped the money, and turned China inwards. The Indian ocean was open once again for countries whose expeditions were considered breathtaking if they managed to send three ships a quarter of the size of one of Zheng's junks.

Three years before Zheng reached the eastern coast of Africa, an impoverished European nation surprised Rome, and probably itself, with the conquest of a Muslim bastion on the northern coast. King John had won the admiration of his subjects by protecting the independence of Portugal from the widening ambitions of Castile. In 1415, a swarm of small sailing craft crossed the 15 miles of water between Portugal and the Muslim port-city of Cueta. The governor of Cueta did not take this threat seriously; he even sent back a Berber force that had come to protect the city. King John lost only eight men when Cueta was captured on 21 August 1415. Muslims were slaughtered, the main mosque converted into a church, and King John declared that all his sins were forgiven now that he had washed his hands in infidel blood. The Pope agreed. He declared it a victory of the Crusades.

Three of John's sons from his English queen Philippa (daughter of John of Gaunt), Duarte, Pedro, and Henry, fought at Cueta and were knighted. Henry's astrologers had foreseen a noble future, but as the youngest and furthest from the throne, glory appeared a remote possibility. His father gave him the kind of job that is often meant to keep third sons busy. In 1319, through a Bull of Pope John XXII, the Order of Christ had been formed to 'defend Christians from Muslims and to carry the war to them in their own territory'. Henry became grandmaster of this Order in 1417. For a hundred years Portugal had done little about such lofty ambitions. It was so poor that it did not have enough gold for its own coins, and used Moroccan currency. Gold was the only coin acceptable to a trader with valuables and luxuries from the east like spices and silks, and its price had multiplied as trade drained away what little there was. The conquerors had marvelled at the quality of homes they found in Cueta.

At the age of 25, Henry moved to the Algarve, which the Knight Templars had conquered from the Muslims; according to some of his more fervent admirers, he also took a vow of chastity. Henry became the patron of explorers, encouraging seamen to track the African coast. If nothing else, the ships could always bring back plunder and slaves. (Aristotle propounded the theory that Africans were natural slaves, which does not make this evil any more acceptable.) The first black slaves arrived in 1441. Slavery was common in an age when might was right; at least one Muslim country, Saudi Arabia, continued the practice into the twentieth century. Prince Henry allotted himself one-fifth of the plunder, including slaves; the Order of Christ was awarded one twentyfirst. When slaves were cheap, fourteen of them could be traded for one Arab horse; later, the ratio changed to six slaves per horse.

In 1437 Henry attempted to fulfil a more difficult part of his mission. He attacked Tangier. Tangier was not Cueta, or at least not yet. The Portuguese were defeated and Henry's younger brother Fernando taken prisoner. The Moroccans offered to exchange a prince for a port, but Henry scoffed at the thought of evacuating Cueta to save a brother. Fernando, who kept pleading for rescue, died after five years of captivity. He was declared a martyr.

Despite success in the west, Rome was apprehensive. All dreams of an alliance with Mongols had soured because Hulegu's heirs converted and joined the 'scourge' instead of eliminating it. The joy of Christian victories in Spain was diluted by the Ottoman upsurge; by 1453, that veritable symbol of Christian faith on the doorstep of Europe, Constantinople, had fallen. The Ottomans had replaced the defeated Arabs as the new and conquering guardians of the 'false' faith. Worse, the great Christian powers were uninterested in another Crusade. Only Spain and Portugal displayed any enthusiasm, and they were at odds over the potential wealth that the new adventurism promised.

On 8 January 1455, clearly at the urging of the ascendant Portuguese (although the decree was careful to note that this was *not* done at their urging), Romanus Pontifex Nicholas V issued a Bull. The rights of conquest east of the cape of Bojador were given to King Afonso and his heirs, and Henry, 'and not to any others'. Christian ships also required a licence from Lisbon, even if they wanted to do no more than fish in Portuguese waters.

Afonso, the 'true soldier of Christ' was given a mission: 'invade, search out, capture, vanquish, and subdue all Saracen and pagans whatsoever, and other enemies of Christ wheresoever placed, and the kingdoms, dukedoms, principalities, dominions, possessions, and all moveable and immoveable goods whatsoever held and possessed by them and to reduce their persons to perpetual slavery . . .'

The most interesting part of the Bull was the world strategy it envisaged: it said that Henry

> would best perform his duty to God in this matter, if by his effort
> and industry that sea might become navigable as far as to the In-
> dians who are said to worship the name of Christ, and that thus he
> might be able to enter into relation with them, and to incite them
> to aid the Christians against the Saracens and other such enemies
> of the faith, and might also be able forthwith to subdue certain
> gentile or pagan peoples, living between, who are entirely free
> from infection by the sect of the most impious Mahomet [sic] . . .

A second Papal Bull, issued in 1456, extended the jurisdiction of the Order of Christ 'all the way to the Indians'. Nicholas V's world-view still echoes through a think tank or two in Washington, Tel Aviv, and Delhi, of a trilateral alliance that can squeeze the Muslim nations in between.

Afonso raised an army of 12,000 fresh holy warriors, and minted a new, appropriately named, coin, the *cruzado*. This army never reached Constantinople, but it did cross the straits of Gibraltar to capture Alcacer Ceguer, next to Cueta, in 1458. In 1471 Afonso made a business decision; he contracted the voyages of discovery to slave merchants and shifted state resources to another holy war, against Morocco. He raised another army of 30,000 with three hundred caravels and the larger carracks, and seized Arzilla, which, like Cueta decades earlier, was largely undefended. Two thousand Muslims were killed, 5,000 enslaved, and 800,000 gold doubloons taken as booty. The victors marched on to Tangiers (the birthplace of that famous Muslim world-traveller Ibn Batuta). Portugal was now on the road to somewhere. The king assumed a title he felt he deserved: Afonso the African.

Exploits at sea justified the claim. In 1471 Alvaro Esteves crossed the equator, near an island he named Sao Tome. Spain also began to stir. The prospect of Portugal reaching the spice of India before Spain hurt. India was believed to contain one-third of the world's population, and much more than that of the world's production of spice. Arab merchants based in the famous south Indian port city of Calicut, who often sent it on the same ships that brought pilgrims to Mecca, controlled the trade in spices. The merchants of Venice had virtual monopoly over the next stage, to Europe, by which time the price had multiplied astronomically. A ducat's worth of spice in Calicut fetched between 60 and 100 ducats in Venice, and multiplied further by the time it was sold for gold in western Europe. Pepper was the king of this trade. It was both health food and preservative of this age. Apart from its reputed medicinal properties, it was rubbed, along with salt, into meat stored for the long winter or long sea voyages. Spices became an all-purpose need, for cosmetics as well as an antidote to the plague.

In 1478 a Spanish fleet was defeated by the Portuguese off west Africa. The competition between the neighbours was finally resolved by Rome in June 1494 by the treaty of Tordesillas, in which the famous 'Pope's Line' divided the world between Portugal and Spain. Portugal got the east; Spain was told to stick to Columbus' direction. In 1496 Manuel ascended the Lisbon throne. First things came first. About a hundred thousand Jews had taken shelter in Portugal from the Inquisition, and Muslims still lived there. He decreed that within ten months both would either have to leave Portugal or baptize. It was not so simple either. All children below 15 would be baptized in any case, so parents would have to choose between their children or their faith.

On 7 July 1497 Vasco da Gama prayed all night at – where else? – Henry's chapel. The following morning an oath was taken: they would die rather than fail. Barefoot, in plain tunics, candles in hand, the men knelt to receive absolution. The Papal Bull was read out. For some unknown reason, Vasco da Gama, resplendent in a gilded cross suspended from a scarlet cloth, vowed that he would not cut his beard till he had returned from Calicut. The wind was favourable, and the crusade of three ships, *San Gabriel*, *San Rafael* and *Berrio*, flying the blood red crucifix of the

Order of Christ, sailed from Lisbon. Such was their zeal that landfall came after more than 4,000 miles.

Their first encounter with Arab infidels was at Mozambique, a small port that has now given a country its name. The governor, who owed allegiance to the state of Kilwa, thought these white men had come to trade. He also thought that they were Turks. When he came on board and politely asked to see a copy of their Quran, the Portuguese did some quick thinking and fudged. They left shortly after. Such meek behaviour would be rare.

The Portuguese side of this story has been told in great detail by the soldier-diarist on board, Alvaro Velho. The Indian account of the first visit by the Portuguese is precise to the point of indifference: they came, they saw, they did not trade. Velho's narrative details the gruesome spirit of this holy war. Vasco da Gama took pleasure in torturing Muslims by pouring boiling pork fat on their skins. It was ironical then that he reached India thanks to a Muslim navigator, who was forever afterwards cursed by his brethren for showing the way. Ahmed ibn Majid was such a regular on the route to India that he was also known as the Moor of Gujarat. He was an extraordinary sailor, astronomer and poet. Perhaps he came aboard the *San Gabriel* because he liked the wine, as he admitted. He took the ships back into the northern hemisphere (there were cheers and thanks offered to God), and from a point called *Saif al Tawil* (the Long Sword), he steered due east and reached Calicut in twenty three days. The return journey over the same distance took Vasco da Gama three months. On 18 May 1498 he reached Calicut after the longest sea voyage in history.

On the way to meet the *raja*, or zamorin, Vasco da Gama stopped at a temple under the mistaken impression that this was a church of a strange Christian sect. It is possible that he mistook the mother and child for a version of Jesus and Mary. In fact, he had knelt before Krishna and Devaki.

Rajah Mana Vikrama was lying on a couch, his body bare, chewing betelnut and spitting into a gold bowl held by a page when Vasco da Gama called on him. He saw the presents – wash basins, coral, scarlet hoods, jars of honey – and turned away in contempt. Parsimony almost cost the Portuguese captain-general his life. The next day the Portuguese were detained, and only released when four Nairs pleaded for his life because they had given their word of honour guaranteeing da Gama's safety. Calicut would rue this dent to Vasco da Gama's pride.

On his return to Lisbon the hero was welcomed with a gift of 20,000 gold *cruzados* and Manuel declared that he was now 'Lord of Guinea, and of the Conquest, the Navigation and Commerce of Ethiopia, Arabia, Persia and India'. He wrote to Ferdinand and Isabella that India had 'Christians', although they were not strong of faith, but they would be useful in 'destroying the Moors'. The holy war should now be pursued with greater ardour, he advised.

On 8 March 1500, thirteen ships with 1,200 men, including German and Flemish gunners, commanded by a young aristocrat, Pedro Alvares Cabral, left for the first exercise in gunboat diplomacy. Mana Vikrama was seated on a throne this time, wearing a *lungi*, the local form of sarong. He was offered a treaty of friendship, which he accepted; and an order to expel all Muslims, which he refused. In the harbour, Cabral seized an Arab ship. On land the Portuguese compound was attacked by the Arab merchants. European cannons blazed. Cabral seized ten merchant ships and their crew were burnt alive in full view of the citizens. (Three elephants found in the cargo were eaten.)

In 1502 Vasco da Gama sailed again, this time with twenty five ships and 'much beautiful artillery'. On the way he stopped a pilgrim ship and burnt every one of the seven hundred Muslims going to Mecca. Calicut was devastated with cannon power. Prisoners were paraded after their hands, ears, and noses had been hacked. Their feet were tied together, their teeth broken, and they were thrown into a boat, which was set on fire. Mana Vikrama received a message that he could cook a curry of this human flesh. When a Brahmin was sent to negotiate with Portuguese his lips were cut off and his ears replaced with those of a dog. By 1503 the Portuguese felt strong enough to leave a permanent settlement with five ships at Cochin, a neighbouring principality that they had befriended, or cowed down into friendship.

Inevitably there was a reaction in the Muslim world at this new and terrible power. Sultan Qansuh as Gawri of Egypt threatened retaliation against the Christians living in Jerusalem. The prior of St Catherine's monastery on Mount Sinai went to Rome and Lisbon to negotiate, but Manuel told him that Portugal was only doing its duty. This duty included laying waste to Mecca and the destruction of the tomb of the 'false prophet' in Medina. Muslim Sultans were generally contemptuous of sea warfare, a sentiment they shared with most monarchs, and prone to dismiss sea battles as 'grocers' wars', but once Arabia was threatened, the Ottoman empire finally did give battle.

In 1507 Admiral Amir Husayn led a convoy of twelve ships with 1,500 men and cannon to the Gujarati port of Diu. The governor of Diu, Malik Ayyaz, had an extraordinary history. He was born in Russia, converted to

Islam after being enslaved, and reached India where he rose in the service of the Gujarat court. Ayyaz accepted secret terms from Almeida. On 2 February 1509 Ayyaz's home fleet stood by as Almeida's eighteen ships with forty guns, higher in the water, ran repeatedly across Husaya's and destroyed them. Husayn reported to Constantinople that he had been betrayed by a man who had been born a Christian.

Manuel had already added another title to his kingdom, Estado da India. Afonso de Albuquerque achieved what Manuel flaunted. Portugal was however in search of a sea empire more than a land one, and its immediate strategic needs were served by an island off the west coast of India that lay midway between Calicut and Gujarat. Albuquerque shared every predecessor's thirst for Muslim blood, and is generally described as 'great', but he was the only Portuguese captain-general to lose a battle at Calicut. He made amends in 1510 by marching into Goa, an island offering safe anchorage in the worst weather. It was part of the Muslim state of Bijapur. The Portuguese again enjoyed good fortune for most of the defence force had been withdrawn to fight another war. Albuquerque wrote to his king, Manuel, after four days of bloodthirst in Goa that left 6,000 Muslims dead: 'No matter where we found them, we did not spare the life of a single Muslim; we filled the mosques with them and set them on fire . . . Apart from Goa being so great and important a place, until then no revenge had been taken for the treachery and wickedness of the Muslims towards Your Highness and your people.'

He decreed that he would not allow Muslims to live in Goa, and hanged a dashing officer, Rodrigues Diaz, for bedding a captive Muslim woman. A second decision was to have more lasting impact. Portuguese were allowed to marry local women provided they were 'whitish' in colour. A new community was born into the splendid Indian mix. Before he died at the age of 63 in 1515, Albuquerque attempted to fulfil one great personal and national dream, the conquest and devastation of Mecca and Medina. He attacked Aden but had to retreat with heavy losses.

The first European colony in India, Goa, was thus established in India sixteen years before Babur marched through the Hindu Kush to establish the Mughal empire. The Portuguese presence in India outlasted even the British empire, but that is a statistical victory. Portugal was not able to achieve that strategic alliance with non-Muslim Indians that would pin down Ottoman power sprawled between India and Europe. Instead, it was confined to Goa while the Mughals became one of the great imperial dynasties of history. It was left to another Christian power, Britain, to end Muslim rule in India after seven hundred years, almost exactly the period that Muslim dynasties ruled in Spain.

The British, or at least the East India Company, declared their first war in India during the reign of Aurangzeb, the last of the six great Mughals. In 1686, Sir Josiah Child, a militant governor of the East India Company based in London, thought that he could extract trading rights in Bengal through gunships. He may have been encouraged in such a view by his official in Surat, who thought that he could blow off the Mughal navy with his fart. The first chapter of the war between the British and the Mughal empire would not end so pleasantly for the Honourable East India Company.

Blame it once again on pepper. Dutch merchants suddenly raised the price of pepper from 3 shillings to 8 shillings a pound. On 24 September 1599, eighty London businessmen formed an association, raised capital of some 30,000 pounds, and sought a royal charter to trade in the east. Permission from James I came in 1600. The number of subscribers rose to two hundred and seventeen and capital more than doubled to over 68,000 pounds. In 1608 the first ship of the East India Company berthed in India.

British interest in Indian trade was already evident. The first English mission to the Mughal court was led by William Hawkins, an old hand at diplomacy who spoke Persian and Turki. He set foot in India on 28 August 1608 and reached Agra with a letter from King James in 1609. The Emperor, Jahangir, was apparently delighted with his company and called him the English Khan, but did not consider him important enough to mention in the official memoirs, *Jahangirnama*. Williams left in 1611, frustrated and angry with the Jesuits who, he believed, had outwitted him. Europeans had been petitioning the Mughal court for exclusive trade rights from Akbar's time. Lack of success only sharpened the rivalry.

Trade wars were not a metaphor, either. The first mention of Britain in Jahangir's annals is the record of a naval battle in 1612 that the British won against the Portuguese. Jahangir had, like the other Mughals, little interest in the sea, except to ensure the safety of *hajj* pilgrims from his empire but was however impressed by English naval ability. In 1612, a royal *firman* permitted the East India Company to start its first trading post at Surat. It set up a factory, with agencies in Ahmedabad, Agra, and Ajmer.

The second mission on behalf of King and Company reached India in 1615. Sir Thomas Roe was an Oxford and Middle Temple man, had explored the Amazon (for which he was knighted), and sported a carefully

groomed moustache plus a Van Dyke beard, along with a prickly temperament. He treated the Mughals as inferiors. Jahangir deflated him by asking
why, if the British king was so grand, his presents were so ordinary. Sir
Thomas replied as best he could, saying that as the emperor lacked nothing, anything presented to him would be equally worthless. Sir Thomas
disliked India as much as he disliked Turkey, and advised the Company to
stick to sea and silence in India; profit would be a better objective than
garrisons and wars. This makes Sir Thomas a bit unique: he was wrong
both about Turkey and India.

The East India Company became more Indian after the Dutch massacred the British in Amboyna in 1623, and expelled them from Indonesia.
Profits were good from the beginning, with an annual return of 25 per
cent on capital. Forts became necessary to protect those profits. In 1640
the Company moved to the east coast, acquiring Madras, and built Fort St
George. In 1661 Charles II received a distant island as dowry when he
married Catherine of Braganza; the Portuguese called it Bombay. In 1668
the crown rented out Bombay, officially part of the royal estate of East
Greenwich in Kent, for ten pounds worth of gold, yearly, 'for ever'. The
'for ever' ended in 1739.

In 1650, Prince Shuja, son of Shah Jahan and governor of Bengal, gave
permission to the Company to trade for a lumpsum payment of Rs 3,000,
and the first factory opened in Hooghly. The western bank of that river
turned into a mini-Europe. The Dutch came next door to Chinsurah, the
French downriver to Chandernagore, and the Danes to Serampore.

Things were, perhaps, going too well; employees were becoming mil-
lionaires with deals on the side, siphoning off business that should have
gone to the employer. One such fortunate buccaneer was an American in
the Madras office. Elihu Yale is now better known for the university he
funded in Connecticut than the private trade he did at the Company's
expense with Siam and Canton. Trade had brought the Company to India;
profits altered its ambitions.

In 1687, Sir Josiah Child wrote from London to the governor of Madras
that the new charter was to lay the foundations of a British dominion in
India for all time to come. He argued that events were forcing the Company
to create a sovereign state on the subcontinent. Child was father to empire.
He was convinced that India needed the Company more than the other
way around, and declared war on the Mughal empire following a breakdown
in negotiations over trading rights in Bengal. The Company man in Hooghly,

Job Charnock, was more prudent. With barely three hundred and eighty soldiers and two ships, he risked nothing more adventurous than skirmishes against the Mughal governor, Qasim Khan. The Mughal navy seized Bombay in 1689, and the following year Company officials had to seek a humiliating pardon from Aurangzeb, who restored their trading rights in both Bombay and Hooghly after indemnity and promise of good behaviour.

The crisis persuaded Job Charnock to search for a more defensible spot than Hooghly. He located a village called Sutanuti protected by marshes on one side and the river on the other. He anchored there in August 1690, and, with some difficulty, obtained the *zamindari*, or land rights, to three adjoining villages, Sutanuti, Govindapur, and Calcutta, for an annual rent of Rs 12,000. A factory came up. A fort was built, and named after William of Orange. A capital was born.

As Rudyard Kipling wrote, Calcutta was

> *Chance directed, chance erected*
> *Laid and built*
> *Upon the silt*
> *Palace, mire, hovel, poverty and pride*
> *Side by side.*

Pride and poverty still live side by side in Calcutta.

In 1717 the head of the Company in Calcutta, John Surman, reached the court of Farrukhsiyar in Delhi along with his friend and interlocutor, an Armenian merchant called Khwaja Israel Sarhadi. The emperor had been brought up in Bengal when his father was posted as Mughal governor, and toys for his nursery had come from England. Surman came bearing more adult toys. Heavy bribes to courtiers, and medical attention to the emperor's groins might also have helped. Negotiations were nonetheless still tough, and agreement was reached only when the British threatened to withdraw from Surat. After a century of pleading and one futile show of strength, the Company had won.

On the last day of 1716 the emperor put his signature to a *firman* that the British called their Magna Carta in India; the Mughal court acknowledged that such a favour had never been granted to any European nation. The Company had a mandate from the emperor, and could legally act in defence of its perceived rights; it was allowed to trade, acquire land, and settle where it wanted to in Bengal, all for an annual payment of Rs 3,000.

In precisely forty years Robert Clive used this *firman* to justify the legality of his advance to Plassey.

The many reasons for the defeat and death of Nawab Siraj ud Daula of Bengal and Bihar within a year of his accession; the story of his infirmity and the infidelity of ambitious lords in his court like Mir Jaffar belong to another book. This much is however relevant: with the defeat of Siraj ud Daula, Muslim power began to evaporate in north India.

The first round went to Muslims. On 15 May 1756 Siraj ud Daula left his capital Murshidabad for his last hurrah. On 20 June he captured Fort William when the British panicked and fled. That night, forty three of the fifty five British prisoners suffocated and died after being locked up in a 18'x14' cell used previously to confine drunken soldiers, infamous now as the Black Hole of Calcutta. Whether Siraj ud Daula ordered this, or whether he was rueful, is less important than the reaction. The British were horrified. They would have tried to recapture Calcutta in any case, but the Black Hole added a moral zeal to their cause.

Robert Clive was born on 29 September 1725 near Market Drayton in Shropshire. When he was seven, his uncle remarked in a letter about his fierce imperiousness, and wanted to inculcate in the lad meekness, benevolence, and patience. It was good for Britain that he failed. The owner of a private school he went to predicted that if this child survived, few names would be greater than his.

Clive was 17 when he got a job as a writer in the East India Company on a salary of five pounds a year. He took his time getting to India; the ship he boarded in March 1743 reached Brazil, blown off course by inclement weather. He was so broke by the time he reached Madras that he had to borrow twice from the captain and accept a gift of shirts and stockings from a kindly fellow passenger. By the time he sailed for England on 23 March 1753 Clive was a military hero, with a fortune to his name. His contemporaries grudged him neither wealth nor fame. He received a grand welcome in England and was elected to Parliament. The House of Commons was however a dull place in comparison to India for a man who was not yet 30. Clive returned to Madras in August 1756 as deputy governor. In six weeks he was on his way, as commander of the land forces, to recapture Calcutta. Clive wrote to the Secret Committee in London on 11 October: 'I flatter myself that this expedition will not end with the retaking of Calcutta only: and that the Company's estate in these parts will be settled in a better and more lasting condition than ever.' The British empire was not built without foresight.

On 2 January 1757 Calcutta fell to the British without resistance. Over the next six months Clive split the Bengal court by offering to make Mir Jaffar the new *nawab* in return for help to the British. The forces arrayed at the decisive battle of Plassey indicate just how much help Clive needed. He had eight hundred Europeans, 2,200 sepoys, and a couple of guns. Siraj ud Daula put into the field 35,000 infantry, 15,000 cavalry, fifty three pieces of cannon, a French artillery unit, and allies who brought 5,000 horses and 7,000 infantry. On the eve of battle, ten of the seventeen members of the British council of war voted against attack, including Clive. He only changed his mind after receiving an assurance from Mir Jaffar that their pact held.

Siraj ud Daula was a pathetic field commander. Most of the day went in desultory shelling by his cannon until a sharp shower in the afternoon drenched the ammunition. Mir Jaffar watched from the sidelines, unwilling to put his soldiers into the fray even when Siraj begged him to do so. A misunderstanding by units who had engaged the British led to a calamity. They were told to pause; they thought that they had been ordered to retreat. They ran. The British received the gift of Bengal from one fool and one traitor. Robert Clive lost four British and fifteen Indian soldiers.

When Clive entered the capital on 29 June (protected by two hundred European and three hundred Indian soldiers) he wrote, 'The city of Murshidabad is as extensive, populous and rich as the city of London with this difference, that there are individuals in the first possessing infinitely greater property than any in the last city.' The Portuguese too had found Calicut far more impressive than Lisbon.

On 30 July Emperor Alamgir II ratified a recommendation made by Robert Clive confirming Mir Jaffar as *nawab* of Bengal and Bihar. There was no illusion now about who was giving the orders. Siraj was killed by Mir Jaffar's son Miran; and Miran was struck dead by lightning three years later, which made for excellent *deux ex machina* when this story became part of the ouvre of travelling theatre groups of Bengal. Mir Jaffar became destitute rewarding top Company officers from his depleted treasury. He was forced to hand out 2,340,000 pounds in 'gifts'. Clive was at the top of the list. In addition Clive was awarded a *mansab* of 6,000 foot and 5,000 horses, honoured with the title of Zabdat ul mulk Nasib ud daulah Colonel Shahat Jung Bahadur, and given the large tract of twenty four Parganas, making him the largest landowner in Bengal. When the counting stopped he was at least 400,000 pounds wealthier. Clive was not embarrassed. As he told a parliamentary committee later in England, 'A great prince was dependent upon my pleasure; an opulent city lay at my mercy; its richest bankers bid against one another for my smiles . . . Mr Chairman, at this moment I stand astonished at my own moderation!'

The prospects of the Mughal emperor in Delhi seemed not much better than that of his defeated *nawab* in Bengal. Just as the British were the real power in Bengal, the Marathas had taken control of the north. It seemed just a matter of time before the Mughal in Delhi was replaced by a Maratha claimant. However, one last jihad saved Muslim rule for a hundred years, and kept it alive for the Christian musket to deliver the final volley.

The origins of Maratha power lie in the genius of Shivaji, born in 1630, who began to literally gather a kingdom through a string of fortresses in the rugged mountain range called the Western Ghats, east of Mumbai and west of Bijapur in the Deccan. Shivaji defeated a Bijapur attempt to bring him into submission, and then kept Delhi at bay through a combination of wit, strategy, and military ability. The anti-Hindu policies of his contemporary, Aurangzeb, cast a perhaps unintended light on Shivaji, whose radiance was not communal. However, his successes against Aurangzeb persuaded some later historians to turn him into a standard-bearer of Hinduism as a counterpoint to Aurangzeb.

The kingdom that Shivaji had nurtured came to maturity during the decline of the Mughals. After Shivaji's death on 4 April 1680, the Marathas dwindled under uncertain successors; it was not until Balaji Vishwanath became *peshwa*, or chief minister, on 17 November 1713 that Maratha fortunes began to revive. By 1719 Balaji had become a major player in national politics, at a time when the crown in Delhi was passing from severed to uneasy head with a frequency as alarming to rulers as the ruled.

By 1737 the Marathas were raiding the suburbs of the capital. They watched coolly, as Nadir Shah destroyed Delhi in 1739; by 1741 they had taken control of the fertile land of Malwa. When they added unity to wealth, they became masters of India. They created a loose confederacy of the great families of Scindia, Holkar Bhonsle and Gaekwad in 1749 with the *peshwa* in Pune at its head. By 1758 the Marathas had taken Lahore and carried their march up to Attock on the Indus, and by that December Delhi was also theirs, although they took care not to disturb the sedentary emperor. None of the competing warlords of this period felt confident enough to remove the titular Mughal, no matter how notional his authority. They were not worried about him; they were more worried about one another.

In 1760 the Marathas were at their zenith and looked invincible. Their revenue-writ ran throughout India outside the British territories of Bengal, Madras, and Northern Sircars; and Hyderabad, Awadh, and the smaller principality of Rohilkhand, all three under Muslim *nawabs*. The year began in triumph for the Marathas with victory over the forces of the nizam of Hyderabad at Tandulaja on 24 January. In August they were back in Delhi. It seemed only a matter of time before the veneer of Mughal rule would be replaced by the substance of a *peshwa* on the throne at Red Fort. There was corresponding consternation amongst the Muslim nobility and intelligentsia, short of unity, ideas or ability, but suffering acutely from the wounds of an age passing before their eyes.

In that moment of depression, one leading Muslim cleric could think of only one answer: jihad. Shah Waliullah (1703–62) belonged to a blue-chip ancestry, descended from the second Caliph, Omar, through a central Asian-Turkish family. His father, Abdur Rahim, had been a court intellectual: mystic theologian as well as respected historian, one of the compilers of *Fatwa-e-Alamgiri*, a chronicle of Aurangzeb's reign, and founder of the Rahimiyya Medressa in Delhi. By seven, Waliullah was a *hafiz*, or a person who could recite the Quran from memory. He completed his formal education by 15, and took charge of the seminary at 17 after his father died. His reputation as a scholar was well established by the time he went on *hajj* in 1730; he has over a hundred books and monographs to his name.

He analyzed this decay through the illumination of the Quran. Victory, Allah said, was the reward of faith; ergo, decline was the consequence of decadence. His prescription was a return to the first principles of the Quran and the Sunnah. Erwin Rosenthal makes a key observation about Shah Waliullah in *Islam in the Modern National State* (Cambridge University Press, Cambridge, 1965): 'The important feature of this remarkable presentation of the tenets of Islam is that it originated in an Islamic environment free from any European influence decades before the French Revolution.' Sir Muhammad Iqbal, one of the greatest Indian poets of the twentieth century and an ideologue of the Pakistan movement, saw Shah Waliullah as the first Muslim of the subcontinent with a new spirit; others called him the bridge between the old and the new. 'The time has come,' Shah Waliullah wrote in his most famous work, *Hujjat Allah al-Baligha,* 'that the religious law of Islam should be brought into the open, full dressed in reason and argument.' The precepts of the Quran would prevail over European thought, he argued. He attacked imitation of the West and urged Muslims to return to the simplicity and spirit of the time of the Prophet and the first two Caliphs.

Shah Waliullah prayed to Allah and turned to Afghanistan. He wrote a letter to the 'pearl of the age', the Afghan King Ahmad Shah Abdali, who had carved a kingdom out of the domain of Nadir Shah, inviting him to save Islam in India with a jihad against the Marathas. This letter has been included in the excellent *Sources of Indian Tradition* (Viking, Harmondsworth, 1991), edited by Ainslee T. Embree:

> In this age there exists no king, apart from His Majesty [Ahmad Shah], who is a master of means and power, potent for the smashing of the unbelievers' army, far-sighted and battle-tested. Consequently a prime obligation upon His Majesty is to wage an Indian campaign, break the sway of the unbelieving Marathas and Jats, and rescue the weaknesses of the Muslims who are captive in the land of the unbelievers. If the power of unbelief should remain at the same level (God forbid!), the Muslims will forget Islam; before much time passes, they will become a people who will not know Islam from unbelief. This too is a mighty trial: the power of preventing that is attainable for His Majesty alone, by the favour of the beneficent God . . . In the name of Almighty God we ask that he [Ahmad Shah] expend effort avidly for a holy war against the unbelievers of this territory, so that in the presence of Almighty God a fine reward may be inscribed in His Majesty's book of deeds, so his name may be recorded in the register of holy warriors . . . so in the world innumerable foes may fall at the hand of the heroes [ghazi] of Islam, so Muslims may obtain rescue from the hand of the unbelievers. The victory of Islam is the destiny of the entire community; so, wherever there is a Musalman, [the Muslim warrior-kings] will love him on a part with actual sons and brothers; and wherever there is a warlike unbeliever, they will be like raging lions.

The victory of Islam, said Shah Waliullah, is the destiny of the entire community. This was the bargain that Allah had promised His believers.

Jihad may have seemed less viable to Abdali than booty. He was another of those invaders who improved their local GNP by regularly looting India. We have no evidence that he replied to Shah Waliullah's letter, but this was one incursion into India when booty was not on his mind. He fashioned an alliance with the two principal Muslim kingdoms of the north, Rohilkhand and Awadh, and appeared to the north of Delhi. The confrontation came in

January 1761, at the third battle of Panipat. Against the odds, and against the tides of the age, it proved to be a catastrophe for the Marathas.

The army that the Marathas mobilized in 1760 was the largest and most splendid ever raised under their banner. Skirmishing went on for some two and a half months. The Muslims succeeded in cutting the communication lines of the enemy, leading to a shortage of supplies that in turn forced the day of battle. It took place on 14 January.

The Maratha left was under the command of a Muslim general, Ibrahim Khan Gardi, who had resisted every temptation to switch sides in the name of religion. There was, generally, less Hindu-Muslim rigidity on eighteenth century battlefields than we have been led to believe. As Ian Raeside, who has translated the Maratha chronicles of this battle, notes, 'Of course the difference of religion was always there to be called upon at need, as an ultimate justification for pre-existing rivalry, but the Muslims saw no difficulty in calling upon the support of the Hindus to fight fellow-Muslims, and vice-versa. There is scarcely a single religiously homogenous army to be found throughout the history of eighteenth century warfare.' There was however little doubt on either side about the stakes at the third battle of Panipat. A victory for the Marathas would have handed the throne of Delhi to a Hindu monarch for the first time since the defeat of Prithviraj in the twelfth century.

It was, coincidentally, Ibrahim Khan Gardi who almost broke the Abdali line, but Abdali was a better strategist. Waiting for the Marathas to exhaust themselves, he counter-attacked with 10,000 fresh troops in the early afternoon. At about a quarter to three, 'in a twinkling of the eye, the Maratha army vanished from the field like camphor', taking Maratha ambitions along with it. Abdali attributed his victory to Allah in a letter he wrote later to Madho Singh, Raja of Jaipur: 'Suddenly the breeze of victory began to blow and, as willed by the Divine Lord, the wretched Deccanis suffered utter defeat . . .'

The third battle of Panipat was the last and least successful jihad in India. Abdali did not want the crown of Delhi; he returned to Afghanistan, the Marathas to their principalities. For the dormant Mughal emperor it was a pyrrhic victory; for the Marathas a historic defeat. In truth, the Muslims had lost their empire, and Hindus had not found theirs. This was the dilemma that searched for an answer. For Shah Waliullah, Abdali had saved a Muslim throne from one set of infidels. His son, Shah Aziz would discover that Abdali had only created space for another.

One day after the Marathas disappeared from the field of Panipat, something equally dramatic happened in the south of India. Comte de Lally, son of an Irish Jacobite, governor-general of all French establishments in India and commander-in-chief of its armies, surrendered Pondicherry to the British, making the East India Company as powerful in the south as it was in the east. The British conquest of India is conventionally dated from the victory at Plassey. After 1757 the British picked up parts of India like ripe fruit from the trees of an untended and unclaimed garden.

Over the next fifty years the British took command of the future of India through a series of major victories against adversaries far more competent than Siraj ud Daula. Superb politics and better drill crushed the options of men who are icons of the nationalist oeuvre: Hyder Ali and Tipoo Sultan in the south, Chet Singh and Mahadji Scindia in the north. In 1764 the British confirmed their supremacy in the east by defeating an alliance of Delhi, Awadh, and a disobedient Bengal at the battle of Buxar. Their principal adversaries were however Mysore in the south and the Marathas elsewhere. In 1787 the redoubtable Tipoo Sultan of Mysore even sent an emassary to Constantinople for help against the British. He was badly informed about the Caliph's abilities. In 1792 Tipoo was defeated and killed.

The Marathas fought a long war. Arthur Wellesley, who served in India at this time, would claim that his victory over them at Assaye was more difficult than his victory over Napoleon in Waterloo. In September 1803, a Bengal army under General Gerard Lake, defeated a Maratha army at Patparganj, entered Delhi and made the hapless Mughal ruler a virtual pensioner. With the end of the second Maratha war in 1804 Governor General Richard Wellesley could talk of an empire rather than possessions. The British were now masters of India.

A cry was heard across the Islamic world: that Muslims must rediscover the strength to protect the House of Islam from Christian nations that were encroaching upon its territories. It rose first from outside the political establishment and found support among the people.

Shah Aziz was in Delhi when Gerard Lake occupied the Mughal capital in 1803. He issued a *fatwa* that unbelievers had seized power and India could no longer be considered a House of Islam. His student, Sayyid Ahmad Barelvi, took the next step and launched a jihad against the British that would trouble the Raj long after Barelvi's death. And through the Ottoman lands roamed a man with a similar mission, whose ideas would inspire the Muslim brotherhood of the twentieth century.

10

THE BARGAIN GOES SOUR

Never will Allah change the condition of a people until they change
it themselves.

[From Verse 11 of Surah 13, Al Rad, or The Thunder]

When Caliph Abdulhamid II advised him, in a helpful way, to get
married, Sayyid Jamal ad Din Afghani threatened to get himself
castrated. Even the great Saladin had a normal family life, and was known,
as a teenager, to sip a bit of wine. However, such banal needs as sex and
family were unacceptable distractions for a man with a single mission: to
launch a pan-Islamic jihad against the power and inexhaustible will of
Great Britain, superpower of the age and fountainhead, in his view, of
Christian imperialism.

He called himself Afghani, but he was an Iranian Shia born near
Hamadan in Asadabad. One reason for this may have been his irritation at
the Shia-Sunni divide, which prevented the unity of Muslims. He made
every effort to conceal his own Shia birth, for most Muslims are Sunnis.
This restless visionary was born in either 1838 or 1839. After an education
in a seminary he went to Kandahar. Either his polemics or his politics
made him a difficult resident. From Afghanistan he was forced to move to
Constantinople; in 1871 he was in Cairo, where his criticism of the Khedive
Ismail and Britain won him admirers. In Cairo, Muhammad Abduh became
his *murid* (disciple). Disciple does not quite define the intensity of a
relationship between a *pir* (master) and a *murid* but the English language
was not created for the Islamic ethos.

By 1879 he had become too inflammatory for Egyptian sensitivities as
well, and moved to Hyderabad in India, where he launched a vitriolic

attack on an educationist who wanted Muslims to befriend the British, Sir Sayyid Ahmad Khan. In 1884 Afghani went to Paris where Abduh joined him; the next year he was back in Iran where he tried to get Shah Nasr ul Din to enlist Russia in the anti-British cause. The Shah did not oblige, so he went to St Petersburg himself and stayed for two years. Although his claim of an audience with Tsar Alexander II was fiction, he did persuade Moscow to permit publication of the Quran and Islamic literature.

Through the expanse of the Ottoman empire, the capitals of Europe, Afghanistan, and the rumbling heart of the British empire, this itinerant missionary left whirlpools of conviction that retained their energy long after he had left. Wilfred Cantwell Smith calls Jamaluddin Afghani the first intellectual to define the contours of the conflict between Islam and the Christian West (*Islam in Modern History,* Princeton, New Jersey, 1957). Nikki Keddie comments that Afghani's relevance lies not so much in the enunciation of the problem as in the construction of the answer (*An Islamic Response to Imperialism*, University of California Press, Los Angeles, 1968). Afghani's prescriptions, which did not always find immediate sympathy, discovered their momentum with the collapse of alternative models, and still constitute the basis for radical Islamic movements that bridge the second millennium with the third. Afghani's favourite quotation from the Quran was from Verse 11 of Surah 13, The Thunder: 'Verily, never will Allah change the condition of a people until they change it themselves.' If governments were too compromised, then the Muslim masses needed to take up the challenge against Christian imperialism without their consent.

The Western-Christian advance from Africa to India, Afghani argued, could be reversed by pan-Islamic unity and a jihad supported by modern science, technology, and rational behaviour. He urged the revival of science and technology in Muslim education, lamenting their collapse after the golden era of Arab power. Afghani dismissed the Western charge that the Quran was anti-modern and inconsistent with a scientific temper. As others had argued, Afghani also stressed that the modern Muslim needed the inspiration of the Salat al Salih, the pious ancestors, whose jihad had succeeded because of their unswerving faith in the Quran and the Prophet. Pan-Islamic unity, he stressed, could coexist with nationalism.

You did not have to be exceptionally perceptive to recognize the wretched state of the Muslim world in Afghani's time. One last burst of passion preceded the formal burial of the Mughal empire in 1857, when

Muslim and Hindu sepoys revolted for a variety of reasons against British rule and dragged a number of princely families to join their cause. The Raj trembled but survived, and revenge was severe. During the mutiny, the British prevailed upon the Caliph, Abdul Mejid, in Constantinople to issue an edict saying that the Muslims could not describe their mutiny as a jihad. Abdul Mejid was in no position to oppose a vital British interest.

In the Ottoman empire the reforms inspired by the West had failed to deliver. Selim III (1788–1807) heard Napoleon dream, loudly, of Constantinople, and thought the answer lay in making the army more European. Mahmud II (1808–39) raised a conscription force trained by Europeans and lost Greece and Algeria. Mahmud curbed the power of the *ulema* and gave equality to all citizens. Everyone could now wear the *fez*. Europe applauded politely in public, and sneered in private. By 1829, Russia had seized Ottoman territory in the Caucasus (names which are familiar once again, Chechnya and Daghestan) and proclaimed itself protector of the twelve million Orthodox Christians in the reduced Ottoman empire. This had one unintended consequence. Muslims in Tsarist Russia sent a counter-appeal to the Caliph to become their guardian, as did Muslims in India after 1857. Muslims were however seeking the protection of their Caliph in vain; Turkey was barely able to protect itself. By the 1870s Russia had encouraged Bulgaria, Bosnia, Serbia, and Montenegro to rebel against Istanbul.

Caliph Abdulhamid was persuaded by Afghani that only Islam, not reforms, could hold his disintegrating empire. He set out to woo his subjects rather than foreigners. He constructed the railway line from Damascus to Medina for pilgrims, and tried to increase Arab participation in the administration of the empire. It was however too little and much too late. Britain had begun to use the promise of Arab independence against Turkey.

In Afghani's thesis, while Islam was threatened by both London and Moscow, Britain was the Great Satan. Britain, he believed, had not only the means but also the will to control the world. Its grip on India was absolute, and its growing reach in Africa and the Middle East were indicative of its appetite. Afghani wanted nothing less than a declaration of a pan-Islamic jihad against Britain. He was certain about mass support for such a call.

Shah Nasr ul Din of Persia discovered Afghani's strength when in 1890 he granted the tobacco concession to a British company. Afghani circulated a pamphlet in Tehran against economic imperialism and appealed to the people to overthrow their government. Under Afghani's prodding, a *fatwa* was issued by *Hajji* Mirza Hussein Shirazi: 'In the name of Allah, the Merciful, the Compassionate, today the use of tobacco in any form is war against the Imam of the age.' The concession was eventually cancelled. But the anger that Afghani had unleashed had not exhausted itself. In May 1896 Shah Nasr ul Din was assassinated by a man called Mirza Riza, a disciple of Afghani. Afghani was thrown out of the country in January 1891, forcing him towards Basra and Baghdad. From there Afghani went on to London, then as now a good place to foment sedition, even against Britain.

Afghani wanted an assault on British power from the heart of British rule; this is why he was so incensed with leaders like the knighted Sir Sayyid Ahmad Khan who advocated Muslim-Christian friendship, and even quoted the Quran in support. Afghani was shocked and angry at what he considered to be the betrayal of the Islamic cause. He labelled Sir Sayyid a *dajjal*, an Islamic equivalent of the Anti-Christ, in a devastating critique titled *The Materialists in India*, issued on 28 August 1884. His opening sentence sets the tone: 'The English entered India and toyed with the minds of her princes and kings in a way that makes intelligent men both laugh and cry.' As for Sir Sayyid: '. . . he took another road in order to serve his English masters, by sowing division among the Muslims and scattering their unity'. Afghani continues:

> His doctrine pleased the English rulers and they saw in it the best means to corrupt the hearts of the Muslims. They began to support him, to honour him, and to help him build a college in Aligarh, called the Muhammedan College, to be a trap in which to catch the sons of the believers in order to bring them up in the ideas of this man, Ahmad Khan Bahadur. Ahmad Khan wrote a commentary on the Koran and distorted the sense of the words and tampered with what God had revealed. He founded a journal called *Tahdib al Akhlaq* which published only what would mislead the minds of the Muslims, cause dissension among them, and sow enmity between the Muslims of India and other Muslims [especially] the Ottomans. These materialists became an army for the English government in India. They drew their swords to cut the throats of Muslims, while weeping for them and crying: 'We kill you only out of compassion and pity for you, and seeking to improve you and make your lives

comfortable.' The English saw that this was the most likely means to attain their goal: the weakness of Islam and the Muslims.

Afghani's end was controversial. In London he was befriended by an Englishman called Wilfrid Blunt. In 1892 his mentor Abdulhamid invited him to Constantinople but began to suspect that Afghani had been compromised by a British agent, and co-opted into plans to promote an Arab Caliphate of the sort that Lawrence of Arabia went on to create two decades later. A life that had been so vibrant ended in some gloom. He died in 1897 of cancer of the chin. As Keddie puts it:

> At the time of his death he was apparently attended by only one person, a Christian servant, and his death brought no great reaction in either the East or the West. Only later, when his pan-Islamic, unapologetic, and anti-Western ideas began to be picked up by a growing body of Muslim writers, was he once again eagerly and widely read, and regarded as a modern Muslim hero . . . Afghani initiated the partial transformation of Islam from a generally held religious faith into an ideology of political use in uniting Muslims against the West.

Abduh abandoned thoughts of jihad but worked for reform through the application of Quranic tenets to a modern idiom. His disciple Rashid Rida started a periodical called *Al Manar* or The Lighthouse. His most important political heir was Hasan al Banna, who founded The Society of Muslim Brothers, more familiar as the Muslim Brotherhood in 1928. The pacifism of Abduh and Rida gave way to a programme of social, political and, if necessary, military action. Afghani's legacy was safe.

Blunt may or may not have been a British agent, but the British were nothing if not careful. They understood jihad. They had just dealt with one in India. The jihad that Shah Waliullah had initiated in 1761 against the Marathas was continued by his son Shah Aziz against the British. The principal firebrand was Sayyid Ahmed Barelvi.

Barelvi was born in 1786 in the district of Rae Bareli in the United Provinces. He entered the Shah Waliullah seminary at 20, where he befriended Shah Ismail, Waliullah's grandson. By the time the two went on *hajj* in 1822–3 they were both well-known. Barelvi's *Sirat al Mustaqin* (The Straight Path) and Ismail's *Taqwiyat al Iman* (Strengthening the Faith) had been printed in lithographic editions. In Arabia Barelvi found the ashes of a fire that warmed his heart.

Muhammad ibn Abd al Wahhab was born in Najd in Arabia in the same year, 1703, as Shah Waliullah. Their thinking was influenced by similar anguish. Both attributed decay to infidel influences that had corrupted the pristine principles of Islam. Both demanded a jihad: Shah Waliullah against the infidel, and Wahhab against 'corruption' within.

The Wahhabis began by targetting trees and tombs: tree-adoration, they said, was a relic of a pre-Islamic past, and tombs had acquired devotees despite the injunction against saint and relic worship. His home town did not much care for his zeal and Wahhab found refuge in 1744 in a market town called Diriya, whose chief was Muhammad ibn Saud. Saud became a convert to the cause. He banned decadent luxuries like jewellery, gold, and silk, and the even more decadent music, dancing and poetry. This was complemented by victory on the battlefield, reinforcing faith. The death of Wahhab in 1787 did not stall growth or aggression. In 1791 the Wahhabis defeated the sheikh of Mecca, and in 1797 even reached Baghdad.

By 1801 Saud ibn Abdul Aziz, grandson of Muhammad ibn Saud, had some 100,000 troops under his command. He invaded the holy city of Kerbala in 1802. In 1803 he captured Mecca and demolished all the structures constructed over the graves of Islam's heroes. In 1804 the Wahhabis took Medina, and even skirmished with the British in the Gulf. Selim got the shock of his Caliphate when a pilgrims' caravan from Constantinople was not permitted to perform the *hajj*. A Caliph unable to ensure the safety of a pilgrimage was bad news.

In 1812, Mahmud II sent a force under Muhammad Ali Pasha from Cairo to end this insurgency; by 1819, Diriya had fallen and the incumbent, Abdullah ibn Saud, was sent to Constantinople, where he was beheaded. That was not the end of the story. The Sauds would get their Arabia a little over a century later with British help.

The Wahhabi spirit found a second home in India. The dialectics of the Wahhabi and Waliullah movements were not similar, but the British were convinced that the essence was the same. It was the British who described the Indian jihad as 'Wahhabi'. Barelvi was a deceptively gentle, calm man prone to trances, of medium height, with a flowing beard that touched his chest. He preached three themes: the unity of God; the equality of man; and the pollution of Indian Islam through its contact with idolatrous and superstitious Hinduism.

Sir William Hunter, commissioned by the British government to understand these difficult people called Muslims, termed Barelvi a bandit and an impostor in his report, *The Indian Mussalmans* (first published in 1871. But he also recorded:

> He [Barelvi] appealed with an almost inspired confidence to the religious instinct, long dormant in the souls of his countrymen, and overgrown with superstitious accretions which centuries of contact with Hinduism had almost stifled Islam . . . I cannot help the conviction that there was an intermediate time in Sayyid Ahmad's [sic] life when his whole soul yearned with a great pain for the salvation of his countrymen, and when his heart turned singly to God.

Barelvi persuaded the three principal Sufi orders of India, Chishti, Naqshbandi and Qadiri, to join his revival, which he called the *Tariq e Muhammadiya*, or the Way of Muhammad. In 1821 he established a base in Patna from where a massive network of missionaries spread into rural India. When he left for *hajj* by boat down the Ganges to the port in Calcutta, the crowds were overwhelming. The welcome he received on his return in October 1823 befitted an *imam*. His followers had begun to call him a *mahdi*; he became a symbol of deliverance for Muslims who had lost faith in their kings and élites.

In 1824 Barelvi visited Afghan tribes around Peshawar, and heard stories of persecution by the Sikhs. He promised a jihad. On 21 December 1826 a *fatwa* was proclaimed; in 1830 the holy warriors surprised everyone but themselves by seizing Peshawar. Barelvi had coins struck in his name, declaring himself to be 'Ahmad the Just, Defender of the Faith, The glitter of whose sword scatters destruction among the infidels'. One infidel's sword glittered a little more sharply. A Sikh force captured Barelvi and killed him while he was escaping to the safety of Muslim Awadh in 1831.

The British, consistent in their policy of weakening an enemy without strengthening a friend, were not entirely unhappy at the jihad within the Sikh kingdom, but became concerned when it spilled over, through various rivulets, into their territory. Their concern turned to alarm when a Bengali from Chandpur in Barasat, Nisar Ali, more famous as Titu Miyan, who had met Barelvi, rebelled against the harsh economic measures of Bengali Hindu landlords who guaranteed the revenue of the Raj. Regular Company troops were called in to end this upsurge. Titu Miyan died in battle in 1831.

Martyrdom gave new life to this movement. Rebellion was in the air, but without a leader and without direction, driven only by emotion. Disparate groups were scattered across India, fomenting discontent that played its part in the outburst that is called the Mutiny of 1857. The *Risala-Jihad*, a war song of one of the groups, extolled the rewards of martyrdom and left little doubt about intentions: 'Fill the uttermost ends of India with Islam, so that no sounds may be heard but Allah! Allah!'. The poetry of ferment was heard in cities. A *kasida* (lament) written by Maulvi Karam Ali of Kanpur stressed the obligation of jihad against the infidel; an ode by Maulvi Niyamatullah predicted the coming of a king who would deliver Muslims from the (Christian) Nazarenes 'by the force of the sword in a Holy War'. Maulvi Muhammad Ali announced the success of another *mahdi* in graphic detail: 'even the very smell of government being driven out of their heads and brains', etc.

The hard core was not deflected by the fate of mere battles; even the collapse of the Mutiny left it unbowed, if isolated. A pamphlet, *Jama Tafseer*, printed in Delhi in 1867, insists that Indian Muslims had only two options: either jihad or emigration from India, which the Christians had converted into a House of War. Those who deterred Muslims from this path were placed in the category of the Hypocrites mentioned in the Quran:

> Let all know this. In a country where the ruling religion is other than Muhammadanism, the religious precepts of Muhammad cannot be enforced. It is incumbent on Mussalmans to join together and wage war upon the infidels. Those who are unable to take part in the fight should emigrate to a country of The True Faith . . . Oh Brethren, we ought to weep over our state, for the Messenger of God is angered with us because of our living in the land of the infidel. When the Prophet of God himself is displeased with us, to whom shall we look for shelter?

In 1865 the magistrate in Patna recorded his concern: 'They have under the very nose and protection of government authorities, openly preached sedition in every village of our most populous districts, unsettling the minds of the Mussalman population, and obtaining an influence for evil as extraordinary as it is certain.' Hunter admitted that 'a network of conspiracy has spread itself over our Provinces, and that the bleak mountains that rise beyond the Punjab are united by an unbroken chain of treason-depots with the tropical swamps through which the Ganges merges into the sea'. Jihad was described as 'a source of chronic danger to the British power in India'.

Between 1850 and 1857, that is, *before* the Mutiny, the British had to send sixteen expeditions, using 33,000 regular troops, to quell disturbances. Says Hunter

> about 30 years ago, it seemed as if a fanatic confederacy had firmly established itself in the heart of southern India. Sir Bartle Frere informs me that the Wahhabi organization of the day included a brother of the Nizam [of Hyderabad] who was to have been raised to the Haidarabad [sic] throne . . . It is not the Traitors themselves whom we have to fear, but the seditious masses in the heart of our Empire . . . and no one can predict the proportions to which this Rebel camp, backed by the Mussalman hordes from the westward, might attain, under a leader who knew how to weld together the nations of Asia in a Crescentade [the British term for Jihad].

Muslims were 'a class whom successive Governments have declared to be a source of permanent danger to the Indian Empire'.

When the British drum was beaten to proclaim the transfer of power from the East India Company to the crown after the mutiny, the drum-beaters were told to increase their decibel levels in Muslim neighbourhoods. British policy assumed, with reason, that Muslims would remain their most determined opponents as they had suffered most from British success. In the 1860s, conspiracy trials took place against the so-called Wahhabi leaders in Patna. Although Wahhabi passions had nothing to do with this incident, it was still noted that a Muslim prisoner had assassinated the Viceroy Lord Mayo in 1872 while he was visiting the Andaman islands. The assassin was an Afghan.

It was Lord Mayo who raised the question that William Wilson Hunter was asked to answer. Dr Hunter, member of the Bengal Civil Service, who became the first director general of statistics, produced a seminal report in 1871 titled *The Indian Mussalmans: Are They Bound in Conscience to Rebel*

Against the Queen? Hunter was not averse to prejudice, but his answers to this question left a deep impression on both the government as well as the Hindu gentry and educated professionals, teasingly referred to as the 'Bengali *babu*'. Hunter described Hindus and Muslims as the deadliest of enemies; attributed extra-territorial loyalties from Constantinople to China to the Muslims, called Hindus the 'real natives'. The Hindu had 'unquestionably the higher order of intellect' but the Muslims were a 'superior race', at least until the British came, because of their courage and political organization.

The Muslim clergy that Dr Hunter consulted had a straightforward response to the theme-question: Were Muslims bound by conscience to be disloyal to the English monarch? No. The Hanafi, Maliki and Shaafi schools all pronounced that so long as the practise of Islamic law was permitted in the British empire (what is known as Muslim personal law), it was a Dar al Islam, a House of Islam. It did not matter whether Christians were in power or not so long as Muslims could live by their law. The Shia answer sounded more practical but was more artful: a jihad is valid only when the armies of Islam are led by the rightful *imam*, when there are enough arms and sufficient warriors with requisite experience, when generals are in possession of their reason, and there is enough money to finance the war. As they did not know of any generals in possession of the requisite reason or funds, the question of jihad did not arise.

Hunter and his fellow civil servants took up a subsequent question: how could the Raj break the stranglehold of 'these misguided Wahhabis' over the Muslim masses?

Education. James O'Kenealy, who was in charge of prosecutions against the Wahhabis, wrote: 'I attribute the great hold which the Wahhabi doctrines have on the mass of the Muhammedan peasantry to our neglect of their education.' E.C. Bailey, home secretary to the Government of India in 1870, commented: 'Is it any subject for wonder that they [Muslims] have held aloof from a system which, however good in itself, made no concession to their prejudices, made in fact no provision for what they esteemed their necessities, and which was in its nature unavoidably antagonistic to their interests, and at variance with all their traditions?' Teach them, defuse their anger, and make them part of the system.

The first census of British India took place in 1872. It divided communities into four categories. Aryans (Brahmins and Rajputs), Mixed, Aborigines and Muslims, which is at least indicative of the sociology of the period. The 1881 census identified over fifty million Muslims in India, or one-fifth of the total population; forty per cent of them lived in Bengal. These twenty million Bengali Muslims formed over half the population of the province. Ten million Muslims lived in Punjab. About 14 per cent, or less than six million, lived in the Gangetic heartland, a statistic which has not changed much. In Punjab, Muslims spoke Punjabi, in Bengal, Bengali, and in the United Provinces and Bihar the élite spoke Urdu and the mass their local dialects.

With the old nobility destroyed after 1857, and the clergy snuffed out after their spirited pop-up revolts, the leadership of Muslims shifted to what is known as the *sharif* class: Hunter's alleged 'haughty foreigner'. There was some truth in the *sharif* identification with Central Asians and Persians. There is an interesting story about Sayyid Mahmud, the younger son of the pro-British educationist Sir Sayyid Ahmad. In 1869 he was sitting in the India Office in London looking at pictures of semi-clad natives in the just-published *The People of India*. An Englishman approached him and asked, 'Are you a Hindustani?' Sayyid Mahmud looked up from the book and stuttered, yes, but not an 'aborigine'. His ancestors, he explained, had come from a foreign country.

This attitude had serious implications for the politics of democracy as it emerged in the twentieth century. On the one side, it reinforced a growing accusation against Muslims that they lived in India but were loyal to foreign lands. The passionate Muslim effort to retain the Ottoman Caliph as the custodian of Mecca and Medina and the movement led by Mahatma Gandhi for better peace terms after Turkey's defeat, was more grist to such mills. Later, the Muslim League's demand for a separate homeland provided all the confirmation required.

There was however also a contradiction in the Indian Muslim attitude. The *sharif* class of central India, with fair skin and almond eyes, too often displayed a racist contempt for fellow Indian Muslims who did not resemble their 'haughty foreigners'. They looked down upon converts from the lower castes, who did not have the physique of the 'conquerors of India'. A certain Dr James Wise, civil surgeon of Dhaka, did some research in the 1870s on the Muslims of eastern Bengal and found that the only difference between the Hindus and the Muslims was the Muslim beard and the nature of the loincloth the two communities wore: Muslims preferred the colourful *lungi* and Hindus the plain white *dhoti*. He compared fifty Hindus and Muslims in Dhaka jail on the basis of age, height, weight, girth of chest; there was no variation. The children of Pathans and Turks, and the Sheikhs and Syeds of the Gangetic belt, could not co-opt Bengali Muslims, who were as 'puny' as Hindus, into their concept of the 'real' Mussalman. The derision extended, even more stupidly, to disregard for a language as beautiful as Bengali, while the 'Bengali *babu*', clerk and magistrate of the empire in Calcutta, became an object of caricature. Such racism was responsible for the partition of Pakistan and the emergence of Bangladesh in 1971.

There was one unexpected side-effect of this syndrome. The Hindu élite of Calcutta and Bengal, the intellectuals produced by Presidency College and Macaulay's minute on the role of the English language in the empire, called the *bhadralok,* and the *zamindars,* the landlords who exploited the peasants, shared this contempt for the Muslim peasantry and laced it with the casteism that is one of the traditional evils of India. The *bhadralok*, who had no social problems with the Muslim *sharif* of the north, dismissed Bengali Muslims as converts from the 'dregs of Hindu society'. Bengal, consequently, became a fountainhead of divisive politics. It used to be said, largely by Bengalis, although in fairness they were not the first to articulate the sentiment, that when Bengal gets a cold, India sneezes. When the Bengali *bhadralok* were unable to stomach the prospect of adult franchise in their Muslim-majority province, India did not catch a mere cold. It caught Partition.

Hundreds of years of 'Muslim' power did not translate into material reward for the overwhelming majority of the Muslims. The large majority of Punjabi and Bengali Muslims were either poor and illiterate peasants or urban labour, driven to British factories by the absence of capital for traditional Indian manufactures. In the countryside, economic power, through land ownership or moneylending at cruel rates of interest, had consolidated into the hands of a small class of Hindus. (The Hindu peasant was no better off than the Muslim.) In Bengal and Punjab, where linguistic, cultural, and ethnic identification between Hindus and Muslims was far stronger than in United Provinces (UP) and Bihar, this economic factor played a major role in the growth of the Partition idea. In UP and Bihar, the economic condition of Muslims was not very different. Only three per cent of Muslims, for instance, were literate, but the Muslim élite was closer, culturally and emotionally, to their own community than to Hindus.

After the failed jihad, the British were far more comfortable with the *sharif* than with the clergy among the Muslims, just as they preferred to deal with lawyers and the emerging professional middle class among the Hindus. These were elements who could be taught the language of the ruling class, English, and hopefully be inducted into the management of the empire.

The war that took place between Hindus and Muslims under British rule was in the mind: the intelligentsia of both the communities, outside the discipline of power, became rebels in search of a cause. The history of the ninety years between 1857 and 1947 has too often been viewed through the perspective of consequence rather than cause; from the ideological compulsions of post-1947 India and Pakistan, and post-1971 Bangladesh, rather than the processes that led to the great divide. As Partition was a visible victory for Muslim separatism, it has been natural to trace the evolution of the Muslim mind from post-Mughal despair to the language and politics of the pro-Pakistan movement.

This is a line that can be drawn through Urdu poetry, from the wondrous irony of the last Mughal poet, Ghalib, to the satire of an Indian in British India, Akbar Allahabadi; to the anguish and intellect of a Muslim in search of answers, Iqbal; and to the despair of a Pakistani leftist, Faiz, who found the answer hollow. Ghalib's poetry lives beyond the chronicle of events; Akbar Allahabadi's satire, which laughed at Muslims as much as at the British, was rooted in time. Iqbal has been dismissed by purists as an Urdu Kipling, but he mirrored the passions that coursed through the Indian Muslim's heart.

Iqbal's most famous work, *Shikwa*, is a complaint to Allah, a story of pain (*kissa-e-dard*). It became an anthem of the Muslims of this subcontinent after it was recited at a gathering in Lahore in 1909. It was a lament and a challenge. The poet asked Allah why He was unfaithful to Muslims when they remained faithful to Him. For the first time since the dawn of faith, Allah did not seem to be keeping His bargain with His believers. (The translation, by the well-known Indian litterateur Khushwant Singh, was published by Oxford University Press, Delhi, 1981.) These stanzas illustrate the pain:

> *Hai baja shewa-e-taslim mein mashhoor hain hum*
> *Kissa-e-dard sunate hain kee majboor hain hum.*
>
> We won renown for submitting to Your will – and it is so;
> We speak out now, we are compelled to repeat our tale of woe.

Aa gaya ain larhai mein agar waqt-e-namaz
Qibla-ruh ho ke zamin-bos hui qaum-e Hijaz
Ek hi saf mein kharhe ho gaye Mahmud o ayyaz
Na koi banda raha, aur na koi banda nawaz
Banda-o-sahib-o-muhtaj-o-ghani ek huey
Teri sarkar mein jo pahunche toh sabhi ek huey.

In the midst of raging battle if the time came to pray,
Hejazis turned to Mecca, kissed the earth and ceased from fray.
Sultan and slave in single file stood side by side,
Then no servant was nor master, nothing did them divide.
Between serf and lord, needy and rich, difference there was none.
When they appeared in Your court, they came as equals and one.

But what is the reward of such devotion?

Ummate aur bhi hain, unme gunahgaar bhi hain
Izz wale bhi hain, maste-mai-pindar bhi hain
Unme kaahil bhi hain, ghafil bhi hain, hushiar bhi hain
Saikron hain ki tere naam se bezaar bhi hain.
Rahmatein hain teri aghiyaar ke kashaanon par
Barq girti hai to bechaare Mussalmaanon par?

There are people of other faiths, some of them transgressors.
Some are humble; drunk with the spirit of arrogance are others.
Some are indolent, some ignorant, some endowed with brain,
Hundreds of others there are who even despair of Your Name.
Your blessings are showered on homes of unbelievers, strangers all.
Only on the poor Muslim, Your wrath like lightening falls.

The clergy lost the battle against the British in the nineteenth century. Indian Muslims turned to other avenues, to politics, to education, and, as we can see from Iqbal, sometimes even to poetry. Despair has many manifestations. Eventually, one of them would become violent.

11

THE WEDGE AND THE GATE

All well in the Cabul Embassy.

[The final telegram sent by Major Sir Pierre Louis Napoleon
Cavagnari to the Viceroy in India on 2 September 1879, one day
before his death.]

The first American to interfere in the internal affairs of Afghanistan
was a Quaker from Pennsylvania with an unmistakeable name, Josiah
Harlan. Like Elihu Yale, he had come east to make his fortune; adventure
was a bonus. In 1823, undeterred by the absence of any medical training,
he enlisted with the Bengal Artillery as an assistant surgeon and went off
to fight a war in Burma. In 1826 he headed north, for the small Punjabi
town of Ludhiana, attracted by a king without a kingdom. Shah Shuja had
been dethroned in Kabul by Dost Mohammad Khan and found refuge
with the British, who had learnt the value of pawns on this vast Indian
chessboard. (Rivalry for power was literally inbred in Afghanistan. Dost
Mohammad, for instance, had seventy two brothers or half-brothers; they
did not always keep count of sisters then.) Harlan claims that he disguised
himself as a dervish in order to spy for Shah Shuja in Kabul and was
rewarded with the title 'Companion of the Imperial Stirrup'. The honour
was less than imperial, but Harlan did go to Kabul, and – clearly a
mercenary without prejudices – became an aide to Dost Mohammad,
who sent him on a punitive and successful military expedition to Bukhara.
When Harlan returned to Kabul in 1839, he heard stories of a great army
being sent by the British to depose his paymaster and did what any prudent
adventurer would have done, deserted. In 1841 he found his way back
from Kabul and retired in the slightly less turbulent city of San Francisco.

The British were the first empire builders since Asoka the Great to expand from the east. Europe came to Afghanistan two thousand years before they did, with Alexander, who left behind a flourishing Afghan-Macedonian-Buddhist kingdom. The other great world-conqueror, Ghengis Khan, also subjugated the land some fifteen hundred years later, but he left behind only the memory of devastation in Herat, an oasis city on the crossroads of the most profitable trade routes of the world for at least three thousand years. Muslim armies began to march through the country from the mid-seventh century towards the Oxus valley. Afghans say that God had a pile of rocks left over after creation, and so he made Afghanistan. The Almighty certainly used up much of His collection, for a vast, flat plain stretches from the northern border without serious undulation till Siberia.

A glance at the map confirms the obvious: Afghanistan is both the wedge and the gate to India. The Afghans, Ghaznis, and Ghoris, who raided and ruled from the eleventh century onwards, understood this. When Babur established the mighty Mughal empire he took care to secure Kabul first. His grandson Akbar, also considered great, took out further insurance with a splendid fort at Attock, that towers over the confluence of the dark, stained Kabul river and the clear, sparkling Indus as both enter the plains. (The dark and light waters travel together, dividing the river, for perhaps half a mile before a reluctant merger of identities.) India was secure from the west so long as the Attock fort guarded access to the plains of Punjab from the Khyber pass. The decline of Mughal power is correctly attributed to Nadir Shah, the first invader to breach that pass since Babur.

Modern Afghanistan is generally dated from a dynasty established by one of Nadir Shah's Pashtun generals, Ahmad Shah Abdali. In 1747 a nine day *loya jirga* (meeting of tribal chiefs) elected him leader of the Durrani clan by placing grass on his turban as pledge of its loyalty. Abdali ruled from Kandahar; his son Taimur Shah shifted the capital to Kabul in 1772 and brought the whole of Afghanistan under his rule. In 1780, through a treaty with Bukhara, the Oxus, or Amu Darya, was confirmed as the northern boundary, while its eastern territories extended beyond the Indus to Peshawar.

In the second half of the eighteenth century, the British either neutralized or defeated every Muslim *nawab* or Hindu *raja* till they could legitimately call themselves masters of India. Only the Punjab remained beyond their grasp thanks to the grip of the extraordinary Sikh Maharajah Ranjit Singh who understood that power grew out of the barrel of a disciplined gun. However, a strong Punjab also served as an effective buffer, a comfort that crumbled when Ranjit Singh's heirs destroyed in a decade what had taken a generation to build.

With the kings defeated, the nature of the challenge to the British changed to something unusual; it became subversive rather than offensive. Instead of formal armies representing a state, the British encountered inspired armies without recognized leaders, or inspirational leaders without recognized armies. Soldiers and peasants took up causes that their leaders were too weak or too cowardly to voice. The most powerful of the these wars was what the British called the 'Sepoy Mutiny' of 1857, when, using secret signals to coordinate, the people revolted and nearly broke the Raj. The Indians had passion, the British had organization; after the initial tidal wave, it was a no-contest.

The most pervasive challenge in the nineteenth century came through a series of jihads; no sooner did the authorities snuff out one menace in the east than another broke out in the centre or west of their sprawling geopolitical map. The most successful of these jihads saw the brief 'liberation' of Peshawar by Syed Ahmad Barelvi, with the help of Afghan tribes, from Sikh rule. Within twenty years of this episode, the British would encounter the ferocity of the *ghazis* when they made their first serious error and invaded Afghanistan. (The *ghazi* is of course the holy warrior of the Quran). When the emir deserted the *ghazi* he fought alone.

The British tried hard to understand the mind of the Muslim they were dealing with, but were never quite able to grasp what this fervour was all about; they were unable to come to terms with a cause that might be beyond a king or country. Percival Spear has a perceptive comment (*The Nabobs: A Study of the Social Life of the English in 18th Century India,* Oxford University Press, 1963):

> An important factor was the prejudices or presuppositions which
> each side brought to the encounter. On the British side there was
> previous experience with Africans in west Africa and the West Indies,
> with Red Indians in America, with Muslim Turks and Arabs in the
> Levant and north Africa. To the British of those days the African
> was a savage and a slave, or a potential one; the Red Indian was
> looked on with respect, but was definitely wild or primitive. The

Turk and the Arab were neither of these, but they were involved in a tradition of enmity dating from the Crusades. Muslims were infidels; they were held to be cruel, licentious, perfidious as well as brave. Were not the Moguls and many Indians Muslims? . . . When the Moguls were seen to have lost their power and Marathas not to have inherited it, both Muslims and Hindus fell in cultural as well as political estimation.

More, therefore, than the revival of any Indian power, the British in India worried about the envy of Europe. All the three great European powers of the time, England, France, and Russia, had India in their sights. The first two had already dueled in India. France, though defeated, revived its hopes in the age of Bonaparte. Napoleon instigated the first serious British interest in Afghanistan, for the conqueror was widely expected to take Alexander's route through Persia after he reached Egypt in 1798 with 38,000 troops and a hundred and seventy intellectuals. Although Nelson's naval victory over the French eased fears it did not eliminate them. The eminent British civil servant Monstuart Elphinstone visited Peshawar in 1809 to seek help from the Afghans in the event of Napoleon invading, while Charles Metcalfe signed a treaty with Ranjit Singh that assured the British of Sikh support in case Napoleon reached his western gates. In return, the British guaranteed the territorial integrity of the Sikh kingdom; they kept their word to Ranjit Singh as long as he was alive. In 1814 Britain came to similar quid pro quo terms with Persia, offering Persia help if it was invaded. When Persia, under threat from an aggressive Russia, invoked this pact in 1826, it discovered that the British were busy elsewhere.

The first Britishers to cross the Khyber were an elderly horse breeder and a young lawyer-clerk, who reached the fabled pass in 1824 on their way to Bukhara. William Moorcroft and George Trebleck did actually reach Bukhara via Kabul in February 1825, to the consternation of some of their civil service compatriots in Calcutta who had predicted disaster for such foolhardiness. Moorcroft's epic journey charted the course that the empire would take within less than fifteen years of his death. In the event, the government would prove to be more foolhardy than the pioneer.

Moorcroft was hired by the East India Company at the grand salary of Rs 30,000 a year for something completely different: to breed better horses. This was however too mundane a destiny for a temperament as tempestuous as his. He came to India as superintendent of stud, and lived up to this designation in private life too. It was not simply a matter of having a wife, Mary, in England and a second, Purree Khanum (literally, Fairy Begum), the mother of his two children Anne and Richard, in India. That was common practice before the fishing fleets brought single women and stern chaplains to the Raj. The natives had a sly, but witty, term for this convenience: the *bibi* (white woman) had been replaced by the *bubu* (a Hindustani word meaning sister). As puns go, this is not bad at all. While the *bibi* received regular letters from the sahib, the *bubu* ran the house, taught him Hindustani, nursed his brow, and shared his bed.

Moorcroft was 52 when he left Calcutta in 1819. The government's attitude was clear in its duplicity; he could go anywhere he liked so long as the government could not be blamed if anything went wrong. Such standard policy for spies seems not to have changed. On 6 March 1820 Moorcroft left British India when he crossed the Sutlej on inflated buffalo skins. Not even the most gullible princeling believed that Moorcroft had come for better horse semen, although he did maintain that pretence. His regular reports to Calcutta proved to be espionage of the highest class. He was welcomed hospitably in Peshawar in December 1823, from whence he proceeded to Kabul through the Khyber.

The spy sent one message from the cold: one regiment of the Raj would be sufficient to overthrow Dost Mohammad and replace him with the British protege, Shah Shuja. Moorcroft was yet another champion of a phrase that echoed Robert Clive's dictum: to stand still is to perish. This philosophy impelled what was called a 'forward policy'. That, explained Moorcroft, was the only way to thwart the Russians. He met them in Bukhara, which he entered on foot as an infidel was not allowed through the city gates on horseback. He was impressed by the thousand-year citadel, a great library, some three hundred schools, gardens, canals – and markets stockpiled with Russian goods as well as Russian slaves. (When, later, Russia used this slave trade as a pretext for invasion, the Muslims could not understand the accusation. Russia, they argued, enslaved its own people through serfdom; why should it complain about slavery elsewhere?)

The Russian threat was not fanciful, even if you eliminated some of the more exotic interpretations. The Russian urge southwards has its share of explanations apart from old-fashioned domination and a route to warm waters. A persuasive one is that Russia needed open space for strategic defence. Space can be as defensible as a wall; this was the principle on which the British cantonments were created in India. In front of every cantonment there was open space, or *maidan*, to ensure an unrestricted field of fire. Dominion and security were not unmixed with a crusading element. The Cossacks, who rode under the banner of Ivan the Terrible (or Great) and captured the Muslim city of Kazan on the upper Volga in 1552, made it a point to convert women and build churches whose bells announced the spreading power of a deeply Christian empire. Peter the Great's imagination was not restricted to the Islamic world (he took Estonia, Latvia, and part of Finland in 1721) but his principal dream was to win back Constantinople for Christendom. Peter's first foray towards Central Asia ended in disaster when an army of 3,500 was massacred in Khiva. He shifted his attention towards the Caucasus, the spectacular range that divides Europe from Asia for about 650 miles from the Caspian to the Black Sea. In 1722 Russia entered Daghestan, opening the passage to the Muslim Caucasus.

The Muslim armies of the seventh century swept into Persia and Central Asia but stopped before these high mountains and forbidding people; the Persians believed that the king of the jinns lived in the snows of these impenetrable peaks. Islam came to this region through Sufi missionaries, particularly of the Naqshbandi order. The Chechens, Circassians, Avars, and Daghestanis were converted rather than conquered, while Georgia and Armenia remained Christian.

In 1734 Russia advanced in both the east and the west, defeating the Kazaks and taking Crimea. Russia's focus, ability, and determination sharpened further under Catherine the Great, when at least one of her ambassadors declared that the future belonged to Russia and America. That might have been true of the distant future, but not of the immediate. The British lion had life in him yet. The defeat of Napoleon's 600,000-strong Grand Army in 1812 and Wellington's victory at Waterloo released the energies of Russia and Britain from European preoccupations, enabling both to embark on empire-building on a scale unprecedented in European history. Tsar Alexander I added some 200,000 square miles to his realm and British analysts like Sir Robert Wilson, who had been a military observer during the burning of Moscow, reported that he planned to conquer Constantinople and also to enter India through Persia. Russian armies were now operating on both sides of the Caspian, using Orenburg as their base. By 1825 Russia had crossed a west-east line from the north of the Caspian to the Aral, and to the Lake Balkhash. (It was this advance that worried Persia.) In 1839–40, Khiva enjoyed its last victory when it repulsed 5,000

Cossacks and 2,000 Khirgiz under General V.A. Perovsky, but the persistence was unflagging. In 1865 Russia captured the prized city of Tashkent; by 1868 Bukhara and Samarkand were under Russian rule and Khiva at last fell in 1873. Within another decade Russia was a handshake, or a gunshot, away from Herat.

A century seems brief when punctuated by dates, but the struggle was not easy nor the outcome inevitable. If the Russian advance was piecemeal rather than a continuous sweep it was also because resistance came from those irregular armies who held on to the banner of jihad when their emirs had capitulated. Not all the emirs surrendered easily either; men like Nasrullah Khan of Bukhara combined guile, confidence, commerce, and the horrors of an invidious kind of incarceration to hold their kingdoms: his favourite prison for infidels was Siyah Chah, a pit about twenty feet deep in which select prisoners lived with vermin, rats, insects and the rotting corpse or two. However, the most famous of the jihad banners was raised in the Caucasus, a puritan black standard that held up the Russians in a long and brutal war under the leadership of a man who has become an Islamic legend, Imam Shamyl.

Muslim Caucasus remembers it as the age of *Sharia*. It was the time, goes a popular belief, when a Chechen girl would not marry a young man unless he had leapt over a stream, jumped over a rope held at shoulder height, and killed a Russian. The first jihad, they say, was led by an Italian Jesuit known as Elisha Mansour, who had converted to Islam and was sent by the Ottoman Sultan to fight against the Russians. He was defeated in 1791 and taken prisoner. The resistance was nourished by the *ulema*, most notably Mullah Muhammad Yaraghi, a Sufi scholar, and his disciple, Ghazi Mullah, an Avar from Daghestan. Their message was familiar: jihad would not succeed against the Russians unless they adopted the *Sharia* completely, and forsook their traditional laws, called the *aadat* (the word has travelled to India, where it is the Urdu for 'habit'). Unity and purity was their answer to the crusades of the Russian Orthodox Church and the Tsars. In 1829 Ghazi Mullah travelled the region preaching that nothing, not obedience to *Sharia*, not giving alms, not prayer, and not even the pilgrimage would be accepted by Allah if a Russian existed in their midst. Their marriages would be illegal and their children bastards until they ejected every single Russian. He was proclaimed *imam* at a gathering in the mosque of Ghimri, where he formally gave the call for a jihad. Ghazi Mullah and his *murids* (disciples or followers) won their first encounter with the Russians in the forests south of Grozny. The Russian reaction was severe, and Ghazi Mullah was driven back to Ghimri. The story goes that when the Russians took Ghimri, they found Ghazi Mullah dead, but seated, legs folded, on his prayer carpet, one hand on his beard and the other pointing towards the sky.

Only two *murids* survived. One of them was Shamyl. Four soldiers confronted him as he stood at the doorway of a house. Tall, well built, he seemed to pause as if to let them take aim, then suddenly leapt over them, cut three down from behind but was bayoneted in the chest by the fourth. He pulled the steel out of his chest, killed the fourth soldier and then jumped over the wall and vanished into the dark. This is how the people remember their hero.

Born in 1796 into a noble family of Daghestan, Shamyl became renowned for his Islamic scholarship by his early twenties. In 1828 he went on *hajj*. After the defeat at Ghimri in 1829, he was accepted as the *imam* of the jihad. He built up a mobile army of some six thousand *murids*, with a *naib* or a deputy at the head of each unit of 500. For ten years this army wrought havoc on the Russians until it was finally encircled and defeated in 1839. Despite the loss of one wife and a baby, Shamyl escaped. In 1840 he was back with a new army, the same black banners, and once again on a victory march. The Russians offered to pay for his head by its equivalent weight in gold: the blood-money was rising. It was only in 1858 that Imam Shamyl was finally subdued; he surrendered after a last stand in June 1859, when the Russians threatened to slaughter his whole family if he did not give himself up alive. He was banished to the outskirts of Moscow, where he lived till 1869, when he was allowed to leave for Mecca and Medina. Crowds turned out to cheer him as he travelled through Turkey to the holy cities, where he died in 1871.

The legend lives, of course. The jihad lives too in the Caucasus.

If the *murids* of Caucasus trapped the Russians, then the *ghazis* of Afghanistan stopped the other great contemporary power of Europe.

In 1833 the British posted a spy in Kabul and called him a 'newswriter', surely the first instance of compatibility between two separate professions. He was a deserter and wanderer called Charles Masson who was paid Rs 250 a month, a commitment that Calcutta made clear it would disown if discovered. He was a good and honest spy. He reported that Kabul (unlike Kandahar) was tolerant, classless, civil, and hospitable, where even Hindus and Armenian Christians got justice from Dost Mohammad, who was loved by the people and employed the sword only when every other strategy had failed. In 1832 a promising British officer, Alexander Burnes, received permission to travel up to Bukhara, a journey that took two years. He put on a turban and robes, shaved his head, dyed his beard black, began to eat with his fingers, and renamed himself Sikander. When Dost Mohammad asked him why he had taken all this trouble if he was not a spy he answered that he only wanted to avoid being stared at. The explanation was found plausible for a *sahib*. In 1836 the new governor-general of India, Lord Auckland asked Burnes to make a second visit to Kabul and Central Asia, ostensibly to promote trade. By this time, the 'forward policy' had taken a further step forward. Calcutta had decided to seize what it could on its western frontiers and control what it could not seize.

In 1844, once again preceded by 'travellers' who mapped the routes, General Sir Charles Napier took the province south of Punjab and Afghanistan, Sind. His triumphant telegram has become a famous pun; it used just one word, '*Peccavi*': 'I have sinned'. The Anglo-Sikh wars after the death of Ranjit Singh brought Punjab into the British fold in the same decade, just in time, one might add, for it was Punjab that saved the British Raj during the mutiny of 1857. The third objective, Afghanistan, would prove more complicated.

Worries about Russia intensified when it supplied 'guests' to Persia for an assault on Herat in 1837. It needed the appearance of two British gunboats in the Persian gulf to lift that siege. In December 1837 a Russian turned up in Kabul, purportedly with a letter from the Tsar. It proved to be a letterhead rather than a letter, because it was not signed. Burnes, who was also in Kabul, did the decent thing and invited Captain Ivan Viktorovich Vitkevich, 30, an officer with the Cossacks, over for dinner. The captain's visit did not amount to much in Kabul but it became the provocation that Calcutta was seeking. In March 1838 Dost Mohammad was given an ultimatum: 'You must desist from all correspondence with Persia and Russia; you must never receive any agents from them . . .' The Afghan responded that the British asked for everything and gave nothing. Burnes was recalled in April, only to be handed orders for a third visit to Afghanistan, this time along with an army. He was also, at the age of 33, promoted to lieutenant colonel and knighted. The British foreign secretary Lord Palmerston was convinced that the attack on Herat indicated a deeper Persia-Russia alliance aimed at the British empire and recommended the replacement of Dost Mohammad with the more pliable Shah Shuja.

He was evidently unaware of Shah Shuja's Afghan nickname: *'Shah-e-kumnaseeb'* or the unfortunate Shah.

The head of this expedition was Sir John Macnaghten; Emily Eden, a contemporary visitor, tartly observed that Sir John spoke Persian better than English although he preferred Sanskrit. On 1 October 1838 the Simla manifesto accused Afghanistan of support to Persian designs. The Army of the Indus was mobilized to invade Afghanistan: 9,500 men from Bengal and Bombay, and 6,000 (mainly Hindu) troops under the nominal command of Shah Shuja. It had 30,000 camels, enough sheep for ten weeks' dinner, and 38,000 camp followers: water carriers (like the loyal Gunga Din), stretcher bearers, cooks, fortune tellers, fiddlers, nautch girls and, for the pious, wives. There was much drama and dramatics along the way. Auckland himself came up to meet Ranjit Singh, but the Sikh was sharp enough not to let this army pass through Punjab. It marched and bribed its way through Sind and the Bolan pass towards Kandahar, where Shuja was 'coronated' in front of a few hundred indifferent Afghans. In Ghazni, an informer pointed out the one gate that had not been reinforced, and it was effectively mined by Lt Henry Durand of the Bengal Engineers. Appropriately, it was Kabul gate. The Army of the Indus lost a mere seventeen men. Kabul fell without a fight, as it was to do again in 1879, 1978, and 2001. Dost Mohammad fled, sought and got sanctuary in Bukhara. Shah Shuja and his mostly Hindu troops settled down to enjoy their good fortune. The British garrisoned Ghazni, Kandahar, and Jalalabad, occupied Quetta and Khyber to secure their communications, and sat back to dream of Herat, 'Chinese Tartary', and even Siberia as their future gifts to Queen Victoria. Shah Shuja shifted a household of several hundred wives and retainers to the citadel of Bala Hissar, despite a request from the British that they be permitted to use that fort as their garrison. Shah Shuja refused because the British would be able to peep into his harem from the ramparts. The British did not press their point. They should have, dealing as they were with an unfortunate Shah.

Life was good in Kabul. Sir Alexander, now also a knight of the Durrani order, led the way with his preference for local, dark-eyed damsels. There was polo, champagne, Madeira, hermetically sealed salmon and splendid dinner parties for the *sahibs* and *memsahibs*. In 1840 Lord Palmerston was predicting that the Cossack and the sepoy would meet in the centre of Asia, Afghanistan, to decide the fate of the continent. Kabul reported to Calcutta that Afghanistan was 'supernormal'. That was surely why a dysenteric, 59-year-old Major General William Elphinstone arrived in mid-1841 as the new commander in chief, to a 'recuperative' posting. He had won his spurs at Waterloo and rested on them ever since. So normal was the situation in Kabul that the British cut the subsidy, another polite word for bribe, to the Ghilzais who in turn blocked the Khyber pass. It seemed a minor fuss in Kabul.

On 2 November 1841 a crowd gathered before Burnes' mansion chanting his old pseudonym: 'Sikander! Sikander!' When he went to the garden to meet them, he was hacked to pieces. The British did nothing. No one knew anything about this leaderless insurrection. It was leaderless, but not clueless. A battle ensued that lasted till 23 November. Lady Florentina Sale (quoted by Meyer and Brysay in *Tournament of Shadows*) has left an account of the 'Ghazeas' rushing towards the British in 'scenes depicted in the battles of the Crusaders'. At last a leader appeared. Akbar Khan, son of Dost Mohammad, arrived with a group of Uzbegs. The British, surrounded, now wanted to negotiate their way out of a calamity. Akbar Khan offered them safe passage, giving vent to his anger only at one point when he told a group of negotiators led by Macnaghten, 'You'll seize my country, will you?!' Macnaghten was killed. The tattered remains of the élite Kabul force were allowed to leave the city on 6 January, only to be mowed down by the Ghilzais as they struggled towards the fort at Jalalabad. Only one man, Dr William Brydon, reached that fort on 13 January. (Brydon was a great survivor. He also survived the epic siege of Lucknow during the Mutiny.)

The so-called Army of Retribution forced the Khyber in April 1842, relieved Jalalabad, and marched to Kabul in September where it met up with another army from Kandahar. There was some display of anger, and an expected number of hangings, but the revenge was superficial. Dost Mohammad Khan was given back his throne. The British might have saved themselves their greatest humiliation in Asia if they had never removed him to begin with.

Dost Mohammad lived till 1863. His favourite son, Akbar, was already dead. As plenty of heirs were available, the battles for succession lasted five years until Sher Ali emerged victor. He was the first of the modernizers. He opened English schools, introduced postal services and, most modern of all, actually paid the troops on time. He sought good relations with the British, coming to attend Lord Mayo's *durbar* in 1869. Mayo's assassination by an Afghan prisoner in the Andaman islands was never attributed to Kabul, and his successor, Lord Northbrook, even offered

British troops to Sher Ali in the event of a Russian threat. In 1874 however Benjamin Disraeli formed a Tory government in London and the forward school was back.

In 1875 Edward Robert Bulwer Lytton was named Viceroy despite his reluctance to go to India because of a 'medical condition' (he had piles, which made him slouch when seated on the viceregal throne). Lord Salisbury, then secretary of state for India, gave Lord Lytton some sensible advice before he left for India: if you believe the doctor, nothing is wholesome; if you believe the priest, nothing is innocent; if you believe the soldier, nothing is safe. Lord Lytton chose to believe the soldiers. Lytton did not require much persuasion to agree that the empire needed to secure Afghanistan. That meant, at the very least, an army in Quetta, a railway to Khyber, and political agents in Kabul, Kandahar, and Herat. The borders of Asoka and Akbar were at the Hindu Kush; the Raj wanted nothing less. Lytton sent a blunt message to Sher Ali: hand over control of foreign policy to a resident British mission in Kabul or face the consequences. Sher Ali argued that if he conceded a mission to Britain he could not refuse one to Russia. Lytton retorted that if Sher Ali did not listen he would have to go. If Afghanistan did not behave, it would be carved up into three regions. Gentler souls in London warned that three Afghanistans might be three times as troublesome, but the Viceroy had set his course. Russia had its own claimant to Kabul, Abdur Rahman, waiting for the dice to turn his way, and helped raise the temperature with a military mission to Kabul. Lytton cabled London that Sher Ali was both savage and insane. Sher Ali halted a provocative British military mission at the Khyber only to discover that there was no Russian help to back him. He lost nerve, but it was too late. At three in the morning of 21 November 1878 Lytton telegraphed Lord Cranbrook, the secretary of state for India: '*Jacta est alea.*' The die is cast. Thirty thousand troops moved, this time wearing *khaki*: half of them up the Khyber, 6,500 through the Kurram valley, and 12,000 through the Bolan pass.

As usual, Kabul fell without a fight. Sher Ali fled, to die on 21 February 1879 at Balkh. The British installed Yakub Khan, described as a wretch by his father. In March 1879 he conceded every British request, including the transfer of the Khyber pass for an annual rent of 60,000 pounds, through the treaty of Gundamak. Lytton congratulated himself and announced celebrations.

Major Sir Pierre Louis Napoleon Cavagnari had an Irish mother, a

French father, and English nationality. When he crossed the border into Afghanistan as head of an eighty one member British mission he was welcomed with a feast that ended with Russian tea and coffee laced with opium. In Kabul the band played *God Save the Queen* after a seventeen gun salute. He settled down in a home adjoining the Bala Hissar fortress. There is some dispute about Yakub Khan's role; and if he actually was behind the unrest that broke out as early as in September, he knew how to keep a secret. On 2 September Cavagnari sent a cable to Peshawar on the newly laid telegraph line: 'All well in the Cabul Embassy.'

The following morning soldiers from Herat, demanding their pay from Yakub Khan, were told to get their money from the British overlords. Cavagnari was having his breakfast when they appeared. In a battle that lasted eight hours, the whole British mission was massacred.

On 5 September Lord Lytton was informed. Everyone in that mob, he raged, was guilty: soldier, civilian, *mullah*, or peasant. That was one indication that the attack was not by mutinous soldiers alone. Major General Sir Frederick Roberts took Kabul again for his country in October. Yakub Khan abdicated. General Roberts announced rewards for information, from Rs 50 to Rs 120 per head, and eventually eighty seven Afghans were hanged by the military tribunals of the time. That was not however the end of the story. In December some 10,000 *ghazis* besieged the British cantonment in Kabul, forcing the general to cable for reinforcements. In January the Russian protégé Abdur Rahman, a grandson of Dost Mohammad, began a march from the north. Lytton, who had started the whole misadventure to stop Russia, now cabled London that as a native was necessary, he was recommending early public recognition of Abdur Rahman! On 22 July Queen Victoria graciously provided that 'recognition'. That too was not the end of the story. On 27 July another irregular army of 20,000 *ghazis* – and there was no talk of back pay this time – destroyed a British contingent of 2,500 at Maiwand, while the 3,000-strong British garrison of Kandahar was besieged by an army under Ayub Khan, a brother of Yakub Khan. General Roberts became a hero when, after a rapid march from Kabul, he relieved Kandahar. Roberts was wise enough to note that the less the Afghans saw of the British, the less they would dislike them. He advised Russia to do the same, in her own interest. In 1907 Britain and Russia agreed to leave Afghanistan alone. The great game was over for precisely seventy years when the Russians restarted it.

The British kept Khyber and claimed that Kabul's foreign policy was still dictated by them, but such delicacies mattered less once the infidel was out of the country. Even this anomaly was cleared up in the third Afghan war, the first started by the Afghans. An exhausted Britain with a heavily depleted army was in no mood for more battles in 1919, and granted Afghanistan what is called her "independence". The Durrani dynasty continued to rule until Zahir Shah, who came to power in 1933, was overthrown by a coup of leftist army officers. His relative, Sardar Mohammad Daud became president of the Republic of Afghanistan in 1973, backed by a socialist political party with an urban base, the Parcham. The leader of Parcham was Babrak Karmal. Tsarism was back in business, this time in the guise of the Union of Soviet Socialist Republics. Pakistan's Prime Minister Zulfiqar Ali Bhutto countered by promoting a small Islamic party. Three of its leaders were forced to flee to Peshawar: Gulbuddin Hekmatyar, Burhanuddin Rabbani, and Ahmed Shah Masood. Each was to become an international star during the jihad against the Soviet invasion of Afghanistan that started in the winter of 1978.

In April 1978 Daud was killed by his own supporters. The Parcham, riven by greed for power, split into the Khalq (People) and Parcham (Flag) factions. Daud's successor Nur Mohammad Taraki was also murdered by friends turned enemies, and Hafizullah Amin took over for a while. The Soviet army and KGB troops seized Kabul in the last week of December 1978 and placed Babrak Karmal on what was now a socialist throne. Kabul once again fell without a fight. A country that had either been too remote or too exotic for America suddenly became its opportunity base. One and a half million Afghans died and the world was a different place by the time the defeated Soviets withdrew in 1989.

The Pakistani journalist Ahmed Rashid, author of the excellent book *Taliban: Islam, Oil and the New Great Game in Central Asia* (I.B. Tauris, London, 2000) narrates the story of a dinner hosted by prime minister Benazir Bhutto in April 1989. Among her guests was Lt Gen. Hameed Gul, chief of ISI, the intelligence agency that spearheaded the Pakistan effort against the Soviet occupation. [Jihad, one should note, interrupting the story, was an eminently respectable word in the West at that time, and American senators were tripping over their tongues in order to be photographed with jihadis like Ahmed Shah Masood. Pakistani leaders like the dictator General Zia ul Haq would laugh that American politicians would put one toe across the border into Afghanistan, get themselves photographed, and rush off to their constituencies to pose as war veterans. I quote General Zia from one of the many conversations I had with him.] Rashid asked the most powerful general in 1989 whether he was not playing with fire by encouraging jihad. General Gul replied: 'We are fighting a jihad and this is the first Islamic international brigade in the modern era. The Communists have their international brigades, the West has NATO, why can't the Muslims unite and form a common front?' It was such thinking that later converted the jihad against the Soviet Union into a jihad with a larger mission.

America dismissed the threat from the aftermath as of little consequence. In a famous remark Zbigniew Brzezinski, national security adviser to Jimmy Carter, asked whether a few stirred up Muslims were more important than the defeat of the Soviet Union and the liberation of eastern Europe. Among those stirred up Muslims was Osama bin Laden, who first came to Peshawar in 1980 with the gushing support of Prince Turki bin Faisal, head of the Saudi intelligence agency, the Istakhbarat. In 1984, Osama's friend and perhaps mentor Abdullah Azam set up the Makhtab al Khidmat, or Centre for Service; from here originated the network that became Al Qaida.

In August 1996 Osama bin Laden issued his first call for jihad against the United States for, among other things, occupying Saudi Arabia, as 20,000 American troops remained on the soil of Arabia even after the war against Iraq was over. 'The walls of oppression and humiliation cannot be demolished except in a rain of bullets,' said that declaration.

In February 1998, Al Qaida and its associates issued a manifesto in the name of the 'The International Islamic Front for Jihad against Jews and Crusaders'. It said: 'For more than seven years the United States has been occupying the lands of Islam in the holiest of places, the Arabian peninsula, plundering its riches, dictating to its rulers, humiliating its people, terrorizing its neighbours, and turning its bases in the peninsula into a spearhead through which to fight the neighbouring Muslim peoples.'

The solution? 'The ruling to kill the Americans and their allies – civilian and military – is an individual duty for every Muslim who can do it in any country in which it is possible to.'

That call to jihad was issued from Afghanistan, but the jihad itself would not have been possible without the help it received, both individual and institutional, from Pakistan. Pakistan emerged from the most unusual circumstances, partitioned out of India in the last days of British rule, to become a homeland for Muslims. The passions of that birth still shape the politics of two powers, India and Pakistan, that are now nuclear. The past never leaves the present on the Indian subcontinent.

12

HISTORY AS ANGER,
JIHAD AS NON-VIOLENCE

They [Muslims] were not satisfied merely with looting, they destroyed temples, they demolished idols, they raped women. The
insult to other religions and the injury to humanity were unimaginable. Even when they became kings they could not liberate themselves from these loathsome desires. Even Akbar, who was famed
for his tolerance, was no better than notorious emperors like
Aurangzeb.

[Saratchandra Chattopadhyay, an eminent Bengali novelist,
in a speech in 1926]

A history of anger and a literature of revenge divided India and created
Pakistan.

On the evening of 12 January 2002 Pakistan's fourteenth head of state
and third general to take over in a coup, Pervez Musharraf, appeared on
television to make a much-awaited speech. The anticipation was justified.
President Musharraf, addressing his nation, his neighbourhood, and the
world, declared that Pakistan would no longer tolerate the extremists and
terrorists who had created a 'state within a state' in the country, become
a law unto themselves and a threat to the world. The time had come to
end their jihad. 'The extremist minority must realize,' he said, 'that Pakistan is not responsible for waging armed jihad in the world.'

'Sectarian terrorism has been going on for years,' President Musharraf
declared in a speech that was as courageous as candid. 'Everyone is fed up
of it. It is becoming unbearable. Our peace-loving people are keen to get
rid of the Kalashnikov and weapon culture. Everyone is sick of it . . . The day
of reckoning has come. Do we want Pakistan to become a theocratic state?'

'We are conscious,' he said,

> that we need to rid society of extremism and this is being done
> right from the beginning . . . Some extremists, who are engaged
> in protests, are people who try to monopolise and attempt to
> propagate their own brand of religion. They think as if others are
> not Muslims. These are the people who considered the Taliban to
> be a symbol of Islam and that the Taliban were bringing Islamic
> renaissance or were practising the purest form of Islam . . . I
> want to ask these extremists as to who was responsible for mis-
> leading thousands of Pakistanis to their massacre in Afghani-
> stan? . . . [Some] mosques are being misused for propagating and
> inciting hatred . . . I would like to inform you that a number of
> terrorist rings have been apprehended . . . The writ of the gov-
> ernment is being challenged. Pakistan has been made a soft state
> where the supremacy of law is questioned . . .

It could not have been easy for a President of Pakistan to make that
speech. President Musharraf could have kept quiet, but he was different
from his predecessors in that he was honest enough to admit that this
cancer had reached the bloodstream.

How did a homeland for Muslims become a homeland for Muslim
terrorists? Fundamentalists who could not capture power at the inception
of Pakistan gradually created a parallel state with two objectives: the indoctrination of young minds through those *medressas* that were under
their control, and the declaration of jihad against a succession of enemies:
India, Russia, the United States of America and, periodically, their own
government. Afghanistan under the Taliban became a formal ally of this
state within a state. More important and less obvious was the use they
made of one government or the other for their wars. Funds came, discreetly or in the name of a higher cause like religious education, from
Saudi Arabia; no one questioned where those funds went. There were
other security blankets. The jihad against the Soviet Union was of course
financed and armed by the West and most of the Muslim world, and
resources poured into that war are still visible in the Kalashnikov culture
that President Musharraf mentioned. The United States and Britain have
long distanced themselves from that jihad, but the parallel state of Pakistan continues the holy war against Russia through its support for Chechens.

The jihad against America came into its own in the 1990s and was not without its friends in the Pakistan and Saudi establishments. Washington's influence has made it impossible for a contrary voice to be heard after 11 September 2001, but it cannot prevent the contrary whisper.

The Pakistan government could always be counted upon to provide support to the jihad against India, for this was its declared undeclared war. Many extremist organizations cleverly exploited this sanction to serve a larger agenda. The jihad against India, widely supported by the people and the government, became the true sustenance of the state within the state, and also a cover for terrorists who were deployed for other wars. Pakistan's anger against India is larger than the problem over Kashmir, and needs to be fully understood. A terrorist cause can always find use for an argument, and India provided one. The roots of anger run deep.

The literature of revenge raged through the second half of nineteenth century, its apex in the most literate and political city of the country, Calcutta. Calcutta was the capital of the British Raj as well as the capital of Indian intellect. One powerful strain of thought dwelt on a single question: what had gone wrong with Hindus? How had they permitted centuries of Muslim rule in Delhi and Bengal, and then become the collaborative clerks and professionals of the British, the notorious 'Bengali *babu*'?

Who, or what, is the Bengali *babu,* asked a master of Bengali prose and fiction, and the most influential intellectual of that period, Bankimchandra Chattopadhyay (1838–94). His answer was devastating.

> Like [the god] Vishnu the *babu* will always lie on an eternal bed. Like Vishnu again, he will have ten incarnations: clerk, teacher, Brahmo, broker, doctor, lawyer, judge, landlord, newspaper editor and idler. Like Vishnu, in every incarnation he will destroy fearful demons. In his incarnation as a clerk, he will destroy his attendant, as a teacher he will destroy the student, as station master the ticketless traveller, as Brahmo the poor priest, as broker the English merchant, as doctor his patient, as lawyer his client, as judge the litigant, as landlord his tenants, as editor the innocent gentleman, as idler the fish in the pond . . . He who has one word in his mind, which becomes ten when he speaks, hundred when he writes and thousands when he quarrels is a *babu*. He whose strength is one-time in his hands, ten-times in his mouth, a hundred times behind the back and absent at the time of action is a *babu*. He whose deity is the Englishman, preceptor the

Brahmo preacher, scriptures the newspapers and pilgrimage the National Theatre is a *babu*. He who declares himself a Christian to missionaries, a Brahmo to Keshabchandra, a Hindu to his father and an atheist to the Brahman beggar is a *babu*. One who drinks water at home, alcohol at his friend's, receives abuse from the prostitute and kicks from his boss is a *babu*. He who hates oil when he bathes, his own fingers when he eats and his mother tongue when he speaks is indeed a *babu* . . . O King, the people whose virtues I have re- cited to you will come to believe that by chewing *pan* [betel], lying prone on the bed, making bilingual conversation and smoking to- bacco, they will reconquer India.

[This translation is from Partha Chatterjee's *The Nation and its Fragments: Colonial and Postcolonial Histories,* Oxford University Press, New Delhi, 1993.]

The mordant wit is brilliant; the pain of impotence palpable in the last sentence.

Some answers of the time verged on the fantastic. The first history of India printed in Bengali, *Rajabali,* appeared in 1808 and was written by Mrityunjay Vidyalankar, a Sanskrit teacher at the East India Company's Fort William College. He rationalized the defeat of the last Hindu emperor of Delhi, Prithviraj Chauhan, in 1162, with a comforting story. One of the two wives of Prithviraj's father was a demoness who forced her husband to eat human flesh. Frightened, the second wife ran away to her brother, where she gave birth to Prithviraj. When he grew up Prithviraj, in a form of Oedipal revenge-atonement, killed his father and fed his flesh to twenty one women. Patricide however always demands a price. That was why Prithviraj lost his kingdom to a demon, a 'Yavana'. Muslims, in this world- view, are the demons who came from foreign parts to rule India.

Bankim had no time for such fables. As he exclaimed in 1880 to fel- low-Bengalis at the start of a series of lectures: 'We have no history! We must have a history!' 'Even the Oriyas,' he lamented, 'have their his- tory . . .' (Oriyas, people of the neighbouring province, were looked down upon by the superior *babu*.) Bankim rejected history based upon the court records of Muslim princes and emperors because 'Anyone who uncritically accepts as history the testimony of these lying, Hindu-hating Mussalman zealots is not a Bengali'. (The Bengali Muslim did not quite fall into the purview of Bankim's Bengali nation.)

163

What Bankim wanted was an inspirational history that would resurrect Hindus made supine by continuous defeat. The British and Muslims, in his view, were both foreign invaders although the British were more civilized. Indian nationalism was therefore synonymous with Hindu nationalism. The finest articulation of this belief is in his best remembered ode, *Vande Mataram,* a hymn to the goddess Durga, who protects the Motherland in both her benign and destructive manifestations, nourishing it with her love and cleansing it of demons.

Bankim wanted a holy war as well, a Hindu national holy war. He urged it repeatedly in popular novels like *Anandmath*, a story about a conflict between ascetics of the Naga Dasnami sect and a Muslim *nawab* during a famine in 1770. Hindu peasants found their answer: 'Unless we throw these dirty bastards [Muslims] out, Hindus will be ruined . . . When shall we raze mosques to the ground and erect Radhamadhav temples in their place?' The refrain of this novel is 'Kill the low Muslims'. The historian Tanika Sarkar, in an illuminating essay (printed in *Making India Hindu*, Oxford University Press, New Delhi, 1996), from where I have taken the translation of the texts used here, writes: 'Perhaps the most significant way in which Bankim served as a bridge between nineteenth-century Hindu revivalism and the later, anti-Muslim, violent politics was by providing an immensely powerful visual image of communal violence and by giving it the status of an apocalyptic holy war. He stamped the image indelibly on the imagination of communal politics by fusing the impulse of community violence and revenge with the spectacle of a feminine body.' The image of a raped mother/motherland was exceptionally evocative.

Bankim's most powerful characters are women, for men had let the nation down and women preserved their original temper with inner steel. The Bengal Renaissance needed its Dark Ages, and found it in Muslim rule; it needed its Golden Past and found it in fragments, some real, some imagined. Bankim compared Bengalis to Athenians, for Bengalis had once conquered Sri Lanka and Indonesia. When Bankim visited such a glorious past, and then saw the 'effeminate' *babu* around him, satire was his only consolation. Simple 'effeminacy' was no explanation; Marathas and Sikhs, who were indigenous, had defeated the British in their time. Hindus had lost their desire for liberty, he worried. Power was not just brute force; it came also from courage, enterprise, solidarity, persistence, and attitude. Europeans had power because they worshipped power. Hindus had become so captivated by spirituality that they had lost their taste for the practical.

This was doubly unfortunate because the solution lay in a true understanding of Hinduism, which, he argued, was the greatest of all religions for it was both practical and philosophical, and shorn of all hypocrisy.

Lord Krishna, central figure of the epic *Mahabharata,* hated war but understood the need for it, and so when he went to war he became invincible. Bankim writes: 'Krishna is the true ideal for man. Krishna himself was householder, diplomat, warrior, lawgiver, saint and preacher; as such, he represents a complete human ideal for all . . .' One had to return to this ideal by clearing the haze of orthodoxy and superstition that had overtaken Hinduism. Intellect remained the finest virtue of the Bengali, but perhaps the worship of intellect had made the Bengali neglect his physique, making him effete. This permitted raw brutes like Muslims to conquer Hindus, destroy temples and – this motif was constantly stressed – rape Hindu women.

Such contempt for Muslims was lucidly expressed by another of Bengal's popular novelists, whose books have been turned into films and whose fiction is part of school texts. Saratchandra Chattopadhyay discussed the *Bartaman Hindu-Mussalman Samasya* (The Present Hindu-Muslim Problem) in a speech to the Bengal Provincial Conference in 1926, later printed in *Hindu Sangha.* Its premise was that Hindu-Muslim unity, particularly of the kind fostered by Mahatma Gandhi, was a dangerous illusion as 'Battles for a false cause can never be won'. The two communities had irreconcilable political aspirations, and Muslims were hypocritical when they sought the support of Hindus for their own ends. 'The truth is that if Muslims ever say they want to unite with Hindus, there is no greater hoax. The Muslims came to India to plunder it, not to establish a kingdom.'

Facts were irrelevant to such analysis; prejudice never too far away. 'They [Muslims] were not satisfied merely with looting, they destroyed temples, they demolished idols, they raped women. The insult to other religions and the injury to humanity were unimaginable. Even when they became kings they could not liberate themselves from these loathsome desires. Even Akbar, who was famed for his tolerance, was no better than notorious emperors like Aurangzeb.' The destruction of temples was on par with rape of women as a constant of this dialectic.

Muslims would never attain the culture that Hindus possessed:

> But if the essence of learning is width of the mind and culture of
> the heart, then there is no comparison between the two communi-
> ties . . . Unity can only be realized among equals . . . A thousand

years has not been enough time, nor will another millennium suffice . . . 'Hindu-Muslim unity' is a bombastic phrase . . . We must sacrifice this illusion. It is useless for us to try to shame Bengali Muslims by saying that seven generations ago they were Hindus, therefore they are related to us by blood: fratricide is a sin, so show little pity.

Lack of culture made Muslims barbaric, brutal, fanatic, and rapist. There was no difference between the poor and the rich Muslim, both were barbaric, just as high culture was shared by all Hindus, irrespective of their class or wealth. Cruelty was synonymous with Islam: 'All that we [the passive Hindu] do is compile lists of all instances of their cruelty, oppressiveness and hostility towards us and all we ever say is this: "You have killed us, you have broken our idols and kidnapped our women. In this you have been very unjust, and have caused us great pain. We cannot continue to live like this." Do we ever say more than this, or do more than this?'

He continued: 'Hindustan is the homeland of the Hindus. Therefore it is the duty of the Hindus alone to free this nation from the chains of servitude. Muslims look towards Turkey and Arabia, their hearts are not in India.' Hindu-Muslim unity could never promise freedom, as Gandhi argued. 'I ask you this – can our country be freed by fraud? When Hindus come forward and vow to free their country, then it will matter little whether a few dozen Muslims lend their support or not.'

There were some curious examples offered in support of this position. 'When America fought for her independence, the majority of her people supported the British. How many Irish people supported the Irish freedom movement? The Bolshevik government that is in power in Russia has not the support of even one per cent of the people.'

The past was reshaped to fit convictions. The image of Siraj ud Daula, the Muslim *nawab* defeated by Clive, for instance, was bounced around. While the secular-nationalist school ignored Siraj's less savoury traits and recreated the battle of Plassey as a patriotic war against the British, Hindu-nationalist historians welcomed the outcome as the moment of Hindu liberation from Muslim rule. Jadunath Sarkar describes this dawn (*The History of Bengal Vol 2. The Muslim Period, 1200-1757*, Dacca, 1948):

On 23rd June, 1757, the middle ages of India ended and her modern age began. When Clive struck at the *nawab* . . . the

country's administration had become hopelessly dishonest and in-
efficient, and the mass of people had been reduced to the deepest
poverty, ignorance and moral degradation under a small, selfish,
proud and unworthy ruling class. Imbecile lechers filled the
throne . . . the women were even worse than the men. Sadists
like Siraj and Miran made even their highest subjects live in constant terror. The army was rotten and honey-combed with treason.
The purity of domestic life was threatened by the debauchery fashionable in the Court and the aristocracy and the sensual literature
that grew up under such patrons.

So on it went. You have to dislike Muslims with some seriousness to write
with such vehemence. Jadunath Sarkar wrote that India began an economic recovery under the British, even while other Indians, like Jawaharlal
Nehru in *Discovery of India* (Calcutta, Signet, 1946) noted that Siraj's
commander-in-chief at Plassey was a Hindu, and categorized the land
revenue policies of the British as 'pure loot' and 'outright plunder', leading directly to the famine of 1770 that killed 'over a third of the population of Bengal and Bihar'. Sarkar was honoured with a knighthood.

Jaya Chaterjee's brilliant work *Bengal Divided, Hindu Communalism
and Partition (1932–47)* (Cambridge University Press, 1996) places such
history in its contemporary political context:

In writing of the Renaissance in this way, Jadunath Sarkar did not
merely celebrate British rule, or simplify a complex history. He
denied Muslims a place in the history of modern Bengal. The
Muslims, his epilogue suggests, had had their 'period' (from 1200
to 1757), during which time they brought upon Bengal nothing
but bloody and unrelieved barbarism and tyranny. In the modern
age, the age of culture and enlightenment, they had no place.
Modern Bengal was the creation of the Hindu *bhadralok* (gentry).
They had made Bengal what it was – albeit with the help of 'light'
'borrowed' from the British – the centre of India's civilisation. By
rights, therefore, Bengal belonged to them. The Renaissance, from
this viewpoint, became a symbol not only of a culture that was
bhadralok, but also of a Hindu Bengal from which Muslims were
excluded. It was construction that also denied the Muslims any
title to Bengali nationality.

The Indian National Congress, formed in 1885, sought to channelize the sway of political demand and supply through a political platform that was larger than any specific community. The response of the Raj was to gravitate around politicized communities.

One consequence was the formation of the All India Muslim League on 30 December 1906 in Dhaka. Its avowed objective was to promote 'loyalty' to the British and 'advance the political rights and interests of the Mussalmans of India' through separate electorates. There was one prominent Muslim, noted the Aga Khan, the first President of the League, in a letter to the British official wielding the baton, Dunlop Smith, who 'came out in bitter hostility toward all that I and my friends had done and were trying to do . . . He said our principle of separate electorates was dividing the nation against itself.' That prominent Muslim was a thirty year-old lawyer called Mohammad Ali Jinnah.

The Muslim League was rewarded in the Morley-Minto reforms of 1909, which granted Muslims separate electorates. Hindu-Muslim tensions had already been provoked by the partition of the huge and unwieldy province of Bengal by Lord Curzon on 16 October 1905. Bengal then included Bihar and Orissa, and had a population of some 79 million. A good administrative case could have been made for cutting Bengal down to size, but Muslims were sold a pup. They were told by senior government officials that they were being freed from Hindu domination as they would have a clear majority in the new province of East Bengal, with 18 million Muslims and 12 million Hindus. Strong passions, backed by colourful oratory, swept through influential sections of the Hindu community, and even caused a near-split in the Congress. Lord Curzon, who had engineered this division, shrugged that Bengalis like to 'howl until a thing is settled and then they accept it' but the anguish of this howl unnerved his successors. Bengal was reunited in 1911, this time leaving loyal Muslim leaders wondering about the value of their loyalty.

The bridge that Muslim leaders like Sir Sayyid Ahmad had built to the British began to crumble. In 1910 Jinnah organized a unity conference in Allahabad following which the League passed a resolution favouring greater cooperation with the Congress. The Congress and the League began to hold their sessions in the same city so that there could be crossover participation. In Lucknow in December 1916 they signed a 'pact'. Congress accepted separate Muslim electorates, and Muslims in turn relinquished their right to vote in both separate as well as general constituencies. It was a dramatic breakthrough. It also came at a swivel point, when the world, as it does periodically, had changed.

On 8 May 1901, a walrus-moustached Englishman who had already made one fortune out of Australia's goldfields but not yet exhausted his energies, received a document from the Shah of Iran for twenty thousand pounds sterling in cash, giving him exclusive rights to look for, find, and sell natural gas, asphalt, and petroleum from anywhere in the Persian empire. William Knox d'Arcy thereby bought the first concession of the region. By 1904 his investment began to look foolish. In Britain however, First Sea Lord Admiral Sir John Fisher had decided to convert the navy's fuel from coal to oil, and his only assured supplies were from a small oil field in Borneo and a larger one in Burma. He persuaded his government to treat oil as a defence priority and place more funds in the hands of d'Arcy. The government asked the Burmah Oil Company to become d'Arcy's partner.

A little before dawn on 26 May 1908, near the very small town of Masjid as Suleyman (The Mosque of Suleyman) a rig began to tremble. D'Arcy cashed in some nine hundred thousand pounds worth of Burmah shares. In 1911 and 1913, London obtained commitments from Bahrain and Kuwait that no concessions would be given without British assent. By 1914, with war ahead, the British government had purchased 51 per cent of Burmah Oil Company to ensure oil to the navy at a guaranteed price. Deserts suddenly became worth a sea-power's attention.

Turkey had not been indifferent to its troubles as the Caliphate slipped from senility into terminal decline. The 1890s seethed with insurrection. A Committee of Union and Progress was formed in Salonica by, among others, Mustafa Kemal. The Anglo-Russian entente of June 1908 unhinged Turkey's foreign policy, which had traditionally played off the two powers. In July some army officers took to the hills. A desperate Sultan Abdulhamid announced censorship and elections to Parliament in autumn. It did not save him. In 1909 a triumvirate of Enver, Talaat, and Jemal Pasha deposed the Sultan; on 29 April he was packed off by train to Salonica at 2.45 in the morning, and his first eunuch hanged on the Galata bridge. His brother Reshad, who wrote poetry and supported the Young Turks, was placed on the throne. High on the agenda of the new government was improving relations with the Arabs; there was even talk of a dual Turk-Arab monarchy modelled on the Austro-Hungarian empire.

One of the last decisions taken by Abdulhamid was to make Huseyn ibn Ali, descendant of the Prophet through his daughter Fatima, emir of Mecca in 1908. There was trouble in Arabia from the young Abdul Aziz bin Saud, descendant of the family that had given the Wahhabis their brief phase of glory. What Huseyn ibn Ali did not know was that ibn Saud was in touch with the British through William Henry Irvine Shakespear (there was no 'e' at the end), a former officer of the Bengal Lancers. Ibn Saud would describe Shakespear as the greatest European he had known, but then he did not know too many. London was initially cool to such mutual admiration, but Shakespear's moment came in 1914.

Turkey joined her neighbours, Austria, Hungary and Germany, against Britain, France, and Russia. In January 1915 Shakespear 'recognized' ibn Saud as the independent ruler of Nejd, and offered him Britain's protection. The green Wahhabi banner fluttered on behalf of the Union Jack. Shakespear died in the course of their first joint raid, a failure, but ibn Saud lived to fight another day. In June 1916 His Majesty's Government approved the supply of 1,000 Mausers, 200,000 rounds of ammunition, and a £20,000 loan.

By 1918 Turkey's jihad had failed. The Muslims of India, apprehensive since the beginning of the First World War, were alarmed at the 'annihilation of the military power of Islam in the world' and were determined to do something about it, even if they did not know precisely what. Writing to Lord Chelmsford on 6 September 1916, the then secretary of state for India, Austen Chamberlain, noted: 'The Muslim community of India is, I think, the only community under the British flag which habitually prays for a foreign sovereign, and does not offer prayers for the King.' The foreign sovereign was the Caliph. The British tried to dampen pan-Islamic sentiment by making a distinction between the Caliph and the Ottoman government, and assuring Muslims that Mecca and Medina would never be attacked, nor would there be any interruption in the pilgrimage. That was scant comfort. While Muslims were groping for an effective response to the Christian conquest of their holy places, Mohandas Karamchand Gandhi entered their lives.

It was always difficult to maintain Gandhi in poverty; later, as the poetess Sarojini Naidu trenchantly observed, it also became expensive. When Mohandas Karamchand Gandhi left Cape Town for London on 18 July 1914 by third class passage, the company took care to accord him VIP status. The only real privilege that the Mahatma wanted was a diet of nuts and fruit. He had progressed from vegetarianism and become a nutarian.

Gandhi took a circuitous route to India because he wanted to call on his ailing mentor Gopal Krishna Gokhale, then convalescing in Europe. Two days before he reached England on 4 August, war was declared. Indian notables in London gave the hero of the South African struggle a handsome welcome. On 8 August, Gandhi was felicitated at Cecil Hotel. The most notable of those present was a fellow Gujarati, lawyer and politician, Mohammad Ali Jinnah. Among those who regretted their inability to come due to 'pressing engagements' were Lord Curzon, Keir Hardie, Ramsay MacDonald, and Lord Crewe, the secretary of state for India. Jinnah was effusive about Gandhi. Responding, Gandhi advised the Indian leadership to 'think imperially in the best sense of the word and do their duty'. He offered to mobilize Indians for a medical service unit on the European battlefield.

Lord Crewe was sceptical, and perhaps wisely. Long before this medical unit reached the killing fields of France, it had begun a struggle against the British. Gandhi protested that British students had been made section leaders over adult Indians. It required correspondence and a conference to arrange a truce. Then Gandhi caught pleurisy during open-air training in the autumn chill. The government had no appetite for a war casualty of this kind, particularly as Gandhi refused to listen to his doctor, Jivraj Mehta, and eat better food. His diet, at the time, was groundnuts, bananas (ripe and unripe), lemon, tomatoes, grapes, and, when in a mood for luxury, olive oil. The government pleaded with him to leave for India. If there was still a war in progress by the time he recovered, the Empire would doubtless find ways in which Gandhi could serve.

Gokhale offered some sharp advice. When in India, he told Gandhi, keep your eyes open and mouth shut for one year. On 19 December Gandhi left for Bombay, travelling second class. His ship was allowed to berth at Apollo Bunder in Bombay on 9 January 1915, an honour reserved for royalty, viceroys, and famous sons of the land.

The first important thing that Gandhi did in India was to change his clothes. He donned a dhoti, Kathiawadi shirt and turban, all products of Indian mills. Clothes make the Mahatma.

The second important thing he did was to irritate Jinnah. As in London, Jinnah was selected to deliver the welcome address at a reception for Gandhi, this time by Gujarati businessmen. Gandhi interrupted him in mid-eloquence to say that as everyone present was a Gujarati, why was Jinnah speaking in English? Thirty-two years later Jinnah would create a nation whose official language was Urdu without knowing a word of Urdu.

On 3 June 1915 two Indians were honoured on the King's birthday list. Rabindranath Tagore was knighted and Gandhi received the Kaiser-e-Hind medal. In December, Gandhi attended the Lucknow session of the Congress, where Jinnah was the star. A Congress delegate from Champaran, in Bihar, Rajkumar Shukla, pleaded with Gandhi to go back with him to 'wash away the stain of indigo'. Gandhi, who had never heard of Champaran, and barely of indigo, was moved sufficiently by Shukla's persistence and agreed to go to Champaran for 'a day or two'.

Gandhi reached Patna, the capital of Bihar, by train from Calcutta on the morning of 9 April 1917. He first went to the home of an eminent lawyer, Rajendra Prasad. The host, blissfully unaware of the honour, was on holiday at the seaside. A servant took one look at Shukla, a second at Gandhi, and turned them out. Gandhi remembered a friend of his student days in London from Patna, Mazharul Haq. A surprised Haq made friend Gandhi comfortable.

He began his enquiry into the state of indigo workers. On 13 April, he was ordered to leave. Gandhi refused. On 16 April he clambered atop an elephant in the face of a strong, dust-laden west wind at nine in the morning for the last lap into Champaran. At noon a police sub-inspector arrived to escort him to the collector. They left for Motihari by bullock cart, but on the way Gandhi was served a formal order to leave the district. He defied it. He was threatened with arrest under section 188 of the Indian Penal Code.

Thousands of peasants crowded at the district magistrate's court on 18 April. Glass panes and doors broke under pressure; armed police were summoned to keep the people out. The government lawyer requested the magistrate to postpone the case. Gandhi intervened to ask why. He wanted to plead guilty: 'As a law-abiding citizen my first instinct would be, as it was, to obey the order served upon me. But I would not do so without doing violence to my sense of duty to those for whom I came . . . I have disregarded the order served upon me not for want of respect for lawful authority, but in obedience to the higher law of our being, the voice of conscience.'

The reluctant magistrate fudged, anxious for an opportunity to release Gandhi. The Mahatma seemed equally determined to be condemned. 'I do not wish to waste the time of the court and I plead guilty,' he said. Leave the district now, do not return, and the case will be withdrawn pleaded the magistrate. Gandhi replied that he would make Champaran his home after his prison sentence. The magistrate hesitated. An order would be passed at three. At three, he postponed a decision a second time. On 20 April the magistrate informed Gandhi that the lieutenant-governor of the province had ordered that the case be withdrawn.

Gandhi had raised the stakes; and the government had blinked. A course was set for the next three decades. Gandhi had displayed for the first time the weapons he would use against the British empire: a contagious fearlessness; an unrelenting conscience; and non-violence. He said that at Champaran he had forged a weapon 'by which India could be made free'.

On 6 February 1919 the government of India introduced two bills in the Imperial Legislative Council on the recommendations of a committee chaired by Justice Rowlatt. The second was called the Anarchical and Revolutionary Crimes Act of 1919, and created special courts for quick trial, without leave to appeal, and with the power to consider evidence thus far inadmissible under the Indian Evidence Act. On 18 March 1919 it became law. Gandhi announced civil disobedience in protest. He also decided to close down India for a day, on 6 April. This new weapon was called a hartal, a Hindi word that has become part of the English lexicon.

The lieutenant-governor of Punjab, Sir Michael O'Dwyer, was determined to prevent people from becoming what he called 'Congress-minded' and on 10 April ordered the internment of two local leaders, a Hindu and a Muslim, Satyapal and Dr Saifuddin Kitchlew under the Defence of India Act. A protest procession in Amritsar was stopped at a railway crossing; the police opened fire, and killed a number of Punjabis. Anger led to violence, and half a dozen English bank officers were killed in their offices, buildings were burnt and telegraphs lines cut. On 11 April their funeral passed off quietly. That evening, Brigadier General R.E.H. Dyer arrived in the city.

The following day arrests began. All gatherings were banned. On 12 April, agitators announced that they would hold a public meeting at 4.30 p.m. at Jallianwala Bagh, an open area about the size of Trafalgar Square, and enclosed almost entirely by walls. No effort was made to prevent the meeting from taking place in the midst of a fairground, milling with non-political families. Brigadier General Dyer reached after it began. No warning was given. He ordered his troops to fire, at a range of a hundred yards until the ammunition was exhausted: 1,650 rounds hit the trapped, dense crowd in ten minutes, killing three hundred seventy nine men and women, and wounding a further two hundred. Brigadier General Dyer marched his men back the way they had come. He had done his duty, he said later. On 15 April the government cordoned Punjab with censorship and martial law.

Gandhi, unaware of the Punjab details, but worried about violence, suspended the agitation against the Rowlatt bills. He was not allowed to visit Punjab, but stories seeped through. Tagore renounced his knighthood on 30 May, calling the Jallianwala incident a savagery 'without parallel in the history of civilized governments, barring some conspicuous exceptions, recent or remote'.

The year 1919 was a nodal point in the young nationalist movement when anger for different reasons forged a common purpose between Hindus and Muslims. Gandhi himself could not have asked for more.

Muslims were livid that for the first time in history the holy places were controlled by a Christian authority. On 24 November 1919 an All-India *Khilafat* (or Caliphate) Conference was held in Delhi to discuss the 'peace celebrations' of the British at the end of the great war. The conference became a display of Hindu-Muslim fraternity. Gandhi presided and spoke in Urdu. His first sentences said it all:

> It ought not to appear strange for the Hindus to be on the same platform as the Muslims in a matter that specially and solely affects the Muslims. After all, the test of friendship is true assistance in adversity and whatever we are, Hindus, Parsis, Christians or Jews, if we wish to live as one nation, surely the interest of any of us must be the interest of all . . . We talk of Hindu-Muslim unity. It would be an empty phrase if the Hindus hold aloof from the Muslims when their vital interests were at stake.

Excited Muslim leaders responded by promising to give up beef (cow slaughter was a troublesome problem in a Hindu-majority country), but Gandhi insisted that Hindu cooperation would be unconditional: 'Conditional assistance is like adulterated cement which does not bind.' Maulana Abdul Bari, a regular fire-breather in the Muslim cause, responded: 'Muslim honour would be at stake if they forgot the cooperation of the Hindus. I for my part say that we should stop cow-killing, irrespective of their cooperation, because we are children of the same soil.' The excitable Maulana Hasrat Mohani urged Gandhi to do something dramatic against the British, 'give us something quicker, and speedier' to remove the British from India. Gandhi could not think of an appropriate word in Urdu or Hindi for a 'quicker, speedier' concept that had begun to occur to him. He fell back upon English: Non-cooperation.

In January 1920 an élite assemblage of Hindu and Muslim leaders called on Lord Chelmsford. The viceroy did a foxtrot around the rebels; he offered to finance a visit to London. Never averse to foreign travel, Maulana Mohammed Ali accepted the onerous responsibility of visiting London. On 17 March Lloyd George stripped the Ali deputation of all illusions. Turkey would be shorn of her empire; the victorious European powers would control the holy places. The response in India was instant. March 19 was declared a day of national mourning.

'A loyalty that sells its soul is worth nothing.' These nine words formed the heart of the resolution moved by Gandhi on 19 March 1920 at the *Khilafat* Committee meeting in Bombay. Indians would not sell their soul to the British. Gandhi insisted on non-violence, but graciously pointed out that he would not come in the way of a violent jihad by the Muslims if the non-violence failed. He may have been buying Muslim loyalty for the moment, but that speech in Bombay had more omens than he knew. The Muslim mind could not understand the sanctity of non-violence; there was no precedence for a non-violent jihad for the liberation of the holy places. Muslims however lent their full support to Gandhi's strategy.

On 1 August 1920, Gandhi returned his Kaisar-e-Hind gold medal to Lord Chelmsford, 'not without a pang,' in protest against the wrongs done to 'my Mussalman countrymen'. The treaty of Sevres was signed on 10 August: the straits were handed over to an international commission, eastern Anatolia divided between Armenia and Kurdistan, and Greece was given Izmir and eastern Thrace. The Caliph described it as Turkey's death blow. Indian Muslims felt his pain.

The Congress approved of Gandhi's programme at a special session in Calcutta between 4 and 9 September by a narrow margin of 144 to 132, reflecting the growing Hindu doubts about a struggle to liberate India in the name of the Caliph. Moving the resolution, Gandhi said that he was neither a saint nor a dictator, just a practical politician. All the Muslims at that Congress session supported Gandhi. Only one opposed him, because he hated the idea of mixing religion with politics. That was Jinnah. Rabindranath Tagore was sceptical about the power of such sweeping non-cooperation, but the people rose against British rule as in a dream. Peasants were convinced that 'Gandhi Raj' was going to replace the British Raj in a year's time. Anger at their misery demonstrated itself in sundry forms. In many areas peasants stopped payment of rent to landlords because rent was incompatible with their Gandhi Raj. The Mahatma discouraged such diversions, but some of his socialist disciples saw nothing very wrong in such manifestation of economic discontent. Not everyone agreed that if only Indians spun and Gandhi weaved they would become free.

In Kerala, a tenants-rights agitation had begun from 1916 among the restive Moplahs, a Muslim community, against largely Hindu landlords. Some *Khilafat* leaders, relieved at a jihad that had become violent, gave this a religious twist. They promised a glorious Muslim state upon the success of their agitation. On 29 August 1921 the police raided a mosque in Tirurangadi to search for arms. Rebellion ensued. Police stations, government offices, and landlords' homes were attacked. '*Khilafat* Republics' were set up by some Muslims and Lord Reading, now Viceroy, told London that it was actual war. It however became more a war against Hindus than the British. Hundreds of Hindus were killed and some forcibly converted. Government repression was severe: 2,337 rebels were killed and 45,404 taken prisoners. On 20 November, in an Indian 'Black Hole' incident, sixty six bodies of Moplah prisoners were found in a railway wagon, asphyxiated.

The newspapers on the morning of 8 February 1922 had another story to tell. On the fifth, a procession was taken out in a village called Chauri Chaura in Gorakhpur district of United Provinces. The constables on duty had taunted some stragglers. The police beat up their leader, Bhagwan Ahir, and opened fire on protestors, who torched the police station. Twenty-two constables were burnt alive.

Gandhi suspended the campaign nationwide. Satan, he said, had taken over. Jawaharlal Nehru and other Congress leaders in detention, young and old, who had no private communication with Satan, could not believe what they were hearing. Later explanations that Gandhi offered were not as irrational, but neither were they convincing. The British, who had not dared to arrest Gandhi, picked him up on 10 March and sentenced him to six years in prison.

Suddenly, as if some strange light had been switched off, India returned to slumber. Not a soul protested when Gandhi was jailed. There was never again such unity in a shared cause between Hindus and Muslims. From that point on, they began to wander in different directions.

About fifteen years later, Muslims rediscovered a leader they had rejected when under Gandhi's spell, Jinnah.

13

ISLAM IN DANGER ZONE

The Muslim League has given you a goal which in my judgment is
going to lead you to the promised land where we shall establish
our Pakistan. People may say what they like and talk as they like.
Of course he who laughs last, laughs best.

[Jinnah in a speech to the All India Muslim Students' Federation
on 26 December 1941]

How did a non-practicing, chain-smoking Muslim lawyer, who liked a
drink, barely knew the basics of Islam, could speak no language other
than English, preferred to dress in an immaculate suit, almost settled
down in England, snubbed *mullahs* for dreaming of an Islamic state,
abhorred Gandhi for his hymn-chanting politics, and dreamt of becoming
an Indian Ataturk, single-handedly create Pakistan? Pakistan was meant to
be a solution to the problems between Hindus and Muslims. Why did
India and Pakistan sink into such bitter hatred, and start a war that became
a school for terrorism?

Mohammad Ali Jinnah was born nine weeks before his birthday. He
came into the world on 20 October 1875 as Mohammad Ali Jinnahbhai.
After his first encounter with the western world, at the élitist Christian
Mission High School, Christmas seemed a better birthday and so he
amended the date to 25 December 1875. His name also sounded too
native, so he chopped off the *bhai* suffix. When he was called to the bar
at Lincoln's Inn in London in 1893 he took his degree as Jinnah.

His three great interests as a student in London were law, which he
studied; theatre, which he frequented; and politics, which he fancied. Jinnah
was superb in whatever he chose to do. Those who underestimated his

sense of theatre, or the power of his set-piece speeches, or his knowledge of the right moment to intervene, did so at their peril.

His most useful contact in London was the great Zoroastrian business-man-scholar Dadabhai Naoroji, whose pioneering study, *Poverty and un-British Rule in India* became the basis of the nationalist critique after it was published in London in 1901. Dadabhai was the first Indian to be elected to the House of Commons, as a Liberal from Central Finsbury in 1902. He thanked an English education for his success and was always helpful to Indian students in London. Jinnah worked as his secretary for a while. The prevailing image of Dadabhai in India is of an old man, because he was over 80 when he came to Calcutta to preside over the 1906 Congress session. Jinnah helped draft the presidential address.

By 30, Jinnah was already among the élite in the growing national movement. His political line was clear and radical. He became a sharp critic of the pro-British Sir Sayyid Ahmad who had already divided India into two nations in his speeches. Conviction took precedence over popu-larity. He opposed the partition of Bengal in 1905 and attacked Curzon for dividing Hindus and Muslims with a stroke of the viceregal pen. Jinnah refused to become a member of the All-India Muslim League, founded on 31 December 1906 in Dhaka. He warned Muslims not to fall prey to the British game of 'divide and rule' and called the League's demand for separate electorates poisonous. His career, at the bar and in public life, flourished. In 1910 he became the first non-official in the Viceroy's Ex-ecutive Council and stoutly defended Gandhi, then in South Africa, when Lord Minto censured the latter as seditious. Some hardline Muslim Leagu-ers like Maulana Hasrat Mohani became so antagonistic to Jinnah that they labelled him a Hindu agent, and there was little more abusive in their political lexicon.

Understandably, the early Jinnah was much admired in Congress circles: the poetess Sarojini Naidu even found his humour as gay and winning as a child's, his intuition as tender as woman's, and the man himself rational, practical, and splendidly idealistic.

The low point of Jinnah's career coincided with the rise of Gandhi. The confrontation between their different roads to a similar goal came at the Nagpur Congress session in 1919. Jinnah, lawyer and constitutionalist, had distanced himself from both the theme and the structure of the movement demanding restoration of Mecca and Medina to the Ottoman Caliph. He rejected pseudo-religious mass hysteria, and could not quite comprehend why the holy places should become less holy under British administration. Not a very good Muslim in his personal life, he did not relate to the horror felt by other Muslims at the prospect of Christian sovereignty over Mecca and Medina. The community did not forget what Jinnah did not know, that the Prophet Muhammad himself had warned that there should never be two religions in Arabia.

Gandhi was not interested in the Prophet's injunctions either, but the politician in him seized the chance to enter Muslim affections. The Muslims at the Nagpur session of the Congress in 1919 cheered the man who worshipped Ram rather than Allah. Jinnah was heckled. The more aggressive of the Ali brothers, Shaukat, threatened to lynch him. Jinnah stood his ground. He warned Gandhi about the dangers of mixing religion with politics and walked out of the Congress. He never returned.

Politics shifted to constitutional methods after Gandhi's abrupt failure in 1922. A section of the Congress, led by Motilal Nehru, even participated in the elections of 1923. Jinnah was his usual rapier self in the Central Legislative Assembly. The story of his exchange with finance member Sir Basil Blackett is oft-repeated. During a debate in January 1925, Jinnah accused Sir Basil of proposing a budget that was more helpful to Britain than to India. Sir Basil denied the accusation. Jinnah told him to repeat the denial with hand on heart. When the finance member did so, Jinnah turned to the Speaker: 'In that case I submit, Sir, that the Hon'ble finance member has no heart.'

The only memorable thing that Gandhi did in the rest of the 1920s was to publish a patchy autobiography about some sensational experiments he had conducted with truth. Readers got a prismatic view of his highly unusual sex life. A renewed effort to arrange a Hindu-Muslim agreement on constitutional reform failed in 1927; all it achieved was a split in the League, if that can be described as an achievement. An effort by the government to push forward a draft constitution through the Simon Commission is remembered now only for the boycott it provoked. In 1928 the Congress made its own effort to draft a constitution which failed amid accusations of ambivalence.

On 19 June 1929 Jinnah wrote to the new Labour Prime Minister Ramsay MacDonald urging a round table conference. The Viceroy, Lord Irwin, accepted the proposal on 31 October, but the Congress placed a cart before this horse. India would have to be given dominion status first. At the end of the year the Congress upped its demand to full independence. Jinnah thought that Gandhi was unsuited to modern times, and asked Heaven to help Mr Gandhi. He was always particular about using 'Mr' when addressing Congress leaders. Fifty-eight delegates were invited to the first round table conference, inaugurated by King George V on 12 November 1930. Gandhi called the meeting worthless without the Congress.

Ten weeks of confabulation later, it was clearly not worth much. Jinnah gave up. He bought a mansion in Hampstead, opened chambers at King's Bench, settled down in London with his doting sister Fatima and daughter Dina, got a poodle as a pet, a chauffeured Bentley as a convenience, and began practice before the Privy Council. (His wife Ruttie, a Parsi, married young and died young. The only time Jinnah cried in public was at her death although they were already estranged.)

In London, Jinnah discovered Mustafa Kemal Ataturk through a book. He picked up *Grey Wolf: An Intimate Study of a Dictator* by H.C. Armstrong and became a fan of the Turk who first saved and then reformed his country. Jinnah told his sister that if he ever got as much power as Ataturk he would westernize Indian Muslims.

The second round table conference, from 7 September 1931, promised far more than it delivered. Gandhi's participation heightened expectations, but he used this London visit principally to raise the profile of India's independence movement with the British people. Gandhi mingled with the working class and became a media star; a veritable loincloth in winter. The half-naked *fakir* called on a double-breasted King. King George V remarked that his visitor did not seem to have enough clothes; Gandhi responded that the King wore enough for both of them.

Negotiations at the round table conference got sucked into the same communal mire as before. As the Aga Khan remarked in his memoirs, the hair-splitting got so fine that it became unreal. Jinnah kept largely silent. This was interpreted as either indifference or weakness. Jinnah got a shock when he was not invited to the third round table conference in November-December 1932. His ego needed repair; it could only heal in India. One glimmer of light came from Bombay where, in his absence, voters of his reserved-Muslim constituency had elected him unopposed to the Central Legislative Assembly. In January 1935 he sailed for Bombay to serve his voters. It was a journey as significant as that Gandhi had made in January exactly twenty years earlier, in 1915.

Jinnah returned with a vengeance. His opportunity lay in the turmoil created by British efforts towards a new constitution for India, a process that began with the Simon Commission and culminated in the Government of India Act of 1935. While the British were in no mood to share power in Delhi, they permitted responsible government in the provinces with a much larger electorate (there were 30 million voters in 1937, as against six and a half before).

Decisions punctuated this process. Ramsay MacDonald announced an appropriately named Communal Award in 1932. Hoping to spread representative government to the provinces, it allocated seats in their legislatures according to the perceived 'importance' (as distinct from demographic strength) of different communities. The electorate was separated and the system rigged to ensure a balance that suited the empire. In Bengal, for instance, Europeans got 25 seats out of 250 although they constituted 1 per cent of the population. Hindus were allotted eighty seats (seventy for upper castes and ten for untouchables) when they constituted 44 per cent of the population according to the 1931 census. Muslims were allotted a hundred and nineteen seats (including two for women), and they too were under-represented as they constituted 54 per cent of Bengal's population.

However, the Hindu élite's reaction revolved around a single fact: Muslim seats outnumbered Hindu seats by a large margin when in the previous Bengal Council Hindus had forty six seats against thirty nine for Muslims. Their worst fear was a Bengal ruled by a Muslim majority.

On one side there was lament at the 'reversal' of Plassey. The British, who had saved Bengali Hindus from barbaric Muslims by Clive's victory at Plassey, were now handing power back to the barbarians. B.C. Chatterjee, the leader of the Hindu Sabha, called it a betrayal. More moderate voices wanted special consideration for the high state of Bengali Hindu culture. The maharaja of Burdwan presented a petition, signed by the most respectable names in Calcutta, arguing that 'The Hindus of Bengal, though numerically a minority, are overwhelmingly superior culturally, constituting as much as 64 per cent of the literate population . . .' Congress leaders either supported this mood or prevaricated.

Muslim withdrawal symptoms from the Congress began after the sudden abortion of the *Khilafat* struggle. The reaction and rhetoric of 1932 seemed to confirm every Muslim suspicion that the Congress in Bengal was not secular, but a thinly-veiled Hindu party. The most popular Muslim leader of the time, whose eventual tilt towards Jinnah would prove decisive, A.K. Fazlul Haq, told the *Statesman* on 12 October 1933: 'I am prepared to be hanged if I cannot demonstrate to the satisfaction of any judge that the

Hindus of Bengal constitute the very personification of communalism based on intense selfishness.' Jinnah began to pick up the various strands of Muslim anxiety scattered across the huge subcontinent and knit them into a single canvas. His first test came in the elections of 1937. He failed. Muslim League candidates did particularly badly in the large Muslim-majority provinces of Bengal, Punjab, Sind, and the Frontier. The Congress triumphed, winning seven hundred and eleven of the 1,585 provincial seats reserved for caste Hindus, and most of the untouchable seats as well. However Jinnah could take consolation from the fact that if the Muslims had not voted for him, they had not voted for the Congress either. The Congress contested only fifty eight of the four hundred and eighty two seats reserved for Muslims, and won just twenty six. Jinnah may not have become the sole spokesman of the Muslims, but he could keep pushing the argument that the Congress represented only the Hindus.

Part of Jinnah's problem was that the League had decayed into insignificance. It did not have a serious presence in a pivotal province like Bengal. Men who would later become synonymous with the Muslim League, like the merchant Hassan Ispahani and politician Huseyn Shaheed Suhrawardy, formed a United Muslim Party for the 1937 elections with the help of the influential British-era *nawab* of Dhaka. (It is not widely known that the *nawabs* of Dhaka were of Kashmiri origin, and had initially made their money as hide merchants. Abdul Ghani was given the title in 1875, made hereditary two years later for loyalty to the Raj in 1857.)

Jinnah exploited the defeat of 1937 better than the Congress used its victory. Congress leaders formed governments in the provinces, but did not quite appreciate that while this might be heady to start with, running a government was a headache. Jinnah picked up every instance of real or imagined injustice to Muslims by Congress governments to widen the distance between Muslims and Gandhi. He judged, accurately, that the further they moved from Gandhi the closer they would now come to him, for the Muslim League was the only national banner to which they could turn to make their case in Delhi. Jinnah neatly eliminated alternative formations that might attract Muslims. He simply co-opted regional leaders into the national League on whatever terms they sought. They could carry on exactly as before, except that they would now do it under the crescent on his banner. By 1938, the two most powerful Muslim leaders in India outside the League, both premiers in their provinces, Sir Sikander Hayat Khan in Punjab and Fazlul Haq in Bengal, joined the Muslim League.

Party structures were in any case loose. Gandhi insisted that the Congress was an umbrella shielding whoever travelled the broad path towards unity and freedom. Jinnah made the Muslim League a similar umbrella for whoever wanted to travel the narrow path towards a still-unclear Muslim emancipation. Jinnah brought clarity to his cause through sparring. When Jawaharlal Nehru, during the election campaign of 1937, declared that there were only two forces in India, the British and the Congress, and that opponents of the Congress had nothing to do with the masses, Jinnah hammered him with an emotive cudgel. 'I refuse to line up with the Congress,' he replied from Calcutta. 'There is a third party in this country and that is the Muslims.' Nehru, who had also started life in Saville Row suits but changed to homespun cotton, exhibited heartfelt contempt for this man who could not speak an Indian-origin language, remained indifferent to economic issues, and used mass hysteria to bait his net. Jinnah, in turn, accused Nehru of arrogance, but he did get out of those suits, at least for part of the time, and began to sport a long coat called *shervani* and a cap. This was better suited to his new message: Islam was in danger.

Here, certainly consciously, Jinnah had fertilized a fear from the Islamic subconscious. This was the dread of being forced to live in *Dar al Harb*, or a house of war, in which Muslims would not be allowed to practice their religion with any freedom. Jinnah, in acceptable language, and many of his lieutenants in coarse phrases, equated a Congress India with Hindu rule. Preachers and *mullahs* propagated that Muslims would not be allowed pray publicly in their mosques on Fridays, or read the Quran, if the Hindus came to power. The propaganda was effective.

Jinnah cleverly converted the religiosity of Gandhi into a weapon against the Congress. Gandhi would often fantasize about creating a 'Ramrajya' in India, the ideal state that existed during the time of Lord Ram. It was a popular motif symbolizing equality and a full stomach for the peasant, an image of idealism that Hindus could respond to. Jinnah turned it into an image of a domineering Hindu state. He converted 'Ramrajya' into a Muslim nightmare. Gandhi never hid his anguish at such misrepresentation, but after the formation of the Congress governments in 1937 the Muslim mood began to flow against him.

An umbrella needs a firm hand to stand up against the pressure of strong winds. The Congress umbrella splayed when it tried to protect India from a world war outside and a civil war within. On 3 September 1939 Britain declared war on Germany. India, as part of empire, became party to that war through a decision made in London. The Congress, uncertain about how to use the war for its own objectives, asked all Congress governments formed after the 1937 elections to resign. Jinnah announced a day of deliverance and asked Muslims to offer thanks to Allah.

He also offered thanks to Winston Churchill, giving full support to the war effort from the Muslim nation waiting to be born. The British were grateful for one Indian leader who was neither confused nor exploitative. Jinnah did not waver when Britain seemed on the brink of defeat. The Congress went to sleep on the horns of this dilemma, with painful consequences.

Jinnah placed a single proposal on the table, and waited until it was propitious to convert it into a demand. The proposal was made at Lahore, a city that can legitimately claim to be the birthplace of both modern India and Pakistan. In 1929, at Lahore, the Congress asked for India's freedom; in 1940 the Muslim League asked for Pakistan.

Pakistan was never mentioned in the Pakistan resolution of the Muslim League, moved late in the afternoon on 23 March 1940 and adopted by acclaim the following day. It would be scandalous to accuse Jinnah of clumsy phrasing, but he permitted it. The draft was prepared by the premiers of Punjab and Bengal, Sir Sikandar Hayat Khan and the 'Lion of Bengal' Fazlul Haq, who chaired the subjects committee. The third paragraph read:

> That it is the considered view of this Session of the All-India Muslim League that no constitutional plan would be workable in this country or acceptable to the Muslims unless it is designed on the following basic principles, viz., that geographically contiguous units are demarcated into regions which should be so constituted, with such territorial readjustments as may be necessary, that the areas in which the Muslims are numerically in a majority, as in the North-Western and Eastern zones of India, should be grouped to constitute Independent States in which the constituent units shall be autonomous and sovereign.

What did it mean? One Muslim state, or more? Within India or without India? The ambiguity may have been deliberate. There have been suggestions that the Bengal leader Fazlul Haq deliberately introduced the doubt to create space for a future independent Muslim Bengal, which would make Lahore the birthplace of Bangladesh as well. There was however no ambiguity in Jinnah's mind, which was made clear to the media that flocked around him during formal conversations with government and at public meetings. On 27 June 1940 Jinnah met Lord Linlithgow at the viceregal palace in Simla. In a note on the meeting he recorded that the viceroy had promised him that there would be no final scheme without the 'previous approval of Muslim India' and that the Pakistan resolution had become the 'universal faith of Muslim India'. In a typical speech, on 26 December 1941, Jinnah told the All India Muslim Students' Federation, 'The Muslim League has given you a goal which in my judgment is going to lead you to the promised land where we shall establish our Pakistan. People may say what they like and talk as they like. Of course he who laughs last, laughs best.' Jinnah would laugh last, but a hint of uncertainty would cloud that laugh.

He knew he had to wait till the war was decided. Churchill's defeat in the post-war general elections (the 'Order of the Boot' in his own phrase), cleared the last hurdle before India's freedom. The British government was divided over Jinnah's dream with his partisans determined to reward a leader who had been so faithful to the war effort, and a section apprehensive about the enormous consequences of dividing India. Lord Wavell, the second last viceroy, thought that you could not change geography, but he was dealing with those who wanted to make history.

The results of the 1945–6 elections were unambiguous. The Congress swept the general Hindu constituencies. The Muslim League won 86.7 per cent of the total Muslim vote cast for the Central Assembly and 74.7 per cent of the vote for the provinces. The Congress got 1.3 and 4.67 per cent of the Muslim vote respectively. Jinnah often said that the only thing that Muslims and Hindus had in common was their slavery to the British. He had made his point. On 2 June 1947 the British parliament passed the India Independence Act. It gave independence to two nations.

Lord Mountbatten, the last viceroy and the first governor general of India, wrote to London in Personal Report No. 17 dated 17 August 1947 that the Karachi programme for independence celebrations had to be changed from lunch to dinner because Jinnah had forgotten that it was the Muslim holy month of Ramadan, when Muslims fast. Id came four days after Pakistan was born. There was little to rejoice about as millions of refugees crossed unknown borders through trails of blood and hate. Jinnah's own health had collapsed. A disease kept secret, tuberculosis, compounded by cancer of the lungs, had ravaged him. That did not stop him smoking or drinking. The man who wanted to westernize the Muslims made one serious attempt to lay the course for the future of the country he had created.

He spoke extempore when Pakistan's Constituent Assembly met for the first time in Karachi on 11 August; that speech was written somewhere in his heart. As he put it, 'I shall say a few things as they occur to me . . .' This is what occurred to him: ' . . .You are free; you are free to go to your temples, you are free to go to your mosques or to any other place of worship in this State of Pakistan . . . You may belong to any religion or caste or creed – that has nothing to do with the business of the state.' Jinnah dismissed talk of an Islamic state as nonsense. It was not such nonsense to others. Maulana Maudoodi, the founder and ideologue of Jamaat-e-Islami, a religious party that plays an active role in politics, attacked Jinnah for ignoring the Quran. In a speech to the Constituent Assembly, another influential cleric, Maulana Shabbir Ahmad Usmani warned the élite that while they might want the *mullah* to devote his attention to reforming society while they were left free to 'spoil' Muslim society day in and day out, he saw no harm at all if the *mullah* also aspired to power to set up 'a truly Islamic state'.

India accepted her freedom at an hour determined by astrologers. Gandhi refused to celebrate. He was not in Delhi but in Calcutta, picking up the pieces of a lost India. It was left to his heir, Jawaharlal, to welcome India's tryst with destiny at the stroke of the midnight hour.

There was unprecedented Hindu-Muslim violence in the morning. India and Pakistan would see each other only through the virulence of that wall of blood that now divided them. Jinnah was in anguish at the horror he had never imagined. Gandhi was in despair; he may not have lived too long even if he had not been killed when he was.

Nathuram Vinayak Godse acquired an automatic pistol, Number 606824, and seven bullets. He reached his destination at ten minutes to five on the evening of 30 January 1948. No one stopped him at the gates of Birla Bhavan, where Gandhi lived when in Delhi. Gandhi had survived yet another fast unto death, but mortality seemed to hover over his conversations, perhaps because there was too much blood in the air. This fast was not in protest against any British crime, but against the crimes of those he had freed: Hindus and Muslims who had welcomed their independence with slaughter on a scale unprecedented in their history. Non-violence had become a mockery. On 20 January a Hindu refugee from Pakistan was arrested at Gandhi's prayer meeting with a hand grenade, even as a bomb intended for the Mahatma went off harmlessly if loudly about 25 yards away. Gandhi remained serene, looking for all the world like a man who actually believed what he had often prophesised, that he would live up to 125 or 133, the span of service allotted by the *shastras* to those who served humanity.

By the twenty second, Gandhi had recovered sufficiently from his fast to walk unaided on the lawns. That week he gave an interview (quoted in Tendulkar's biography) to the British journalist Kingsley Martin, which turned into a discussion on non-violence. A South African millionaire had once told Gandhi that passive resistance was merely an expedient; what else could the Indians do since they had no army? Jesus, pointed out Gandhi, was the king of passive resisters, and surely you would not describe him as weak? Kingsley Martin wondered how non-violence would work with a tyrant like Hitler. Gandhi laughed and disingenuously argued that he was not a man of government and therefore could not take responsibility for the rationale used by governments. His colleague, Maulana Azad, had been more specific, said Gandhi. Gandhi quoted Azad: 'When we gain power, we shall not be able to hold it non-violently.'

On the twenty eighth, a Congress colleague, Rajkumari Amrit Kaur, came to express concern about his safety. 'If I am to die by the bullet of a madman,' replied Gandhi, 'I must do so smiling.' Just before he retired to bed on the night of Thursday the twenty ninth he recited an Urdu couplet to his granddaughter Manu:

> The spring of this garden lasts but a few days,
> Take a look at its show for a few days.

He woke up at 3.30 on Friday the thirtieth, his usual hour. Prayer, then work. At eight, the regular massage. He looked better, more refreshed after his bath, and began his new ritual of learning how to write Bengali. At nine-thirty he had his breakfast: goat's milk; vegetables, both cooked and raw; oranges; and a mixture of ginger and sour lemons. He then worked on a draft constitution for the Congress that aimed at creating a fresh structure for the organization. After a nap at noon, there were visitors. Some Muslim priests had heard that he was planning to leave the city, and were anxious about their safety in his absence. He reassured them. They left, and he asked for his important letters. 'I must reply to them today,' he said, 'for tomorrow I may not be.' A delegation of refugees from Sind in Pakistan met him after his correspondence was over, and he told them the story of how an angry refugee had advised him to retire to the Himalayas. Gandhi chuckled that he would actually love that: he could then become a double Mahatma and attract even larger crowds. At four on that winter afternoon, the Iron Man of India, the home minister, Sardar Vallabhbhai Patel, came for advice. Nehru and Azad were scheduled to call later in the evening; Gandhi was negotiating peace in the higher regions of the Congress leadership. At 5 p.m. he took out his pocket watch and told Sardar Patel that it was time for public prayers.

Nathuram Godse saw the Mahatma leave his room at about ten past five, leaning on the shoulders of his granddaughters, Manu and Abha. He waited near the point where the Mahatma would ascend the few steps to a platform. Godse opened the safety catch of the gun while it was still in his pocket. Gandhi walked towards him. Godse waited for a clear view. He took two steps towards the Mahatma. A thought stopped him briefly: Manu might be too close to Gandhi and could get hurt, so he waited till he was about three paces from his target. With the gun, incongruously, in his hands, he joined his palms, bowed his head and said *'Namaste'*: this, Godse explained later at his trial, was a gesture in honour of 'whatever useful service [Gandhi] had rendered to the country and the sacrifice he had made in his lifetime'.

Godse moved another step, pushed Manu aside, and pulled the trigger once. Three bullets emerged because he had squeezed too hard. Gandhi faltered, but remained on his feet. Two more bullets followed. Gandhi took the name of the Lord. *'Hey Ram!'* he cried, and fell. A stain grew on the white khaddar that draped him. Gandhi had paid the price for wanting peace with Muslims.

Jinnah, who created Pakistan, began to wonder about the Pakistan he had created. You can hand over power to the chaps from the club, as the British did, but you cannot guarantee that these chaps will retain it for ever. A homeland is not exclusive to those who aspire to play golf. Theocrats will also dream. A struggle between what might be called the Jinnah group and theocrats began in Pakistan. The balance was even till General Zia ul Haq, after hanging the country's first elected leader, Zulfiqar Ali Bhutto, placed the weight of his office heavily behind a theocracy, even as he smiled and smiled before frequent-flyer visitors from the United States. As he had more than one face, Zia could turn in more than one direction.

14

JINNAH REDUX AND THE AGE OF OSAMA

Obey me as long as I obey Allah and His apostle, and if I disobey
them you owe me no obedience.

[Abu Bakr, the first Caliph of Muslims,
upon being named leader of the *umma*.]

Do you threaten a duck with a river?

[A proverb often quoted by Hasan i Sabbah, the Old Man of
the Mountains, when told that his life was under threat.]

Kabul ke baad, Islamabad! . . . Taliban! Taliban!

['After Kabul, Islamabad! . . . Taliban! Taliban!' chanted a
gathering of *mullahs* outside the Lahore High Court on 15 May
1994. They had come for the hearing of a review petition on
the death sentence awarded to two Pakistani Christians, Salamat
and Rehmat Masih, for blasphemy against the Prophet.]

How was jihad knitted into a single mesh beyond the reach of governments, and turned into a war against America? Why did America and
Britain invade a nation they had saved from Soviet domination in the
1980s? How did Pakistan become a playing field for terrorist organizations that launched a holy war wherever they could find an enemy?

As we have seen, Muslim armies began incursions into India, first for
booty, and a lot of it too, during the first decades of the eleventh century,
a little before the Crusades began in West Asia. India's wealth whet the
appetite for more. In the mid-twelfth century, Muslims established themselves in Delhi, and did not leave until the British prised them out after a
bitter war of blood and nerves in 1857. India was always a Hindu-majority

region, but Muslim power lived on, or sometimes limped on, till Britain eliminated it.

The Muslim response swung between anger and anxiety. The jihads of the nineteenth century were crushed by the British; the spirit revived early in the twentieth century, where it merged with the larger nationalist movement under Gandhi. In a unique departure, Gandhi persuaded Muslims into their only experience of a non-violent jihad. It failed.

Muslim politics took a separate, and then a separatist turn. In 1947 a section of Indian Muslims won a homeland, and called it Pakistan. From its inception, Pakistan turned jihad into an instrument of state policy.

Pakistan is the one modern, democratic Muslim nation that might have been. It emerged out of the debris of the Mughal empire, through the hoop of colonialism. The Muslims of the Maghreb and West Asia were not the only communities who had their modern destinies shaped in Europe, although the creation of Israel has given West Asia far greater international visibility. However, two wars began simultaneously, one in 1947 and the other in 1948, and neither has stopped. While there is more available in one bookshop about the conflicts of the Middle East, there is comparative indifference to the passion plays on the Indian subcontinent. Two recent factors should change that. India and Pakistan now threaten not only regional havoc, but also have the capability of spreading nuclear clouds over the richest piece of real estate on earth: those deserts soaked with oil. Also, Pakistan has become a haven for terrorists who have created a 'state within a state'. No one said this more clearly than Pakistan's sixteenth chief executive and the first to show any genuine inclination to challenge this menace, President (and General) Pervez Musharraf. In that nationwide address to his country on 12 January 2002, President Musharraf asked for an end to the culture of jihad that had wounded Pakistan more than it had hurt anyone else. He told the extremist clergy that they must stop encouraging gullible young men into martyrdom. Pakistan had not taken the responsibility for jihad across the world. He would not allow mosques to be misused and seminaries to become schools for hatred; he would end the rule of the Kalashnikov. Pakistan would not become a theocratic state, he asserted. He taunted those fundamentalist *mullahs* who preached jihad from the comfort of their Pajeros; he gave an instance of a *mullah* who had personally killed people in his version of the holy war. These wholesale agents of Islam, like the Taliban and its allies in Pakistan, he said, thought they were leading some 'Islamic renaissance'. All they had achieved was to turn their country into a cesspool of violence and he was determined to destroy this 'state within a state'. No one would be allowed to carry on any jihad, including the jihad in Kashmir, from the comfort of Pakistan, he declared; that era was over. The first reaction of the militant clergy was to sneer at Musharraf, as a man who did not know what he was talking about. However, at least one Pakistani general had set out to undo what another had set in motion. General Zia ul Haq, who seized power in 1977, Islamized Pakistan during his decade in power, and no successor until Musharraf has had the conviction to challenge that legacy. Musharraf may also claim at least as much time to reverse what happened under the cover of the jihad against the Soviet Union in Afghanistan.

America did not care to ask too many questions about its friends in its first Afghan war, because Afghanistan was only a staging ground for a larger conflict against communism and the Soviet Union. Time will tell how much America understands about the forces at play in its second Afghan war, but this too is an episode from a larger world conflict: only the roles are reversed. America is the Soviet Union this time. The nature of battle is different. One army is in the field, and the second is in the shadows. No government was involved in the terrorist attacks of 11 September 2001. They happened.

Some conceptual misunderstanding arises from a word that has become shorthand for all problems: fundamentalism. To most in the West, fundamentalism is some repository of all evil. If however, by fundamentalism you imply conviction in the basic tenets of the faith, then more than ninety per cent of the Muslim population is fundamentalist. Any other term – say, Islamist – appears equally prone to misinterpretation. The better solution might be to use 'fundamentalism', but explain what it does *not* imply.

Most Christians might shrug if asked whether they really believed that Jesus turned water into wine, or raised Lazarus from the dead. Muslims by contrast do not doubt that Allah's angels helped the Prophet at the battle of Badr. Allah is a living god to them, as palpable and meaningful as an ideal parent might be. Muslims do not understand the implicit equation between faith and terrorism that is so often made by Christians whose own faith seems to have lapsed. Equally, there is bewilderment at the charge of hatred. Muslims do not 'hate' the West, or hate Christians, any more or any less than they might 'hate' Buddhists or Japan. However, what they do possess is a deep and powerful anger against the Christian West, an anger provoked by slander against their beloved Prophet, bred by unceasing war, and now nurtured by factors like Muslim impotence against Israel. Israel is viewed as a surrogate of America. It is not the only one. The Muslim street is convinced that most governments of Islamic nations are stooges of America, and this hurts even more. This is their only explanation for American tolerance of Muslim monarchs and despots. One of the most widely-advertised policies of America since the collapse of the Soviet Union has been an insistence upon democracy. Where does this insistence disappear when it comes to a regime like Saudi Arabia's? Washington may want 'free and fair' democracy in Libya, but makes no such call on Egypt. No standard was ever more double. Democracy, however, is noticeable by its absence in the contemporary Islamic world, whether or not its nations are obedient to Washington.

Even Jinnah could not ensure democracy in Pakistan. He knitted a country out of the strands of British policy with iron needles, but those needles were forged in the heat of a movement for democratic rights. The Pakistan idea lived on the claim that Muslims would not get justice where Hindus outnumbered them by three to one. It was a unique rationale for a new nation, plucked out of the British grasp by Jinnah's cold and steady hand.

So what happened to democracy in Pakistan? The only Muslims in the world to enjoy sustained democratic liberty are not in Pakistan, but those who remained in India. Indian Muslims have had more problems than anyone deserves, paying the price for their ancestors, on the one hand, and the success of the Muslim League, on the other, but they remain the only Muslims – and there are now over 150 million of them – with guaranteed democratic rights. It would be foolish to say that democracy has removed their grievances; it has not. As in the case of the wanton destruction of the Babri mosque in 1992, it may have even added to their problems. Resultant riots are often an exercise in lynch mob barbarism, with the administration giving a friendly nod to violence, as in Gujarat in 2002. But democracy has given Indian Muslims the means to punish governments and political parties who are either antagonistic to their sentiments or have betrayed their interests. After the alienation of 1947 they have lifted themselves up and are becoming effective partners in the evolution of a nation state. The charge of tokenism can be easily made about Muslims who have become head of state in India; real power lies with the prime minister. But even a prime minister's job is not completely outside the reach of a minority in today's India. This is, interestingly, what Jinnah wanted for Pakistan: a time when, in the political sense, Muslims would cease to be Muslims and Hindus cease to be Hindus. That is happening in India instead, not because Indians are superior to Pakistanis, but because they have a superior political system. Pakistan's Muslims have had only a fleeting feel of free will.

Even such brief acquaintance is more than Muslims elsewhere have enjoyed. Morocco is a monarchy. Tunisia experienced the slightly disconcerting radicalism of Francophile Habib Bourgiba, and is now content, or not, with one-party rule. Algeria began her independent experience with the liberal autocracy of victorious revolutionaries and then slipped, through failed experiments in elections, to army dictatorship. Sudan stuttered between Quranic law and strongmen like Colonel Jafar Numeiri, and has settled for a dictatorship of ideological convenience. Libya and Egypt replaced decadent kings with the army. Gamal Abdel Nasser gave Egypt hope, and Muammar Gaddafi gave Libya a Green Book, but neither offered their nations democracy.

Syria and Iraq are Baathist, if that means anything any longer. Baath is a Quranic term implying rebirth. Michel Aflaq, a Greek Orthodox Christian, believed that Islamic-Arab socialist nationalism would challenge the 'traditional Islam' of kings and emirs, and terrify Europe with its resurgent power. Aflaq's Arab nationalism was inclusive of all communities, Shia, Sunni, Druze or Christian, but it concentrated state power in the hands of a single party. That has tapered down to single-family rule. The egalitarian Aflaq had no idea he was replacing old dynasties with new ones, and without much class to boot. The communities that he had tried to unite fought bitter wars that deranged Lebanon. Jordan is a liberal kingdom, handed to the Hashemite family as a sop when the Saudis were awarded Arabia. Irrespective of their differences, both the Hashemites and the Sauds know who protects their dynastic rule. The same protection is given to the emirs of the Gulf. All these ruling families invite contempt if not worse from those who have declared jihad on America. Yemen is a small republic with independent traditions, but Yemen too has elections with 93 per cent victories.

The proud nation of Arabia, home of the Prophet, religious centre of Islam, was handed over by imperial British bureaucrats and adventurers to a family in their pay. The Sauds then hijacked the country. There is no instance in history of a nation being renamed after a family: Arabia was never Saudi before the Sauds. Arab potentates believe that they have purchased the loyalty of their citizens – a loyalty that must include, very frequently, tolerance of appalling excess and greed – by doling out some of the oil wealth that they have not appropriated. Man does not live by the air-conditioner alone, even in Saudi Arabia.

Afghanistan replaced a mild monarch with increasingly brutal dictators, culminating in the Taliban whose worst terrorism was against the Afghan people, particularly the women. In Bangladesh, assassins in uniform stained a democratic promise; after much bloodshed and army rule it has turned to genuine elections, proving that there is nothing incompatible between Islam itself and democracy. Democracy is only incompatible with those élites who have turned Muslim nations into their playthings. Malaysia has, in effect, one-party rule, and Indonesia has only recently enjoyed the privilege of a vote. Brunei is a family heirloom. The African countries, irrespective of religion or tribe, have not been able to provide stable democracy to their people.

The Central Asian Muslim nations got independence from the Soviet Union but have not yet surrendered the formula of electing leaders with 99 per cent of the vote. Albania looks lost. Turkey, still straining for Europe, has a democracy whose spine is protected by the army, if that is not a contradiction. A Shah was placed over Shia Iran by the colonial powers. Iran flirted with independence in the heady early-fifties and discovered that the CIA did not approve. The shah returned from brief exile and lorded over the country until Ayatullah Khomeini mobilized this old civilization. A believer and an intellectual, the Ayatullah contributed two important elements to modern Islamic history. He inspired the empowerment of Islam through non-traditional avenues that were encouraged to sidestep their governments to organize and launch their own jihad. He also made a serious attempt to create a modern Islamic state whose tenets would be protected by guardians of the faith, the clergy. This permitted space for a controlled democracy. There was more breathing room than under the absolutism of Shah Reza Pahlavi, but no one should confuse it with free expression of democratic will. The experiment has survived, but there is no evidence that it has worked as well as envisaged. Iran fought a jihad for eight years, not against Israel, but against a fellow Muslim country, Iraq. Both Iran and Iraq told their young men that they would go to paradise on the wings of a heavenly horse if they died in this jihad.

What are the implications? When the street does not have a voice in the affairs of its own nation, it seeks assertion by other means. All Muslims live in two dimensions: one is the circle of nationalism, the other a circle of brotherhood. National identity coexists with commitment to a world-faith, pride in a unique history, and passions that override national boundaries.

In an age of despair the need for a hero who can inspire pan-Islamic victories becomes acute. The situation today is akin to a thousand years ago, when Crusaders conquered Jerusalem and Christians established powerful states in the heart of Palestine, in territory approximate to where Israel exists today. A revival by Zengi, Nuraddin, and above all Saladin lifted Muslims from a morass then. There is no such hero on the horizon now. Despair can become a breeding ground for mavericks who believe in themselves and their version of the faith.

Osama bin Laden is in the tradition of another famous name from the eleventh century, Hasan i Sabbah, the Old Man of the Mountains, who has given the English language the word 'assassin'. The year of his birth is not known, but he died in 1124: that, presumably, is what fame is all about. He was born in a Shia family in Qum in Persia and travelled restlessly when young, serving many masters. In 1090, he finally found a base for his militant creed in the castle of Alamut, on a high rock in the middle of the Elburz mountains, perched above a fertile valley. He did not leave this mountain for thirty four years, until he died. From there he commanded a network of missionaries and terrorists who became the most feared force of their time.

For more than a hundred years the cult of assassins spread terror among both the Christian crusaders and the Arab *emirs* who had permitted Christians to triumph. Hasan i Sabbah promised paradise to martyrs in his cause, apparently with the judicious use of *hashish*, hence *hashishin* and then assassin. They perfected the strategy of suicide missions, and their secrecy was legendary. It reached a point where a Sultan like Saladin could not be certain if his own bodyguards had not become assassins, waiting for a signal from their lord. Assassins made two attempts on the life of Saladin, once in the winter of 1174–5, when he was besieging Alleppo; and then on 22 May 1176 when, disguised as his soldiers, they attacked him with knives. After that Saladin slept under special protection, and only those who knew him personally were allowed to approach him.

When the Old Man would hear of a threat to his own life, he would laugh it off with a proverb: Do you threaten a duck with the river?

The cult's greatest success came at a critical moment during Richard II's Crusade. It was carefully planned and brilliantly executed. Two assassins entered the service of Marquis Conrad of Montferrat, King of Jerusalem, in Tyre, as Christian monks and, after securing his complete confidence, killed him on 28 April 1192. It was the 11 September of its time. The assassins added ingenious salt to this wound by 'confessing' that Richard II had instigated the murder.

However, the romance of the assassin withered when the Arab establishment protected the victories of Saladin. Having found Saladin, Muslims did not need terrorism. The movement drifted into appalling heresy, and ended up on the margins until it was scattered into oblivion by the Mongol Hulegu. (It prospered in oblivion. The modern Aga Khan, head of the Ismailis, is a direct descendant of the Old Man of the Mountains).

There may be a lesson here for modern times. When Saladin gave a call for a jihad against Richard II, response came from as far away as India. The street is still ready, but there is no Saladin. Dictators like Saddam Hussein exploit this disenchantment to divert some of the anger against their own tyranny. The United States, most Muslims believe, only dispenses with those dictators who fall out with Washington; in other words, it is Washington's interest that must always be served, not theirs. The Saud family remains the outstanding example of Washington's tolerance for obedient kings. 'King' is not the most important of the titles of the Saudi monarch; he is also custodian of the holy places. To many Muslims, the Saud family is only the custodian of American oil.

In May 1932 an American and a British explorer-agent had lunch at Simpson's restaurant in the Strand. The American, Francis B. Loomis, former under-secretary of state during Theodore Roosevelt's administration, and now foreign affairs consultant to Standard Oil Company of California (Socal), had invited Harry St John Bridger Philby, just back from a Saudi Arabia that was broke because of falling revenues and the rising royal expenditure of Abdul Aziz bin Saud. According to the unreliable Philby, all the oil concessions of Arabia were available to anyone with a million dollars.

In 1928, American, British, Dutch, and French oil companies had shared the concessions in the conquered parts of the dead Ottoman empire: Standard Oil Company of New York (now Mobil); Standard Oil Company of New Jersey (Exxon); Anglo Persian (British Petroleum); Royal Dutch Shell; and *Compagnie Francaise des Petroles*. Socal was not in the cartel but had begun to explore in Bahrain (it hit pay dirt on 1 June 1932). Within a year of that lunch in 1932, terms were settled with the Saudi government: 30,000 pounds in gold as loan, a further 20,000 in eighteen months, and an annual rent of 5,000 pounds. Socal counted out 35,000 gold sovereigns (literally, on the table of the manager of Netherlands Trading Society) on 25 August

1933 for the title to explore an area four times the size of Britain, and for a further 100,000 pounds gained the rights to Nejd and Kuwait Neutral Zone. By the end of the year Americans were in Hasa, with cranes, girders, cars, lorries, electric fans, showers, and water closets. The rest, as they say, is history. By March 1938 Dammam No. 7 was spewing some four thousand barrels of oil a day. On 18 February 1943 President Franklin Delano Roosevelt issued Executive Order 8926 to under-secretary of state Edward Stettinus in which he summed up America's position: 'I hereby find that the defense of Saudi Arabia is vital to the defense of the United States.' Lend-lease funds were made available to the government. Britain was slowly eased out of the way. American troops were stationed at Dhahran. The interdependence of Washington and Riyadh was established.

There is a saying of the Prophet familiar to those Muslims who have read about their religion: if an *imam* does not protect his people, he shall never smell the perfumes of paradise. In his first speech after being named Caliph, Abu Bakr had said: 'I have been given authority over you but I am not the best of you. If I do well, help me, and if I do ill, then put me right . . . Obey me as long as I obey God and His apostle, and if I disobey them you owe me no obedience.'

Thirteen of the twenty four Caliphs of the Ottoman empire were removed from office after a *fatwa* from the Sheykh ul Islam, declaring that they were no longer able to protect the Muslim because they had forgotten how to serve Allah. The Islamic code has left space for dissent and means for redressal. Dissent may be suppressed in Saudi Arabia but it still travels. Elements of the *ulema* are often the champions of change. One reason why Saudi authorities are generous to religious causes is their anxiety to appease the clergy. It does not always work. In the middle of America's war against Al Qaida and the Taliban, Saudi authorities summoned a highly respected, blind, 80-year-old cleric, Sheikh Hamoud bin Ogla an Shuaibi, to interrogate him on whether he had really issued a *fatwa* against the ruling family. Sheikh Hamoud answered simply: 'Whoever backs the infidel against Muslims is considered an infidel.' The Prophet had said, let there not be two religions in Arabia. The Saudis have altered that; it is now, let there not be two opinions in Saudi Arabia.

As Britain lost its eminence to the United States after the Second World War, the rage shifted from the pre-eminent colonial power to the 'neocolonialism' of America. With the creation of Israel, all three sides of a monotheistic faith, Judaism, Christianity, and Islam, became enmeshed in this conflict. It is less a clash of civilizations and more a struggle for political space, economic power, and national pride underlined by religious differences. The Muslim anguish at departed glory contrasts sharply with Jewish revival after some two thousand years of exile. Muslims need someone to blame, apart from themselves. America is necessary.

The Muslims of undivided India did find their Saladin in the 1930s, although he would have recoiled from such an analogy. There is not a single reference to Saladin in the 421 pages of Stanley Wolpert's *Jinnah of Pakistan* (Oxford University Press, New York, 1984), the most comprehensive English biography of the man who created a nation out of a minority demand. Jinnah did not believe in the traditional heroes of Islamic history; if he had a role model, it was Mustafa Kemal, the Turk who ended the Caliphate.

When did the Muslims become a minority in India? The question is rhetorical, because Muslims in India have always been a minority. However, particularly after the conversions in Bengal, India also had the largest Muslim population in the world, principally converts from the nether regions of the Hindu caste system attracted by the egalitarian promise of Islam. At no point in their long presence in India did Muslims ever demand a specifically Muslim kingdom, or a province exclusive to them. They never felt any need for protection from Hindus.

At what point of their history, then, did they become a 'minority'? The process began with the loss of the Mughal empire and the decimation of the old nobility after the defeat of 1857. The language of power changed from Persian to English, and systems of authority were altered to suit the British interest. New ideas like elections came into play. A complete misunderstanding of elections was unsurprising for no one clearly understood what this animal called a vote was all about; whether it would walk, run, or turn and bite the hand that fed it.

However, when Jinnah got his promised land, he became radically different to the man who had wrested that prize. His speech at the opening of the Constituent Assembly on 11 August was troubled. While he asserted that history would vindicate Partition, he was uncertain now about the last laugh: 'Any idea of a United India could never have worked and in my judgment it would have led us to terrific disaster. Maybe that view is correct; maybe it is not; that remains to be seen.' Maybe?

He told the Constituent Assembly that Pakistan would succeed if its leadership worked for the well-being of the poor, and if they buried the hatchet to ensure that every citizen had equal rights, privileges, and obligations 'no matter to what community he belongs, no matter what relations he had with you in the past, no matter what is his colour, caste or creed, is first, second and last a citizen of this State with equal rights, privileges and obligations, there will be no end to the progress you will make . . . You are free; you are free to go to your temples, you are free to go to your mosques or to any other place of worship in this State of Pakistan . . . You may belong to any religion or caste or creed – that has nothing to do with the business of the State.' He emphasized this repeatedly: 'We are starting with this fundamental principle that we are all citizens and equal citizens of one State.'

He offered a startling thought: 'I think we should keep that in front of us as our ideal and you will find that in course of time Hindus would cease to be Hindus and Muslims would cease to be Muslims, not in the religious sense, because that is the personal faith of each individual, but in the political sense as citizens of the State . . .' This made no sense. Gandhi could have said the same thing.

Jinnah won the argument in India before 1947. Pakistan's tragedy was that he lost the argument after 1947. From there began Pakistan's slippage into administrative chaos, arbitrary rule, and dictatorship that fed the rise of fundamentalist organizations.

The clergy set the pace for an Islamic government from the outset. Pakistan was created because Islam was in danger, they argued. How do you save Islam from danger? Through an Islamic government. Jinnah would have none of that. He dismissed the thought of a theocratic state with contempt, but he was in very poor health, wasting away from disease. He died in Karachi at 10.20 p.m. on 11 September 1948. His body, weighing just seventy pounds, was buried the following day. His principles were buried not much later.

The sovereignty of Pakistan lay with Allah, said the Objectives Resolution of the Constitution moved by his heir, Prime Minister Liaquat Ali Khan, on 7 March 1949. However, Jinnah's vision dominated that resolution, passed after five days of debate: democracy, an independent judiciary, freedom, equality, and minority rights. Not one of these principles was implemented.

On 16 October 1951 an Afghan called Said Khan, who turned out to be a former British intelligence agent, assassinated Liaquat Ali Khan. This set in motion power struggles between a clutch of civilians who should not be dignified by being called leaders.

Khwaja Nazimuddin, who had become governor general after Jinnah, stepped down to become prime minister. Ghulam Muhammad, the finance minister, a Punjabi bureaucrat, stepped up to become head of state. In April 1953, suddenly and without explanation, he dismissed the Nazimuddin government after the latter had proved his majority in the Assembly. Another Bengali, Muhammad Ali Bogra, was apponted prime minister to either please the Bengalis or the Americans, or both. Bogra tried to change the statute that gave the governor general arbitrary powers of dismissal. Ghulam Muhammad responded by declaring an Emergency on 24 October 1954 and threw out not only the cabinet but also the Constituent Assembly. Bogra compromised, accepted the dissolution of the Assembly, and was retained. The first 'Cabinet of Talents', a presumptuous title that Pakistan uses for arbitrary governments, was formed.

In August 1955 an ambitious minister Iskander Mirza took over as governor general with support from the army. A civil servant, Chaudhri Muhammad Ali, was appointed prime minister. Finally, on 29 February 1956 the Constitution Bill was passed. Pakistan became an Islamic Republic and the governor general was renamed president. East Pakistan was unhappy because the Constitution gave both wings equal seats despite the numerical majority of Bengalis in the country. All Muslims were not equal in the Muslim homeland. Three more prime ministers came and went, including Huseyn Suhrawardy who seemed serious about holding elections, and even advocated joint electorates. Mirza ended such hopes on 7 October 1958 by proclaiming martial law and suspending the constitution. The army ended his own hopes a few days later. The army chief, Muhammad Ayub Khan, took over as chief martial law administrator and stayed till street protests forced him to hand over power to another general, Yahya Khan, in March 1969. Yahya Khan was the only Pakistan leader since 1947 to ensure free and fair elections. Maybe he should not have bothered. Those elections led to war and another partition. Bangladesh was born because Bengalis were not accepted as equals by West Pakistan.

There has been agreement in Pakistan on only one policy through all the political turmoil that the country has suffered for over five decades: a jihad against India over Kashmir. The strategy of what might be called arm's length jihad, funded and managed by the secret services, began within weeks of freedom, and would become a pattern with a far wider embrace. The Kashmir war was also launched when there was no dispute between India and Pakistan. Kashmir was not a part of India then.

The British left on 15 August 1947, but India retained the last viceroy, Lord Mountbatten, as its first governor general. Jinnah declined a similar suggestion, but there remained many senior British officials and officers in Pakistan's service. One of them was Sir George Cunningham, the governor of the North West Frontier Province, a tribal province straddling Kashmir and Afghanistan. Sir George recorded in his diary of 17 October 1947 (quoted in Brian Cloughley's *A History of the Pakistan Army*, Oxford University Press, Karachi, 1999):

> [A member of his staff] told me . . . there is a real movement in Hazara [a region of north central Pakistan] for a jehad [sic] against Kashmir. They have been collecting rifles and making a definite plan of campaign, apparently for seizing the part of the main Jhelum valley above Domel [in western Kashmir]. I have warned everyone I could, including the Afridis and Mohmands, of the danger of taking part in anything like this, in case it leads to war between India and Pakistan. I am not quite sure whether it could be made a *casus belli* at present, as Kashmir has acceded to neither Dominion.

There lay the nub. Muslim-majority Kashmir was ruled by a colourful Hindu maharaja, Hari Singh, who dreamt of independence. This was not the only unusual aspect of the problem. The most popular leader of the Muslims, Sheikh Muhammad Abdullah, had bucked the trend and opposed the Muslim League. In his first public meeting in Srinagar after India's independence, on 4 October 1947, Sheikh Abdullah declared, 'I never believed in the Pakistan slogan. It has been my firm conviction that this slogan will bring misery . . .' (There were no elections in Kashmir in 1945–6 because it was a princely state and not formally part of British India.) The Maharaja of Kashmir had signed what was called, accurately, a Standstill Agreement with both India and Pakistan by the terms of which its status was frozen pending a final decision.

However, Pakistan interfered. The preparations for jihad were hardly a secret, as later memoirs were to reveal. H.V. Hodson says in *The Great Divide* (Hutchinson, 1969) that the commander in chief of Pakistan General Sir Frank Messervey, advised Liaquat Ali Khan against such adventurism. Jawaharlal Nehru had a pretty sharp idea of what was going on, and wrote to his home minister Sardar Patel on 27 September 1947: 'The Muslim League in the Punjab and the NWFP are making preparations to enter Kashmir in considerable numbers. The approach of winter is going to cut off Kashmir from the rest of India . . . I understand that the Pakistan strategy is to infiltrate into Kashmir now and to take some big action as soon as Kashmir is more or less isolated because of the coming winter.' Notwithstanding Nehru's anxiety, his government was powerless to do anything until Hari Singh made up his mind.

Vacillation ended when on the night of 21 October 1947 some 6,000 well-armed raiders set off from Pakistan for Srinagar. Hari Singh learnt of the crisis only on 24 October when the lights in his palace went off; the powerhouse at Mahura had fallen. At eleven the following morning the defence committee of the government of India met with Mountbatten in the chair. Nehru was worried about Kashmir; Mountbatten was equally concerned about the fate of some three hundred Britishers living in the Valley. Preparations were ordered for an immediate airlift of Indian troops to Srinagar. An emissary was dispatched to Hari Singh to sign an accession treaty without which Indian troops could not intervene.

The Indian army would never have reached in time to save Srinagar, but help came from an unforeseen source, the raiders themselves. They had been sent on jihad; they dallied to rape and loot. The most horrifying incident was the rape of seven nuns in St Joseph's Hospital. The raiders were still outside Srinagar when the first battalion of the Sikh Regiment landed at the airport on Monday, 27 October. Today the dispute has acquired a nuclear dimension.

Undemocratic governments, searching for legitimacy, pick up help wherever they can find it. Only two men have ruled Pakistan for any length of time; both were generals who seized power through a coup. The first, Field Marshal Ayub Khan, was a 'whisky-general' but could not avoid the temptation of sending irregulars into Kashmir, on the same pattern as 1947. His jihad, in 1965, also failed. General Zia ul Haq, who threw out and then killed the first elected prime minister of Pakistan, Zulfiqar Ali Bhutto, ruled for eleven years from July 1977 to August 1988. If his means were unscrupulous, his theme was piety. It was during his years that Pakistan edged towards theocracy, Osama bin Laden became a warrior of Islam, and made friends with a *mullah* called Omar.

Zia ul Haq wanted to change the date on which Pakistan celebrates its independence each year, 14 August. He felt this great event should be remembered by the Muslim calendar, or the twenty seventh of Ramadan. The suggestion was ignored. He however gave a clear indication of his mind in his first televised speech to the country. Pakistan, he said, had been created in the name of Islam, and would survive only if it stuck to Islam. He considered the introduction of an 'Islamic system' essential.

Zia was sincere in his piety. He was born on 12 August 1924 into a modest family, in the Indian city of Jullundur, and never shed the values that his parents had inculcated, despite an education at St Stephen's College in Delhi, a premier institution of the good and the grand. Neither did life, and war as an officer with the British Indian Army, change his views. The barracks are notorious for making an Englishman out of a man. He would claim later that his formative memory was the vision of his mother struggling, with all her worldly possessions, across the border into Pakistan after Partition, but an officer who had served in Burma, Malaya, and Java was not likely to be as incapable of providing protection to his family as a peasant.

Later, when he survived longer than anyone expected, some of his disenchanted colleagues would suggest he made more use of Allah than Allah made use of him. There were enough sycophants to insist that he was a man of destiny, to use a tired but much-loved phrase of dictators. You could however hardly blame him for thinking so. In August 1950, after his marriage to his cousin Shafiqa, he was posted to the Guides Cavalry, where he impressed his seniors. In 1969 he was seconded to Jordan, where he became hugely unpopular with the Palestine Liberation Organization when he helped organize brutal aggression against refugee camps. On his return, he was given command of the First Armoured Division. In 1976, Bhutto, searching for a general he could trust (Bhutto was an optimist), bypassed half a dozen and made the pious Zia his army chief. It is the sort of thing that confirms your belief in destiny. In July 1977 Zia seized power, after checking with the American ambassador, when Bhutto completely mishandled an election that he had ordered.

Zia's first promise was to hold 'free and fair' elections, possibly as soon as by October. That was his last promise as well, before his death in a mysterious air crash in August 1988. No free elections were ever held by the man who organized a coup to hold them.

Zia eliminated Bhutto through what can only be described as judicial assassination. He manipulated the judicial process and Bhutto was hanged to death in the early hours of 4 April 1979. Zia became a pariah both with the West and the Arab countries, who had genuine regard for Bhutto and were warmly supportive of Bhutto's secret plan to build what was called an 'Islamic bomb' (Pakistan is the only Muslim country with nuclear weapons). American economic assistance was suspended, but Zia's good friend, destiny, helped out.

In 1979 the Shah of Iran was driven from his throne by the street power of Ayatullah Khomeini, leaving America staring at a hole where its best friend had lived. Exactly twenty three days after Bhutto's death, the pro-Soviet People's Democratic Party of Afghanistan, headed by a part-time poet, Nur Mohammed Taraki, seized power in Kabul. This led to widespread protests that, in turn, created rifts in the leadership. Supporters of his own prime minister, Hafizullah Amin, killed Taraki on 14 September. On the evening of 27 December, Kabul went dark. The electricity had been sabotaged. After seven, some 5,000 Soviet troops marched to the palace. Their nominee, Babrak Karmal, was out of Kabul that night, in nearby Dushanbe, capital of Tajikistan, waiting for the call. At three in the morning the formation of a new government was announced. Karmal's first decision was to 'earnestly' demand the presence of Soviet troops that were already in Kabul. On 31 December the Central Committee of the Communist Party of the Soviet Union accepted a document (now declassified) prepared by Comrades U. Andropov, A. Gromyko, D. Ustinov, and B. Ponomarev which noted that Amin had been punished because he began to 'circulate notoriously invented gossips, discrediting the Soviet Union' and was 'practicing confidential contacts' with the American charge d'affaires in Kabul. The Russians also declared victory in the first flush of their Afghanistan adventure. The broad masses, the document added, had 'expressed unconcealed joy' at the overthrow of the notorious Amin. From that moment Pakistan became a frontline state in the war against communism.

Zia had the touch of a successful opportunist. He spurned an offer of $400 million in aid from Jimmy Carter as 'peanuts'. He was right. President Ronald Reagan sent apples: $3.2 billion spread over six years. This was outside what the CIA poured into the war effort, controlled from Peshawar. Zia exploited the American blind eye to push Pakistan's nuclear programme. The Carnegie Task Force Report on non-proliferation in South Asia, published in July 1986, reported that Pakistan had enough stockpiles for one to four bombs annually. India, it added, had the capability of making fifteen to thirty every year.

Zia used his unchallenged authority to propel the Islamization of Pakistan. In his early days, he sought assistance from the Jamaat-e-Islami, a religious-political organization created by one of the most influential Islamic thinkers of the last century, Maulana Abul Alaa al Maududi. Perhaps the Jamaat was misled into believing that Zia would actually share power with them. Zia had no such intention: he had to share power with his fellow generals, and key positions went to generals who shared his views. The most powerful job, after his own, was that of the head of the Inter-Services Intelligence (ISI) directorate, set up by Bhutto.

Zia had forced one vital concession from the Americans. All weapons, training and finance for the war against the Soviet Union would be funnelled only through the Pakistan army, and the CIA would do nothing independently. He had in place his own agency, the ISI.

Just after the Soviet invasion Zia appointed a new ISI chief, Lieutenant General Akhtar Abdul Rahman Khan, an officer in the same 'pious and professional' mould as himself, with three rows of medals, and as proud of his Islamic principles as of his Afghan blood. The ISI was given control of all supplies to the warriors of God. Weapons came from America, Egypt, Saudi Arabia, Britain, France, and Israel; where they ended up depended on the ISI. General Akhtar was in Zia's plane on the day it crashed. By then he had risen to chairman of joint chiefs of staff. Mentor and heir died together.

Zia complemented this with attempts to force through Islamic legislation. Getting public support for such laws, however, faltered on three counts. Strong differences arose between Sunnis and Shias (for instance, over laws of marriage; Shias have a system of 'temporary' [*muta*] marriage that can be extremely convenient for men). Second, there was public resistance to the imposition of punitive punishment that Zia insisted on, like flogging. And then there was old-fashioned corruption and inefficiency: the introduction of the *zakat* or charity law, for instance, led to complaints about the management and disbursal of this money. Zia was unperturbed. He passed a law, making eating or drinking in public during Ramadan a crime punishable by a fine of Rs 500 or a two-month jail sentence. The *mullahs*, typically, were more interested in Talibanization rather than an Islamic society; they appealed for an ordinance under martial law regulations to make beards compulsory for men and the veil for women (The Taliban would later enforce this in Afghanistan). They wanted a religious police that would ensure compliance of five prayers a day, and began learned discussions on whether blood donations were Islamic. Zia was unfazed. The programme he had launched in February 1979 acquired claws in May 1981 when the Federal Shariat Court was created with *ulema* as judges. In August 1982 *ulema* were named to a three-member appellate bench of the Supreme Court on Muslim law.

The tendency of the clergy towards cruel chauvinism became apparent.

In a horrific instance, a blind servant girl, Safia Bibi, was sentenced to fifteen lashes, because she had become pregnant after multiple rape. The rapists were not convicted, for lack of evidence! The power of the clergy, and the spread of seminaries (funded hugely by Saudi money), reached unprecedented levels during the Zia regime, but nothing was enough for the *mullahs*. Zia himself might have wondered about what he had begun. A whisper campaign was started, alleging that he was not a true Muslim but a Qadiani; a heretic who denied that Muhammad was not the last Prophet. Zia had to publicly deny this rumour, but there was no u-turn.

The speed with which the army returned to the barracks after Zia died, and civilians came to power through a democratic process indicates that the country was not convinced about Zia's dose of doctrine and dictatorship. However, that phase of indoctrination had created a large pool of committed fundamentalists who could not be removed from the public life of the country, nor could any future government retake the legislative space that the clergy had occupied with Zia's patronage. Some militants even took up arms against Zia's successor, the liberal, Oxford and Harvard-educated daughter of Bhutto, Benazir. In November 1994 a group called the Tehrik-e-Nifaz-e-Shariat-e-Muhammadi (roughly, those who wanted the laws of Muhammad), wearing their trademark black turbans (the preferred colour of Mullah Omar's turbans too) declared a jihad against Benazir from its base in Malakand in the North West Frontier Province. That very year a conspiracy was uncovered in the army to overthrow Bhutto and declare Pakistan a 'Sunni Islamic' state. The three senior officers involved were Major General Zaheerul Islam Abbassi, Brigadier Mustansar Billah, and Colonel Inayatullah Khan. They, along with some junior officers, had planned to storm a meeting of senior Army commanders on 30 September.

Zia successfully used duplicity with America. While he needed and used American support to survive at home and fight abroad, he gave parallel encouragement to the militancy that would soon confront the West. An event on 21 November 1980 is indicative. The American embassy was torched that day following rumours that American forces based in Saudi Arabia had attacked the Kaaba in Mecca. Zia could barely disguise his pleasure. While America was harnessing Islam against communism, Zia was seeding the country for a war that he himself may not have fully thought through.

America began to wake up to the involvement of Pakistan-based fundamentalists only after the bombing of the World Trade Center on 26 February 1993. On 19 November 1994, Egypt's embassy in Islamabad was attacked by a suicide bomber from Al Jihad, leaving eighteen dead and sixteen injured.

One particularly unfortunate consequence of Zia's policies was the violence against Pakistani Christians. Christians were never part of the politics of Partition, and had been left alone after 1947. However, once Islamic militants turned their attention to the Christian West, themes from a bitter history began to echo in domestic politics. The case of Selamat, Manzoor and Rahmat Masih, indigent Christians who were accused of blasphemy against the Prophet, became a cause celebre as the punishment for such blasphemy in Pakistan is death. On 5 April 1994 fundamentalists gunned down Manzoor as he left Lahore high court. On 15 May that year, *mullahs* demonstrated outside Lahore high court while a review petition on behalf of the Masihs was being heard inside. The slogans outside the court appealed to a group that was still unfamiliar in Pakistan. The Taliban. The *mullahs* urged these religious students (which is what Taliban means) to protect Islam in Pakistan, now being abused by Christians like the Masihs (Masih, incidentally, is a variation of Messiah; Jesus is called Isa Masih in Urdu). '*Kabul ke baad Islamabad...Taliban! Taliban!*' they chanted. After Kabul, they said, the Taliban must take over Islamabad.

Osama bin Laden was 22 when the Soviets invaded Afghanistan. His father, Muhammad, had emigrated from his native Yemen and got his first job with the giant oil company, Aramco − as a bricklayer. By the time Muhammad bin Laden died in 1966, in a suicidal air crash (those searching for psychological clues might want to note this), he owned the world's largest private contractor firm and probably also the world's largest family. He had fifty two children. One of them was destined to become a world figure.

Osama came to Pakistan in 1980, with encouragement from the Saudi intelligence chief, Prince Turki bin Faisal al Saud, and set up office in Peshawar. Any friend of Saudi intelligence was a friend of the ISI, and Osama flourished under the benign eye of General Akhtar. The mandate for the young man was to create a mobile Islamic strike force that could hit a target *anywhere.*

Religious organizations like the Jamaat and the ISI were already looking ahead to a jihad that would liberate all the Muslim nations under Soviet domination in Central Asia after victory in Afghanistan. Zia created, to use Musharraf's phrase, this state within a state; a set of institutions and individuals who would implement a not-so-hidden agenda in both international and domestic policy. Osama used personal funds and institutional support to create what was in effect a private army, mostly Arab, but also with Muslims from across the globe. Osama proved a capable fighter during his occasional stints on the warfront, but his principal contribution was organization and, even at that young age, leadership. When in Karachi, Osama operated from the Binori mosque; the *imam* there was a certain Mullah Omar.

Osama emerged out of the Afghan experience with an unshakeable conviction, which he repeated to anyone who would listen: with insignificant numbers and limited capability, a jihad could defeat even the greatest empire in the world. If the Soviet Union could be humbled, then the same spirit could renew Muslim power and confront Islam's more powerful enemy, America, the superpower that had usurped the oil wealth that Allah had given to Muslims. When Osama returned home to Saudi Arabia, he was welcomed as a hero by its government and the people.

On 2 August 1990 Saddam Hussein occupied Kuwait, convinced he could get away with his audacity. The Arabs, publicly, and America, more discreetly, had been supportive of his war against Iran. The Saudis said thank you in the only way they knew – hard cash. America was relieved to see Ayatullah Khomeini's energies diverted from the Great Satan to a local horror. However, instead of acquiescence, the world mobilized against Iraq. The terrorized Saudi ruling family believed that its turn was next. Osama bin Laden sent his government an offer. He could raise a force of at least 10,000 mujahideen, more than a match for the Republican Guard, against Saddam, he claimed. A Muslim army, he argued, should defend his homeland. For a few days Osama believed that his offer was under consideration. On 7 August he heard the announcement that American troops would protect Saudi Arabia's oil reserves. He was given a private assurance that the Americans would leave once Kuwait had been liberated. When they did not, Osama went public with his resentment. He would make his accusations more explicit later: the Saudi family had betrayed the Muslim people, befriended Christians and Jews, and were no longer fit to be custodians of the holy places. They would, he said, disperse and disappear like the Persian royal family. As for the Americans, he promised that they would leave Saudi Arabia in coffins.

Osama was told to leave Saudi Arabia. The government returned his passport. Osama's first stop was Pakistan, en route to his old haunt, Afghanistan. Liberated Afghanistan was an appalling, self-destructive mess by then. Dr Hassan al Turabi, the soft-spoken, scholarly leader of the

Sudan National Islamic Front, gave Osama and his entourage of Afghan veterans shelter in Khartoum in 1991. Al Qaida, or The Foundation, became the vehicle for his politics, while his shrewd business acumen increased his wealth during his years in Sudan.

Osama began to see himself as a new Caliph, or *imam*, who would safeguard Muslim interests across the world. His allies in the mission were groups like the Egyptian Gamaa al Islamiya and Al Jihad, who had conspired in the assassination of Anwar Sadat. The network grew. Governments in Algeria, Egypt, Tunisia, and Yemen found his hand in their troubles. The world began to explode with bursts of terror in the most unexpected places.

Nothing was more unexpected than the attack at the doorstep of the CIA headquarters in Langley, Virginia, a place where you might expect to find a certain degree of security. In January 1993, a man called Mir Aimal Kamsi shot dead two CIA employees outside the main gate of the CIA headquarters – and escaped, to Pakistan. He was tracked down and flown to the United States on 17 June 1995. The first attack on the World Trade Center occurred in February 1993. Obsessed with Saddam Hussein, an alarmed America chased shadows in Iraq. It was looking in the wrong country. The mastermind was a Pakistani Baluch, a veteran of the shadowy groups that were a law unto themselves in Pakistan.

His name was Ramzi Ahmed Yousef. He told his captors that he wanted to kill thousands of Americans by making the twin towers topple over each other like dominoes.

On 26 February, a Friday, a little before noon, a bomb blast shattered three floors of the parking garage of the World Trade Center, starting a fire. Six people died, and some seven hundred were injured. The plan was to engineer a blast that would fell one tower on to the other, while cyanide gas spiralled up. The tower did not topple, leading to a false sense of invulnerability, and the cyanide gas burnt up in the heat of the explosion. On 5 March 1993 the police made their first arrest: Mohammed Saleh, 26, a Jordanian working in a truck rental company. A van in the rubble had been traced to this company. It was the beginning of a two-year hunt. On 20 February 1995 Pakistan picked up 27-year-old Yousef from a hostel owned by Osama and handed him over to the US authorities.

The blind Egyptian cleric Sheikh Omar Abdul Rahman was also convicted in this case, but he was found guilty only of conspiracy, not the actual execution. His attorney argued that Sheikh Omar was only guilty of believing in his scripture, which he characterized as a profound dilemma.

The FBI accepted that there was no state sponsorship in the bombing, to the despair of those waiting to provoke American action against Iraq.

Ironically, Yousef had flown from his base in Pakistan to the United States in September 1992 with a false Iraqi passport in order to claim political asylum as a dissident Iraqi; a clever touch if ever there was one. After the bombing, he calmly boarded a plane back to Pakistan at JFK airport, this time using another false passport, but provided quite legally by the Pakistan consulate in New York, through another smart bit of deception. On 9 November 1992 he reported to the New Jersey police that he had lost his passport, and gave his name as Abdul Basit Mahmud Abdul Karim, born in Pakistan and reared in Kuwait. He then went to the Pakistan consulate with photocopies of this 'missing passport' and they handed him a temporary document and told him to sort things out when he returned home. He did return home, after bombing the World Trade Center. He remained in Pakistan until arrested, as we have noted, in a hostel owned by Osama bin Laden.

Osama bin Laden also turned east for shelter. By 1996 it became impossible for Sudan to resist regional and American pressure, so Osama was told to pack. This time there was a place for him in Afghanistan, thanks to a government placed in Kabul with Islamabad's assistance. His old friend from the Karachi days, Mullah Omar, was the supreme authority in what was known as a Taliban government.

Mullah Muhammad Omar Akhunzadeh was born in the Maiwand area of Kandahar, where peasants cultivate opium for a living. Those who have met him describe him as tall, thin, and rather elegant. He would speak in an almost inaudible voice, and sport a broad beard and black turban. He was injured thrice in the battles that swept the Taliban to power; wounds that he took pride in.

In 1994 Benazir Bhutto may have been in office, but she was not in charge of the parallel state that continued on its own course, and considered her an abomination. However, she did support the Taliban as it served a major foreign policy interest of Pakistan, being inimical to 'infidel' India. It also appeared to be the only answer to the bitter factional feuds that left Afghanistan ungoverned and sent a steady stream of refugees into Pakistan and Iran. Bandits controlled the highways, and collected money at gunpoint from trucks and travellers. In the summer of 1994 a convoy was held hostage by such bandits on the road to Kandahar. The Pakistan government, obviously, could not intervene. There were however Afghan students in the seminaries who seemed willing to intervene. A nod from the ISI brought guns and permission. About 2,000 students hit the road, freed the convoy, saved two women from a rapacious local commander, and left behind a legend. They went on to take Kandahar, the second largest city in the country. The students were exemplary in their behaviour. There were no revenge killings, and they established peace under a benevolent Islamic law. By February 1995 this movement, now fully armed by Pakistan and funded by the Saudis, who saw them as a solid Sunni wedge against Shia Iran, reached the neighbourhood of Kabul. Kabul did not fall, but Herat did. The first hint of the future came in Herat. A young man suspected of killing two Taliban was hanged from a crane while loudspeakers recited verses from the Quran. On 26 September 1996 the Taliban entered Kabul. They were very different from the group that had entered Kandahar in the pristine days.

The last pro-Soviet President, Najibullah, had found sanctuary in the United Nations office since his fall in April 1992. The Taliban castrated him publicly before killing him. The anti-Taliban forces managed to do in defeat what they could not do in victory, that is, ally with one another. They were however reduced to a rump base in the north of the country, giving them their name, the Northern Alliance.

The Taliban served Pakistan in significant ways, apart from ensuring an increasingly brutal stability. A perennial strategic aim of Islamabad has been to end the two-border squeeze, from both India and Afghanistan. Pakistan did not have to worry about the west with the Taliban in Kabul. The Taliban also became the pride and ally of the 'state within a state' in Pakistan. It was convenient for the government in Islamabad, which could push off those terrorists and groups who could not be given sanctuary in Pakistan because of its vulnerability to America. Osama bin Laden fell in this category.

America was initially reluctant to worry too much. It may have been influenced too by arguments of the 'larger interest', and particularly those advanced by the oil lobby. We have met Socal before, in Saudi Arabia. It now lobbied for a trans-Afghan pipeline from Central Asia to the Indian ocean, whose security and therefore viability, would be guaranteed by an apparently impregnable Taliban.

American reluctance to chase enemies in the region also stemmed partly from embarrassment, for many of the monsters had been created by a Frankenstein called the CIA. When the director of FBI in New York, Robert Fox, suggested on television in 1993 that some of the World Trade Center bombers had received CIA training, he found a transfer order on his desk in a few weeks. Washington could not however be squeamish for ever.

In February 1998 a meeting took place in Afghanistan between Osama bin Laden, Ayman Zawahri of the Egyptian Al Jihad, Rahman Khalil of the Pakistani Ansars, and Abdul Salem Muhammad from Bangladesh, and Abu Yassir Ahmed Taha representing the Maghreb. They agreed to coordinate their efforts through an Islamic Struggle Front. Whether all that happened in 1998 can be directly attributed to this meeting is impossible to confirm, but we can flag the incidents, and add that Osama was never shy about claiming credit for any jihad mission in America. In June he declared war on America through an interview to John Miller of ABC News, and you can hardly go more public than that. The Saudis, worried, exerted pressure on their clients, the Taliban, to persuade Osama to calm down. They already had some experience of Osama's reach. On 13 November 1995 a Saudi-US military office in Riyadh was attacked, killing five Americans; and on 25 June 1996 a housing complex for American servicemen at Khobar Towers was hit by a truck bomb, killing nineteen and injuring more than four hundred. Mullah Omar however made it clear then and later, that Osama was one of them, and would never be handed over.

On 7 August 1998, truck bombs hit American embassies in Dar es Salam, Tanzania, and Nairobi in Kenya. In Nairobi two hundred and forty seven people were killed, including twelve Americans. Ten died in Dar es Salam. President Bill Clinton ordered Osama's death by cruise missiles, and they hit Osama's camps at Khost in Afghanistan and what turned out to be a pharmaceutical plant near Khartoum, on 20 August 1998. The plan was codenamed Operation Infinite Reach. It reached nowhere. American intelligence teams swept through the world for clues. Among the first to be arrested was a Palestinian who had become a naturalized Kenyan, Muhammad Sadek Odeh. Odeh was arrested neither in Palestine nor Kenya, but in Pakistan.

The culture of guns and drugs sponsored by General Zia ate up Pakistan's credibility, and was a permanent threat to its internal stability. On the eve of her visit to the United States in April 1995, Prime Minister Benazir Bhutto remarked that Pakistan's very existence was threatened by this drug-gun culture. Her own existence certainly was. One person who tried to assassinate her was Ramzi Ahmed Yousef, who failed in an attempt to blow up her Islamabad residence, and along with it, her. He did not quite succeed when he bombed the World Trade Center either.

Just before he was sentenced Ramzi Ahmed Yousef told the tough, acerbic US District Court judge, 'Yes, I am a terrorist, and proud of it.' America had made him a terrorist, he said. He told Americans, 'You are more than terrorists. You are butchers, liars and hypocrites.'

Ramzi Ahmed Yousef dreamt of toppling those twin towers. He was arrested; but the towers came down, over eight years later, on 11 September 2001, because that dream was never arrested.

The Taliban, and Al Qaida, and many organizations with a similar dream, can survive without a government, or even a country, because the recruitment is done in the mind. You cannot fight a battle in the mind only with special forces and cruise missiles.

On 7 October 2001 the United States of America answered 11 September. It declared war on the Taliban, Osama bin Laden, and terrorism. The defeat of the Taliban and Osama was complete, but not decisive.

A jihad is never over. In the last week of January 2002 Pulitzer-prize winner John F. Burns, who had earlier done breakthrough reporting on the ethnic-cleansing in Bosnia, sent a story from Azhakhel Bala, Pakistan, to *The New York Times*:

> Little in the manner of Ijaz Khan Hussein betrays the miseries he saw as a volunteer in the war in Afghanistan.
>
> Mr Khan, a college-trained pharmacist, joined the jihad, or holy war, like thousands of other Pakistanis who crossed into Afghanistan. He worked as a medical orderly near Kabul, shuttling to the front lines and picking up bodies and parts of bodies. Of 43 men who boarded a truck to travel with him to Afghanistan in October, he said, 41 were killed. Now with the Taliban and Al Qaida routed, have Mr Khan and other militants finished with jihad?
>
> Mr Khan, at least, said he had not.
>
> 'We went to the jihad filled with joy, and I would go again tomorrow,' he said. 'If Allah had chosen me to die, I would have been in Paradise, eating honey and watermelons and grapes, and resting with beautiful virgins, just as it is promised in the Quran. Instead, my fate was to remain amid the unhappiness here on earth.'

Defeat is only a setback in the holy war. The jihad goes on.

15

SADDAM, BUSH AND THE SHIA JIHAD

The desert is the cradle of the Arab, and Iraq is his grave.

—An Arab proverb

The American response to Pearl Harbour and 9/11 was the same: 'Never again!'

In both cases, American skies had been penetrated with devastating effect, leaving a searing wound that would not easily heal. Both invasions were viewed as forms of deceit. Perhaps the line between them is thin: deception is permissible in the unwritten American code for war, but not deceit. American anger over Pearl Harbour was eventually assuaged by Hiroshima: there were few regrets over the use of an atomic bomb on a collapsing enemy.

11 September 2001 sparked an even greater need for revenge. The most potent symbols of American power were hit: Pentagon, the Twin Towers. The White House became vulnerable. President George Bush escaped into the skies and Vice President Dick Cheney into an unknown hole. More than 2000 people died and 16 acres of downtown New York gaped like some sculptured Guernica. Such startling images of terror had never been seen, each driven deep into the American subconscious by television. It was not a coincidence that the flag draped over the falling statue of Saddam Hussein in Baghdad in April 2003 was the same American flag that had fluttered over the Pentagon on the morning of 9/11.

'Never again' was the theme of subsequent policy. After Japan's defeat in 1945, war returned to the West. The fact that it was cold did not make it less dangerous, or less consuming. The cold war quickly turned into a world war, the third of the 20th century. The American intelligence establishment, unwilling to be surprised again, sought a pragmatic morality. It received permission for covert action.

George Washington, victor of a war against Britain, was the first American President to authorize spying abroad, but the world was too far away for America until the 20th century. No organization did intelligence work outside America until, in the early 1930s the FBI set up shop in Latin America. Branches of the military devised their ways and means on a need to know basis. It was not until after the outbreak of the Second World War that Franklin Roosevelt asked a New York lawyer, William J. Donovan, to draft a plan for such an organization. From this emerged the Office of Strategic Studies (OSS) in June 1942; and although Pearl Harbour was an intelligence failure, the OSS went on to do exemplary work in the war. American tradition reasserted itself after victory and the OSS was abandoned in October 1945.

But Donovan would not be denied. In September 1944 he sent Roosevelt a proposal for a post-war institution that would 'procure intelligence both by overt and covert methods', and coordinate all the various spy operations in different arms of the government. He also wanted authority to conduct 'subversive operations abroad'. Expectedly, existing operations were loath to surrender their independence. They were overruled, if a little patchily. In January 1946 President Harry Truman established the Central Intelligence Group. It sought to please everyone and pleased no one.

The cold war soon began to freeze Europe. The Soviet Union turned Poland, East Germany, Hungary, Romania, Bulgaria and the Baltic states into a protectorate; by February 1948 the democratic government of Czechoslovakia was replaced by a Communist dictatorship. The threat extended beyond East Europe with the real possibility of Communist parties heading elected coalitions in Italy and France. Greece had survived civil war. In the far east Chiang Kai-shek's nationalists were retreating before Mao Zedong. The American response began to sharpen.

The National Security Act became effective on 18 September 1947, and with it were born the National Security Council and the Central Intelligence Agency. The director of the CIA would report directly to the President.

How would the CIA ensure 'Never Again'? One option in 1947 was 'covert operations'. National Security Council Directive 4/A authorized the CIA to conduct covert psychological operations, a polite term for propaganda. After the 1948 Communist coup in Czechoslovakia, General Lucius Clay, commander of American forces in Germany, cabled Washington that war with the Soviet Union 'may come with dramatic suddenness'. This prompted NSC Directive 10/2, which defined the range of covert action that the CIA could plan and execute, throwing in a neat rider '...and that if uncovered the US Government can plausibly disclaim any responsibility for'.

Richard Helms, who joined the CIA at its birth and rose to become director during the terms of Presidents Lyndon Johnson and Richard Nixon, recalls a revealing conversation with Allen Dulles, the legendary head of the organization, in his book *A Look Over My Shoulder* (Random House, New York, 2003). It was January 1953 and Helms had just taken over responsibility for both intelligence collection and covert action operations. Dulles advised him, beginning with the beginning: 'You remember the conniving and the blood spilling that went on when we were trying to sort things out in 1946? What would Central Intelligence be responsible for? Would there even be a service? . . . It was perfectly clear then and it's all down in black and white that the fundamental purpose of Central Intelligence is to prevent anything resembling another Pearl Harbour . . . And as of 1948 it's been equally clear that we have full responsibility– all of it specified in NSC 10/2, documented and legal–for most aspects of *covert action* operations.'

There were no limits to covert operations. Regime change is not a 21st century war cry. It was part of a superpower's strategic needs, and the United States sought to destabilize governments in every continent, whenever it felt its vital interests were sufficiently threatened, with full authority from the President in each case, for the rest of the 20th century. As long as it lasted, the Soviet Union did the same thing, only more brutally, and bled to death when a regime change in Kabul went wrong. The United States and the Soviet Union had defined their line of control across Europe. The rest of the world was open game for their diplomatic, defence and intelligence establishments.

The most successful American covert action did not take place in East Europe, since it was off limits, but in an oil-soaked nation on the borders of the Soviet Union. The most vital of interests was involved, oil. The year was 1953, and it was an authentic Dulles triumph that sent church bells pealing through the establishment. The methodology was very different, but the mission in 1953 was much the same as the mission in 2003: a government that had become hostile to western interests had to be removed. In 1953 the means was covert action; in 2003 it was called pre-emptive strike. In the first instance, it was Iran; in the second, Iraq.

The consequences of decisive events are both immediate and long-term. Covert action in Tehran saved the pro-American Shah of Iran in 1953 but it also helped create the conditions for the success of an Islamic revolution 25 years later, in 1979. Where will Iraq be two decades after George Bush liberated the country from Saddam Hussein?

Events in Iran mesh easily with those of its neighbour, Iraq, particularly since Iran and Iraq are the only two Shia-majority nations in the Islamic world. Iraq became the first home of the Shia community in Islam, when the cousin and son-in-law of the Prophet Mohammad, Ali ibn Abi Talib, the first Caliph (or Imam) of the Shias and from whose trials and tribulations the Shia movement begins, made the garrison town of Kufa his capital.

Iraq and Iran trace their civilizations to the beginnings of recorded history. George Bush Junior's war on Iraq has brought some of this history to general attention, although Bush may not be aware that the Sumerian government offered the first recorded tax cut as well as declared the first formal war. It did not, however, do the two simultaneously. What the Greeks called Mesopotamia and we now call Iraq has been a centre of the civilized world since man began to write, ruled in turn by Sumerians, Akkadians, Babylonians, Hittites, Hurriyans, Kassis, Assyrians, Arabs and Turks. Half the Old Testament is Iraq-based, and the Talmud was written here. But the word 'Iraq' (meaning flat, sunny plains) was put into currency by geographers in the Islamic period, who also took care to differentiate between 'Persian Iraq' in the northeast and 'Arab Iraq' in the southwest.

Islam came to Iraq when Khalid ibn Walid, perhaps the most venerated of the early Muslim warrior-generals, started a four-year campaign along the Euphrates in 637, five years after the death of the Prophet, that eventually took the Muslims into the heart of the Sassanid Empire. The Persians were shocked and awed by their decisive defeat at the battle of Qadisiya, near Najaf, in 638. Persian forces included elephants, which were neutralized by Muslim suicide squads who slipped through enemy ranks to slice open their bellies. (There is nothing new about suicide missions.) A proverbial sandstorm that blew into enemy eyes provided the cover for the last Arab charge that dispersed the Persian army. The

217

Sassanid monarch Chosroes escaped to the eastern edge of his empire where he was killed by one of his own satraps. Umar, who was Caliph, ordered his troops to garrison the cities of Basra and Kufa.

The early years of Islam, as we have noted earlier, saw both unexpected success abroad and unbelievable turmoil at home, including civil wars over the leadership of a nascent community. The Prophet did not name a successor when he died in 632. Ali was bitterly disappointed when, by consensus, Abu Bakr was named the first Caliph. In 634 Abu Bakr was succeeded by Umar ibn al-Khattab, whose ten years in office turned Islam into a regional superpower. Ali again dissented, but accepted the will of the elders. In 644 there was much deeper dismay, and this time with better cause, for the third Caliph Uthman's reputation was not above controversy. Uthman belonged to the powerful Meccan family of Umayyads, and while his 12 years in authority were marked by some superb military triumphs (including a great victory against the Byzantines at sea in 654-55, known as the Battle of the Masts), nothing seemed to heal the bitterness within the community. In 656 Uthman was killed by a group of Muslims, who then named Ali as the Caliph.

Uthman's family, the Ummayads, challenged the succession. They were led by Muawiya, governor in Damascus, who not only had strong tribal support but also a battle-hardened army high on confidence after having driven the Byzantines out of Syria.

Ali responded by moving his capital from Medina to the garrison-town of Kufa in Iraq in 656. His followers, known simply as 'Ali shiatu Ali' (or, the followers of Ali, later shortened to Shia) launched their bid for leadership of Muslims in the name of their Imam, Ali, and his direct descendants, from Kufa.

Success was elusive. Two major battles were fought between Ali and Muawiya, in 656 and 657, after which Muawiya sought arbitration on the basis of the Quran. When Ali accepted the offer in the interests of peace, his own hardliners turned against him. One of them was so incensed that he assassinated Ali while he was praying in the mosque that he had built at Kufa. Ali was buried at Najaf, and his magnificent mausoleum has become a shrine for Shias, the third holy place on their map after Mecca and Medina. Najaf also developed into an *Atabat*, or a set of seminaries, and the home of the principal clergy of the community, the centre from which the most important *fatwas* were issued, a virtual Shia Vatican.

The Graveyard of Iraq

If Iraq can be called the graveyard of the Arab, then Najaf is the graveyard of Iraq. Its cemetery stretches for miles, and it is truly a city of the dead. Millions of Shias have either come to die at Najaf, or been brought to be buried near the last resting place of their beloved Imam Ali. The city of the dead calls out to the living; and one Shia who heard the call left India in 1830 for a pilgrimage to Najaf. He never returned. His name was Seyyed Ahmad Musavi Hindi; his grandson was named Ruhollah Khomeini.

Muawiya's death in 680 relit the first conflagration in Muslim history. By this time, Damascus had become the capital of a world power. The empire stretched from north Africa in the west to the border of Afghanistan; it was a prize worth the effort. Muawiya had persuaded, sometimes with the help of the sharp edge of the sword tribal leaders to pledge their allegiance to his son Yazid: he once described the sword as his most effective orator. Ali's second son, Husayn, was unimpressed by the Ummayad sword. He did not give his allegiance to Yazid. Husayn left Medina with just 72 armed followers and women and children for his father's base in Kufa. On the way, at Karbala, he was ambushed by about 4,000 of Yazid's forces. On the tenth day of Muharram. Every single warrior in that group was killed; the women and children were taken prisoner. The image of Husayn, the last of the martyrs, with a sword in one hand and a Quran in the other, is a central image of the Shia lament. Husayn's surviving son, Zain al Abedin, became the next Imam of the Shias.

The difference between Sunni and Shia is political rather than doctrinaire; on the nature of the leader rather than the content of the message. The Shias are not in any sense a deviation from Islam. They accept, like Sunnis, the eternity of Muhammad's message, and him as the last Prophet of Allah. They do not recognize the first three successors of the Prophet as leaders, or Caliphs of the community and offer their allegiance to the fourth, Ali, and his descendants. They base their faith in his dynasty on verse 124 from the second chapter of the Quran, Al Baqarah: 'And remember that Abraham was tried by his Lord with certain commands, which he fulfilled: He (the Lord) said "I will make thee an Imam to the nations".' The promise was extended to Abraham's offspring. Muhammad was a direct descendant of Abraham, and his descendants were his son-in-law Ali's children.

'Wherever Shiites are to be found,' writes Bernard Lewis (*The Middle East: 2000 Years of History From the Rise of Christianity to the Present Day*, Weidenfeld and Nicholson, 1995*)*, 'on this day (of Karbala) they commemorate the martyrdom of the Prophet's family, the penitence of those who failed to save them, and the wickedness of those who killed them, in religious rituals inspired by the potent themes of sacrifice, guilt and expiation. The doctrinal differences between Sunni and Shia Muslims are of minor importance, far less than those that divide the rival churches of Christendom. But the Shiite sense of martyrdom and persecution, reinforced by their long experience through the centuries as a minority group under rulers whom they regarded as usurpers, raised a psychological barrier between them and the Sunni state and majority, a difference of experience and outlook, and therefore also of religious and political attitudes and behaviour.'

The Shia community attracted support because of political and social reasons rather than religious ones. The pro-Arab racism of the Umayyads, who treated Persians as inferior when one of the fundamental tenets of Islam was equality, increased support for the Shias in Persia. The Persians, with a thousand years of empire behind them, had natural disdain for upwardly mobile desert tribes. Dissent invited persecution. Shia memory of Sunni rule is best summed up in the story of the Umayyad governor Al Hajjaj bin Yusuf al Thaqafi who famously said on entering Najaf: 'I see heads ripe for cutting and I am the man to do it.' A sense of oppression married well with the tradition of martyrdom. Karbala became a seminal memory, reinforced each year during the month of Muharram, with its penitential procession of Shia men lacerating themselves with knives and chains as self-punishment for their inability to save Husayn. A poetic line sums up the Shia philosophy: *Islam zinda hota hai har Karbala ke baad.* Or, Islam is resurrected with every Karbala. History made the Shia into a rebel. Rebellion encouraged the doctrine of *ghayba* and *raj'a*, concealment and return: the leader, or the imam, disappears but is not dead, he will return through divine help to deliver the people. Exile and triumphant return is part of the Shia eschatology. On a more practical level, sanction was given to the practice of *taqiyya*. This permits a Shia to dissimulate before hostile authority, to deny his faith in order to preserve it. Radical options are more tempting to a party of the underprivileged.

The most astonishing consequence of Karbala is that Shias, despite their majority, have never been in power in Iraq, a land bequeathed to them by their Imam Ali. From Yazid in 680 to Saddam Hussein in 2003, only Sunnis have ruled Iraq.

In an irony fraught with unintended consequences, George Bush has removed the last Sunni dynasty, the one sought to be created by Saddam Hussein. By ushering democracy, or some form of it, George Bush will enable Shias to rule their original homeland for the first time in more than 1300 years. Bush in that sense has reversed the consequences of the battle of Karbala. Allah too works in His mysterious ways His wonders to perform.

Shias lost battles, but they never lost hope. Their anger played a significant part in the destruction of the Ummayad dynasty, which lasted only 70 more years after Karbala. As misrule fed disaffection, the Shia belief that only a member of the Prophet's family could lead the community began to gather support. On 13 June 747 a black banner of revolt was unfurled in Persia, and quickly spread to Iraq. By 750 the Umayyads were defeated, and the rebels proclaimed their leader, Abul Abbas, the new Caliph, at the Shia stronghold of Kufa. Abbas was nicknamed 'al-Saffah,' or the shedder of blood, when he killed every member of the Umayyad family, bar one. (Only Abdur Rahman escaped and went on to build an empire in Spain.) But once again the Shias were to be disappointed. The Abbasids had exploited Shia slogans during the revolt, but the moment they came to power they turned their sword against suspect friend as easily as against established foe. Abbas turned on the Shias to ensure that the perennial rebels did not rebel against him. His successor in 754, Abu Jaafar al-Mansur, may have been less bloodthirsty but he was no more sympathetic to the Shias. Mansur put about the story that he had a magic mirror, passed on to him by Allah through Adam and Abraham, by which he could see where every rebel was hiding. Mansur believed that the four pillars of his state were the chief judge, the chief of police, the chief tax collector and a postmaster who could spy on all three.

Conscious that Damascus was an Ummayad city, Mansur began to search for an Abbasid capital. Christian monks pointed out a small village from where, according to their holy books, a great kingdom would grow. In July 758 more than a hundred thousand artisans and engineers broke ground. Mansur named the city Baghdad, or the gift of God. In 765

Mansur entered a capital guarded by walls that were 145 feet thick, to live in a palace whose green dome rose 160 feet. By the time Haroun al Rashid came to power in 786, Baghdad had a population of half a million stretched across 25 square miles of city and suburbs. The culture of power became munificent and magnificent. When his treasurer told Haroun that a particular project was too expensive, he replied that no money is ever wasted that leaves a large legacy of praise. For five centuries the Sunni Abbasids sat on the throne of Baghdad, until in 1258 a whirlwind from the east destroyed a still-resplendent capital along with its decayed dynasty.

In August 1257, Hulegu Khan, grandson of Chingiz, had Persia at his feet and Iraq in his grasp. He sent a letter to the Caliph Mostassim which read like a death warrant rather than an invitation to a dialogue. The Caliph was asked to level his capital's mighty walls, abdicate and come over to the Mongols as a hostage. The Caliph may have lost real power, but he had not yet lost his wits: ten days of good fortune, he replied, had seduced Hulegu into believing that he had become a master of destiny. The Mongol's response was sharp: the Caliph, he said, was as crooked as a bow; he would make Mostassim as straight as an arrow. Legend has it that Hulegu consulted two astrologers, a Sunni and a Shia, before he decided to attack Baghdad. The Sunni seer predicted six calamities that would visit anyone who dared to lay siege to the capital of Islam. The Shia astrologer, a man called Nasser, predicted that the only thing that would happen would be the destruction of a dynasty that had outlived its utility. Nasser proved right. When his pretensions had been stripped bare, Mostassim tried obeisance but it was too late. Baghdad's citizens were slaughtered for seven days till there was no one left to kill and nothing left to loot.

Medieval Baghdad was lost in that vengeful week. Its chief glory was not the magic of the Arabian Nights, or the dazzle of its markets, but the wealth of its intellectual life. For centuries the city had been home to a succession of cutting-edge scholars and scientists, nourished by a stable empire. In 830, for instance, Muhammad al-Khawarizmi produced an extraordinarily accurate map of the world for its time, while also creating the astrolabe and discovering the algorithm. There were massive private libraries and hundreds of bookstores; and the science of the Greeks was preserved in translations, particularly in the reign of al-Mamun. This dynasty ended on 21 February 1258 when, at the age of 46, the 37th

Abbasid Caliph was bundled into a sack and trampled to death by Mongol horses.

The Mongols ended the first era of Islam, one controlled by the Arabs who had emerged from Mecca and Medina. Their credibility, dented by suicidal and fractious egotism, had died before their dynasty. It could not survive the hammer blows delivered by the Christian Crusaders who took Jerusalem in 1098 from under the nose of Baghdad and Damascus. The centre of gravity now shifted to what might be called the New Muslims, the Kurds, the Turks and tribes of Central Asia, who would reverse the victories of the infidels and eventually rule Muslim empires that stretched contiguously from North Africa to the edge of Burma. The revival found its first international hero in an Iraqi Kurd, Saladin, but before he could turn the Crusader tide he had to demolish the only Shia dynasty in the first phase of Islamic history.

Curiously, the most successful Iraqi Shia founded a kingdom not in Iraq but in Tunisia. In 910, Abu Abdullah al-Dai, a thread inspector from Basra, reached Tunisia, proclaimed to the Berber tribes that he was the promised Mahdi, and at their head seized power from the Abbasid governor. Abdullah claimed descent from Fatima, the Prophet's daughter; hence his rule was called Fatimid. Abdullah's great grandson, Al-Muizz, turned a kingdom into an empire when he conquered Egypt in 972. Within two years he shifted his court to Egypt and founded the city of Cairo. At one point the Fatimid Empire stretched to Syria, but never managed to dislodge the Abbasids in Baghdad. That period is sometimes called the era of the cold war between Shia Cairo and Sunni Baghdad. Neither, however, could save Jerusalem. Saladin, who held the misrulers of Cairo, Damascus and Baghdad responsible for the loss of Jerusalem, dispatched the dynasty with barely-disguised contempt in 1171. He united Damascus and Cairo and ignored Baghdad. But Saladin's own successors were less than competent and almost lost what their hero had won. Muslim fortunes were saved on the battlefield by the so-called slave-regiment of Mamelukes, a tribe of Turkish Sunnis. They went on to rule Egypt.

The Shias did not find another haven until the Safavids came to power in Persia in the sixteenth century. They made Shiism the state doctrine, and over time changed popular attitudes till Persia became overwhelmingly Shia. For a while the Safavids attempted to extend their rule to Baghdad, contesting the southward thrust of the Sunni Ottomon Turks in the 17th century, but the Turks prevailed. The Shias had lost, consecutively, to the Umayyads, Abbasids and Ottomans. They did not fare any better when the Europeans arrived to Middle East.

MAN OF OTHERS' DESTINY

Europe was expelled from the Levant (the Crusades were a Levant war) in 1291, when the last outpost of the Franks, the fortress of Acre, fell to the Egyptians. The French reappeared in Egypt precisely 508 years later, in 1799. Their commander was Napoleon. Whatever he touched turned into either battle, empire or controversy, so it was not surprising that Napoleon provoked the riddle that would consume the nineteenth century: the Eastern Question.

Egypt was too insignificant for Napoleon's ambitions. He was 30, and another Alexander on the march. He had come to Egypt, then ruled by the Ottoman Turks, to knit a fantasy empire from Paris to Calcutta, with his own throne at Constantinople/Istanbul. He was prepared to convert to the religion of his future subjects, if that was what it took to win their affections. On landing in Egypt he declared that he had become a Muslim. He took Cairo and then moved north to Al Arish in the Sinai, from where he advanced to Palestine, reaching Acre on March 18. The fortress was defended vigorously by the Ottomans, and Napoleon now urged the Arabs to rebel and overthrow the Turkish yoke. In this he foreshadowed T.E. Lawrence (or Lawrence of Arabia) by precisely 115 years. Napoleon, a man of everyone else's destiny, also decided that it was an appropriate moment to offer a homeland for the Jews; he was as ready to be a Zionist as a Muslim in the service of his ambition. From Ramleh, 25 miles from Jerusalem, he asked Israelites to return from exile and restore their civic rights that had been shamefully stolen from them for thousands of years. By simultaneously offering Arabs liberation from Turkey and Jews a new kingdom of David, Napoleon was doing precisely what the British were to do more than a century later, in the First World War.

At St Helena Napoleon fantasized in his memoirs: 'Acre once taken . I would have reached Constantinople and the Indies (India). I would have changed the face of the world.' Unfortunately for him, his destiny, far from taking him to Constantinople, did not take him even to Jerusalem. The Turks refused to be defeated. When, at Mount Tabor, on 16 April

1799 Napoleon destroyed a Turkish army which had come to relieve the garrison at Acre, he thought he had captured the road to Constantinople. There were visions of a triumphal entry into Jerusalem en route to Turkey. But he forgot that this was not the Third Crusade. The British this time were not allies of the French. They were instead allies of the Ottomans.

All events have a background. In 1776 the French had avenged their defeat in the Seven Years War (1756-1763) with a magnificent triumph, when they helped liberate the American colonies. The loss of America concentrated British minds wonderfully in one direction, the east and India. French colonialism was interrupted by Bastille in 1789, but Napoleon arrived to resurrect it. Napoleon calculated that the British could be strangled out of India if France seized Egypt, cut a canal through to the Red Sea, turned the Mediterranean into a French lake, and took a grip on the trade from the East through this new route. The third side of the Eastern Question was framed by Russia, which under Catherine the Great was thirsting for a warm water port in the Black Sea, Odessa. After Odessa the urge towards Constantinople was as large a gleam in the Czarist eye as it was in the French. Britain could afford neither possibility.

The road to India was an important part of strategic thinking in Paris and London. Hesitant to take on the British from the front, across the channel, Napoleon decided to stab them in the back. It was not entirely coincidental that the army he led to Egypt was the one he had assembled for England.

The British knew their road map as well as the French. The moment Napoleon set out for Egypt, William Pitt, Prime Minister of Britain, signed a secret treaty with the Ottomans guaranteeing the territorial integrity of the Ottoman Empire for eight years. And so while Napoleon advanced towards Palestine and Syria, Lord Nelson smashed the fleet that had brought him to the shores of Egypt. The naval guns of Sir Sidney Smith turned against Napoleon during his siege of Acre in April and May 1799. On 20 May, five weeks after the dreams of Tabor, Napoleon admitted defeat. He would describe it as the bitterest moment of his life.

Control of the Middle East became synonymous, for the British, with the defence of India.

The Ottomans obliged Britain in the 19th century through a paradox. They were strong enough to hold on to most of their empire: rumours of their death had been vastly exaggerated. But, unable or unwilling to keep pace with weapons technology, they had also weakened sufficiently to start losing their frontiers. Greece was the first country to become independent, in 1832, after 400 years of Ottoman rule. Predators, including friendly Britain, nibbled at the edges. Britain looked longingly at Egypt and a very unusual man gave Britain her chance. His name was Mehmet Ali.

He was an Albanian who might never have become a Pasha of the Turks in Egypt if his life had not been saved by the British in a battle against the French. If that is not a multinational coincidence then it would be difficult to find one. He commanded an Egyptian regiment against Napoleon in 1799, and was literally driven into the sea where he was rescued by a British ship. His fortunes lifted after Napoleon returned to France, and the Ottomans got back their Arab territories. Mehmet Ali was appointed Pasha of Egypt in 1805. A large degree of autonomy was inbuilt into the structure of such a sprawling empire. Mehmet Ali began to expand the territories under his control, and increase his political distance from Constantinople. Using French military advisers, he built up a modern army and fleet, and in 1830 moved against his Turkish masters. By 1833 he had taken the whole of Syria and posed a direct threat to Istanbul, to the unmasked delight of the French who believed that the Ottoman Empire would soon come under their influence through their surrogate. A desperate Sultan sought help from both the English and the Russians. Lord Palmerston, the British foreign secretary, wavered, waiting to see whether a deal with Mehmet Ali might not be more helpful to his cause. The Russians did not hesitate, but their help to the Sultan came at a heavy price: the Turks promised to close the Dardanelles to all other warships. England intervened, and joined Russia and Turkey against the Egypt-France alliance. Mehmet Ali was defeated, and his bubble exploded after an impressively long life. The Pasha who startled visitors by smoking a diamond-studded hookah would die insane. The European powers joined Turkey in a new treaty, signed in London in July 1841, to preserve the Ottoman Empire. But Europe now also knew that an empire that could not protect itself was available for dismantling. In 1839 Britain occupied Aden.

Direct intervention in the Middle East brought Jerusalem back onto the British political horizon. The Jewish question entered the discourse.

In 1839, just before his collapse, Mehmet Ali gave an audience to Sir Moses Montefiore, the first British Jew to be knighted, who was on his second visit to Jerusalem. Sir Moses had a plan for a grant of land corresponding to between 100 and 200 villages on which European Jews could settle. Mehmet Ali, who wanted Sir Moses to be his business partner in Europe, promised to do everything he could to help this project. The idea of Jewish resettlement had support from high quarters in London, most notably Lord Palmerston, who even sought to persuade Abdulmecid I, Sultan from 1839, through the British ambassador in Istanbul, that it would be in the Ottoman interest to keep a Jewish wedge in Palestine between Turkey and Egypt. This was urged in a formal letter from the foreign secretary to Lord Ponsonby, the British envoy, dated 11 August 1840. Within a week, on 17 August, *The Times* published an editorial praising a plan 'to plant the Jewish people in the land of their fathers...(that was under) serious political consideration'.

The idea of a new Israel had the support of the evangelist lobby, which wanted the Biblical prophecy of the Second Coming fulfilled in much the way that the Bible belt in contemporary America values the existence of Israel. The return of the Jews to Israel is a necessary prelude to the Second Coming. Britain was in its most Christian phase at the time. Empire and religion had similar objectives. But to the Sultan, the idea of a homeland for Jews in Jerusalem seemed irrelevant when the Ottomans had provided sanctuary to the persecuted community ever since they were driven out of Catholic Spain. Jews, for instance, formed the largest ethnic group in Baghdad when it fell to the British after the First World War. The Ottomans did not buy the British argument for Israel. The concept survived a seesaw life until the Balfour Declaration in the course of the First World War made it a part of British policy. The end of that war in 1918 also marked the end of the Ottoman Empire. Priorities had changed. The highest priority for the British Empire now was oil.

JARS OF OIL

The British had only one, and insufficient, source of oil in the first decade of the twentieth century, in Burma. It was drilled by a company owned by Scotsmen and called, simply and accurately, Burmah Oil.

Iraq's oil potential had been the subject of much talk, but insufficient evidence. Nebuchadnezzar, King of Babylon, was said to have thrown rebellious Jews into a burning furnace six miles from Kirkuk, in the heart of what is now Kurdish Iraq; and the locals had set a street on fire to impress Alexander. But Middle Eastern oil was first rediscovered by the West in Persia, since the West did not have access to Iraq's deserts till British and French rule began in the region after 1918.

Persia's epic heroes, Cyrus and Darius, ruled an empire that in the fifth century BC touched India in the east and Greece in the west, and they used oil for both the construction of ship as well as to bind bricks. The penultimate Persian dynasty, the Qajars, heavily influenced by European powers in the 19th century, permitted European exploration, and in the 1890s French geologists reported that Persia had extraordinary reserves.

Baron Julius de Reuter, who made a fortune out of news, would have become even wealthier if he had kept faith in the Persian oil concessions he obtained in 1872 and 1889. But news was clearly easier to manage than a desert. The concessions lapsed, and it was left to a maverick prospector, gambler and racing man (he had the only private box at Epsom apart from the royal family) to create economic history.

We have met William Knox D'Arcy. In 1901 he sent his agent to Tehran to negotiate a concession, which duly materialized after everyone useful (including the man who brought the pipe and coffee to His Majesty Muzaffar al-Din) had received a suitable gift. He had competition from Russia. Russia wanted to build a pipeline from Baku to the Persian Gulf to find an Indian market for its kerosene, and threw a spanner or two, but nothing could argue against the persuasive power of a bribe. D'Arcy sent an extra five thousand pounds to the Shah personally, and the master of Persia signed on the dotted line. D'Arcy won a 60-year concession that allowed him to explore across three quarters of the country.

The journey was less exciting than the start. Initial estimates put the cost of drilling two wells at 10,000 pounds. In 1903 D'Arcy noted ruefully that every purse had its limits, and he could see the end of his own. By 1904 he had lost 200,000 pounds and the venture was on the point of collapse. The British government was concerned that D'Arcy might sell out to private interests or, worse, that either he or the Persians might turn to Russia. The Foreign Office worried about a Russian naval base in the Persian Gulf that could threaten India, and the Admiralty wanted secure oil for the British fleet. London forced Burmah Oil to help D'Arcy survive. It also sent, from India, to protect the drilling, a company of twenty horsemen from the Bengal Lancers under Lieutenant Arnold Talbot (or 'AT') Wilson, a Tarzan kind of figure who was as dedicated to the empire and religion as to physical exercise. (He once saved fare on the ship home by working as stoker.) AT would become the first 'despot of Messpot' when the British conquered Iraq, or Mesopotamia as they originally called it, during the First World War.

The nearest dentist from Maidan-e-Naftan, or the Field of Oil, says Daniel Yergin (*The Prize: The epic quest for oil, money and power,* Simon and Schuster, 1991) was 1500 miles away, in Karachi; and the nearest brothel 150 miles away in Basra. (The code word for the latter was a visit to the dentist, for some reason, perhaps to do with various forms of drilling.) D'Arcy was drilling on a spot known as Masjid-e-Suleiman. By May 1908, Burmah Oil had had enough. Orders were issued that the rigs be dismantled and sent to Burma. They had not reached Persia when a well came alive. At about 4 am on the morning of 26 May 1908 oil was struck. It was the tip of a lake that would become a sea when next-door Iraq's potential was established.

Britain tried to persuade Turkey to remain neutral in the First World War. But the Ottomans, victims of either Russian aggression or British diplomacy for a century, declared for Germany and the Central Powers in October 1914 in what would be the last Jihad call given by an Ottoman Sultan. Turkey's first offensive in the region was towards the Abadan oil refinery in Persian Shatt al-Arab, through which the Tigris and Euphrates enter the sea; the second, in February 1915, across the Sinai towards the Suez Canal. The threat to British interests was serious, and made the Middle East into *the* major theatre of the war. An eager Churchill dreamt of a prize no less than Istanbul via the Dardanelles, and was humiliated at Gallipoli. But there was success elsewhere. The Turkish advance to Suez was repulsed in February 1915, and a Mesopotamian Expeditionary Force made up from the Indian Army sailed in from the Gulf, saved the Anglo-Persian Oil Company's operations and occupied Basra. Basra became not only a launching pad for the Iraq campaign but also the epicentre of a comfort zone for local emirs who survived under British protection. The British were to suffer one severe defeat on the way to Baghdad, at Kut, but the capital of Iraq was taken in April 1917. The second British advance, by the British Egyptian Expeditionary Force, led by (later, Field Marshal) Edmund H.H. Allenby, began from Egypt in December 1916 and reached Jerusalem in exactly one year. (The Turks, after fighting hard all along the way, chose not to defend the city that was holy to all three Semitic religions, Judaism, Christianity and Islam.)

It is often said, when examining the torrid consequences, that British policy during the war was a mess; but that is not quite correct. It was remarkably single-minded and clear. The British had only one policy: to win. They did everything necessary, made every bargain that they needed to irrespective of whether they wanted to keep their word or not. Morality was for the weak-minded. Any support was welcome if a promise was all that was required to buy it. Each deal had a public face as well as a secret life, as allies were to discover.

Herbert Henry Asquith, said to be the first Prime Minister since Pitt the Younger to carry a tipple into the House of Commons, snubbed the idea of a Jewish homeland when it was presented to him by Sir Herbert Samuel, the first Jewish Cabinet minister in a memorandum titled *The Future of Palestine*. Sir Herbert had support from Lloyd George, who remarked that he was more familiar with the cities of the Old Testament than the battlefields of the Western Front. The idea revived when Lloyd George became Prime Minister in December 1916 and Arthur James Balfour his foreign secretary. On 2 November 1917, in a communication of 117 words to Lord Rothschild of the Zionist Federation in Britain, he conveyed the government's approval of a plan for 'the establishment in Palestine of a national home for the Jewish people'. Arabs, at that time, made up 87 per cent of the local population and Jews only 13 per cent. When the League of Nations assigned the mandate of Palestine to Britain on 24 July 1922, it confirmed the pledge.

Between 1915 and 1916, totally contrary promises were made to the Arabs. The British were aware of an Arab nationalist upsurge against Turkish rule. In an effort to instigate a revolt against the Ottoman Empire, the British settled on Husayn ibn Ali, the Sherif of Mecca, and his family as their flag bearers. On 31 October 1914, Field Marshal Lord Horatio Herbert Kitchener, former consul general in Egypt and now war minister, sent a cable to be forwarded to the Husayn family dangling the offer of the Caliphate after an earlier promise of an Arab 'nation' to be created out of the ashes of the Ottoman Empire.

In the spring of 1915 Kitchener sent out a young archeologist and Arabic scholar, T.E. Lawrence, who had done a survey of Sinai for the Palestine Exploration Fund, to Cairo for 'military intelligence', a vague definition that left a great deal of room for individual manoeuvre. Lawrence of Arabia had the whole desert to manoeuvre in, and did so with fertile dexterity. He too conveyed the dream of a future Arab nation. This was put in more concrete form in correspondence between Kitchener's successor in Cairo, Sir Henry McMahon, between July 1915 and January 1916. (Arabs had no idea that this was the same man who had delineated, during his service in India, both the Durand Line dividing Pakistan from Afghanistan and the McMahon Line in 1914 that divides India and China in the eastern Himalayas. Both are still disputed.) The fourth letter, dated 24 October 1915, was crucial, since it sought to define the geography of the nation. The number of times he hedged to protect British interests (through virtual control of government) might well have been interpreted as a guarantee of sincerity about the rest, critically, that Britain was 'prepared to recognize and support the independence of the Arabs'. There was also a mention that French interests would have be considered. McMahon was skilful; he left every party to make of the promise what they would. Husayn ibn Ali, along with the ablest of his sons, Faisal (Lawrence called him 'an absolute ripper') dutifully launched the Arab revolt on 6 June 1916.

He might have been less eager if he had known what McMahon knew, that two bureaucrats in London and Paris were arguing over a different future. In January 1916, a month after Lloyd George became Prime Minister, Sir Mark Sykes, who had once served Britain in Istanbul, and Francois Georges-Picot, who had once been French consul in Beirut, reached a provisional agreement on the map of post-Ottoman Middle East. There was no mention of any Arab homeland. Russia had made a secret claim on the Bosphorus and adjacent Turkish territory; France wanted Syria, a term for the Levant coast (now extending across Syria, Lebanon, Palestine/Israel and Jordan), to protect the Christian minorities as well as to rule. What they got was different. The British red appeared over Iraq and its influence extended across north Persia and Egypt. The French blue started from Acre (they never forgot that fortress) to deep into Turkey along the coast. A small bit of brown in Palestine was left as an 'International Sphere'. Every 'Arab homeland' was heavily predicated by its 'Sphere of Influence'. Emerging realities would alter the details (Turkey proved more resilient than they conjectured, and Russia fell off the allied map), but the contours would hold.

Tsarist approval was obtained by handing out Ottoman Armenia to Moscow. Italy was pacified with a part of Asia Minor, and a final agreement was reached on 18 August 1917, merely awaiting formal Russian ratification. Before it could arrive, the Tsars were overtaken by the October Revolution. Sykes-Picot might never have become public knowledge had the Bolsheviks not handed it out to the press as evidence of imperialist chicanery.

British bureaucrats were horrified when they learnt of the details, not because promises had been violated, but because Sir Mark Sykes had handed over oil-rich Mosul to France. (There might have been less post-war confusion if Sir Mark Sykes had not died suddenly of influenza in 1919 at the age of only 40, but that is only a hypothesis.) Oil had been the big story of the war, and this was tantamount to a scandal. Sir Maurice Hankey, the powerful secretary of the War Cabinet, could not have put it more accurately when he wrote to foreign secretary Balfour after the British occupied Baghdad in 1917 that control over oil supplies was a 'first class war aim'. The British had already taken from Persia what they could: oil production in Persia had risen from 1600 barrels a day in 1912 to 18,000 in 1918 but the demands of war were ravenous. As Balfour put it to the Prime Ministers of Dominions at a conference in August 1918, after explaining that it would be more respectable to become the 'guiding spirit' rather than an imperial presence in Iraq/Mesopotamia, 'I do not care under what system we keep the oil, but I am clear it is all-important for us that this oil should be available.'

It would be, but oil always comes with a price tag.

THE WAR AFTER VICTORY

The British inherited an Iraq that was administered as three vilayets under the Ottomans, with their capitals in Mosul, Baghdad and Basra. Baghdad was a cosmopolitan city: Jews constituted the largest single ethnic group, followed by Arabs and Turks, mainly Sunnis. The rest of the country was different. Shias were in an overwhelming majority, but administrative power continued in the hands of a small Sunni elite, exactly as it had been for centuries. Freedom from Turkish rule meant different things to Sunnis and Shias: Arab nationalism for the former, and liberation from both the Turks and the Sunni Arabs for the latter. The British had no interest in meeting either aspiration; they were too busy with their own needs. When the Shias discovered that nothing had changed, they turned their anger against the new rulers.

When America entered the First World War on the side of Britain and France in 1917 it made a promise that has a familiar tone: it was going to make the world 'safe for democracy'. There was genuine hope among the Arabs when the Armistice in November 1918 elicited a declaration (drafted by the familiar Mark Sykes) that Iraq and Syria would have 'national governments and administrations that shall derive their authority from the free exercise of the initiative and choice of the indigenous population...Far from wishing to impose on the populations of these regions any particular institutions, [the British and French governments] are only concerned to ensure, by their support and adequate assistance, the working of governments and administrations freely chosen by [the people] themselves' (quoted by John Keay in *Sowing the Wind: The Seeds of Conflict in the Middle East,* Murray, 2003). This was on 7 November. On 1 December 1918 Prime Ministers Clemenceau and Lloyd George were celebrating in London. After accepting public cheers they went to the French embassy and made their first deal. What did Britain want, asked Clemenceau, jovially, but not lightly. Mosul and Palestine replied Lloyd George. He got both. Promises made to both Arabs and Jews were betrayed in that one moment. They were never intended to be kept. The Jews would have to await another world war, and the Arabs longer.

If Husayn ibn Ali and his sons thought their status as descendants of the Prophet would fetch them better returns, they were quickly disillusioned. Boundaries were drawn along the Sykes-Picot lines, and remain on the maps today. Syria was created and Britain, as the occupying power, guided by Lawrence, rewarded Faisal, Husayn's son, with its throne. But France had no intention of being diddled out of her post-war empire. France sent the one-armed, blue-eyed General Henri Gouraud, and on 25 July 1920 he entered Damascus at the head of his Moroccan, Algerian and Senegalese troops. The French had no use for ceremony. Faisal was put into a train at the Hijaz railway station. The British welcomed him ceremonially at Haifa, and then left him, sitting on his baggage instead of a throne.

In 1920 the British got their first taste of the future. Their administration had been run by the indefatigable imperialist, 'Acting' Civil Commissioner Wilson. Trouble began to brew in the form of incidents, as he began to demand revenue from a people he had conquered against their will. The San Remo conference in 1920 may have given Britain the legal protection of a mandate, but Wilson was feeling more like King Canute. The Shias, both in the cities of Najaf and Karbala, and in the tribal villages, declared jihad. Keay writes: 'It so happened that in 1920 the month-long fast of Ramadan coincided with the infernal heat of May/June. [there was] an ominous closing of Islamic ranks as Sunni and Shia draped their shared hostility to the mandate in the greed flag of the jihad.' There are parallels with 2003: 'There were no pitched battles; as Lawrence [of Arabia] had demonstrated, Arab tactics did not lend themselves to battles.' The British were called Franji, a term we have encountered earlier: it was used by Arabs to describe the Anglo-French infidels during the Crusades. Official records state that 453 troops (mostly Indians) died, while some 600-odd were missing in action or captured. The British used the Royal Air Force as well as gas against civilians, making them the first government to use chemical weapons in Iraq. Arab losses probably topped 8,500. Wilson lost his job and London realized that it needed an Arab government, even if it were to be in the hands of a puppet.

Churchill, appointed to head the Colonial Office as secretary of state, convened the two-week Cairo conference in March 1921. If you wanted to find the right Arab face for British rule, you had to summon Lawrence of Arabia. Faisal's destiny was worthy of astrology. Churchill first thought of Abdullah, Faisal's brother, for Iraq. But Lawrence won the day for his 'absolute ripper'. The ceremony to place Faisal on the throne of Iraq was held at six in the morning on 23 August 1921. The British official who wrote the acceptance speech almost aborted the occasion when Faisal realized that it included accepting the British High Commissioner as his superior authority. The sentence was quickly deleted. But when the proclamation was over (breakfast was not served) the band played 'God Save the King'. Which king? The duplicity was entirely appropriate. Faisal became yet another Sunni ruler of a Shia-majority land, in a sequence that had survived some extraordinary twists of history. Abdullah was handed a 'vacant lot next door', officially called Transjordan, and now known simply as Jordan. As they pointed out, Egypt had one river, Iraq had two and Jordan had a railway line. For the first few years Abdullah lived in tents since he had no residence. But the Hashemite family still rules in Amman.

THE TIPS OF SPEARS

The Iraqis were distinctly underwhelmed by their new king. To start with, this was the first time that Faisal had set foot in Iraq. He was frank enough to acknowledge that he was 'an instrument of British policy,' which did not endear him to the people he was destined to rule. London had no ideas beyond the obvious, and power remained in the hands of either the British High Commissioner or a Sunni elite, with subsidiary roles given initially to minorities like the Christian Assyrians. Excluded from government, the Shias turned to Iran for assistance in their various struggles, but to little avail. Iran was embroiled in its own travails.

The British took both formal and hard-nosed precautions to protect their power. At one level, they raised Christian levies to protect oil installations. At another, a façade of 'self-rule' was set up. The 1924 Constitution created an elected lower house and a nominated upper chamber. Britain controlled defence and foreign affairs and set up a system of 'advisers'. Their number decreased from 3,000 in 1921 to 100 in 1932 when Iraq was recognized as an independent nation. The High Commissioner preferred to wield his influence both through the palace and the executive civilian ministers, and the vulnerability of governments was one means of keeping them obedient. Simultaneously, favoured ministers seemed to always find a place. There were 59 Cabinets sworn in between 1921 and 1958, and a clever self-server like Nuri al-Said was either Prime Minister or minister in 47 of them. (There were only four Shia Prime Ministers, all of them after 1947.) The charge of neo-colonialism has become a bit of a cliché, but the British were unambiguous about their need for dependant regimes in Baghdad.

Faisal's one lasting contribution to Iraq was the creation of a strong national army. Faisal's dozen years on the throne were untroubled by illusion. There was no attempt made at any form of economic reform in the country, and foreign policy was a matter of taking dictation. His policy on oil was silence. To the people, Arab or Persian, Sunni or Shia, oil was synonymous with nationalism, and betrayal was measured by the barrel.

The search for Iraq's oil had been initiated under Ottoman rule. Calouste Gulbenkian, son of a wealthy Armenian who lived in Istanbul and made his money by importing Russian kerosene, could have become a partner of Anglo-Persian but thought that D'Arcy was 'a very wild cat', a gambler rather than an investor. When D'Arcy hit oil, Gulbenkian adopted a motto: 'Never give up an oil concession.' In 1912 he set up the Turkish Petroleum Company, although there was very little Turkish about it. The partners were Deutsche Bank, Royal Dutch/Shell and the

Turkish National Bank, which was controlled by the British but had Gulbenkian as a 30 per cent partner. The British government, always wary of competition in oil, forced a change in equity and by 1914, when the concession was granted; Anglo-Persian owned 50 per cent of the company, with Deutsche and Shell splitting the rest. Gulbenkian was rewarded with 5 per cent, given equally by the British and Shell. He was ever after called Mr 5 per cent.

The war eliminated the problem of enemies, but created the problem of friends. France did not get Mosul, but would not surrender a claim to Mosul's potential oil. And the American oil companies were not willing to watch from the sidelines while Europe played monopoly in the Middle East. Moreover, a resurgent Turkey under Kemal Ataturk, which had just taught Britain, Russia and their client Greece that its integrity was non-negotiable, was challenging the British-drawn borders and claiming some share of the oil from Mosul as well. The American oil companies appointed a businessman, Walter Teagle (six foot three and 300 pounds with an insatiable sweet tooth) to represent their interests. His brief from Allen Dulles, then chief of the Division of Near East Affairs in the State Department, was simple: the 1914 concession was invalid. On 14 March 1925 a new agreement was signed, opening the door for American companies. In the same year a geological expedition reported that Iraq was probably the richest oil-region in the world. Drilling began in April 1927.

One of the sites, Baba Gurgur, about six miles from Kirkuk, was near Nebuchadnezzar's 'fiery furnace' for the Jews. At 3 am on 15 October 1927, after only 1500 feet of drilling, a roar echoed through the desert, and 95,000 barrels a day gushed out of Well Number One until it was capped on the ninth day.

On 31 July 1928 a contract was signed. Royal Dutch/Shell, Anglo-Persian, the French and an American consortium called Near East Development Company would get 23.75 per cent of the oil each. Gulbenkian kept his 5 per cent, but would sell the oil immediately to the French. This suited him; he preferred cash to crude. A 'self-denying clause' prevented the partners from poaching on one another within what was called the Red Line: at one meeting Gulbenkian asked for a map and drew a thick red line through the Red Sea, Mediterranean, Black Sea, Persian Gulf and Arabian Sea, enclosing Saudi Arabia, Yemen, Oman, Muscat, Trucial Coast, Bahrain, Iraq, Turkey, Syria, Transjordan and Palestine; he excluded Kuwait. The Americans were bitter at how much they had denied themselves in order to please the Europeans they had just saved from Germany and Turkey.

What did Iraq get out of this deal? It got a mention, since it was now the Iraq Petroleum Company. And a promise. A vague assurance was given in 1928 that 20 per cent of profits would be given to Iraq, but was never kept. King Faisal said nothing. But his son was ready to broadcast his feelings.

Ghazi was 21 when he came to the throne on his father's death in 1933. It was perhaps an inopportune moment for an Iraqi monarch to turn on his dynasty's benefactors, for as the extent of Iraq's oil reserves became known, the British grip on Baghdad became tighter. Ghazi was a populist by instinct, and anti-British by conviction. A year at Harrow and a few months at Sandhurst had not made him more amenable. He became an advocate of Arab nationalism. Iraqis united around his message, and discounted his personal incongruities (he was bisexual). He was already a minor hero, having crushed an Assyrian insurrection in 1932 (which he thought had been inspired by the British). As king he wore a uniform and consorted with anti-British officers, while the High Commissioner, Maurice Patterson came under pressure from London to control the berserk protégé. In 1936, Ghazi, with the help of the Army chief General Bakr Sidqi, staged a coup against his own government.

In 1937 he set up a radio station in his palace, Al Zahour, that began to propagate Arab causes and became an instant hit in Syria, Jordan, Palestine and Kuwait. A radio-empowered Ghazi launched a direct attack on British interests by advocating the annexation of Kuwait, then as now under British protection from Iraqi claims. (Incidentally 10 out of 14 members of Kuwait's incipient legislative council voted to unite with Iraq.) Second, Ghazi began to help Palestinians against Jewish settlers.

Patterson demanded that the radio station be shut down. Ghazi ignored him. In an official communication, dated 22 July 1936, the British Foreign Office suggested that King Ghazi either be controlled or removed. General Sidqi was killed in 1937. No one was ever tried for the crime. Pro-British politicians who had fled after the coup drifted back to Iraq after his death, and began to demand that Ghazi be replaced by either his minor son, or his cousin and brother-in-law Abdul-Ilah.

On 3 April 1939, a change of regime took place. The official story was that Ghazi's skull was smashed when the car he was driving hit a telephone pole. But there were no evidence of high speed; the car looked undamaged; and the fatal wound was at the back of Ghazi's head, not the front. The doctor refused to sign the death certificate. There was no post-mortem examination. Two companions who were in the car with Ghazi, Eid bin Said and Ali bin Abdullah, were never seen again. The crowds at Ghazi's funeral procession of Ghazi singled out the pro-British politician Nuri al-Said for abuse. They warned that he would answer for Ghazi's blood. But for the moment Nuri al-Said became prime minister.

The reaction came from the army. In 1941, four anti-British colonels led a coup against the Nuri al-Said. The British helped Abdul-Ilah escape. Rashid Ali al Keilani took over and declared support for Nazi Germany. That was reason enough for what followed. On 19 May they opened military operations and by 30 May they had occupied the country. The Iraqi army did not put up any significant resistance. Rashid Ali fled to Germany. The four colonels were hanged, and their bodies left on display in a public square. Abdul-Ilah returned with the British troops, but the British ruled Iraq directly till 1946. Martial law continued till 1948. A song for schoolchildren that had become popular under the patronage of Ghazi, *Lahat ro'os al hirabi,* or 'The tips of our spears have become visible', was banned. In May 1948 the British withdrew their forces from Iraq, but designated Iraq a 'tributary country'.

The British could hardly remain in Iraq after what had happened in the region.

On 14 February 1947, the British decided to refer their mandate for Palestine back to the United Nations, the successor to the League of Nations. Arab anger took the suicidal form of a boycott and they lost what little chance they had of stating their case. On 29 November 1947 the General Assembly voted, 33 to 13, with 10 abstentions, in favour of the partition of Palestine to create Israel. Britain withdrew. On 14 May 1948 the Jewish National Council proclaimed the birth of Israel. The Arabs declared war, which lasted 15 months and whose fortunes changed from Israeli setbacks to Arab defeat. Iraq dutifully sent troops, and remained the only country not to sign an armistice, but it could not disguise its utter failure. The people had an explanation: their army was sincere, but their rulers were British stooges. The 'foreign hand' was an easy alibi for ineptitude, but it worked. An anti-monarchy, anti-government and anti-British *intifadah*–the term is not new–broke out, with sporadic intensity. Events in the region helped make 1952 a particularly violent year, and one young man came to attention as one of the street-smart organizers. His name was Saddam Hussein. He was born in Tikrit in 1937, two years before King Ghazi was assassinated.

1952 was a year of dramatic events on either side of Iraq. In Iran a quirky old aristocrat, Mohammad Mosaddeq (nicknamed 'Mossy' by Anthony Eden) nationalized the British-controlled oil industry. In Egypt an Army group, self-styled as the Free Officers, overthrew the corpulent King Farouq, yet another monarch foisted upon a nation by the British. America watched with a cool, but always heavily involved eye. Some critics have accused the United States of even being cross-eyed, but it was still broadly supportive of the decolonization that had begun with the freedom of India in 1947. Nor did it believe that the process would be as democratic as in India, and was willing to be helpful to other options. The principal concern was to stop the advance of communism and if a few majors and colonels were willing to do so, so be it. In September 1947 a bright young American intelligence officer, Miles Copeland, flew to a posting in Damascus. After stoking enough embers in Syria, he came to Cairo by 1952, a year in which the simmering capital was getting ready to explode. On 26 January 1952, Black Saturday, Cairo burned with anti-British fervour. The director of Middle East operations in the Middle East for the CIA, Kermit ('Kim') Roosevelt, grandson of Theodore, flew in. Between the two of them they established contact with the Free Officers and Roosevelt helped ease any doubts Washington might have had about the intentions of the Free Officers. The CIA was informed a week before the coup place on the night of 22-23 July 1952, through which Gamal Abdel Nasser eventually took over. There was no bloodshed.

But the great CIA success story was to take place in 1953. In Iran.

HALL OF MIRRORS

The anti-colonial movement in Persia can be dated precisely to 1891. The Qajar king, Nasser al-Din Shah, granted a tobacco monopoly to British Imperial Tobacco Company for the less than princely sum of 15,000 pounds a year. The Shia *fatwa* against the monopoly was issued not in Iran but in Iraq, from Najaf, by Mirza Hassan Shirazi, the leading Shia divine. It banned the use of tobacco by the faithful. Even ladies of the Shah's harem, it was said, obeyed the ban. Jamaluddin Afghani, ideologue of the Islamic movement, was one of the leaders of the agitation. The concession was withdrawn in 1895, marking the first victory of the clergy-bazaar alliance that was to play such a significant part in the politics of the country for the next century. In 1896 Shah Nasser was assassinated by a disciple of Afghani.

The ferment was reinforced by the support of the liberal reformers and in 1905-6, Mozaffar al-Din Shah was forced to create the Majlis-e Shoura-e Melli, or a national consultative assembly in what is known as the Constitutional Revolution. The immediate provocation was the extraordinary influence that Britain and Russia had established on the Qajar court, which extended to their control over revenue decisions. In December 1906 the Shah signed the law reducing his own powers. But he was on his deathbed, and his heir Mohammad Ali Shah reneged on the commitment, abolished the Majlis and arrested the leaders. The struggle took on an armed dimension and in 1909 he was deposed and replaced his 11-year-old son Sultan Ahmad. During the brief life of the first Majlis, the anti-monarchy alliance had already split over a basic difference. The clergy, led by Sheikh Fazlollah Nuri, insisted that the national assembly could only legislate within the scope of the Sharia, while the reformists were dreaming of a French revolution in Persia. The conflict became so bitter that when the reformists returned to power in 1909, Nuri was executed after a summary judgement for resisting the constitutionalist forces. The marginalized clergy were either absorbed as lawyers or teachers, or ignored. They would have to await another era, another leader.

One young man who lionized the memory of Fazlollah Nuri was Ruhollah Khomeini. His father Mostafa had come to Najaf in 1891 for further studies. Born on 24 September 1902, Ruhollah was the third son in a prosperous family. He was only six months old when his father died in mysterious circumstances. In family lore this death is tinged with both personal and political romance, for Mostafa was on his way to meet the Shah when he was killed, and his niece was in love with one of the murderers.

Ruhollah followed his father and studied for a place in the clergy. In a classic Islamic education, knowledge is a cornerstone of piety; one of the Prophet's most quoted sayings is 'Search for knowledge from the cradle to the grave.' The mosque and the *medressa* were once indistinguishable. Islamic education included study of the law, Arabic grammar and rhetoric, logic and theology. In 1917, at the age of 15, wearing the black turban that signified that he belonged to the Prophet's family (the Prophet's colour was black) Ruhollah Khomeini began his higher education. (The environment among students in the seminary was not completely puritanical. One of the popular comments among the students in the medressa was: Half the pleasure lies in talking about pleasure. But Ruhollah himself was an unselfconscious moralist. His wife later said in an interview that he was a virgin when he married and remained faithful to her all his life.)

Khomeini grew up in Persia and would almost certainly have gone to study in Najaf, but the British conquest of Iraq made that option uncertain. Instead, Najaf came to him. Following the revolt of 1920, the British expelled the Shia leadership from Najaf. Qom in Iran became the new Atabat, or the set of seminaries somewhat like an English University town. Khomeini moved to Qom in 1922, to take the first step up the Shia clerical ladder. The hierarchy is well-structured. A student has an *alem,* or teacher, as his guide; guidance is called *taqlid* and imitation is a form of guidance. A *talebeh* (student) can progress to *masalegu* (explainer of problems), and then to *vaez,* or preacher. Then comes, with eligibility, the right to offer *ejtehad,* or interpret the law, before being permitted into the rarified ranks of the *mojtahed* (one who interprets law). *Ayatollah* (or sign of God) was a rank created at the time of the constitutional reform, and is equivalent to the *marja-e taqlid.* The *marja-e taqlid* is a source of emulation for the community. Ruhollah Khomeini became a *mojtahed* at the very early age of 32 or 33.

Iran had become a difficult place for the clergy by the 1930s.

In February 1921 Ahmad Shah was the Qajar monarch when a semi-literate but very sharp colonel of the Cossacks called Reza Khan rode into Tehran at the head of his regiment, arrested the prime minister, the Cabinet along with some 50 politicians of all shades. The Qajars had lost effective power, but no one else had found it. Ahmad Shah submitted to Reza Khan's demands, and made him war minister, a portfolio he used with skill to enlarge his support. He strengthened the army, and in the process strengthened both the country and himself. Reza Khan was made Prime Minister in October 1923. In the summer of 1924 Reza Khan placed a bill before the Assembly to abolish the monarchy and declare a republic. The clergy, horrified at the thought after what a republican Turkey had done to mullahs, opposed the bill. Reza Khan went to Qom and declared that he was dropping the idea of a republic to protect and preserve the glory of Islam. In November 1925 Reza Khan dispensed with niceties, got a bill passed that deposed the Qajars and formed a Constituent Assembly that named him the first monarch of the Pahlavi dynasty.

The glory of Islam was the first to hit the mat. Western surnames were forcibly introduced; men were ordered to wear hats and suits; mullahs had to get a permit to wear their cloaks. On 21 March 1928 Reza Khan's queen unveiled her face at the shrine of Fatima in Qom. Ayatollah Bafqi reprimanded her. Reza Khan entered the seminary, his boots on, horsewhipped the Ayatollah and arrested him. In 1933 the veil was banned. Khomeini never forgave the mullahs who compromised with Reza Khan. Reza Khan believed that his greatest victory was over the Shia mullahs.

Reza Khan was both reformer and nationalist, and saw no difference between the two. He treated Anglo-Persian in a manner similar to the way he treated the mullahs; he could not do away with either entirely, but was determined to limit their space for operation. He challenged the deal made by D'Arcy as a violation of sovereign rights, and when The Great Depression drove oil royalties to unacceptable lows, he surprised everyone by announcing at a Cabinet meeting on 16 November 1932 that he was cancelling the Anglo-Persian concession. Negotiations ensued, and by April 1933 Reza Khan had won significant changes.

But eight years later he overstepped British limits. In August 1941, within weeks of the start of Operation Barbarossa, Hitler's massive war against the Soviet Union, Reza Khan tilted towards Germany. Control of the region and its oil was vital to both sides. In the peace terms that Hitler publicly offered to Britain in a speech on 19 July 1940, he said he would recognize the British Empire on condition that Iraq and Egypt were handed over to Germany. Iran was a neighbour of British India, whose manpower played a critical role on the battlefields. Britain, in concert with Soviet Union, sent in troops, deposed Reza Khan and placed his 21-year-old son Mohammad Reza Shah Pahlavi on the throne.

The guilt of political patricide never left the young man, and it was multiplied by his father's death in exile in 1944. Iran was still in deep poverty, and anger was rising. Moscow saw in this situation an opportunity for the party it supported, the leftist Tudeh; while the clergy had other ideas. The latter had found a fiery leader in Ayatollah Seyed Kashani. Kashani was among those who had been forced to leave Najaf by the British after the 1920 revolution. After 1945 he became associated with the militant Fedayeen-i-Islam, or the Martyrs of Islam. The martyrs were active. In February 1949 a Muslim assassin, posing as a photographer, fired six shots at the young Shah from point blank range but missed: fanaticism can blind you. The Shah was cool, but got the message. He stepped back as politics took a harsh anti-British turn.

Iran's frustration turned into hatred of foreigners. The worst accusation made by a politician was calling him a British agent, and it was made often. Even drought and plague were attributed to the evil British. Hard statistics confirmed emotions. The British government received more from just taxes on Anglo-Iranian (when Reza Khan renamed Persia in 1935 Anglo-Persian's name also changed), than the Iranian government received in oil royalties. The young Shah tried to stem the pressure with a new revenue deal, signed in the summer of 1949, but paradoxically the financial concessions, when they were made public in late 1950, only confirmed the popular view that the British were stealing Iran's oil.

The chair of the Majlis' oil committee was Mohammad Mossadeq. He was a rarity: aristocratic, educated (a doctorate in law), charismatic, and honest. Needless to say the last characteristic was the rarest. In 1949 he became leader of the National Front, a loose coalition that aimed to nationalize the oil industry and limit the monarchy's powers. He demanded nationalization of Anglo-Iranian. Prime Minister General Ali Razmara (also famous for once having rejected a bribe) dismissed the idea in the Majlis in March 1951. Four days later he was assassinated in Tehran's central mosque.

On 28 April 1951, asserting its authority, the Majlis elected Mossadeq Prime Minister. On 1 May, the Shah, under severe pressure from Mossadeq, nationalized Anglo-Iranian. Its new name was Iranian National Oil Company.

The Truman administration was, initially, not entirely unsympathetic to Mossadeq, seeing in him a potential nationalist bulwark against Soviet communism. But the British, more directly affected, called him cunning and manipulative. Perhaps both were right. But this old man who saw visitors in his pyjamas had laid low the biggest British investment in the world.

The Clement Attlee government in London considered what they called Plan Y: military intervention. Its main worry was that the Soviets might use this as an excuse to occupy yet another border country. But the Labour defence secretary, Emmanuel Shinwell, argued that if the British did nothing the Suez Canal could go next. (He was prescient.) The Americans laid a restraining hand and sent Averell Harriman as honest broker. Mossadeq put up the American delegation in a palace belonging to the Shah, whose main reception hall was a Sheesh Mahal, or a hall of mirrors. Harriman also consulted Kashani. Both Mossadeq and Kashani thought the British were untrustworthy. Harriman failed and Mossadeq ordered the last Anglo-Iranian workers to leave. They did, on 4 October, to the strains of Colonel Boogie. In the same month Winston Churchill was re-elected Prime Minister of Britain and Anthony Eden became his foreign secretary. Honourably, Eden sold his personal shares, at a considerable loss, in Anglo-Iranian the moment he took office. He was a gentleman.

For Mossadeq nationalization was politically useful and economically counterproductive. Whenever he gave a call on the radio, hundreds of thousands of Iranians turned out. But demonstrations are no compensation for oil revenues. He tried to protect his flanks by wooing Moscow, sharpening suspicions in the Eisenhower administration that had come to office in 1953. As Dulles, now secretary of state, pointed out at a meeting of the National Security Council, if the iron curtain stretched across Iran and then extended its shadow into the Middle East, 60 per cent of the world's oil reserves would 'fall into Communist control'. The Anglo-American plan to remove Mossadeq went active.

It was called Operation Ajax. Kim Roosevelt drove into Iran in mid-July from Iraq. When the Shah was informed about Ajax he was uncertain whether he was being double- or triple-crossed. Among other things, he suspected old Mossy of being a British agent! In an episode fit for the movies, Kim hid under a blanket on the floor of a car and drove into the palace to personally reassure the Shah of American fidelity.

The code names that the Americans gave the main actors were honest. Mossadeq was that 'old bugger' and the Shah a 'boy scout'. One of Kim's own code names sounded more Chinese than American: 'Mr Scar on Right Forehead.' Kim's anthem for the operation was a song from the musical *Guys and Dolls,* 'Luck be a Lady Tonight'.

For the first 18 days of August luck was being a bitch rather than a lady. Acting to plan, the Shah ordered the dismissal of Mossadeq. But delivery of the order was delayed by three days, enough time for the 'old bugger' to realize what was happening. Mossadeq arrested the messenger and whipped up the street, where massive angry demonstrations took place against the monarchy. The frightened Shah fled, first to Baghdad and then to more congenial Rome where his despondent queen window-shopped, while he indulged in dark speculation about job prospects. But on August 19, his supporters, led by the Prime Minister-designate General Fazlollah Zahedi, suddenly found voice, and support. Zahedi held a press conference in Tehran where he distributed copies of the Shah's order, and a small pro-Shah demonstration appeared on the streets. As if by a miracle, it swelled. Someone had done some planning, because wrestlers, weightlifters and acrobats turned up to provide both entertainment and muscle. Elements of the army and police sent to disperse this demonstration joined the mood. Mossadeq jumped over the wall of his back garden and fled. A journalist informed the Shah in Rome. While the queen wept, he said, 'I knew that they loved me.'

There was nothing miraculous about August 19. The CIA and the MI6 might have lubricated the response, but the bazaar was not in their hands. The Shah was back on the throne because the radical clergy had rallied to his side, led by none other than Kashani, the same Ayatollah who had been anti-British all his life. The reason was ideological. He found the anti-clericalism of some of the Mossadeq supporters unacceptable. Kashani preferred the Shah to the dangers of reform under Mossadeq. The Shah later rewarded the clergy by encouraging their attacks on the heretical Bahai sect, created by Mirza Hossein Ali Nuri (1817-92) when he proclaimed himself a new prophet. It would not be the last time that the Americans and the ulema would unite against a common enemy. There has been some speculation that a more judicious western compromise with Mossadeq might have prevented the backlash against the monarchy that took place two decades later, resulting in the ultimate victory of Kashani's disciple, Ayatollah Ruhollah Khomeini, and the formation of the first clerical Shia state in history.

In the short term, the success of Operation Ajax reinforced Eisenhower's faith in clandestine operations. Kim Roosevelt was more cautious. He made a prophetic statement at a review meeting chaired by John Foster Dulles. He said the CIA had succeeded only because the people wanted the same results. Roosevelt notes in his book, *Countercoup: The Struggle for Control of Iran* (McGraw-Hill, New York, 1979) that he told

Dulles: 'If we (the CIA) are ever going to try something like this again, we must be absolutely sure that people and army want what we want. If not, you had better give the job to the Marines!' A later generation of Americans would give such a job to the Marines, in next-door Iraq.

PACT AND IMPACT

Having saved Iran from the Soviet claw in 1953, America now sought to save the region. In 1955 four neighbours, Turkey, Iraq, Iran and Pakistan signed what was called the Baghdad Pact, meant to constitute a multinational fortress against the Soviet Union but which also managed to worry Egypt to this alliance's west and India to its east. (As a consequence Egypt and India became as close as they were ever destined to be, before they fell apart again.) But the irritation in Iraq at this pact was nothing compared to the passions of 1956, when British, French and Israeli forces invaded Egypt after Nasser's nationalization of the Suez Canal in 1956. It is ironical that when Frederic Auguste Bartholdi conceived of the Statue of Liberty, he first saw her standing at the entrance of the Suez Canal, as an Egyptian peasant representing 'Egypt Bringing Light to Asia'. In 1956 Egypt did bring light to Asia.

Baghdad blazed with protest against the invasion. Among those in charge of the management of the street protests, once again, was Saddam Hussein. He had become an expert in mobilizing the underworld for such politically correct causes, using thugs to beat up shopkeepers, for instance, who might be reluctant to lose a day's trade for future freedom.

His official date of birth is 28 April 1937. It has become fashionable in some quarters now to call Saddam a bastard because his father was missing and presumed dead when he was born. Malice serves little purpose. Saddam (the word means someone who confronts or collides) remained devoted to his mother Subha Tulfah Al Musallat till her death in 1982, and photographs show her to be a tough woman who had seen more of life than she might care to narrate. Subha seems to have been a bit of an early feminist who was ready to converse with men who were not close relations, and who remarried after the disappearance of Saddam's father. Saddam admired her for the manner in which she reared her children through abject poverty and once commented to his official biographer, Amir Iskandar, that he had never been young.

At the age of 10 Saddam went into the care of a glamorous relative: the glamour lay in the reputation, not money. For this uncle, Khairullah Tulfa, was one of the army officers who had been cashiered by the British after the failed Rashid Ali rebellion of 1941, a moment remembered by nationalist officers with shame and anger. Khairullah was only a teacher now, but he kept in touch with army officers of his bent.

After Suez the swirl of nationalism was too turbulent to be controlled by the hopelessly discredited Hashemites in Baghdad. Nasser's pan-Arabism was endorsed by the Baath Party, a secular, idealistic organization born in Syria in the 1940s that had become the principal political force in Iraq as well. By early 1958, Egypt and Syria had formally merged to become the United Arab Republic, although neither country gave up its government. In response, the pro-western brother monarchies of Iraq and Jordan decided that they would also become a 'single' entity called the Arab Union.

On 14 July 1958, the 'Free Officers' of the Iraqi Army, led by Brigadier Abdel Karim Kassem and Colonel Abdel Salam Aref, entered the palace and massacred the royal family. Abdul-Ilah's body was dragged through the streets and dismembered by triumphant mobs; his wife escaped only because she had been left for dead among the pile of corpses. Nuri al-Said, Prime Minister for the 14th time, tried to escape by dressing up as a woman. He was caught on 16 July and killed. They then ran cars over and over again across his body. Parts of his corpse were distributed as trophies. Inevitably a kangaroo court was set up; equally predictably it was called a 'People's Court'. A certain Colonel Ahmad Hassan Al Bakr was among the judges.

The British ambassador Sir Michael Wright took refuge outside the official residence. But he did not have to worry too long. Within 24 hours of the coup a secret meeting took place between Kassem and Sir Michael that lasted for some five hours. Kassem assured Britain that the West had nothing to fear. Iraqi oil would continue to flow into the western markets, and he would ensure that Iraq would not join the United Arab Republic of Syria and Egypt. Proof came immediately. On 16 July an eager Nasser wanted to stop over in Baghdad on his way back to Egypt from Moscow, where he had gone to discuss the Middle East crisis with Krushchev. To his shock, Nasser discovered that he had not been given permission to land by those who were chanting his name.

The West was not taking any chances. American Marines landed in Lebanon to support the government of Camille Chamoun which was battling Nasser-backed insurgents. British troops arrived in Jordan to protect a nervous King Hussein. These forces were equipped to march towards Baghdad. Kassem's assurance, backed by the snub to Nasser, may have saved Iraq an Anglo-American invasion in 1958. The Kassem coup was one regime change that surprised London and Washington, but they would not be caught asleep in Baghdad again.

The mood on the street was akin to 1920 in the sense that Sunni-Shia differences melted in the anger against a government that served the foreign infidel. The level of anger was evident in the thirst for blood. Brutal bands roamed privileged neighbourhoods in the major cities, leaving an unknown number dead. Other coups in the Arab world had been relatively peaceful. When the Syrian army dispatched President Husni Zaim in 1949, there was not a murmur. Nasser's 1952 coup was almost gentlemanly; it was certainly polite. King Farouq sailed off to exile in his royal yacht, taking along some of the country's gold, and although his pashas lost their land, they were unmolested.

Iraq's Free Officers had a mission, but no agenda beyond the seizure of power. Unity at the top crumbled quickly. Before the end of the year Kassem sought to strengthen himself at the expense of his brother officers by taking the support of the Communists. But he was also careful not to antagonize the West, and therefore stuck to his anti-UAR line. Aref, who supported the larger cause of Arab nationalism, foundered because he was inept. He was exiled.

The Baath Party took up the cause with its slogan: One Arab nation, one eternal message. Kassem organized a Communist-led militia, called, in leftist fashion, the Popular Resistance against the Baathists. A virtual civil war followed. Among the Baath activists arrested, in November 1958, was Saddam. There was a charge of murder against him, but such an accusation is often symptomatic of the environment. In any case he was released in six months. In March 1959 the Communists provoked an insurrection in Mosul, which Kassem used to eliminate his opponents. Thousands died. The Baathists targeted Kassem. Now a self-promoted General, he was hit on his arm and shoulder on 7 October 1959 while driving along Al Rashid Street, but survived. Among the would-be assassins was Saddam Hussein. A wounded Saddam escaped first to his hometown, Tikrit, and then crossed the desert to reach the safety of Syria. He was only 22 years old. During those three months he spent in Damascus, he took another significant step towards stardom. He met and was immediately patronized by the Christian founder of the Baathist Party, Michel Aflaq, who made his protégé a full-fledged member of the party. Saddam was sent by the party to a high school in Cairo, from where he passed out in 1961. He depended on a small stipend from Nasser's government. He later told an official biographer that instead of succumbing to Cairo's famous belly dancers he played chess at night. Marriage to his cousin Sajida in 1962 must have come as a relief.

Domestically, Kassem gave his policies a pro-poor sheen (he instituted land reforms); internationally, he benefited from his policy of dichotomy. The British were content as long as the oil flowed and Kassem kept Iraq out of Nasser's reach. But the Americans, more worried about the Soviet Union than Arab unity, saw matters differently. They referred to 1959 as the Year of the Bear, and CIA director Allen Dulles described Iraq as the most dangerous spot on earth.

The alliance between Egypt and Syria broke up in 1961. With Arab unity now in reverse gear, Washington decided that offence was the best defence and that its best bet against Kassem was the Baath Party. Its assessment was correct. The CIA, which had kept in touch with fringe players like Saddam through its Cairo bureau (with the knowledge and implicit permission of the Egyptian authorities, and the evidence lies in Cairo's intelligence dossiers), set heavier wheels in motion. Its operative, William Lakeland, was stationed in Baghdad as an attaché. The contacts with Baath officials in Cairo, Damascus, Beirut were so widespread that they could hardly be kept a secret.

Kassem was informed of an impending coup, among others by the Yugoslavs, and in January 1963 he arrested a number of Baathist Army officers. That in turn pushed the day of confrontation forward. On 8 February 1963 pro-Baath elements of the Army, with eight tanks and four Hawker Hunter aircraft (half the tanks broke down, but the planes worked) moved towards Kassem's residence. The non-partisan sections of the Army kept out of the way, and fighting ended after two days with the death of Kassem. The commanders of the Baathists on the field were General Ahmad Hassan Al Bakr and Khairullah, Saddam's uncle.

The Baathists set up a National Guard to take on the Popular Resistance, and in a campaign that lasted months Communists and their sympathizers were killed in their thousands. Allegations are continuously made that the CIA provided lists of those who had to be eliminated, although why the Baathists should need lists from Americans is hard to fathom. They knew Iraq better than the CIA. American recognition and help to the new regime was immediate, in any case. They flew in arms from Turkey and Iran in April to help the government fight the Kurds, who generally chose any moment of uncertainty to renew their demand for independence. The Iraqis responded by giving Lakeland Russian MiG-21s and T-54 tanks for Americans to analyse. American companies moved in to pick up contracts, among them Bechtel and Mobil. And Saddam came back from Cairo, via Damascus, with instructions from Michel Aflaq for the new government. He was named a member of the President's bureau. It was vague enough a job for Saddam to choose what he wanted to do. He set about organizing a personal power base, through the National Guard.

But life was to get more difficult before it became easy. There was confusion, and serious infighting, often at the point of a gun, within the government, the Baath Party, and various sundry elements that had to be represented in the power structure. From the inner councils of power Saddam once again slipped to castaway, and went underground where he indulged in familiar plotting against the government. He was arrested, and escaped while being transferred from one prison to another (they bribed the guards, who stopped to eat at a café in Baghdad, permitting Saddam and two others to escape in a waiting car). Saddam emerged from those nerve-wracking years convinced that Iraq would only have stability and progress if it were run as a complete dictatorship.

His chance came in 1968, in a coup that has also been described by critics of America, and professional cynics, as the second stage of the CIA-Baath partnership. More relevant is the fact that the credibility of the government had collapsed after the whipping at the hands of Israel in 1967. By the standards of Iraq, the 1968 coup was a piece of cake, or at least a cup of tea. President Abdel Rehman Aref offered a cup of tea to those who came to ask him to quit and agreed to join his sick wife in London. Bakr, Saddam's fellow Tikriti and Khairullah's friend, was the new supremo. Saddam was not named a minister in the first phase but he took an office next to the President. In 14 days he engineered the removal of the defence minister and the prime minister, the latter with the influential use of a gun in his hand. For ten years, Saddam was the 'son' to the father figure Bakr, the vice president to the president, the heir who slowly but surely gathered all the instruments of state into his own hands. He was merciless about it, but mercy was an unrequited virtue in Iraq.

In that first decade of power, the much-vilified Saddam also did a great deal to strengthen his country. He was a far better deputy than a number one. Under an umbrella, the best emerged; without cover, he turned into a tyrant. His finest hour came on 1 June 1972 when he personally supervised the nationalization of oil. Saddam, showing every courtesy to the foreign oil executive who had not taken his threats seriously, neatly cut the ground from their feet and protected his back with a quiet deal with the Soviets. The political fallout was support from the Communist Party that led to the formation of the Patriotic National Front on 17 June 1973 and the inclusion of Communists in the government. The benefits of nationalization were more obvious when the Shah of Iran provoked the OPEC move that led to the dramatic rise in oil prices in 1973. In 1974 Iraq's oil revenue had shot up to $5.7 billion from an absolutely pitiful figure before nationalization.

Saddam made creative use of part of his rising resources, like launching the literacy movement for women. But there was a fatal flaw: a tyrant cannot be progressive. Saddam's use of fear, even dread, as his principal political weapon not only negated the social good he sought to achieve, but distorted national priorities. He created a system based on spies, torture, death and extended-family rule. Soon, the principal use that Saddam made of this oil money was to buy arms.

The best biography of Saddam by far is the one written by Said Aburish (*Saddam Hussein: The Politics of Revenge,* Bloomsbury, 2000). Let the author offer his own credentials: 'As managing director of the consulting firm Growth International (GI), and later as chairman of its successor, Aburish, James and Associates, I participated in both these undertakings (economic development and arms purchases) over a period of five years (from 1974 to 1979).' This is not the place to go into details of Saddam's extensive arms purchases and nuclear programme, or the collusion with the western nations that enabled him to go a long way towards his goals. Some facts are pointers. In addition to the official arms budget, Saddam ordered the Ministry of Oil to set aside 5 per cent of its income for weapons and commissions: in 1981, this fund alone totaled $2.5 billion. Commenting on Saddam's and the Baath Party's links with America, Aburish writes: 'The first phase was Cairo and CIA support for the Baath to carry out the 1963 coup, the second was

American assistance, tacit and otherwise, with the 1968 coup, and the third was helping the Baath to stay in power through selling them equipment such as was provided by Karkar.' Karkar was a financially insignificant deal for mobile phones, worth $5 million, but it needed clearance from the government, and the phones, as everyone knew, were destined for the *mukhabarat,* or the vicious intelligence agency that Saddam used for his regime of fear. Aburish continues: 'In 1975, the year of the Karkar project, the United States Government knowingly helped Iraq obtain the technology to build its first chemical warfare plant. This took place after the Iraqis had made an open request to buy such a plant from the USSR, a request which the Russians turned down. This was unsurprising. The USSR, though trying to keep Saddam to themselves, had never approved of his non-conventional weapons plans and had no wish to help him understand regional adventures beyond their control.' (Moscow also suspected, with good reason, that the Baath alliance with the Communists was cynical. It was proved right in 1977 when Saddam turned against Communists, using surrogates like Tareq Aziz to convey the message that Iraq would never become a Communist country.)

In 1974 an American company, Pfaulder Corporation of Rochester, New York provided a blueprint for a plant that could produce toxic chemicals like Amiton, Paraxon, Demeton and Paratheon, with government permission, but then was prevented by Washington from sending the equipment. But the blueprint was good enough. The Iraqis bought different sections from Italy, West and East Germany. Arburish also participated in the setting up of a nuclear reactor, and provides details of deals with France, Brazil, Germany and Italy. Conventional arms, naturally, were obtained more conventionally.

Israel was the official excuse. But during the 24-odd years of power that Saddam enjoyed, first as deputy and then as dictator, he never really fought a direct war with Israel. Egypt and Syria shut him out of the 1973 war even as he declared bitterly that he had to learn the news from the radio. Iraq rushed troops on its own to the Golan Heights, where the Israelis mauled them in a single encounter. Iraq did not even have tank transporters for its armour units in 1973. The arms purchased by oil wealth, including chemical weapons, would be used against the Shia Islamic Republic of Iran created by Ayatollah Khomeini.

Since fiction seeks to become fact in propaganda, it is unsurprising that Saddam once claimed to be a descendant of the first Imam of the

Shias, Ali. As emotional appeasement this failed miserably. Nor did he win Shia hearts and minds by declaring the birthday of Ali a holiday, and refurbishing the shrines at Najaf and Karbala. The Shias remained distrusted, marginalized and persecuted. This grew worse after July 1979 when Saddam felt strong enough to order his nominal superior, Bakr, to go home and rest. Bakr was obedient, but Saddam followed up in any case with wholescale killings of colleagues in that summer of 1979 (by coincidence, I was visiting Iraq at the time and recall the atmosphere of sheer terror that had overtaken Baghdad). The Shias were soon to become a special target of Saddam.

In 1958 Mohammad Baqr al-Sadr and Mahdi al-Hakim helped the Shias of Iraq organize their first political party, Al Dawa Al Islamiya. Its declared aim was to revive Islam and fight 'atheism' (code name for communism). While Ayatollah Hakim was the senior leader, the future lay with Sadr, who was both a scholar and a fiery orator. The Dawa programme called for adult franchise and democracy, but it would, wouldn't it? Shias constituted some 60 per cent of the population. It also demanded, far more vaguely, an Islamic republic. This provoked a question: were Shias more loyal to their faith than their state? The doubt, which could be interpreted any which way, was periodically dusted up by Saddam to terrorize the community. In 1965 Ayatollah Khomeini came to live in Najaf after being exiled by the Shah.

The compact between the Shah and the clergy in Iran had broken down by the early Sixties. The Shah, now feeling as secure as his father once did when he horsewhipped an Ayatollah in Qom, let loose his dreaded Savak, backed by troops, on the most revered clergy at Feiziyeh in 1963. During the traditional 40-day period of mourning that followed, Khomeini emerged as the pre-eminent leader of the opposition. His confrontation was open. He issued an edict forbidding *taqiyya* or dissimulation. In sermons, he called the Shah another Yazid, the Sunni Sultan who had ordered the death of Imam Hussein. On the morning of 5 June 1963 Khomeini was arrested. Riots broke out; there was shooting; many died. The government had made Khomeini a hero.

In the autumn of 1964 the Shah gave diplomatic immunity to American military personnel, placing them outside Iran's courts. Khomeini spotted his opportunity. He began his sermon on 27 October at the shrine of Fatima in Qom with a line from the Quran that Muslims recite during funerals: 'We come from Allah and to Allah we return.'

253

His theme was evocative. An American cook could assassinate your *marja* and Iran's courts could now do nothing about it. On 4 November he was picked up, driven to the airport and sent into exile in Turkey. Then Tehran discovered that the Turks were more intelligent than they expected. Khomeini was treated with the greatest respect and even affection in Turkey, disarming him completely. The Shah of Iran pressurized the Turks to send Khomeini to Iraq. And so in November 1965 Khomeini arrived in Najaf. One of the first bits of advice he gave to Grand Ayatollah Mohsen Hakim, during courtesy calls made on each other, was to order an uprising. Iraq's Shias were not ready for such advice. It was only when Bakr and Saddam came to power in 1968 that repression against Shias took a nasty edge.

In 1968 a special department was created in the security services to deal with Shias. Dawa went underground. In February 1969 Iran demanded a revision of the 1937 treat that defined the border on the Shatt al-Arab. When Iraq refused, Iran abrogated the treaty. Saddam took his revenge upon the Shias within reach, in his own country. A seminary at Najaf was shut down, censorship imposed on Shia religious publications, religious endowments were confiscated and, in the ultimate sacrilege, alcohol was permitted to be sold in the holy Shia cities. Ironically, Saddam sent feelers to Khomeini hoping to exploit his anti-Shah sentiments for Iraq's use, but Khomeini snubbed him, calling the Baathists as tyrannical as the Shah.

But real tyranny had to wait for Saddam to become a dictator. Could one reason for Saddam's hatred of Shias have been personal? He set up the Office of National Security after the 1968 coup and then gave a loyalist, Nazim Kazzar, what was the most sensitive job in the administration. In 1973 Kazzar nearly pulled off a coup of his own. He had planned to kill Bakr at the airport on his arrival from a state visit to Poland, take over television and radio and declare the end of the 'Tikriti' regime of Bakr, Saddam and Khairullah. On 30 June, the appointed day, Kazzar arrested the defence minister and the Army chief, and held them in a cellar-prison inside the building of the security department. By chance the airplane bringing Bakr back was four hours late. Kazzar panicked. He concluded that the plot had been discovered and the delay was deliberate. He rushed back to his office, picked up his two prisoners and rushed off in a convoy towards Iran. Saddam sent helicopters after him. Kazzar was brought back and executed after a summary trial on 8 July.

Nazim Kazzar was a Shia, and had often privately voiced his resentment of 'Sunni control' of Iraq.

When between 1973 and 1979 Saddam sought to eliminate all potential threats, Shias came for special attention. In December 1974, five senior Shia clerics were executed, leading to sporadic but continued clashes between Shias and the police. Sadr was imprisoned for a while, but on his release returned to the street. In February 1977, on the symbolic 10th of Muharram, he organized a huge demonstration. By this time, Saddam was calling Shias pro-Iranian traitors: he offered $2,500 to any 'pure Iraqi' who divorced a wife from Iran. In this confrontation eight clerics were executed, some 2,000 Shias jailed and about 200,000 expelled. In October 1978 Saddam did Khomeini the biggest favour of his life by expelling him as well. Ayatalloh Khomeini went on to Paris, freedom and international media attention. The political distance from Paris to Tehran was much shorter than it would ever have been from Najaf to Tehran. Within a little more than a year Khomeini was back home in Iran, and the Shah of Iran in exile.

Khomeini had become the undisputed leader of the Shias. In Najaf, Khomeini cast himself as a modern, less peripatetic Jamaluddin Afghani, the inspirational ideologue of the 19th century, whose work has been described earlier (see chapter 10). He was visceral about Muslim rulers who had betrayed Muslims, with special emphasis on the Saudi royal family, and castigated foreigners who would not let Muslims unite. Khomeini's message was straight and sharp: Muslims should preserve their borders and unite their thoughts.

Between 21 January and 8 February 1970 Khomeini delivered a series of lectures in Najaf on the Islamic state that became the basis of the polity he would establish in Iran a decade later. The lectures were preceded by a survey of the 'hopelessness and impotence of the Muslim world'. His thesis was that while Shias must await the return of the Imam for the ideal state, in the meantime the Sharia (law) and the Sunnah (the life of the Prophet) contained all that was required for happiness in this life. Islamic government, he said, was neither tyrannical nor absolute, but Constitutional; it was the rule of divine law over men. The law could only be interpreted by the *faqih,* or the one qualified to do so. But he extended his argument. This model government was not the preserve of Shias; it should serve also for Sunnis since there was no dispute between them on the Sharia or the Sunnah. He argued that only 'agents of imperialism' had spread the idea that the clergy should keep out of politics. He summed this up neatly: 'The Prophet was a political person.'

Khomeini's sharpest opponent in Najaf was the pro-establishment Grand Ayatollah Abolqassem Khoei. The story of his successor may not be definitive but it is a marker. Towards the end of the Iraq war of 2003, with the fall of Baghdad, or at least the fall of Saddam Hussein's statue in Baghdad, imminent, Tony Blair sent Sheikh Abdul Majid al-Khoei, in a special aircraft from London to Najaf, with the specific mission of mobilizing the Shia community on behalf of the Anglo-American invasion. On Monday 7 April, from Najaf, Sheikh Majid called upon Shias to support Britain and America. On Tuesday he suggested neutrality. On Thursday he was hacked to death inside the gold-domed mosque of Ali. While the identity of the assailants has been lost in the confusion, friends of Khoei accused the Jamaat-e-Sadr-Thani of inciting the killing. The leader of this group was Moqtada Sadr, son of Mohammad al-Sadr, founder of the Dawa and deputy of Khomeini in Iraq until he was executed by Saddam Hussein. Memory runs as deep as faith in Iraq.

Saddam Hussein escorted Empress Farah of Iran in December 1978 when she called on Grand Ayatollah Khoei to plead for his help against the revolution that Khomeini had inspired. Khoei told her that Iran had gone mad to oppose the Shah and gave her a ring as a gift for the monarch. Khomeini called Khoei *Aqa-e Sarshenas,* or Mr Well-Known. The younger firebrand Sadr declared Khomeini leader of the Shias, and a chant arose in Najaf: '*Ash al Khomeinin wil Sadr weddine lazim yantaser!*' ('Long live Khomeini and Sadr, and faith will prevail!'), and '*Kulana lak fada Khomeini!*' ('We are for you to sacrifice, Khomeini!').

On 16 July 1979 Saddam made himself absolute dictator of Iraq. Taking care to inform Jordan and Saudi Arabia–according to others, keeping the CIA in the know as well–Saddam ordered President Bakr to resign. Aware of the alternative, Bakr appeared on television to 'nominate' Saddam to his job.

1979 was the year of power, purges, executions and state terrorism in Iraq. 1980 was the year of populism, much of it thin fiction. Elections for instance were held for the national assembly with 40 per cent seats reserved for Shias but to call them elections is stretching the truth.

BALANCE OF POWERLESS

Saddam Hussein and Ayatollah Khomeini came to power in the same year, one by conspiracy and murder; and the other wafted up on a mass uprising. There was instant stir among all the Shia communities in the region—in Iraq, Saudi Arabia, Bahrain and Kuwait. Khomeini became their *marja-e-taqlid* or source of emulation. There were even riots in tightly controlled Saudi Arabia, in the oil-rich Shia province of Hasa, in February 1980. But the key was Iraq. Khomeini called on his fellow Shias to overthrow the 'un-Islamic' Baath. Sadr proclaimed himself Khomeini's deputy in Iraq and issued a fatwa against membership in Baath. Saddam's response was predictable. Ayatollah Hakim was sentenced to life imprisonment on a bogus charge, but later allowed to go to Iran. Thousands were arrested for being 'Khomeinites', hundreds executed. The seizure of the American embassy in Tehran on 4 November 1979, and Khomeini's support for the move, gave Saddam an opportunity to twist his anti-Khomeini stance into pro-American postures. He followed this up by unequivocal condemnation of the Soviet invasion of Afghanistan that winter.

On 1 April 1980 there was an assassination attempt on deputy prime minister Tareq Aziz while he was visiting Mustinsiriya University. On 5 April, membership of Dawa became a crime punishable by death. Death followed. On 6 April Sadr and his greatly respected sister Amina were arrested. On 9 April the two were executed. Riots broke out. Shias disappeared in their thousands. Saddam crowed: 'I am the son of Ali, and I kill with his sword!' He certainly began to fantasize about his abilities and about his role in the Arab world. He would be their saviour.

As border skirmishes with Iran increased, positive signals began to emerge from Washington. In April 1980 Zbigniew Brzezinski, Jimmy Carter's national security adviser, said that there were 'no fundamental incompatibility of interests between the United States and Iraq'. This was also fundamentally compatible with the needs of Arab regimes in the American camp that were more than apprehensive about the impact of Khomeini's rhetoric.

To understand why Khomeini, ideological heir of Afghani, Nuri and Kashani, terrified the pro-American Arab regimes we need to examine, briefly, his worldview. He saw his Islamic revolution in Iran as the beginning of a process of Muslim revival rather than an end in itself. It would be given to Iran, and to him, to reverse the decline of the

Muslim world, and the usurpation of its natural resources by the West. He had no doubt about which superpower was the greater enemy of Muslims. The United States was the Great Satan, and the Soviet Union was a Lesser Satan. This was not a moral judgement; he simply, and accurately, recognized that the Soviet Union was a weaker power. Rather audaciously, he sent a letter to Mikhail Gorbachev inviting the Communists to see the Islamic light, in emulation of the Prophet Mohammad who had sent letters to the major powers of the region, including the Byzantine emperor Heraclius and the Sassanid emperor Chosroes. The occupation of the American embassy in Tehran seemed God-sent because it changed the character of the movement and shifted it into a dimension that Khomeini wanted but had not felt strong enough to express. The confrontation with the Great Satan was now direct and open. Khomeini was fond of a repeating a *hadith* in which he defined his vision: 'My brother Moses was blind in one eye [because he was so worldly]; my brother Jesus was blind in the other eye [because he was so unworldly]. But I have two eyes.' Khomeini, both eyes open, now saw his mission as 'Imam of the Islamic community of the world' and 'Hope of the world's oppressed' in what he called the second Islamic revolution. Internally he began to confront and eliminate from the power structure those who wanted a compromise with the United States, or were less aggressive in their thinking. In their place rose disciples like Hojjat al-Islam Ali Khameini, who took over as the third president of the Islamic Republic on 20 October 1981. An eloquent orator, Khameini had also translated the works of Syed Qutb, a leading ideologue of the Muslim Brotherhood in Egypt, which in turn owed its ideological sustenance to Jamaluddin Afghani. For Khomeini, export of the Islamic revolution became almost as important as its preservation in Iran. Baqer Moin explains: 'He [Khomeini] wanted to turn Iran into a power base for Islam in the world, for without power, he believed, the Islamic movement would get nowhere. The establishment of an Islamic government in Iran was not enough; the 'Islamic homeland' [*vatan-e Islami*] which had been "divided by the imperialists and ambitious, tyrannical rulers" had also to be liberated.'

We know who the imperialists were; but whom did he mean when he spoke of ambitious, tyrannical rulers? The answer was given many times, but never as clearly as in his last will and document. His 29-page will was written in 1982 and revised in 1987, and indicates his thinking at this crucial phase of the development of his revolution. He described the Saudi monarch as a traitor to Allah. Muslims 'should curse tyrants, including the Saudi royal family, these traitors to God's great shrine, may God's curse and those of His prophets and angels be upon them...King Fahd spends a large part of the people's wealth every year on the anti-Quranic, totally baseless and superstitious faith of Wahhabism. He abuses Islam and the dear Quran.'

There was no question in Riyadh or Amman or Kuwait that Khomeini had to be stopped. On 5 August 1980 Saddam reached Saudi Arabia via Jordan, wearing his military uniform and carrying a gun. His meeting with Crown Prince Fahd lasted ten hours during which he informed the Saudis about his plans. On 17 September Saddam reneged on the Algiers agreement of 1975 by which half of the Shatt al Arab had been ceded to Iran. On 22 September 1980 more than 2,000 Iraqi tanks entered southwest Iran. Saddam Hussein thought the war would be a matter of days, or at best weeks, leaving him the undisputed king of Arabs and master of the Middle East. By the time it ended eight years later, it had mutated into something substantially different.

Those who dismiss the eight-year war between Iraq and Iran as pointless make one point, but miss another.

Such complicated historical events do not lend themselves to easy definitions, and often outstrip their original intentions. The calculations of Saddam and his fund-raisers would have succeeded if Iraq had been what it told its friends it was, an Israel of the 1967 variety. Saddam fantasized that he could defeat Iran in a six-day blitzkrieg; and even if this went wrong, he would take only weeks to bring the upstart revolution to its knees. But Iran proved to have both geographical depth and a new-found will against what the Iranians called Saddam's *tarhib* and *targhid* (terror and bribes).

It did not turn out, possibly to the surprise of both sides, to be a Shia-Sunni war. In Iraq the Dawa was banned and Sadr was dead, and there was no Shia insurrection in favour of Iran. This would have been too simplistic. Issues like nationalism were involved, which Khomeini recognized: recall his message saying that Muslims should keep their national boundaries but unite their thoughts. The war was a conflict between the power of the state and the power of an idea, and both sides knew that a victory for either would change the future of the region.

Saddam made surface attempts to poach on the religious space: the *kalimah* began to appear behind him on television; the Quran was recited more often on radio; and he began to be photographed in mosques. He also tried to simultaneously sharpen traditional Arab-Iranian hostility: the battle of Qadisiya, in which Arabs had defeated Persians, entered his rhetoric, while he himself became another Khalid ibn Walid and referred to Iranian cities like Khezestan by old names such as Arabistan.

Without Arab cash Saddam could not have fought the war. Iraq had reserves of $35 billion before the war began, and nothing after it. Saudi Arabia and Kuwait gave him interest-free loans and grants of up to $50 billion (the exact figure is disputed). Jordan provided end-user certificates for arms dealers to ensure that Iraq could manoeuvre around the embargo on arms sales. Iran, curiously but logically, found unusual, if secretive, friends in Israel and the United States. Israel could not afford a victorious Iraq and in what became known as the Irangate scandal, supplied vital Tow anti-tank missiles to Iran with American permission.

Henry Kissinger regretted, famously, that both sides could not lose. But of course both sides did lose. Iran lost the momentum of revolution, and the Islamic fire with which Khomeini wanted to burn the regimes of the Muslim world remained in the hearth, to appear after his death in more careful and guarded ways. Iraq, and Saddam, lost far more. As Saddam himself told *Time* magazine (19 July 1982), if the two superpowers had wanted to stop the war they could have. But why would they want to? By the time Iran accepted the ceasefire on 18 July 1988, both Iran and Iraq were drained. Iran retreated into itself in order to rebuild its strength. Saddam, in a dangerously irrational and demanding mood, opted for megalomania.

The consequences of that war, rather than the war itself, shifted the tides of history over the next 15 years. Saddam had started this war as much for his neighbours as for himself. But by March 1983 their generosity began to wane. And while America and Britain opened food credits for Iraq, that was not where the big bucks were. In December 1983 Ronald Reagan sent a special envoy with a handwritten letter to Saddam. The emissary's name was Donald Rumsfeld. In November 1984 Tareq Aziz returned the gesture with a visit to Washington. Coolly, in November 1985 Reagan also approved of the sale of Tow anti-tank missiles to Iran via Israel. America's intention in the region was not to create a balance of power. It was to create a balance of the powerless.

At the end of the war, Iraq owed $35 billion to the West, $11 billion to the Soviet Union and around $50 billion to Saudi Arabia and Kuwait. Saddam expected to be bailed out by his Arab brothers. Instead he discovered that the brothers had other things to do. Iraq was broke. Lower prices had driven oil revenues, which had been around $25 billion before the war, to $14 billion, and nearly all of this was eaten up by military needs. Arab leaders called on Baghdad to congratulate Saddam Hussein on his 'victory' but left their wallets behind. Kuwait's Crown Prince Saad dropped by in February 1989 and Saddam offered him a non-aggression pact in exchange for cancellation of debt. Kuwait did not respond. Instead, Kuwait had already increased its oil production to offset lower prices, ignoring Saddam's increasingly desperate plea that higher prices should be protected by agreed production quotas. Under pressure, and still full of self-grandiose, Saddam became as irrational as a gambler who has seen a pile of riches turn into a mountain of debt.

On 17 July 1989, Saddam gave his first warning to his erstwhile friends, calling their behaviour a conspiracy to drive Iraq towards famine. On 23 February 1990 at a meeting of Arab heads of government in Amman, Saddam demanded that $30 billion of Iraq's debt be cancelled. At the Arab League meeting on 28-30 May that year in Baghdad, he offered a deal to Kuwait: forget the war loans, lease two islands on the edge of the Gulf to give Iraq an outlet to the sea, add another billion dollars as a sweetener and buy peace. The Emir of Kuwait was impassive. But when he approached Saddam the next day to discuss the border issue, Saddam replied that he had a surprise waiting for Kuwait and all would be well. On 25 July Saddam had his fateful meeting with the American ambassador in Baghdad, April Glaspie. She solemnly parroted the standard State Department line that America had no opinion on Arab conflicts. April Glaspie then went off on a probably much-needed holiday. On 31 July a meeting was held in Jeddah to reconcile Iraq-Kuwait differences, with Prince Abdullah in the chair. Kuwait told Iraq: don't threaten us, we have important friends.

On 2 August 1990 Iraqi paratroopers and tanks occupied Kuwait in four hours.

The American-British-Australian invasion of Iraq in March 2003 is the penultimate chapter of a conflict that began on 2 August 1990 as a consequence of a war that Saddam Hussein launched against Iran on 22 September 1980.

CREATIVE DESTRUCTION

Mobile telephone companies depend heavily on humour to make money from SMS but on 23 March 2003, the day George Bush and Donald Rumsfeld launched their 'shock and awe' campaign against Saddam Hussein's Iraq, the message that gathered speed did so because of its chill rather than its warmth. 'Is it a coincidence that war started on the 3rd day of the 3rd month of the 3rd year of the 3rd millennium? Is this the start of the Third World War?'

In the first week of April 2003, a former head of CIA, James Woolsey, gave testimony before Congress. This was not the start of the Third World War for him, but the Fourth (the Third World War, quite correctly, was the cold war between the West and the Soviet Union). Woolsey predicted that the Fourth World War would last longer than the previous three: the first had lasted four years, the second five and third forty.

It is commonplace now that the American war party's plans were ready long before the war. On 15 September 2001, says Bob Woodward in *Bush at War* (Simon & Schuster, 2002), 'Paul Wolfowitz put forth military arguments to justify a U.S. attack on Iraq rather than Afghanistan.' Why? Because while 'attacking Afghanistan would be uncertain...Iraq was a brittle regime that might break easily. It was do-able.' Wolfowitz, now deputy defence secretary, was knocking at the order, offering opportunity. The idea was much older than 9/11, and dated back at least to 1997 when a group that called itself, a bit grandly, The Project for a New American Century, mapped out a post-Saddam Iraq which would, in partnership with other pro-American regimes and Israel, keep the natural resources of West and Central Asia safe for the West. Wolfowitz was one of the members.

9/11 spurred this lobby, particularly since many of them were at different levels of the Bush administration. On 20 September, 40 neo-conservatives sent an open letter to Bush to overthrow Saddam, and destroy the Hezbollah, adding for good measure that he should invade Syria and Iran if they did not cut links with the Hezbollah. Such lobbying is par for the course in Washington, and one would not give it credence if George Bush had not given it attention. Creative destruction was the term applied to the proposed Bush mission. Serious commentators like Norman Podhoretz demanded victory in 'World War IV–the war against militant Islam'. Less serious ones, but no less influential, like Richard

Perle thought that it might not be a bad idea to seize Mecca along with the oil fields, just to prove who had the muscle. On 21 September 1992 a 33-page document outlining a National Security Strategy was issued by the Bush administration, taking the wheels of the new foreign policy beyond containment and deterrence. It was specific in its warning: the USA would not permit any nation to reduce the huge lead it had built up in military capability since the fall of the Soviet Union. (Currently, the United States spends more on its defence than the rest of the world put together.) The distinguished American diplomat Harry Barnes described the coming era as 'permanent war for permanent peace'. A twist in the new mantra took the concept further. America would contemplate a pre-emptive strike even if the threat were uncertain.

Wolfowitz explained this to the *New York Times Magazine* (22 September 2002): 'In fact, there's no way you can prove that something's going to happen three years from now or six years from now. But these people (Saddam) have made absolutely clear what their intentions are, and we know a lot of about their capabilities. I suppose I hadn't thought of it quite this way, but intentions and capabilities are the way you think about warfare. Proof beyond a reasonable doubt is the way you think about law enforcement.' The magazine added: 'Wolfowitz says he believes Sept. 11 has awakened us to a world where certainty is an expensive luxury.'

It gets more expensive when uncertainty is dressed up as certainty. No one could have been more certain than George Bush about the weapons of mass destruction he knew he would find after the defeat of Saddam Hussein. This is the White House shopping list that sent America to war: 500 tonnes of mustard and nerve gas; 25,000 litres of anthrax; 38,000 litres of botulinum toxin; 29,984 banned munitions able to deliver chemical agents; 18 mobile biological warfare factories; aerial vehicles to discharge anthrax, gas centrifuges to enrich uranium and of course several dozen Scud missiles. In his State of the Union speech in 2003, Bush had thanked British intelligence for the invaluable information that Saddam Hussein had tried to buy 500 tonnes of uranium from Niger. This was dropped from the chargesheet when it proved to be based on some very shoddy forgery.

The credibility of the war had self-destructed even before it began. This was why George Bush managed the unique feat of creating a peace movement before any war had begun. What Bush could not appreciate was that anti-war sentiment did not correspond to support for Saddam. This was especially true of the Muslim reaction. Many Muslims saw a much larger picture, in which Saddam was not their ally, but a dangerous irritant and intrusion. This larger picture was painted on evidence provided by a few friends of George Bush.

One of them is Franklin Graham, son of Billy, whose description of Islam as 'a very evil and wicked religion' has been repeated often enough to become infamous. Just after the 1991 Gulf war, Graham tried to improve the world by sending tens of thousands of Arabic New Testaments to Saudi Arabia. Graham also believes that Islam and Christianity are destined to be at war till the imminent Second Coming. This could have been dismissed as peripheral, were it not for the fact that he is a friend of George Bush and was invited to the Pentagon for its 2003 Good Friday prayer service, at precisely the time when the Pentagon was mobilizing for war against Iraq. The signal was not lost on those who saw this as a war against Islam as much as a war against Iraq.

Islamophobia has seeped down to lower layers of the American Right. On 21 April 2003 Dan Smith reported in the *Sacramento Bee* that less than two months after leaving office Shawn Steel, a former Republican Party chairman of California, was calling Islam 'a diseased religion' at Loyola Marymount University in Los Angeles. Steel became more 'specific' at the University of Southern California: 'The disease of Islam must be rectified. It's kill or be killed.' Admittedly this is excess, but when excess threatens to become conventional wisdom we need to take it seriously.

The June 30, 2003 issue of *Time* magazine had an excellently researched cover story ('Should Christians convert Muslims?'). It reported at length on the intense evangelical movement that had targeted Muslim nations and societies for conversion. This predates 9/11, because before the Afghanistan war evangelists who had taken the risk of entering a Taliban-controlled country were evacuated by mutual agreement. *Time* reported that dissimulation was one of the techniques being widely used through what were internally described as 'Jesus mosques'. They were run by pretend-Muslims (the women in burkas) who sought to lure believers with the correct recitation of the *kalimah* before indoctrination began.

Iraq was the newest target in this effort to pierce 'Satan's armour'. Diplomacy, one of the pseudonymous missionaries quoted in the article pointed out, does not work with Satan. *Time* reported a scene from a classroom for evangelical students organized by the U.S. Center for World Mission, in Queens, New York. One of the quotations used in that class was from the U.S. Attorney General John Ashcroft: 'Islam is a religion in which God requires you to send your son to die for Him. Christianity is a faith in which God sends His son to die for you.' *Time* noted: 'After his comment was publicized in late 2001, Ashcroft said it referred to terrorists and not to mainstream Muslims, but the point seemed lost on ["Barbara", the teacher of the class].' Barbara (a pseudonym) had no illusions about her mission: 'Islam is the terrorist. Muslims are the victims.' She added, after the prayer at the end of the class: 'We pray that the weapon of mass destruction, Islam, be torn down. Lord, we declare that your blood is enough to forgive every single Muslim. It is enough.'

Is it any wonder that Muslims increasingly believe that the 'weapon of mass destruction' that the American Right, and its temporary leader George Bush, is searching for is not chemical or nuclear arms, but Islam.

This might be a worst-case scenario, but the Muslim street saw the Iraq war in ways significantly different from the best intentions that Washington and London might have had. This is why events are being overtaken by the law of unintended consequences. The Anglo-American occupation of Iraq has induced a radical response among the previously uncommitted, or indifferent (it would be a mistake to consider every radical a fundamentalist, even if all fundamentalists are part of the radical response). Ibn Khaldun's theory of rise, fall and renewal, that destiny can be changed by a return to first principles, is at work.

At the height of the 2003 war, a *hadith* was repeated in Friday sermons and prayers across the Islamic world. It said: 'The hour (of judgement) shall occur when the Euphrates unveils a mountain of gold over which people will fight.' That gold is of course oil. It was followed by a second hadith: 'The cause of the great war before the final conflict will be Christians. First, Christians and Muslims will ally to conquer a common enemy. But Christians will be treacherous and claim victory on their own strength, driving Muslims to arms against them.' The interpretation is apparent. There was an alliance between Muslims and Christians in the war against the atheist Communists in Afghanistan, but after the victory, the Christian West claimed that it was their victory alone and betrayed their Muslim allies by turning against them.

The alliance of the evangelist lobby with the oil lobby in the Bush administration confirms this hadith for an increasing number of Muslims.

THE ALIBI SYNDROME

Perhaps George Bush, worried too much by the horrifying thought of military failure in his war against Saddam Hussein, did not spend enough time thinking about the meaning of success. By one yardstick, the height of Bush's power can be measured very easily, by the depth of Arab impotence. Or at least the impotence of Arab governments. It can be argued that after Vietnam America learnt to choose its enemies with more care than its friends, a vital lesson. Bush in particular is a soft-target war-maker. Wars can be won in three days or three years. Their aftermath is more troublesome. Bush has altered the political landscape, but in ways he may live to regret. By removing Saddam, he has done Iraq the kind of favour he does not sufficiently understand.

Saddam Hussein was an usurper who exploited Iraqi nationalism to protect his tyranny. It would be a mistake to romanticize the fall and disappearance of Saddam. He was more clever than powerful. He milked, as much as he could, Arab anger against Israel and neo-colonialism. But being a tyrant, he was a problem rather than a solution.

Saddam Hussein belonged to what might be called the 'alibi' category of post-colonial, Third World leaders, men who used a multiplicity of excuses to protect their dictatorships. Their origins were usually legitimate. Many of them did genuinely battle their way to power, in freedom movements against either foreign powers or in internal struggles against monarchies of the kind that the British left behind when they withdrew from their Arab colonies.

But leadership quietly became indistinguishable from dictatorship, and dictatorship morphed into tyranny as individuals became 'indispensable' to either national security or nation-building. (Jawaharlal Nehru and Nelson Mandela are two extraordinary exceptions.) Failure only reinforced their greed for power, instead of persuading them to leave office. The leader rose above the law, and above the people. Institutions were either ignored, or misused. There is nothing Islamic about this syndrome. It extends to Robert Mugabe in Zimbabwe and the Kim dynasty in North Korea. The reasons change, but the objective does not, which is the preservation of a dictatorship protected by an Army-party oligarchy. Such dictatorships often become hereditary because it is convenient. In the absence of law and institutions, the squabble for succession between illegitimate candidates can become vicious enough to destroy the system itself.

In the neighbourhood of Israel, Israel has become the excuse for Army-oligarchies that remain immune to any suggestion of democracy. The excuse can hardly stand up to any scrutiny; these regimes have done as little as they possibly could for Palestine. Hosni Mubarak has retained his grip over a politically dynamic country for a quarter of a century, and as age begins to ask its inevitable questions, thoughts of dynasty hover over Cairo. Damascus accepted dynasty. As would have Baghdad, despite the fact that Saddam's son was a known murderer. Where monarchies thrive, succession is genetic.

The distance between power and people continues to grow. Power generally prevails, except when wrecked by an explosion. In Iraq the explosion was artificially induced, but the ripples will appear both on the surface and as an undercurrent that will invade the region, perhaps travelling along the oil beds under the desert, or whispered from mosque to mosque. The motives for anger against the establishment often differ, and sometimes overlap. An explosion can have many components that react until critical mass is reached. Saudi Arabia is an implosion waiting to happen. Corrective steps can always be taken, in Saudi Arabia as anywhere else. But democracy, the only real answer, is not a gift that can be given in parts, string first, followed by wrapping paper while the real object is kept dangling on a string for delivery on some unspecified date.

Fear of freedom is the motif of most ruling clans in the Muslim world. In a few cases the establishment has been sensible enough to appreciate that this is a means to disaster. Indonesia and Bangladesh are untidy examples, but they are examples nevertheless. A slew of television news channels in the Arab world could be the glimmer of a new dawn, for they will foment change even as they report. A crisis encouraged their birth, and war sustained their birth. The Arab channels, led by Al Jazeera, can thank George Bush for the second Iraq war as much as CNN thanked his father for the first one.

Who will occupy the political space that George Bush cleared in Baghdad? That is the hinge around which the future of the region will turn. If America keeps its commitment to democracy, then Iraqi nationalism will take on a Shia hue. It will be influenced by the lament and anger of its own anguished past. Iraqi Shias believe that they have been oppressed and wronged throughout Islamic history, but defeat has redoubled their commitment to their faith. Life for them is a constant

267

struggle between *haq* (truth) and *batel* (falsehood). This will link with Muslim anger elsewhere, irrespective of whether it is Shia or Sunni.

They will seek to challenge the West by the terms of reference set by Ayatollah Khomeini, as the Hezbollah has done. Shias will have state power in the two major nations of the Middle East, Iran and Iraq; and while this does not mean that the two countries will synchronize every policy, it does mean that it will enable them to lead the Islamic response to any perceived, or actual, Western political or economic hegemony. The conflict over the gold of the Euphrates is not over. This emerging Shia power might prefer disguise before it feels strong enough to assert itself. Shias practised taqiyya with the Ummayads, Abbasids and Ottomans; there is no reason to believe that they will spare George Bush the problem of discovering what their real, long-term intentions are. If America chooses to pre-empt this development, as is possible, then the disguise will come off. Patrick Seale put it well in *Gulf News* on 25 April 2003: 'It seems inevitable that the United States and the Shiites (sic) of Iraq must soon find themselves locked in a struggle for power. This is because the Shiites—some 60 per cent of the population—are the only indigenous force able to challenge the American military presence and, conversely, because the U.S. Army in Iraq is the only force able to prevent a Shiite seizure of power.'

The survival of the Islamic Republic of Iran against difficult odds, and the success of the Hezbollah in Lebanon, have bolstered Shia self-belief. The Hezbollah calls itself an Islamic struggle movement, and considers 1982 a pivotal year in its history. That was when Israel invaded Lebanon and occupied Beirut, the second Arab capital, in its lexicon, to be occupied (the first is Jerusalem). The Hezbollah does not believe that it could have succeeded without the ideological leadership of Ayatollah Khomeini and his categorical definition of the enemy, the Great Satan, and its stooges, the *munafiqeen,* or the hypocrites. The Hezbollah believes that it drove Israel out of Lebanon, a singular success story in a long history of defeat. It took 18 years of faith to do so.

PAST TENSE

When in February 1258 the killing stopped and the looting paused in Baghdad, Hulagu, grandson of Chingiz Khan, creator of the sole superpower of his age, asked the Baghdad *ulema* or religious heads a straight question: 'Which man is better as a sovereign? An unbeliever who is just, or a Muslim who is unjust?'

The question is not substantially different from the one posed to the people of Iraq by George Bush. The 13th century clerics were silent until one of the sages, Radiuddin Ali, wrote down the collective answer: 'The unbeliever who is just should be preferred to the unjust believer.'

It would be convenient to report that this is where the matter ended. But there was more than one response, and delivered over time. No one seriously suggested that the Abbasids be restored to the throne; that era was dead, killed by its own excesses and buried by the Mongol avalanche, just as the self-destructive Baathists were interred by the American onslaught. But to reject the Abbasids was not synonymous with accepting the Mongols.

The Mongols made all the right noises. They promised that the new government would be run by Iraqis, and did not advertise the difference between control and administration. Hulagu retained Ibn al-Kamiya, who had served the Sultan and betrayed him, as the vizier or prime minister. Till today Arab schoolchildren repeat the sentence, 'Cursed by God be he who curses not Ibn al-Kamiya.' Hulagu's forces had a few anti-Abbasid Muslims, just as the Americans had Kurds in the van. But guilt was never very far away from their minds. One of them, Teghel Argun, slipped away from Mongol ranks after he witnessed the destruction of Baghdad. He was later captured by the Mongols and put to death in the marketplace of Tabriz.

Some Muslim chieftans compromised with the new power. Azizuddin Kavus offered Hulagu a magnificent pair of leather boots as a gift. He had his own portrait drawn on the boots so that he could always be at Hulagu's feet.

Others tried craft. The old and wily Badruddin Lulu, on being summoned to Hulagu's presence, promised his terrified followers that he would emerge from the encounter with his honour intact. He hinted that he would actually tweak the Mongol's ears. He did. He offered Hulagu a pair of rare pearls and then asked for the honour of placing them on the conqueror's ears. He was granted permission. He tweaked the ears while placing the earrings, and glanced at his entourage to indicate that he had lived up to his promise.

But there were also those who responded to this crisis by discovering conviction. The first to stand up to Hulagu was Nassir, sultan of Syria, whose strength did not justify his defiance. Hulagu sent him an ultimatum: Resist, and face annihilation; accept and find safety. Nassir replied: 'Resistance to you is obedience to God...If we slay you, our prayers will have been answered. If you slay us, we go to Paradise.'

On 12 September 1259 the Mongols marched into Syria, with the usual results. Cities fell and were destroyed but Nassir remained in the field. He had bought time. Behind him a great revival was taking place under the Mamelukes in Egypt. And in front of him, Hulagu was suddenly diverted—by an election. Hulagu got word that the Great Khan had died and turned towards home for the *Ordu*, or the election of the new chief by family, clan and leaders. In his absence, the Mamelukes defeated the Mongols in the defining battle of Ain Jalut on 3 September 1260. That was the end of Mongol invincibility. Even though Hulagu returned to Syria he no longer aroused the same dread.In a fascinating twist, Hulagu's brother, Berkai, leader of the Mongols in Russia, announced in an open letter that he and his four brothers had converted to Islam. He charged Hulagu with the destruction of Baghdad, and in alliance with the Mamelukes sent an army through the Caucasus, which defeated Hulagu on 13 January 1263. Hulagu died on 8 February 1265. He was 48.

There has never been a time when the Islamic world was under such pressure as in that era. Jerusalem was lost, and even after it was taken back by Saladin, the threat from the West was constant and severe. From the east appeared the Mongols to ravage and rule, while Crusader armies, dreaming of an alliance with the Mongols, swarmed in from the west till Egypt, Syria and Palestine all seemed lost. The new saviours were the Turks, the Mamelukes in Egypt and later the Ottomans who eventually linked Cairo with Constantinople. Within ten years of the fall of Baghdad the Mongols were either destroyed or assimilated; and within another 25 the last Crusader stronghold had fallen. History, of course, does not repeat itself although it has been accused of imitation.

Pride in the past will not determine the course of events in this century, but, as James Woolsey predicted, it could be a long Fourth World War. Listen to the voices.

Craig Smith of the *New York Times* was in Karbala, to see Shia passion during the first Muharram after liberation from Saddam Hussein's tyranny. A white-turbaned Sheikh Muhammad Thamer told him on 21April 2003: 'Our celebration (at release from Saddam) will be perfect only when the

American occupier is gone and the Iraqi people are able to rule themselves by the principles of Islam.' Sheikh Tamer is deputy to Grand Ayatollah Ali al-Sestani. An unnamed chanter in the procession told the reporter: 'The Americans are not our enemy, but they are not our friend. We want an Islamic state and we need to see that the Americans intend to leave our country.'

Sunni voices to the east of Iran had a similar message for Carlotta Gall of the same paper a fortnight later (her story appeared in the *International Herald Tribune* of 7 May 2003 under the headline 'Taliban gather openly in Pakistan and talk of return'). She was told by 26-year-old Abdul Karim, a Taliban: 'We don't like the Americans, and Karzai is a puppet of George W. Bush...We want an Islamic government in Afghanistan.'

It is not important that every Muslim believes that this is true. But war is fought by believers, whether in Washington or on the Muslim street. George Bush has multiplied the number of Muslims who believe in jihad. For such Muslims this jihad will end only when they are convinced that their lands have been rid of American domination and are truly Dar ul-Islam again.

In 1899 Teddy Roosevelt won the Spanish-American war, liberated Cuba and got the Philippines for his country as a bonus. Rudyard Kipling, poet of the British Empire, had been urging the American President to take up the white man's burden, since he suspected that the shoulders of his own country's imperialists were beginning to sag a bit. That burden was heavier than it seemed. When Philippines guerillas of Squinaldo fought back American troops, the *New York World* published a ditty:

> We've taken up the white man's burden
> Of ebony and brown;
> Now will you tell us, Rudyard
> How we may put it down?

That's always the difficult part, isn't it?

GLOSSARY

Akhara:	Or Byayam Samiti, a physical culture club for young men in India.
Atabat:	Set of seminaries.
Alem:	Teacher or guide.
Ayatollah:	Sign of God.
Azaan:	The Islamic call to prayer, delivered five times a day.
Batel:	Falsehood.
Begs:	Turkish nobles.
Bhadralok:	Gentry of Bengal, came into their own in the nineteenth century.
Bibi:	Hindustani word for wife.
Bubu:	Hindustani word for sister.
Cruzados:	Portuguese coins.
Dajjal:	The Islamic equivalent of the Anti-Christ.
Dar ul Harb:	House of War
Dar ul Islam:	House of Islam
Devshirme:	Gathering, method of enlisting Janissaries.
Dhimmi:	Christians and Jews, protected in Muslim lands and given a status under Islamic law.
Dhoti:	An unstitched white cloth worn in India by men, mainly but not exclusively by Hindus.
Ejteha:	Interpretation of law.
Fajr:	Morning, also the pre-dawn Muslim prayer.
Faqih:	One qualified to interpret law.
Fakir:	Beggar, but also one who has surrendered everything for the love of God.
Fatih:	Conqueror, Turkish.
Fatwa:	The decree of a recognized theologian, based on the Shariah.
Fez:	Turkish hat with tassels, a signature of the Caliphate.

Firdaus:	The best and brightest part of Paradise.
Firman:	Royal order.
Furqan:	Title of Surah 25 of the Holy Quran, The Criterion.
Ghayba :	Concealment.
Ghazal:	Romantic Urdu poetry.
Ghazis:	Warriors of Allah.
Hadith:	Compilation of the Prophet's sayings.
Hafiz:	A person who can recite the Quran without reference to text.
Hajj:	The pilgrimage to Mecca.
Hakim:	A doctor.
Hanif:	A person who accepted monotheism but was neither a Christian nor a Jew before the revelation of Islam.
Haq:	Truth.
Hartal:	A general strike, turned into a political weapon by Mahatma Gandhi.
Hashish:	Drug, familiar enough these days.
Hejira:	The emigration of the Prophet from Mecca to Medina along with his devoted companion Abu Bakr; start of the Muslim calendar.
Houris:	The much-dreamt of damsels of paradise, a reward for martyrs.
Ihram:	Two unstitched, seamless pieces of white cloth that are worn by all those visiting Mecca on pilgrimage.
Ijma:	Consensus, along with *Ijtihad* (independent judgment), using *Qiyas* (analogy), *Istihsan* (equity and judgment), *Istislal* (public interest), *Urf* (custom) and *Istidal* (legal reasoning) as means of interpreting law.
Imam:	Islamic priest who leads the community.
Intifadah:	Uprising.
Iqra:	Read. First word of revelation to the Prophet from Allah through the angel Gabriel.
Janissaries:	An elite guard of the Ottoman empire, originally recruited by force in Christian domains like the Balkans; young men were taken to Constantinople, converted and made guardians of the empire.
Jatis:	Castes or communities in Bengal and India.
Jatra:	Travelling theatre groups of Bengal.
Jiziya:	Poll tax imposed on infidels under Islamic law.
Kalimah:	The statement of faith in Islam, proclaiming that Allah is one and that Muhammad is His messenger.

Kasida:	Poetry of lament in Urdu.
Keffiya:	Arab headgear.
Khalifah:	The original of Caliph.
Khutba:	The Friday sermon in a mosque.
Khwaja:	A title given to Sufis who have achieved leadership of their order or have gained respect and admiration of the people.
Labbaika:	The praise and adoration of the unity of God.
Lingam:	Symbol of Lord Shiva's seminal power.
Lungi:	A piece of cloth, sarong-like, worn by men in India, mainly by Muslims but not exclusively.
Mahdi:	The promised priest of Islamic tradition, who will come periodically to cleanse the faith of impurities and restore Muslims to their original glory.
Majnoon:	A possessed person, often a poet, subject of more derision than admiration.
Mansab:	A system of rank and status in the Mughal empire in India.
Marja-e taqlid:	Source of emulation for the community.
Masalegu:	Explainer of problems.
Maulvi:	Muslim priest.
Medressa:	Islamic seminary.
Mimbar:	Place in a mosque from where the Imam leads the prayer.
Mojtahed:	He who interprets law.
Mufti:	A senior Muslim priest.
Mukhabarat:	Intelligence agency that Saddam used for his regime of fear.
Munifiqeen:	Hypocrites who betrayed the Prophet.
Murid:	Disciple.
Murtadd:	Apostates who left Islam after the death of the Prophet and would not accept Caliph Abu Bakr's leadership.
Namaste:	A form of greeting in India.
Naus:	Portuguese ships.
Nawab:	A prince in India.
Ordu:	Election of a new Mongol chief by family, clan and leaders.
Peshwa:	Maratha chief minister.
Pilav:	An excellent delicacy made of rice and mutton.
Pir:	Sufi master.
Poulains:	The community that emerged out of intermarriage between Crusaders and local Arabs.
Qadi:	An Islamic judge; a high post in any Islamic government.
Qalandar:	A Sufi, lost in the love of Allah.

Qiblah:	The direction in which Muslims turn to prayer; it was once Jerusalem and then became the Kaaba in Mecca.
Rai's:	Gentry in India.
Raj'a:	Return.
Raja:	A king in India.
Rakhi:	A thread tied by a sister on her brother's wrist to symbolise her love.
Rikaah:	Part of the prayer (*namaaz*).
Saf:	The line in which Muslims stand during community prayers, in mosques or elsewhere; people take their place in line in order of arrival without distinction of rank, as every Muslim is equal before Allah.
Salat al Salih:	The pious ancestors, companions of the Prophet.
Sanatan Dharma:	Hinduism.
Shahadah:	A proclamation of faith in Islam.
Sharia:	The Islamic law based on the Quran and the sayings of the Prophet.
Sharif:	The rich among Indian Muslims, many of whom trace their ancestry to the invaders from Central Asia.
Sherbet:	A sweet drink, non-alcoholic.
Shervani:	A formal longcoat in India.
Shikwa:	Urdu word for complaint.
Sindoor:	Red vermillion powder that is a mark of marriage in Hinduism and placed in the parting of the hair by women.
Souk:	Arab market.
Swaraj:	Hindi for self-rule. The slogan *Swaraj, swadharma, dharmatattwa* meant National Rule, National Religion, National Identity.
Talebeh:	Student.
Taqiyya:	Permission granted to a Shia to dissimulate before hostile authority, to deny his faith in order to preserve it.
Taqlid:	Guidance.
Targhid:	Bribe.
Tarhib:	Terror.
Tasnim:	Fullness, opulence; *tasnim* is the fountain in paradise whose drink is better than the purest wine.
Tawhid:	The unity of Allah.
Ulema:	Religious heads.
Umma:	The Muslim brotherhood.
Umra:	The lesser pilgrimage.

Vaez:	Preacher.
Vatan-e Islami:	Islamic homeland.
Vazier:	Generally, prime minister.
Wali:	Leader.
Zamindars:	Landowner-class of India.
Zanjabil:	Refreshment of paradise, a heavenly wine based on ginger.

A SUGGESTED READING LIST

A theme such as the subject of this book is inevitably weighted by texts that, common sense suggests, are not going to be bedtime reading. This list is designed to provide further, and in a surprising number of cases, entertaining illumination into the innumerable corners of history through which we have travelled. You might be happy to learn that, thanks to an environment that has encouraged reprints, good bookstores might be as useful a place to find these books as a library. Three basic texts are the foundation for any study of Islam: the Holy Quran being the foremost. I have used Abdullah Yusuf Ali's classic translation as the standard reference (*The Holy Quran: Text, Translation and Commentary,* Islamic Propagation Centre International, Amana Corporation, 1989). It also has an extremely useful index. The second basic work is the *hadith* or the sayings of the Prophet Muhammad, left for posterity in four major collections. I have used the collection of Imam Bukhari published at a very reasonable price by Kitab Bhavan in Delhi in 1987. The third is the great biography of the Prophet written by ibn Ishaq and translated by Alfred Guillaume (*The Life of Muhammad,* Oxford, 1955). One has sought Arabic as well as English sources for the great events of the early period; this was possible thanks to fine translations that are now available. There is a marked revival of interest in original works, and many institutions have used their resources to bring them to a larger audience. One excellent instance is the translation of the *Baburnama* and the *Jahangirnama,* the court histories of two great Mughal emperors of India, brought out by the Smithsonian Institute in 1996 and 1999 with Oxford University Press, New York. I, however, have used the more traditional translations by the Beveridges done in the first quarter of the twentieth century.

A Viceroy's India: Leaves from Lord Curzon's Notebook, Introduced by Elizabeth Longford; Sidgwick & Jackson, London, 1984.

Aburish, Said. *Saddam Hussein: The Politics of Revenge,* Bloomsbury, 2000.

Afnan, Soheil M. *Avicenna: His Life and Works*, George Allen & Unwin, London, 1958.

Aga Khan, H.H. *The Memoirs of Aga Khan*, Simon and Schuster, New York, 1954.

Ahmad, S. Hasan. *Iqbal, His Political Ideas at the Crossroads,* Printwell, Aligarh, 1979.

Ahmad, Aijaz. *Lineages of the Present: Political Essays,* Tulika Print Communication Services, Delhi, 1996.

Ahmad, Aziz. *Studies in Islamic Culture in the Indian Environment*, Oxford University Press, Delhi, 1969.

Ahmed, Rafiuddin. *The Bengal Muslims, 1871-1906: A Quest for Identity,* Oxford University Press, Delhi, 1981.

Ajami, Fouad. *The Dream Palace of The Arabs: A Generation's Odyssey,* Vintage Books, New York, 1998.

Akbar, M.J. *India: The Siege Within – Challenges to a Nation's Unity,* Penguin, London, 1985.

Akbar, M.J. *Nehru: The Making of India*, Viking, London, 1988.

Akhund, Iqbal. *Memories of a Bystander: A Life in Diplomacy,* Oxford University Press, Karachi, 1997.

Al-Biruni, *Al-Biruni's India: An Account*, tr. E. Sachau, Chand, Delhi, 1964.

Alam, Asadollah. *The Shah and I,* I.B. Tauris, London, 1991

Albuquerque, A. *Commentaries of Afonso de Albuquerque.* tr., W. de G. Birch, 4 Vols. London, 1875-84.

Ali, Chaudhri Muhammad. *The Emergence of Pakistan*, Columbia University Press, New York, 1967.

Allami, Abu'l-Fazl. *The Ain-i-Akbari. Vol. 1*, Oriental Books Reprint Corporation, New Delhi, 1977.

Allen, Charles. *Soldier Sahibs,* The men who made the North West Frontier. Abacus, London, 2000.

Anderson, Walter K. and Damle, Shridhar D. *The Brotherhood in Saffron: The Rashtriya Swayamsevak Sangh and Hindu Revivalism,* Vistaar Publications, Delhi, 1987.

Anwar, Raja. *The Terrorist Prince: The Life and Death of Murtaza Bhutto,* Vanguard Books, Lahore, 1988.

Arberry, A.J. *Sufism*, London, 1950.

Armstrong, Karen. *Muhammad: A Western Attempt to Understand Islam,* Victor Gollanz, London, 1991.

Armstrong, Karen. *A History of Jerusalem: One City, Three Faiths,* Harper Collins, London, 1997.

Armstrong, Karen. *Holy War*, Macmillan, London, 1988.

Athar Abbas, Saiyid. *Shah Abdul Aziz: Puritanism, Sectarian Polemics and Jihad,* Marifat Publishing House, Canberra, 1980.

Attar, Farid al-Din. *Muslim Saints and Mystics,* tr. A.J. Arberry, Routledge and Kegan Paul, London, 1966.

Battuta, Ibn. *Travels in Asia and Africa 1325-1354,* Routledge and Kegan Paul, London, 1984.

Baxter, Craig. *The Jana Sangh: A Biography of a Political Party,* University of Pennsylvania, Philadelphia, 1969.

Beha ed Din. *The Life of Saladin,* Committee of the Palestine Exploration Fund, London, 1897.

Bibliotheca Indica: A Collection of Oriental Works; The Tabakat-i-Akbari (Or A History of India from the Early Mussalman Invasions to the thirty-sixth year of the reign of Akbar) of Khwajah Nizamuddin Ahmad, tr. B. De, Asiatic Society, Calcutta, 1913.

Biddulph, John. *Tribes of Hindoo Kush,* Ali Kamran Publishers, Lahore, 1986.

Brown, Judith M. *Gandhi's Rise to Power: Indian Politics 1915-1922,* Cambridge University Press with Blackie India, 1972.

Burnes, Alexander. *Cabool,* Being a personal narrative of a journey to, and residence in that city, in the years 1836, 7 and 8, Munshiram Manoharlal Publishers Private Limited, New Delhi, 2001.

Burton, Richard F. *Pilgrimage to Al-Madinah and Mecca,* Tylston and Edwards, London.

Busbecq, Ogier de. *Turkish Letters.* Sickle Moon Books, London, 2001.

Busteed, H.E. *Echoes from Old Calcutta: Reminiscences of the days of Warren Hastings, Francis and Impey,* Rupa, Delhi, 2000.

Cantwell Smith, Wilfred. *Modern Islam in India; A Social Analysis,* V. Gollancz, London, 1943.

Cantwell Smith, Wilfred. *Islam in Modern History,* Princeton University Press, 1957.

Chagla, M.C. *Roses in December: An Autobiography*, Bharatiya Vidya Bhavan, Bombay, 1974.

Chand, Tara. *History of the Freedom Movement in India,* Government of India Publications Division, Delhi, 1977.

Chandler, David. (general editor) *The Oxford Illustrated History of the British Army,* Oxford University Press, Oxford, 1994.

Chatterjee, Joya. *Bengal Divided: Hindu Communalism and Partition, 1932-1947,* Cambridge University Press, 1996.

Chatterjee, Partha. *The Nation and its Fragments: Colonial and Postcolonial Histories,* Oxford University Press, New Delhi, 1993.

Chatterjee, Partha. *Nationalist Thought and the Colonial World,* Oxford University Press, New Delhi, 1986.

Chatterji, Bankim Chandra. *Anandamath,* tr. and adapted from original Bengali by Basanta Koomar Roy, Orient Paperbacks, New Delhi, 1992.

Chaudhuri, Nirad C. *Clive of India: A Political and Psychological Essay,* Barrie & Jenkins, London, 1975.

Ciardi, John. *The Inferno: Dante's Immortal Drama of a Journey Through Hell,* Mentor, New York, 1982.

Cloughley, Brian. *A History of the Pakistan Army: Wars and Insurrections,* Oxford University Press, Karachi, 1999.

Cooley, John K.E. *Unholy Wars: Afghanistan, America and International Terrorism,* Penguin, 2000.

Currie, P.M. *The Shrine and Cult of Muin al-din Chishti of Ajmer,* Oxford University Press, Bombay, 1989.

Daniel, Norman. *Islam and the West: The Making of an Image,* The University Press, Edinburgh, 1958.

Dupree, Louis. *Afghanistan,* Princeton University Press, 1980.

Eden, Emily. *Up the Country: Letters from India.* Curzon Press, London and Dublin, 1978.

Elst, Koenraad. *Ayodhya and After: Issues Before Hindu Society,* Voice of India, Delhi, 1991.

Embree, Ainslee T., Hay, Stephen. ed. *Sources of Indian Tradition – Volumes I and II,* Viking, Delhi, 1988, 1991.

Ferrier, R.W. *A Journey to Persia: Jean Chardin's Portrait of a Seventeenth Century,* I.B. Tauris, London, 1996.

Fisher, Michael H. *A Clash of Cultures: Awadh, the British and the Mughals,* Manohar, Delhi, 1987.

Fletcher, Richard. *Moorish Spain,* Phoenix Giant, London, 1992.

Friedman, Thomas L. *From Beirut to Jerusalem,* Anchor Books, Doubleday, New York, 1990.

Fyzee, Asaf A.A. *Outlines of Muhammadan Law,* London, 1949.

Gabrieli, Francesco. *Arab Historians of the Crusades,* Dorset Press, New York, 1989.

Garrett, John. *A Classical Dictionary of Islam,* Rupa, Delhi, 2000.

Geertz, Clifford. *Islam Observed: Religious Development in Morocco and Indonesia,* The University of Chicago Press, Chicago, 1968.

Gerald of Wales. *Opera,* J.S. Brewer. ed. Longman and Company, London, 1861.

Ghazals of Ghalib: Versions from Urdu. ed. Ahmad, Aijaz, Oxford University Press, Delhi, 1994.

Gibb, H.A.R., and H. Bowen. *Islamic Society and the West*, London, 1957

Gibb, H.A.R. *Modern Trends in Islam*, London, 1945.

Gibbon, Edward. *Decline and Fall of the Roman Empire*, Seven Volumes. AMS Press, New York, 1974.

Glubb, John Baggot. *The Grea Arab Conquests*, Prentice Hall Inc., Englewood Cliffs, New Jersey, 1963.

Godse, Nathuram. *Why I assassinated Mahatma Gandhi*, Surya Bharti Prakashan, 1993.

Golwalkar, M.S. *Bunch of Thoughts*, Jagarana Prakashana, Bangalore, 1966.

Gommans, Jos J.L. *The Rise of the Indo-Afghan Empire. c. 1710-1780*, Oxford University Press, Delhi, 1995.

Goodwin, Goodfrey. *Islamic Spain: Architectural Guides for Travellers*, Penguin, London, 1990.

Gopal, Sarvepalli. *Anatomy of a Confrontation: The Babri Masjid-Ram Janmabhumi*, Viking, 1991.

Gopal, Sarvepalli. *Jawaharlal Nehru: A Biography*, Oxford University Press, 1984.

Gordon, Stewart. *Marathas, Marauders, and State Formation in Eighteenth-Century India*, Oxford University Press, 1994.

Guillaume, Alfred. *Islam*. Penguin, London, 1954.

Guillaume, Alfred. *The Life of Muhammad*, Oxford, 1955.

Gupta, Narayani. *Delhi between two Empires 1803-1931*, Oxford University Press, Delhi, 1981.

Habib, John S., *Ibn Saud's Warriors of Islam: The Ikhwan of Najd and their Role in the Creation of the Saudi Kingdom*, 1910-1930, E.J. Brill, Leiden 1978. Humanities Press/ New Jersey, 1978.

Hall, Richard. *Empires of the Monsoon*, Harper Collins, London, 1998.

Harrison, Selig S. *India: The Most Dangerous Decades*, Oxford University Press, 1960.

Harvey, Robert. *Clive: The Life and Death of a British Emperor*, Hodder and Stoughton, London, 1998.

Hasan, Mushirul. *Nationalism and Communal Politics in India*, Manohar, New Delhi, 1991.

Heber, Bishop, R. *Narrative of a Journey through the Upper Provinces of India*, John Murray, London, 1849.

Helms, Richard. *Look Over My Shoulder*, Random House, New York, 2003.

Henderson, Michael. *Experiment with Untruth: India Under Emergency*, Macmillan, New Delhi, 1977.

Hersh, Seymour M. *The Samson Option: Israel's Nuclear Arsenal and American Foreign Policy*, Random House, New York, 1991.

Hersh, Seymour M. *Kissinger, The Price of Power*, Faber and Faber, London, 1983.

Herzog, Chaim. *The Arab-Israeli Wars,* Arms and Armour Press, London, 1982.

Hiro, Dilip. *Islamic Fundamentalism*, Paladin, London, 1988.

Hitti, Philip K. *History of the Arabs*, Macmillan, London, 1937.

Hobsbawm, Eric. *The Age of Empire, 1875-1914,* Random House, New York, 1989.

Holden, David and Johns, Richard. *The House of Saud,* Sidgwick and Jackson, London, 1981.

Holt, P.M. *The Age of the Crusades*, Longman, London, 1986.

Hopkirk, Peter. *The Great Game*, John Murray, London, 1970.

Hopkirk, Peter. *Setting the East Ablaze*, John Murray, London, 1970.

Hunter, W.W. *The Indian Mussalmans.* Lahore, 1968, repeat from the 1871 edition.

Huntington, Samuel P. *The Clash of Civilizations and the Remaking of the New World Order*, Simon and Schuster, New York, 1966.

Hyam, Ronald. *Empire and Sexuality: The British Experience,* Manchester University Press, 1992.

Ibn Jubayr. *The Travels of Ibn Jubayr*, tr. R.J.C. Broadhurst, Jonathan Cape, London, 1952.

Ibn Khaldun, *The Muqaddimah: An Introduction to History*, tr. F. Rosenthal, ed. and abridged by J. Dawood, London, 1978.

Iqbal, Mohammad. *The Reconstruction of Religious Thought in Islam*, Javid Iqbal, Ashraf Press, Lahore, 1951.

Irving, Washington. *Tales of the Alhambra,* Ediciones Miguel Sanchez, Granada, 1994.

Islam and Revolution. Iman Khomeini's Writings and Declarations: Tr. and annotated by Hamid Algar, KPI Ltd, England, 1985.

Jackson S.J., Paul. tr. *Sharafuddin Maneri: The Hundred Letters,* Better Yourself Books, Bombay, 1985.

Jaffrelot, Christopher. *The Hindu Nationalist Movement and Indian Politics 1925 to the 1990s,* Penguin, Delhi, 1993.

Jalal, Ayesha. *The State of Martial Rule. The Origins of Pakistan's Political Economy of Defence,* Vanguard, Lahore, 1991.

Jalal, Ayesha. *The Sole Spokesman. Jinnah, the Muslim League and the Demand for Pakistan,* Cambridge University Press, 1985.

Juvaini, Ata-Malik. *Genghis Khan: The History of the World Conqueror,* tr. and ed. J.A. Boyle, University of Washington Press, Seattle, 1997.

Kabir, Humayun. *Muslim Politics 1906-47 and Other Essays,* Firma K.L. Mukhopadhyay, Calcutta, 1969.

Kaye, John William. *Lives of Indian Officers,* A. Strahan and Co., Ludgate Hill, Bell and Daldy, York Street, Covent Garden, 1867.

Keay, John. *India: A History,* Harper Collins, London, 2000.

Keay, John. *The Gilgit Game,* Oxford University Press, Karachi, 1993.

Keay, John. *The Honourable Company – A History of the East India Company*, Harper Collins, 1991.

Keay, John. *Sowing the Wind: The Seeds of Conflict in the Middle East*, Murray, 2003.

Keddie, Nikki. *An Islamic Response to Imperialism,* University of California Press, 1968.

Khan, M. Ayub. *Friends not Masters, A Political Biography*, Oxford University Press, London, 1967.

Khan, Roeded. *Pakistan – A Dream Gone Sour,* Oxford University Press, Karachi, London, 1998.

Khan, Sultan M. *Memories and Reflections of a Pakistani Diplomat,* The Centre for Pakistan Studies, London, 1997.

Lawrence, T.E. *Seven Pillars of Wisdom: A Triumph,* Anchor Books, Doubleday, 1991.

Lelyveld, David. *Aligarh's First Generation,* Princeton University Press, 1977.

Lewis, Bernard. *The Political Language of Islam,* The University of Chicago Press, Chicago and London, 1988.

Lewis, Bernard. *The Middle East: History of Civilisation,* Weidenfeld and Nicolson, 1995.

Lewis, Bernard. *Islam and the West,* Oxford University Press. New York, 1993.

Lewis, Bernard. *The Jews of Islam,* Princeton University Press, 1984.

Lewis, Bernard. *The Assassins,* Saqi Books, London, 1985.

Lichtenstadter, Ilse. *Introduction to Classical Arabic Literature,* Twayne Publishers Inc., New York, 1974.

Lewis, Bernard. *The Middle East: 2000 Years of History From the Rise of Christianity to the Present Day,* Weidenfeld and Nicholson, 1995.

Lings, Martin. *Muhammad: His Life Based on the Earliest Sources*, George Allen and Unwin, London, 1982.

Maalouf, Amin. *The Crusades Through Arab Eyes*, tr. John Tothschild, Al Saqi Books, London, 1984.

Maalouf, Amin. *Samarkand,* tr. Russell Harris, Abacus, London 1994.

MacMunn, George. *The Martial Races of India,* Mittal Publications, Delhi, 1979.

Making India Hindu: Religion, Community, and the Politics of Democracy in India, ed. David Ludden, Oxford University Press, Delhi, 1996.

Mansel, Philip. *Constantinople: City of the World's Desire 1453-1924*, Penguin, London, 1995.

Manucci, Niccolao. *A Pepys of Mogul India 1653-1708*, Srishti Publishers and Distributors, Delhi, 1999.

Mason, Philip. *Skinner of Skinner's Horse*, Clarion Books, Delhi, 1979.

Mason, Philip. *A Matter of Honour: An Account of the Indian Army and its Officers and Men*, Penguin, London, 1974.

Masselos, Jim. *Indian Nationalism*, Sterling, Delhi, 1985.

Memoirs of Lt. Gen. Gul Hassan Khan, Oxford University Press, Karachi, 1993.

Metcalf, Barbara Daly. *Islamic Revival in British India: Deoband, 1860-1900*, Princeton, 1982.

Meyer, Karl E. and Blair Brysac, Shareen. *Tournament of Shadows: The Great Game and the Race for Empire in Central Asia*, A Cornelia and Michael Bessie Book, Washington, 1999.

Miles, Jack. *Christ: A Crisis in the Life of God*, Random House, London, 2001.

Minault, Gail. *The Khilafat Movement: Religious Symbolism and Political Mobilization in India*, Columbia University Press, New York, 1982.

Moon, Penderel. *The British Conquest and Dominion of India*, Gerald Duckworth, London, 1989.

Morris, James. *Heaven's Command: An Imperial Progress; Pax Brittanica; Farewell the Trumpets: An Imperial Retreat* (Trilogy), Penguin, London, 1979.

Mottahedeh, Roy. *The Mantel of the Prophet. Religion and Politics in Iran*, Penguin, London, 1987.

Muhammad, Iqbal *Reconstruction of Religious Thought in Islam*, London, 1934.

Muhammad, Iqbal. *The Secrets of the Self: Allama Iqbal's Asrar-i-Khudi*, Introduction by Reynold A. Nicholson, Lahore, 1955.

Muhammad Iqbal: Shikwa and Jawab-i-Shikwa; Complaint and Answer: Iqbal's dialogue with Allah, tr. Khushwant Singh, Oxford University Press, Delhi, 1981.

Mujeeb, M. *The Indian Muslims*, Allen and Unwin, London, 1967.

Mukhopadhyay, Tarun Kumar. *Hicky's Bengal Gazette, Contemporary Life and Events*, Subarnarekha, Calcutta, 1998.

Nasr, Seyyed Hossein. *Ideals and Realities of Islam*, London, 1966.

Nasr, Seyyed Hossein. *Islamic Art and Spirituality*, Oxford University Press, 1990.

Nehru, Jawaharlal. *Discovery of India*, Signet Press, Calcutta, 1946.

Newby, Eric. *A Short Walk in the Hindu Kush*, Picador, London, 1974.

Niazi, A.A.K. *The Betrayal of East Pakistan*, Oxford University Press, Karachi, 1998.

Nicholson, Reynold A. *The Mystics of Islam*, Arkana, 1989.

Page, David. *Pakistan: Past and Present*, Stacey International, London, 1977.

Page, David. *Prelude to Partition: The Indian Muslims and the Imperial System of Control, 1920-1930*, Manohar, New Delhi, 1982.

Palmer, Alan. *The Decline and Fall of the Ottoman Empire,* John Murray, London, 1992.

Panikker, K.M. *Malabar and the Portuguese*, Bombay, 1929.

Parrinder, Geoffrey. *Jesus in the Quran*, Oneworld Publications, England, 1965.

Pirzada, Syed Sharifuddin (ed). *Foundations of Pakistan: All India Muslim League Documents*, National Publishing House, Karachi, 1969.

Potter, David C. *India's Political Administrators: From ICS to IAS,* Oxford University Press, Delhi, 1996.

Prasad, Bimal. *The Foundation of Muslim Nationalism, Pathway to India's Partition, Volume I; A Nation within Islam: Pathway to India's Partition Volume II.* Manohar, Delhi, 1999 and 2000.

Raeside, Ian. *The Decade of Panipat (1751-56)*, tr. from Marathi, Popular Prakashan, Bombay, 1984.

Rashid, Ahmed. *Taliban: Islam, Oil and the New Great Game in Central Asia,* I.B. Tauris, London, 2000.

Reif, Stefan C. *A Jewish Archive from Old Cairo*, Curzon Press, Surrey, 2000.

Reston Jr., James. *Warriors of God: Richard the Lionheart and Saladin in the Third Crusade,* Faber and Faber, 2001.

Rodinson, Maxime. *Mohammed*, tr. Anne Carter, Penguin, London, 1971.

Rodinson, Maxime. *Islam and Capitalism.* Penguin, London, 1997.

Roosevelt, Kim. *Countercoup: The Struggle for Control of Iran, McGraw-Hill*, New York, 1979.

Rosabi, Morris. *Khubilai Khan: His Life and Times,* University of California Press, Berkeley, Los Angeles, 1998.

Rosenthal, Erwin. *Islam in the Modern National State,* Cambridge University Press, 1965.

Runciman, Steven. *History of the Crusades*, Cambridge University Press, 1951.

Russell, Ralph and Islam, Khurshidul. *Ghalib: Life and Letters*, Oxford University Press, Delhi, 1994.

Ruthven, Malise. *Islam in the World*, Penguin, London, 1984.

Said, Edward W. *Orientalism: Western Concepts of the Orient,* Penguin, 1995.

Salik, S. *Witness to Surrender*, Oxford University Press, Karachi, 1978.

Sampson, Anthony. *The Seven Sisters: The Great Oil Companies and the World They Made*, Hodder and Stoughton, London, 1975.

Sanyal, Usha. *Devotional Islam and Politics in British India: Ahmad Riza Khan and his Movement 1870-1920*, Oxford University Press, Delhi, 1996.

Sarkar, Jadunath. *The History of Bengal.* Vol. 2. *The Muslim Period 1200-1757,* ed., Dacca, 1948.

Saunders, J.J. *The History of Mogul Conquests,* Routledge and Kegan Paul Limited, London, 1971.

Segev, Tom. *One Palestine, Complete: Jews and Arabs under the British Mandate,* Little, Brown and Company, London, 2000.

Sengupta, Nitish. *History of the Bengali-Speaking People,* UBS Publishers' Distributors Limited, Delhi, 2001.

Sharar, Abdul Halim. *Lucknow: The Last Phase of an Oriental Culture,* tr. and ed. E.S. Harcourt and Fakir Hussain, Paul Elek, London, 1975

Sharma, Dasharatha. ed. *Rajasthan Through the Ages, Vol. 1.* Rajasthan State Archives, 1966.

Singh, Khushwant. *A History of the Sikhs, 2 Volumes,* Oxford University Press, Delhi, 1977.

Sleeman, W.H. *Rambles and Recollections of an Indian Official,* London, 1844.

Spear, Percival. *The Nabobs*, Curzon Press, London and Dublin, 1980.

Stein, Aurel. *On Alexander's Track of the Indus*, Phoenix Press, London, 2001.

Stephens, Ian. *Pakistan: Old Country, New Nation,* Pelican, Great Britain, 1964.

Studdert-Kennedy, Gerald. *Providence & the Raj: Imperial Mission and Missionary Imperialism,* Sage Publications, Delhi, 1998.

Talbot, Ian. *Pakistan: A Modern History,* Hurst and Company, London, 1998.

Tendulkar, D.G. *Mahatma: The Life of Mohandas Karamchand Gandhi,* 8 Volumes, Government of India Publications Division, Delhi, 1951.

The Days of John Company: Selection from Calcutta Gazette 1824-1832, Das Gupta, Anil Chandra. ed. West Bengal Government Press, Calcutta, 1959.

Tod, Colonel James. *Annals and Antiquities of Rajasthan or The Central and Western Rajput States of India, ed. W. Crooke,* reprint, Oxford University Press, London, 1920.

Trench, Charles Chenevix. *Viceroy's Agent*, Jonathan Cape, London, 1987.

Troll, Christian. *Sayyid Ahmad Khan: A Restatement of Muslim Theology,* New Delhi, 1978.

Tuker, F.I.S. *While Memory Serves*, Cassell, London, 1950.

Verrier, Anthony. *Francis Younghusband and the Great Game,* Jonathan Cape, London, 1991.

Viceroy's Personal Reports. In the series *India, The Transfer of Power*, HMSO, London, 1980, 1981, 1983.

Waliullah, Shah. *Shah Waliullah ke Siyasi Maktubat*, ed. Khaliq Ahmad Nizami, Delhi, 1969.

Watt, W. Montgomery. *Islam and the Integration of Society,* Routledge and Kegan Paul, London, 1961.

Weir, Alison. *Eleanor of Aquitaine*, Pimlico, London, 2000.

Wheatcroft, Andrew: *Infidels: The Conflict between Christendom and Islam 638 - 2002,* Viking, 2003.

Willey, Peter. *The Castles of the Assassins,* Craven Street Book, George G. Harrap, London, 1963.

Winius, George D. and Vink, Marcus P.M. *The Merchant Warrior Pacified. The VOC (the Dutch East India Company) and its Changing Political Economy in India,* Oxford University Press, Delhi, 1994.

Wink, Andre. *Al-Hind: The Making of the Indo-Islamic World, Volume I, Early Medieval India and the Expansion of Islam. Seventh to Eleventh Centuries,* Oxford University Press, Delhi, 1990.

Wolpert, Stanley. *Jinnah of Pakistan*, Oxford University Press, New York, 1984.

Woodward, Bob. *Bush at War*, Simon & Schuster, 2002.

Yergin, Daniel. *The Prize: The epic quest for oil, money and power,* Simon and Schuster, 1991.

Younghusband, Francis. *The British Invasion of Tibet*, The Stationary Office, London, 1999.

Zakaria, Rafiq. *The Man Who Divided India,* Popular Prakashan, Mumbai, 2001.

Zakaria, Rafiq. *Muhammad and the Quran,* Penguin, Delhi, 1991.

Zakaria, Rafiq. *The Struggle Within Islam,* Viking, Delhi, 1988.

THUMBNAIL SKETCHES

Muslim names pose a problem for those used to the alphabetical order of English usage. We have used an arbitrary convenience by taking the first name as the starting point for everyone.

A.K. Fazlul Haq: A fiery Bengal Muslim leader of the Indian independence movement, who organised the peasantry and later joined the Muslim League. He was one of those who drafted the Pakistan resolution at Lahore.

Abd al-Muttalib ibn Hisham: Abdullah's father, the Prophet Muhammad's grandfather.

Abdallah bin al-Zubayr: Rebel who seized the Holy Cities after the death of Muawiya.

Abdul Ghani: First Nawab of Dhaka, given the title in 1875.

Abdul Qadir: Leader of the Algerian Jihad against the French; with the support of the *ulema* and villagers went to war with the French, was defeated and exiled in 1847 to Damascus.

Abdul Rahman ibn Abdullah al-Ghafiki: The great emir or *wali* of Andalusia (Muslim Spain) whose victorious march was finally stopped at the battle of Poiters in 732.

Abdul Uzza (nicknamed Abu Lahb): The Prophet's uncle, who conspired against his life.

Abdullah Azam: Osama bin Laden's friend and perhaps mentor who set up the Makhtab al Khidmat, or Centre for Service; from here originated the network that became the Al Qaida.

Abdullah ibn Saud: Founder of the Saudi dynasty.

Abdullah ibn Ubayy: Leader of Hypocrites, of the Khazarite clan of Awf in Medina, who conspired against the Prophet.

Abdullah: Prophet Muhammad's father.

Abdur Rahim: The Indian theologian Shah Waliullah's father, Mughal court intellectual: mystic theologian as well as respected historian, one of the compilers of *Fatwa-e-Alamgiri,* a chronicle of Aurangzeb's reign, and founder of the Rahimiyya Medressa in Delhi.

Abdur Rahman: Ummayad prince who escaped the massacre by the Abbasids in June 750 and established the Ummayad dynasty from Cordoba in Spain.

Abu Bakr: Prophet Muhammad's close friend, who was with him during the *Hejira*; chosen by consensus as the first Caliph after the death of the Prophet.

Abu Sufyan: A leader of the Quraysh who fought against the Prophet at Uhud, but later converted to Islam.

Abul Fazl: Mughal Emperor Akbar's court intellectual and chronicler.

Abul Kalam Azad: Scholar, journalist and pre-eminent Congress leader of the Indian independence movement.

Aga Khan: Head of the Ismailis and first president of the All India Muslim League, in 1906; descendent of Hassan, Sabah, the old man of the Mountains.

Ahmad Beg: A soothsayer who read Akbar's future in the blade-bone of a sheep, predicted victory for him at the second battle of Panipat.

Ahmad Shah Abdali: Nadir Shah's Pashtun general who went on to become a great Afghan king and was victor of the third battle of Panipat against the Marathas.

Ahmed ibn Majid: The Moor of Gujarat, extraordinary sailor, astronomer and poet, who showed Vasco da Gama the way to India.

Ahmed Shah Masood: Afghan leader who fought the Russians and then the Taliban; was assassinated just before September 11 changed the world in general and South Asia in particular.

Aisha: Prophet's wife who became a leader in her own right after his death.

Akbar: Third and greatest of India's Mughal emperors.

Akbar Allahabadi: Indian Urdu poet and satirist of the 19th and 20th centuries.

Akbar Khan: Warrior son of Afghan leader Dost Mohammad Khan who was removed by the British in 1839.

Al-Lat, Al-Uzza and Manat: The three most revered pagan goddesses of pre-Islamic Mecca, denounced in the Quran as false deities.

Al-Malek al-Adil: The great Saladin's brother.

Al-Malik al-Kamil: Egyptian sultan, heir of Saladin, contemporary of Frederick II, who handed over Jerusalem peacefully, and temporarily, after a truce with Crusaders in 1229.

Alexander Burnes: British emissary to Afghanistan in 1832 who renamed himself Sikander; was knighted at the age of 33 for his courageous adventures.

Ali: Prophet's son-in-law, a great hero of Islam, always addressed respectfully as Hazrat Ali.

Allan Octavian Hume: British civil servant who founded the Indian National Congress.

Alvaro Velho: Portuguese soldier-diarist on Vasco da Gama's first voyage to India.

Ambalal Sarabhai: Indian cotton mill owner against whom Gandhi led a workers' strike in 1918.

Amir Husayn: An Ottoman admiral who lost a decisive naval engagement to the Portuguese off the Gujarati port of Diu in 1507.

Amr ibn Luhaiy: Said to have introduced idolatry into the Kaaba.

Anandpal: Hindu Shahi king of Peshawar in the 11th century.

Arthur Wellesley: Later, Duke of Wellington, commander of British forces in wars against Marathas and Tipoo Sultan.

Aurangzeb: Sixth and last of the great Mughals.

Aurobindo Ghosh: Bengali revolutionary who established the Pondicherry ashram in South India.

Austen Chamberlain: Secretary of state for India in September, 1916.

Ayesha: Ibn Hassan's wife, mother of Boabdil, the Last Moor of Granada.

Ayyub al-Ansari: Companion of the Prophet, one of the commanders of the Ummayad army during the second siege of the Byzantine capital in 668. His grave was discovered in 1453 after Muslims took Constantinople, and is a shrine.

Babrak Karmal: Leader of the Parcham, a socialist political party with an urban base in the Republic of Afghanistan in 1973; later, ruler with Soviet support.

Babur: Founder of the Mughal empire in India.

Badruddin Tyabji: Third president of the Congress; first Muslim to become president of the party.

Bahira: A Christian monk in Islamic lore who recognized and foretold Muhammad's destiny.

Bankimchandra Chattopadhyay: Brilliant Bengali author and polemicist of the 19th century.

Beha ed Din: Historian, chronicler of Saladin.

Bichitr: Mughal miniature master.

Bihruz: Saladin's father Najm ad-Din's friend.

Bilal: An African slave, who was bought and freed by Abu Bakr and who became a cult figure among Muslims.

Boabdil: The Last Moor of Spain, also called El Zogoybi, or The Unlucky, or El Rey Chico, the Boy King.

Chakravarthi Rajagopalachari: A major figure of India's independence movement, first Indian governor general after Mountbatten's term.

C.F. Andrews: A pastor who was a close associate of Mahatma Gandhi and

Rabindranath Tagore, and a friend of India. Gandhi called him *Deenabandhu* (friend of the helpless), and "Christ's Faithful Apostle." He contributed greatly to promoting appreciation in the West of Gandhi.

Catherine of Braganza: Portuguese princess who became the wife of Britain's Charles II and whose dowry included an unwanted city called Bombay.

Charles Metcalfe: British official who signed a treaty with Ranjit Singh that assured the British of Sikh support in case Napoleon arrived at the western gates of the subcontinent.

Charles Napier: British general who conquered Sind, the province south of Punjab and Afghanistan in 1844.

Charlesmagne: Holy Roman Emperor, who laid the foundations of Christian revival in west Europe.

Chengiz Khan: Description unnecessary.

Chosroes: Persian monarch during Prophet's lifetime.

Comte de Lally: Son of an Irish Jacobite, governor-general of all French establishments in India and commander-in-chief of its armies who surrendered Pondicherry to the British.

Constantine XI: The last Byzantine Emperor.

Dadabhai Naoroji: Zoroastrian businessman and scholar, first Indian to be elected to the House of Commons, as a Liberal from Central Finsbury in 1902.

Dahir: Brahmin king of largely-Buddhist Sind during the first Muslim invasion of India in 711.

Dina Wadia: Daughter of the father of Pakistan, Jinnah.

Dost Mohammad Khan: Afghan king in 1839 during the first Afghan war. The British replaced him with Shah Shuja, but gave him back his throne.

Duarte, Pedro and Henry: King John's sons who fought at Ceuta and were knighted after they established the first Christian foothold in Muslim Africa.

Dunlop Smith: British bureaucrat who encouraged the creation of the Muslim League.

E.C. Bailey: Indian Home secretary in 1870.

Edmund Allenby: British military commander who took Jerusalem in the First World War on 9, December 1917.

Edward Lytton: Viceroy to India in 1875.

Elihu Yale: Governor of the East India Company in Madras, who created a substantial private fortune by questionable means, part of which he donated to a school in Connecticut.

Elisha Mansour: Believed in the Caucasus to be an Italian Jesuit who converted to Islam and was sent by the Ottoman Sultan to fight against the Russians.

Eschiva: Wife of Count Raymond of Tripoli.

Eulogio and Paul Alvarro: Spanish priests in Muslim Spain who invited martyrdom and inspired the clergy against Muslim rule.

Faiz: Major Urdu poet of India and Pakistan.

Fakhr ad-Din: An emir in Cairo, friend of Frederick II.

Fariduddin: Popularly known as Baba Farid, a Sufi mystic of Punjab.

Farrukhsiyar: Weak and spoilt Mughal emperor who granted a *firman* to the East India Company, which the company celebrated as its magna carta.

Fatima: Jinnah's sister.

Fatimah: Hazrat Ali's wife.

Firoz: A Christian slave from Syria who assassinated Umar, the second caliph.

Francois Bernier: A French traveller to India in the Mughal days.

Frederick Roberts: British major general who took Kabul in October 1879, the second Afghan war.

Fulk: King of Jerusalem during Saladin's time.

Gesu Daraz: Nasiruddin Chirag Dehlavi's disciple who took the Chishti order south to Gulbarga.

Ghazi Mullah: Disciple of Mullah Muhammad Yaraghi in the Caucasus in the 19th century during the Jihad against Russia.

Godfrey of Bouillon: Crusader king who conquered Jerusalem in the First Crusade. On 15 July 1099, his soldiers were the first to break through to Jerusalem, and took part in the subsequent massacre of the Jewish and Muslim residents of the city. On 22 July he was named ruler of Jerusalem.

Gopal Krishna Gokhale: Indian political leader, mentor of both Jinnah and Gandhi.

Gulbuddin Hekmatyar: Leader of the Hezb-e-Islami, the strongest force in the Jihad against the Soviets.

Guy of Lusignan: King of Jerusalem who took over after Baldwin V died in 1186.

Hagar: Abraham's wife, mother of Ishmael, to whom Allah showed the spring of Zamzam near the Kaaba.

Haji Bektash: Patron dervish of the Ottoman Janissaries.

Hamida: Mughal emperor Humayun's wife and Akbar's mother.

Hamza: The Prophet's uncle, whose liver Hind ate after the battle of Uhud.

Haroon ur Rashid: The best known of the Abbasids caliphs.

Hasan al Banna: Leader of the Muslim Brotherhood, an intellectual heir of Jamaluddin Afghani.

Hasan: Ali's son, Prophet's grandson, brother of Husayn. Hussayn was martyred at Karbala.

Heraclius: Byzantine emperor at the time of the Prophet.

Hind: Quraysh leader Abu Sufyan's wife, famous for her tastes in battlefield food.

Hulegu: Brother of Kublai, grandson of Chengiz.

Humayun: Babur's son and second Mughal emperor.

Ibn Hassan: Boabdil's father who fell in love with a Christian captive Zoraya.

Ibrahim Khan Gardi: A Muslim general who fought with the Marathas against the Muslim confederacy in the 3rd battle of Panipat.

Ibrahim Lodi: The Indian king in Delhi defeated by Babur in 1526.

Imad ad-Din Zengi: Ata-beg of Mosul, the man who launched the counter-offensive against the Christian kingdoms of Palestine, and set in motion the revival that culminated with Saladin's conquest of Jerusalem.

Jadunath Sarkar: Bengali historian.

Jamaluddin Afghani: Nineteenth century visionary who argued that the Western-Christian advance from Africa to India could be reversed by pan-Islamic unity and a modern Jihad supported by advances in science, technology and rational behaviour. He also urged the revival of science and technology in Muslim education.

Jawaharlal Nehru: Lawyer, author, visionary, Gandhian and first Prime Minister of India.

Jivraj Mehta: Gandhi's doctor in London in 1914.

Job Charnock: Exotic East India Company adventurer, merchant, founder of Calcutta.

John Fisher: Admiral who took forward the process of changing the British Navy from coal-fired to oil-fired ships in the first decade of the 20th century.

John Macnaghten: Head of a British expedition sent to replace Dost Mohammed in Afghanistan with Shah Shuja in the first Afghan war. Emily Eden, a contemporary visitor, tartly observed that he spoke Persian better than English although he preferred Sanskrit.

John of Damascus: Born about forty years after Prophet Muhammad died, established the dialectic of the Christian theological response against Islam, also rebutted Quran on Christianity. Made a Saint.

John Surman: The head of the East India Company in Calcutta who obtained the *firman* from Farrukhsiyar.

Josiah Child: A militant governor of the East India Company, the first to dream of an Indian empire.

Josiah Harlan: Disguised himself as a dervish in order to spy for the British in Kabul before the first Afghan war, first American to interfere in the internal affairs of Afghanistan.

Kemal Ataturk: The Turkish general, reformer and nationalist icon who dispensed with the Caliphate.

293

Khadija bin Khuwaylid: The Prophet's first wife.

Khalid ibn Walid: A brilliant commander and strategist who defeated the Byzantines and helped conquer Jerusalem; one of Islam's legendary warriors.

Khwaja Israel Sarhadi: John Surman's friend and interlocutor, an Armenian merchant who helped the British get their *firman* from Farrukhsiyar.

Khwaja Muinuddin Chishti: Founder of the Sufi-Chishti order in India, a venerated saint whose grave in Ajmer is visited by both Muslims and Hindus.

King Afonso: The 'true soldier of Christ' who was given a mission by the Pope: to 'invade, search out, capture, vanquish, and subdue all Saracen and pagans whatsoever, and other enemies of Christ wheresoever placed, and the kingdoms, dukedoms, principalities, dominions, possessions, and all moveable and immovable goods whatsoever held and possessed by them and to reduce their persons to perpetual slavery.'

King Faisal I: The Hashemite prince who fought alongside Lawrence of Arabia in the First World War against the Turks, and who was rewarded, after more than one heartbreak, with the throne of Baghdad in 1921. He died in 1933.

King Ghazi: King Faisal I's son and Iraq's first 'nationalist' ruler. Using the power of the throne, and, more interestingly, the reach of the radio, he challenged British control of his country. He died in a mysterious car crash that had all the fingerprints of an assassination.

Leo: Soldier who seized power from Emperor Theodosius III and saved the Byzantine empire from the Muslims in 716.

M.A. Ansari: Led an Indian Muslim medical team to the Caliphate in 1912 as a gesture of solidarity.

Mahadji Scindia: Ruler of Gwalior in 18th century who fought the British.

Mahmud (of Ghazni): Afghan ruler who sacked the temple of Somnath.

Malik Ayyaz: Governor of Diu in the sixteenth century, betrayed Ottoman admiral Amir Husayn in 1509 and enabled Portuguese naval victory.

Mana Vikrama: Malabar king during Vasco da Gama's invasion of India, valiantly fought the Portuguese all his life.

Mansur al-Hallaj: The first Sufi to come to India.

Manuel: King of Portugal in 1496.

Michael O'Dwyer: Lieutenant governor of Punjab during the Jallianwalla outrage.

Michael Scot: Frederick II's astrologer, also credited with the translation of Aristotle that reached Europeans through the Arab scholar, Ibn Rushd, known to the west as Averroes.

Mir Jaffer: A lord in Nawab Siraj ud Daula's court, who sold his master to Robert Clive.

Miran: Mir Jaffer's son.

Mirza Riza: A disciple of Jamaluddin Afghani.

Monstuart Elphinstone: A much admired nineteenth century British civil servant.

Motilal Nehru: Lawyer, hero of India's independence movement and father of Jawaharlal Nehru.

Muawiya: Hind's son, first of the Ummayad caliphs.

Muhammad Abduh: Afghani's *murid* or disciple.

Muhammad bin Qasim: Arab general who conquered Sind in 711-712.

Muhammad ibn Abd al Wahhab: Founder of the reformist, puritan Wahhabi movement in the eighteenth century.

Muhammad ibn Saud: Chief of market town called Diriya, ancestor of Saudi ruling family; contemporary and disciple of Wahhab.

Muhammad Iqbal: Indian poet extraordinary.

Muhammad Qasim Nanautvi: Along with Rashid Ahmad Gangohi, founder of the *medressa* in Deoband in 1867.

Muhyi ad-Din: Poet and cleric who prophesied Saladin's conquest of Jerusalem: 'he who takes the Gray Castle in Safar will take Jerusalem in Rajab.' He was the *qadi* chosen by Saladin to deliver the first Friday sermon in Jerusalem after Saladin's victory.

Nadir Shah: Son of a camel driver who rose to be Shah of Persia; sacked Delhi, looted India, laughed at impotent Mughal emperors and took the Peacock Throne and the Kohinoor diamond to Persia.

Najm ad-Din: Head of a prosperous Kurd family of Tovin, in Armenia, father of Saladin.

Nathuram Vinayak Godse: Gandhi's assassin.

Nisar Ali: More famous as Titu Miyan, declared a jihad in the nineteenth century against the harsh economic measures of Bengali Hindu landlords and the British Raj that in turn squeezed the landlords.

Nizamuddin Auliya: A great Sufi divine, whose grave at Delhi is a place of pilgrimage.

Nur ad-Din Mahmud: Zengi's successor in Syria during the twelfth century.

Ogier de Busbecq: Hungarian ambassador to Constantinople.

Osama bin Laden: Description unnecessary.

Pedro Alvares Cabral: Young aristocrat who led the first Portuguese exercise in gunboat diplomacy in 1500. Cabral set out for India with 13 ships and 1200 men, and offered Malabar King Mana Vikrama a treaty of friendship, which he accepted. When the king refused to obey the Portuguese order to expel all Muslims, Cabral seized ten merchant ships and burnt their crew alive in full view of the citizens.

Peter the Great: The Tsar of Russia, took Estonia, Latvia and part of Finland in 1721, he opened the Russian drive to Caucasus, but failed in his dream to win back Constantinople for Christendom.

Peter the Venerable: Abbot of Cluny, whose *The Abominable Heresy or Sect of the Saracens* was a typical work of its age in its anger against the Islamic 'heresy'.

Pierre Louis Napoleon Cavagnari: Headed an 81-member British mission to Afghanistan after the second Afghan war. On September 3, 1879, soldiers from Herat, demanding pay from Yakub Khan, the British protégé, turned their guns on the British overlords. Cavagnari was killed in the ensuing battle that lasted eight hours.

Qasim Khan: Mughal governor in Bengal in the seventeenth century, when Job Charnock was the East India Company man in Hooghly.

Qutbuddin Bakhtiyar Kaki: Sufi saint, disciple of Khwaja Muinuddin Chishti.

R.E.H. Dyer, Brigadier General: The cold British officer who ordered the wanton massacre at Jallianwalabagh, Punjab, in 1919.

Rabindranath Tagore: Great Bengali author, poet, composer, painter and winner of the Nobel Prize for literature in 1913. Returned his knighthood after Jallianwala.

Rajkumar Shukla: Peasant who took Gandhi to Champaran and its infamous indigo plantations.

Ramsay MacDonald: Labour Prime Minister in 1929.

Rana Sangha of Mewar: Rajput prince defeated by Babur at Khanwa in the sixteenth century.

Ranjit Singh: Brilliant one-eyed genius and founder of the Sikh empire.

Raymond: Count of Tripoli, a dove during the wars against Saladin was allowed to escape during the crusader rout at Hattin.

Reshad: Made Caliph by Young Turks after his brother Abdul Hamid was deposed.

Reynauld of Chatillon: A French carpetbagger who came to the Holy Land with the Second Crusade in 1147 and became the principal hardliner in the wars, was beheaded by Saladin.

Richard the Lionheart: Second son of Henry and Eleanor, greatest of the Crusaders, legend in his lifetime.

Robert Clive: East India Company factor who started life in India at a salary of five pounds a year, built both an immense fortune for himself and an empire for his company and country.

Robert Wilson: British analyst who was a military observer during the burning of Moscow by Napolean.

Saladin Ayyubi: The great Saladin.

Sallam ibn Mishkam: Leader of a Jewish tribe that Abu Sufyan got in touch with before the Battle of Uhud.

Saratchandra Chattopadhyay: Eminent Bengali novelist of the twentieth century, who did not believe that Hindus and Muslims could live in unity. 'The Muslims came to India to plunder it, not to establish a kingdom,' he said.

Sardar Mohammad Daud: President of the Republic of Afghanistan in 1973 after the overthrow of King Zahir.

Saud ibn Abdul Aziz: Grandson of Muhammad ibn Saud.

Sayyid Ahmad Barelvi: Shah Aziz's student, launched a jihad against the British.

Shah Alam: Emperor during Mughal decline, became a pensioner of the British Raj.

Shah Aziz: Shah Waliullah's son.

Shah Ismail: Shah Waliullah's grandson.

Shah Jahan: Fifth Mughal emperor, built the Taj Mahal for his wife Mumtaz Mahal.

Shah Shuja: British nominee for King during the first Afghan war.

Shah Tahmasp: Contemporary Persian ruler who helped Humayun win back his kingdom in India.

Shah Waliullah: A Muslim theologian who laid an intellectual framework for Islamic resurgence and inspired a jihad against the Christian victors of Delhi.

Sharafuddin Maneri: Established the Firdausi order in Bihar, India, the fourteenth century.

Shaukat Ali: Along with his brother Mohammad Ali, leader of the Khilafat movement.

Sher Ali: Son of Dost Mohammad Khan, was the first of Afghanistan's modernizers. He opened English schools, introduced postal services in Afghanistan; also sought good relations with the British.

Sher Shah Suri: Afghan who interrupted the Mughal empire.

Shirkuh: Saladin's uncle, Najm ad-Din's brother, and a great general who brought Egypt under Damascus rule.

Shivaji: Extraordinary leader of the Marathas who carved a kingdom for his people.

Shyama Prasad Mukherji: One of the founders of the Jana Sangh.

Siraj ud Daula: Nawab of Bengal and Bihar whose defeat at Plassey handed the province to the British in 1757, who never looked back till 1947.

Sophronius: Patriarch of Jerusalem in 637, during the first Arab conquest of the Holy City.

Subuktigin: Turkish slave who ascended his father-in-law Alptigin's throne in Ghazni.

Taimur Shah: Afghan king Ahmad Shah Abdali's son.

Tarik ibn Ziyad: Arab general who along with Musa ibn Noosier began the conquest of Spain in 711.

Thomas Roe: James I's envoy to the Mughal court.

Turki bin Faisal: A prince who was head of the Saudi intelligence agency, the Istakhbarat, in the 1980s when Osama bin Laden worked in harmony with Saudi authorities.

Ubaydallah: General who brought Husayn's severed head from Karbala and gave it to the despot Yazid.

Uthman bin Talha: Keeper of keys at Kaaba during Prophet's time.

Vallabhbhai Patel: Gandhi's disciple and first deputy Prime Minister of India.

Vasco da Gama: A hero in Portugal, a villain in India, found route to India and established Portuguese presence.

Wajid Ali Shah: Last Muslim Nawab of Awadh, deposed by the British.

William Elphinstone: Major General who was British commander-in-chief in Afghanistan in 1841.

William Hawkins: Led first English mission to the Mughal court of Jahangir, spoke Persian and Turki.

William Henry Irvine Shakespear: A former officer of the Bengal Lancers, friend and mentor of ibn Saud.

William Hunter: British bureaucrat and author of a famous study on Indian Muslims, published in 1871.

William Knox d'Arcy: An Englishman who received a document from the Shah of Iran for £20,000 – in cash – giving him exclusive rights to look for, find and sell natural gas, asphalt, and petroleum from anywhere in the Persian empire.

William Moorcroft: Horse breeder, traveller, pioneer who explored the route to Khyber and up to Bukhara. Was initially hired by the East India Company at a salary of Rs 30,000 a year to breed better horses but no one believed he went to Kabul for semen.

Yazid: Hind's grandson, Muawiya's controversial and hated son.

Zaynab, Ruqayya, Fatima and Umm Kulthum: Muhammad's daughters.

Zbigniew Brzezinski: National security adviser to US President Jimmy Carter.

Zheng He: Also called San Bao, or Eunuch of the Three Jewels, led seven armadas from China to Africa between 1405 and 1433.

Ziadatallah: Emir of Tunisia, who created a Muslim state in Sicily by the first quarter of the ninth century.

Zulfiqar Ali Bhutto: Former Pakistan Prime Minister.

A RELEVANT CALENDAR

570:   Prophet Muhammad is born.

611:   The angel Gabriel appears to the Prophet with the revelation of the Holy Quran during Ramadan.

614:   Jerusalem captured by Sassanid Persians May 5.

622:   Byzantine emperor Heraclius uses sea power to outflank the Persians: sends an army through the Aegean Sea and surprises the Persians at Issus.

622:   The *hejira*, Prophet emigrates to Medina.

624:   Battle of Badr, won against odds by the Prophet.

625:   Heraclius' armies reach Mosul, where another victory leads to a treaty on the basis of status quo and the return of Jerusalem and the True Cross to Christians.

628:   Heraclius goes on foot to keep his vow and restore the True Cross to Jerusalem; gets a letter from Muhammad asking him to accept Islam.

630:   Prophet Muhammad enters Mecca.

632:   The Prophet dies.

634:   Byzantines are defeated by Muslims at the battle of Ajnadain, first Arab victory in the Muslim-Christian confrontation.

634:   The first Caliph, Abu Bakr, dies on August 23.

636:   Muslims defeat Byzantine forces at the battle of Yarmuk, opening the way to Jerusalem on August 20.

637:   Jerusalem falls to Arabs in July.

653:   Muawiya, governor of Syria, marches to Bosphorus in first attempt at Constantinople.

656:   Ali asked to become caliph after Uthman's death.

656:   Battle of Camel between Ali and Aisha.

657:   Ali encounters forces of Muawiya at Siffin in Syria.

664: Muawiya, now caliph, sends an expedition under Khalid ibn Walid, who crosses Anatolia, but fails to reach Constantinople.

670: Muawiya's armies reach Constantinople in a major offensive.

678: Muslims accept defeat, turn back from Constantinople.

680: Muawiya dies.

680: Husayn martyred by Muawiya's son Yazid's troops at Karbala.

688: Construction of the Dome of the Rock begins.

711: Muslims enter Spain, Goths defeated at Guadalete by a small Muslim army of some 11,000 soldiers.

711: A Muslim army enters Sind, on the Indian sub-continent, commanded by a young man, Muhammad bin Qasim.

712: Muhammad bin Qasim drives Dahir, the king of Sind, out of his capital, Debal.

714: Arab conquest of what is now the south of Pakistan is complete.

717: Muslims begin second siege of Constantinople, ordered by Caliph Suleyman on August 15.

722: Christians win Battle of Covadonga, interrupt Muslim advance in Spain.

731: Andalusia (Muslim Spain) gets a new emir, or *wali*, Abdul Rahman ibn Abdullah al-Ghafiki.

732: Al-Ghafiki crosses through Aragon and Navarre and defeats the Duke of Edo at Arles on the banks of the Rhone.

732: Pavement of Martyrs, or Battle of Tours takes place on the banks of the Loire in October: France is saved from Muslim conquest. Al-Ghafiki dies during this battle.

750: Abul Abbas, a general, invites 80 Umayyad nobles to his home for dinner, slaughters them, ends Ummayad dynasty; the only important prince to survive is Abdur Rahman who goes on to establish a great Umayyad dynasty from Cordoba in Spain.

762: Abbasids move capital to Baghdad.

850: Perfectus, a monk in Cordoba, invites death by deliberately challenging Islam, becomes cult figure of martyrs.

870: Muslims come to power in part of Afghanistan.

913: Mansur al-Hallaj, the first sufi to come to India, is executed for heresy on March 28.

977: Subuktigin, a Turkish slave, ascends his father-in-law Alptigin's throne in Ghazni and defeats the neighbouring Shahi king Jaipal.

1008: The Afghan Mahmud of Ghazni crosses the Indus and establishes a base in Punjab.

1024: Mahmud of Ghazni sets off on a winter campaign for Somnath in October.

1026: The revered Hindu temple of Somnath is destroyed and looted by Mahmud of Ghazni.

1061: Count Roger invades Muslim Sicily; Sicily returns to Christendom by 1091.

1085: Frankish knights fight alongside Spaniards to recover Toledo, which falls to Alfonso VI. Pope Gregory VII forms a militia called the Knights of St. Peter, and orders their mobilisation when Turks score major victories over Byzantines in 1071 and 1074.

1095: Byzantine emperor Alexius Comnenus I asks the Pope for help to clear Turks from Anatolia which they have taken after the battle of Manzikurt in 1071.

1095: The Crusades begin when Pope Urban II, addressing a tumultuous gathering of knights, priests and laymen, grants remission of all sins to anyone who joins the holy war against Muslims, to help Comnenus and then to recover Jerusalem on November 25.

1099: The great Crusader conquest of Jerusalem is marked by the horror of massacres of Muslims and Jews on July 15.

1113: The Pope, through a bull, puts the Order of the Hospital under Rome's direct authority, and in 1136 gives it the authority to use arms.

1119: The Order of the Temple is created to protect pilgrims. The Hospitalars and Templars become major bulwarks of Christian armies.

1137: A son is born to a Kurd notable, Najm ad-Din, at Tarkeet, whom he names Yusuf ibn Ayyub.

1144: Zengi, the first in a great line of Muslim king-warriors, takes Edessa, the first of the four kingdoms established in the first Crusade.

1146: Louis VII and his wife Eleanor of Aquitane kneel before St. Bernard of Clairvaux at Vezelay, who promises the couple permanence in paradise if they undertake what becomes known as the Second Crusade, a direct reaction to the fall of Edessa.

1147: Second Crusade begins.

1163: Sultan Nuruddin of Syria, successor of Zengi, sends his general Shirkuh, Saladin's uncle, to conquer Egypt and unite it with Syria.

1169: Cairo falls and Shirkuh proclaims himself king of Egypt in January 8.

1169: Shirkuh dies. Saladin, his young nephew, is named king of Egypt in March.

1174: Nuruddin begins to raise an army against Saladin but dies of a heart attack on May 15. Saladin now takes over Syria, thereby bringing Egypt and Syria under one command by 1175, is proclaimed Sultan of both as well as guardian of Mecca and Medina.

1183: Saladin takes the Gray Castle of Aleppo in the month of Safar, fulfilling an old saying that whoever captures Aleppo in Safar will conquer Jerusalem in Rajab.

1185: King of Jerusalem, Baldwin IV struck with leprosy, dies.

1187: Saladin gives the call for jihad to liberate Jerusalem in March.

1187: Saladin breaks camp at Ascalon and starts the last stage of his march to Jerusalem on September 19.

1187: Saladin's assault on Jerusalem begins on September 26.

1187: Saladin enters Jerusalem on October 2.

1187: Archbishop of Tyre, Josias, boards a ship with black sails to indicate he is in mourning and heads for Europe to rouse Christains for a Crusade against Saladin in November.

1190: Richard I and Philip II meet on the fields of Burgundy with their armies; start their march to the Holy Land in July.

1191: Philip lands in Palestine in six ships on April 20 and Richard follows on June 8.

1192: Richard finally returns to Europe on July 6, after a great Crusade that made his name a legend, but left Jerusalem in Muslim hands.

1192: In India, Muhammad Ghori defeats Prithviraj at the battle of Tarain. Muslim rule reaches Delhi.

1193: Saladin dies on March 4.

1195: The Moroccan Almohads defeat Castile's Alfonso VIII in Spain, briefly checking Christian resurgence.

1204: Constantinople is sacked, not by Muslims, but by the knight of a Fourth Crusade manipulated by Venice and Genoa.

1212: Alfonso VIII, with contingents from Aragon and Navarre, marches to Las Navas de Tolosa and destroys the Almohads on July 16.

1218: Saladin's successor, Sultan al-Malik al-Kamil, nearly loses Egypt to the Fifth Crusade, before he regains all by 1221.

1219: St. Francis of Assissi crosses the Nile during the Fifth Crusade to try and convert none other than Sultan al-Kamil

1221: Fifth Crusade is defeated at Damietta in Egypt.

1227: Pope Gregory IX bans the *azaan* in Christian dominions.

1228: Frederick the II, leader of the 'Bloodless' Crusade, reaches Acre.

1229: Accord is signed between Frederick and al-Kamil over Jerusalem for a truce of ten years, five months and forty days by the Muslim calendar. Muslims peacefully hand over Christian holy sites in Jerusalem to the Fifth Crusaders. There is uproar, anguish among Muslims on February 24.

1236: The great mystic and Muslim saint Khwaja Muinuddin Chishti dies in Ajmer, India.

1236: Fernando III of Castile conquers Cordoba, capital of Andalus and the prize of Spain.

1237: Muhammad ibn Yusuf ibn Nasr establishes the last great Muslim dynasty of Spain, at Granada.

1239: Frederick and al-Kamil truce ends; Muslims recapture Jerusalem.

1248: Fernando enters Seville as victor on December 22.

1249: The final offensive of the Crusades, the seventh, under Louis the IX of France, drops anchor at Damietta. Egyptians abandon the field.

1249: Sultan Najm ad-Din Ayyub of Egypt dies on August 30. The Crusaders, although they suffer reverses elsewhere, move towards Mansura, where the Egyptian army is camped.

1250: The Egyptian army, camped at Mansura, suddenly finds Frank cavalry in its midst; is in tatters except for one unit, the Turkish-cavalry of Mamluks on February 10.

1250: Muslims, inspired by the leader of the Mamluks, Baibars, achieve yet another astonishing reversal and defeat the Crusaders on April 7.

1250: Baibars walks into the camp of the Sultan, al-Muazzam, strikes him with his sword and leaves him to die; the Mamluk era begins on May 2.

1258: Mongol Hulagu Khan is at the doors of Baghdad.

1260: Baibars defeats the rampaging Mongols at the battle of Ain Jalut in Galilee.

1291: Mamluk Sultan Khalil destroys the kingdom of Acre and eliminates Christian power, though not the Christian presence, from Palestine.

1319: Through a Bull of Pope John XXII, the Order of Christ is formed to 'defend Christians from Muslims and to carry the war to them in their own territory'.

1366: Murad I shifts Ottoman capital to Edirne in Europe.

1402: Taimur defeats and imprisons Bayezid, the Ottoman Sultan.

1415: Cueta captured by King John of Portugal; for the first time, Europe finds a toehold in Muslim Africa on August 21.

1417: Henry the Navigator becomes grandmaster of the Order of Christ.

1418: The great Chinese sea admiral, Zheng He, a eunuch, reaches Malindi on the east African coast with his fabulous armada.

1421: Murad II becomes Sultan, leads second Ottoman expedition against Constantinople; fails.

1437: Henry the Navigator attacks Tangier.

1453: The Ottoman Sultan Mehmet gives a call for jihad to conquer Constantinople in May.

1453: Constantinople falls, and with it ends the Holy Roman Empire of the Byzantines.

1453: Grave of Prophet's companion Ayyub al Ansari found by Turks by the walls of Constantinople.

1454: George-Gennadios Scholarius consecrated and enthroned in the Church of Holy Apostles, signalling the new Ottoman policy of accommodation towards Christians on January 5.

1455: The Yedi Kule (Seven Towers) are built on edge of the Sea of Marmara to reinforce the defences of Constantinople.

1455: A Bull is issued by Pope Nicholas V who wants an alliance between the Christian powers of the west and Indians, who he mistook for heretic Christians since they were not Muslims, in order to squeeze the 'Saracen' empires in between on January 8.

1456: Second Papal Bull extends the jurisdiction of the Order of Christ 'all the way to the Indians'.

1459: Ottoman Sultan Mehmet builds a mosque at the site of the grave of Abu Ayyub Ansari, which becomes a point of pilgrimage.

1471: Portugal's Alvaro Esteves crosses the equator.

1483: Boabdil is captured by the Castilians.

1485: Castilians seize Ronda.

1492: Castilians enter Alhambra on January 1: the last Muslim kingdom in Spain has fallen, the last sigh of the Last Moor, Boabdil, is heard.

1496: Manuel ascends the Lisbon throne.

1498: Vasco da Gama reaches Calicut with the help of a Muslim navigator on May 18.

1507: Amir Husayn, an Ottoman admiral, leads a convoy of 12 ships with 1500 men and cannon to the Gujarati port of Diu, to confront the growing Potuguese "menace" on the Arabian Sea.

1517: Ottoman Sultan Selim assumes the title of caliph after he defeats the Mamluks and hangs the last one from the gates of Cairo.

1519: Babur starts for Kabul from Uzbekistan, and establishes a kingdom in Afghanistan on April 25.

1521: Suleyman the Magnificent conquers Belgrade.

1522: Rhodes falls to Suleyman.

1526: Babur enters Delhi after he defeats the Afghan Ibrahim Lodi at the first battle of Panipat in April.

1527: Babur gives orders for the jihad against the vast confederation led by Rana Sangha to destroy the Mughals on February 26.

1527: Babur defeats at the battle of Khanwa on March 17.

1528: Mir Baqi, a Mughal noble, builds a three-domed mosque without minarets in Ayodhya, allegedly at the spot where a temple commemorating the birthplace of Lord Ram, stood.

1540: The Afghan-Indian Sher Shah Suri defeats Humayun at the battle of Kanauj, interrupting the Mughal empire in May.

1555: Ogier de Busbecq, the Hungarian ambassador, reaches Constantinople on January 20.

1599: 80 London businessmen form an association, raise capital of some 30,000 pounds and seek a royal charter to trade in the east on September 24. Permission from James I comes in 1600. The East India Company is born.

1608: The first ship of the East India Company berths in India.

1609: William Hawkins reaches Agra with a letter from King James.

1612: British win naval battle against the Portuguese off the coast of India.

1612: A royal *firman* from Delhi permits the East India Company to start its first trading post at Surat.

1622: On May 9 Janissaries seize their Sultan, Osman 'in the name of the law' and take him to the Seven Towers where he is strangled around the neck while his testicles are, literally, squeezed to death.

1622: Janissaries revolt against the reforms of Mahmud II who begins to Europeanise the army, forsaking those 'ancient traditions'.

1623: Dutch massacre the English in Amboyna, effectively ending the company's interest in Indonesia on February 15.

1630: In the western part of India, Shivaji is born.

1640: East India Company acquires Madras, and builds Fort St. George.

1650: Prince Shuja, son of Mughal emperor Shah Jahan and governor of Bengal, gives permission to the Company to trade for a lump sum of Rs 3000, and the first factory in Bengal opens in Hooghly.

1661: Charles II receives Bombay as dowry when he marries the Portuguese Catherine of Braganza.

1668: Crown rents out Bombay, officially part of the royal estate of East Greenwich in Kent, for ten pounds worth of gold, yearly, 'for ever'. The 'for ever' ends in 1739.

1680: Shivaji dies on April 4, having challenged the Mughals and established the Maratha kingdom in the West.

1683: Ottoman general Kara Mustafa Pasha is defeated at Vienna by a coalition of the Holy Roman Empire, the Pope, Venice and Poland. He prefers death to humiliation at Constantinople.

1686: Buda falls to Austrians.

1686: East India Company declares an ambitious war on the Mughal empire.

1687: Sir Josiah Child, the proactive chief of the East India Company, writes to the governor of Madras in which he dreams of an English dominion in India.

1690: Having lost a war they started, East India Company officials seek pardon from the Mughal emperor Aurangzeb.

1690: Job Charnock founds Calcutta after Hooghly is considered too vulnerable.

1703: Muhammad ibn Abd al Wahhab is born in Najd in Arabia, in the same year as Shah Waliullah in Delhi.

1707: The sixth and last of the great Mughals, Aurangzeb, dies.

1711: Peter the Great defeated in his quest for Constantinople.

1716: Emperor Farrukhsiyar signs a *firman* which the British describe as their Magna Carta in India. The Company is allowed to trade, acquire land and settle where it wants to in Bengal, all for an annual payment of Rs 3000.

1722: Russia enters Daghestan, opening the passage to the Muslim Caucasus.

1725: Robert Clive is born near Market Drayton in Shropshire on September 29.

1734: Russia defeats the Kazaks, and takes Crimea.

1738: Belgrade is retaken by the Ottomans.

1739: The Persian Nadir Shah sacks Delhi, takes the Kohinoor diamond and the peacock throne as part of a fabulous booty.

1748: The Afghan ruler Ahmad Shah Abdali begins incursions into India.

1749: Marathas create a loose confederacy of the great families of Scindia, Holkar, Bhonsle and Gaekwad with the Peshwa in Pune at its head.

1756: Nawab Siraj ud Daula captures the company's Fort William in Calcutta on June 20.

1757: On June 23, Robert Clive, aided by defector Mir Jafar, wins Bengal on the battlefield of Plassey; the British empire is effectively born.

1758: Marathas occupy Delhi in December.

1761: A decisive battle takes place between Marathas and a Muslim coalition led by Ahmad Shah Abdali; Marathas routed, ending their dream of replacing Mughal emperor on January 14.

1764: British defeat an alliance of Delhi, Awadh and a disobedient Bengal at the battle of Buxar; road opens to Delhi for the East India Company's armies.

1786: Sayyid Ahmed Barelvi, leader of a jihad against British in India, is born in Rae Bareli.

1787: Muhammed Wahhab dies in Arabia.

1787: Tipoo Sultan of Mysore sends an emissary to Constantinople for Ottoman help against the British; appeal is fruitless.

1792: Tipoo Sultan is defeated and killed by the British.

1803: A Bengal army under General Gerard Lake defeats a Maratha army at Patparganj, enters Delhi and makes a hapless Mughal emperor its virtual pensioner in September.

1803: Saud ibn Abdul Aziz, grandson of ibn Saud, captures Mecca and demolishes all the structures upon the graves of Islam's heroes.

1803: Shah Aziz, Shah Waliullah's son, issues a *fatwa* that unbelievers have seized power after British occupation of Delhi and India can no longer be considered a House of Islam.

1804: The Arabian Wahhabis take Medina, and even skirmish with the British in the Gulf.

1812: Ottoman Sultan Mahmud II sends a force under Muhammad Ali Pasha from Cairo to end the Wahhabi insurgency after a pilgrims' caravan from Constantinople is not permitted to perform the *hajj*.

1817: Sayyid Ahmad Khan, pro-British Indian Muslim reformer, is born on October 17.

1819: Wahhabi stronghold Diriya falls and the incumbent, Abdullah ibn Saud, is sent to Constantinople, where he is beheaded: Ottomans end Wahhabi revolt.

1821: Barelvi returns from *hajj* in October.

1821: Greece demands freedom from the Ottomans.

1826: Some 20,000 Janissaries sweep through the streets and storm the Topkapi, shouting that they do not want the practices of infidels and demand preservation of the past in the name of the Prophet Muhammad on June 13.

1826: Janissaries abolished; some 6000 executed and 5000 exiled on June 17.

1829: Russia seizes Ottoman territory in the Caucasus (Chechnya and Daghestan) and proclaims itself protector of the 12 million Orthodox Christians in the reduced Ottoman empire.

1830: Barelvi's holy warriors seize Peshawar in the north-west of India.

1830: Serbian state established as Ottoman empire begins to falter.

1831: Barelvi killed while escaping after defeat.

1833: Greece becomes independent of the Ottomans.

1838: Sayyid Jamal ad Din Afghani, the ideologue of Islamic unity against 'Western Christian imperialism' born.

1839: Britain occupies Aden.

1853: Tsar Nicholas I tells British ambassador in St. Petersburg, 'We have a sick man on our hands.' He is referring to Turkey.

1856: Alliance of England, France and Turkey defeats Russia in Crimean war.

1856: For the first time since 1453, church bells are permitted to ring, by the authority of an imperial decree, in Constantinople.

1857: 'Sepoy Mutiny' in India against the British.

1858: The last Mughal, Bahadur Shah Zafar removed from throne by British after mutiny is crushed.

1859: Imam Shamyl gives himself up to Russia after a long jihad in Caucasus in June.

1860s: British conduct conspiracy trials against Indian Muslim leaders in Patna who have launched jihad against the Raj; the British label them 'Wahhabis.'

1865: Russia captures the prized city of Tashkent.

1868: Bukhara and Samarkand come under Russian rule.

1869: Six Muslims and four Hindus under the leadership of Sir Sayyid Ahmad Khan, present petition for what becomes the Aligarh Muslim University in India.

1870s: Russia encourages Bulgaria, Bosnia, Serbia and Montenegro to rebel against Istanbul.

1872: British Viceroy Lord Mayo is assassinated by an Afghan Muslim prisoner while visiting the Andaman islands.

1872: First census of British India takes place.

1873: Khiva falls to Russia.

1875: Mohammad Ali Jinnah born on October 20, but later, under influence of Christian school environment, changes his birthdate to December 25 because 'Jesus was born on Christmas Day'.

1877: Bulgaria gets autonomy from Constantinople.

1879: Afghani moves to Hyderabad in India where he lives for two years and tries to persuade Muslims to stop cooperating with the Christian rulers of India.

1885: 72 delegates gather in Bombay, with A.O. Hume in the chair, to ask for jobs in the civil service for Indians through competitive exams, and legislatures to which they can elect their representatives. The Indian National Congress is born on December 28.

1888: Sayyid Ahmad Khan claims the Congress has been created to subjugate Muslims under Hindu rule in April.

1893: Jinnah called to the bar at Lincoln's Inn in London.

1896, May: Persia's Shah Nasr ul Din is assassinated by a man called Mirza Riza, Afghani's disciple.

1897: Afghani dies of cancer of the chin.

1898: Sayyid Ahmad Khan, now knighted, dies.

1901: William Knox d'Arcy, an Englishman, receives a document from the Shah of Iran for £20,000 – in cash – giving him exclusive rights to look for, find and sell natural gas, asphalt, and petroleum from anywhere in the Persian state.

1902: Dadabhai Naoroji becomes the first Indian to be elected to the House of Commons, as a Liberal representative from Central Finsbury.

1903: The *Risley Paper* is published arguing that the Bengal Presidency in India is simply too large to be governed effectively on December 3.

1905: Lord Curzon's decision to partition Bengal is announced from the British summer capital at Simla on July 6.

1905: Eastern Bengal created with a majority of 18 million Muslims and 12 million Hindus on October 16.

1906: All-India Muslim League is founded in Dhaka on December 31.

1908: Oil struck near the very small town of Masjid-as-Suleyman (The Mosque of Suleyman) in Persia on May 26.

1908: Huseyn ibn Ali, descendant of the Prophet through his daughter Fatima, made emir of Mecca by the Ottomans.

1909: A triumvirate of Enver, Talaat and Jemal Pasha deposes Sultan Abdulhamid.

1910: Jinnah becomes the first non-official in the British Viceroy's Executive Council in Delhi.

1911: The Partition of Bengal is reversed after strong protests.

1911: Italy attacks Tripoli in September.

1914: Mohandas Karamchand Gandhi leaves South Africa's Cape Town for London, en route to India on July 18.

1914: First World War is declared on August 4, Turkey supports Austria and Germany, declares a jihad against England, Russia and France.

1914: Ottoman Caliph declares its last jihad against the Britain-France-Russia alliance in the First World War.

1915: A British officer, Shakespear, recognises Ibn Saud as the independent ruler of Nejd, and assures him of Britain's protection if he goes to war against Ottomans in January.

1915: Gandhi's ship berths at Apollo Bunder in Bombay on January 9.

1915: Two Indians are honoured in the King's birthday list on June 3. Poet Rabindranath Tagore is knighted and Gandhi receives the Kaiser-i-Hind medal.

1915: British Indian Expeditionary Force occupies Basra.

1916: Then secretary of state for India Austen Chamberlain, writes to Lord Chelmsford: 'The Muslim community of India is, I think, the only community under the British flag which habitually prays for a foreign sovereign, and does not offer prayers for the King.' This 'foreign sovereign' is the caliph.

1916: Congress and the Muslim League seal a pact at Lucknow for joint action on constitutional and popular demands.

1916: Arab revolt against the Ottoman Empire.

1917: Jerusalem falls to the British on December 9.

1917: British occupy Baghdad.

1919: Jinnah walks out of the Congress at Nagpur session objecting to Gandhi's volatile mix of religion and politics.

1919: Government of India introduces two bills in the Imperial Legislative Council on the recommendations of a committee chaired by Justice Rowlatt on February 6.

1919: In February, Vallabhbhai Patel, Sarojini Naidu, Umar Sobani, B.G. Horniman, Shankarlal Banker and Indulal Yagnik sign a pledge drafted by Gandhi, to 'refuse civilly to obey these laws'.

1919: Rowlatt Bill gazetted on March 18.

1919: In response, Gandhi organises an all-India *hartal* or strike on April 6.

1919: On April 10, Lieutenant Governor of Punjab Sir Michael O'Dwyer orders the internment of two local leaders, a Hindu and a Muslim, Dr Satyapal and Saifuddin Kitchlew under the Defence of India Act.

1919: British open fire on unarmed, unsuspecting Indians gathered for a fair at Jallianwala Bagh in Amritsar, Punjab on April 12.

1919: Congress demands an enquiry, asks Gandhi to go to Amritsar on April 20.

1919: Tagore renounces his knighthood in anguish and anger over Jallianwala Bagh episode on May 30.

1920: On March 17, Lloyd George informs Maulana Mohammed Ali's deputation that Holy Cities will remain in British control and not be restored to Caliph.

1920: Muslims observe a day of national mourning in India on March 19, with active support from Gandhi, in support of the Caliph.

1920: Gandhi sends back the Kaisar-i-Hind gold medal to Lord Chelmsford on August 1.

1920: Treaty of Sevres signed, the straits are handed over to an international commission, eastern Anatolia divided between Armenia and Kurdistan and Greece given Izmir and eastern Thrace on August 10.

1920: Congress delegates gather between September 4-9 to support Gandhi's idea of a non-cooperation movement, popularly called the Khilafat (or Caliphate) struggle, against the British.

1920: Iraq revolts against British; suppressed by force, including RAF bombing and chemical weapons.

1921: King Faisal I crowned King of Iraq to the tune of 'God save the King.'

1922: On February 5, Gandhi suddenly withdraws this tremendously successful anti-British nationwide agitation because some protesters in an unknown village, Chauri Chaura, have become violent and killed, under provocation, 22 constables.

1922: Gandhi sent to jail for 6 years on March 10; India silent.

1922: Heirs of Mehmet II and Suleyman the Magnificent suffer what is perhaps the ultimate insult: the royal band deserts on November 10.

1922: On November 16, Mehmet Vahideddin, caliph of the Muslims and Sultan of Turkey writes to General Sir Charles ('Tim') Harington, commander of the British forces, seeking refuge and requests transfer from Istanbul.

1922: Last Caliph, Mehmet VI, leaves his palace on November 17.

1924: Caliphate formally abolished in Constantinople on March 3.

1924: Ibn Saud takes over Mecca, declares himself guardian of the Holy Places on October 13.

1926: The last Caliph, Mehmet VI, dies in San Remo.

1929: At Lahore, the Congress asks for 'full' freedom for India.

1930: Fifty-eight delegates invited to the first round table conference, inaugurated by King George V, on November 12 to determine a new Constitution for India.

1932: Saudi family renames Arabia, Saudi Arabia.

1933: King Ghazi succeeds King Faisal I; inspires incipient Arab nationalism.

1937: Congress triumphant in first election in India under new Constitution.

1939: Britain declares war on Germany on September 3.

1939: King Ghazi assassinated.

1940: Muslim League asks for Pakistan at Lahore.

1941: The revolt of the colonels ushers in a brief anti-British government in Baghdad; British conquer and rule whole of Iraq.

1947: The British Parliament passes the India Independence Act on June 2.

1947: Pakistan is born on August 14.

1947: India gains independence on August 15.

1948: A Hindu refugee from Pakistan is arrested at Gandhi's prayer meeting with a hand grenade on January 20.

1948: Gandhi is assassinated by a Hindu fundamentalist on January 30.

1948: Jinnah dies of tuberculosis on September 28.

1948: Israel is born; Arabs lose first war with Israel.

1951: Mossadeq nationalizes oil in Iran.

1952: Egypt's Free Officers overthrow pro-British royalty; Nasser eventually takes over.

1953: CIA organizes coup against Mossadeq; restores Shah of Iran.

1956: Nasser seizes Suez Canal; Anglo-French-Israel invasion of Egypt fails.

1958: Iraq's Free Officers seize power after massacre of royal family.

1963: Baathists triumph in coup against Kassem.

1968: Baathists take charge of Iraq government.

1971: Pakistan is partitioned; Bangladesh is born.

1973: Sardar Mohammad Daud becomes President of the Republic of Afghanistan.

1978: Daud is killed by his own supporters in April.

1979: Saddam Hussein becomes sole dictator of Iraq.

1979: Ayatollah Khomeini rides a revolution to power in Iran.

1980: Osama bin Laden comes to Peshawar for the first time.

1980: Saddam Hussein invades Iran.

1988: Iraq-Iran war finally ends, with both sides defeated.

1990: Saddam Hussein invades Kuwait after his extortionist demands for war 'compensation' are largely ignored by Saudi Arabia and Kuwait.

1991: Saudi authorities spurn Osama's offer of help in the war against Iraq, prefer US ground forces.

1991: Georges Bush Senior liberates Kuwait but spares Saddam Hussein.

1996: In August, Osama bin Laden issues his first call for jihad against the United States, for "occupying" Saudi Arabia, among other reasons.

1996: The Taliban take control of Kabul and set up government on September 26.

1998: Osama bin Laden's Al Qaida and its associates issue a manifesto in the name of the 'The International Islamic Front for Jihad against Jews and Crusaders'.

2001: World Trade Center and Pentagon attacked on September 11.

2001: US begins its war against terror on October 7.

2003: Georges Bush Junior, with Britain's Tony Blair as an ally, invades and occupies Iraq after Saddam Hussein is driven out of power.

INDEX